S.S.F. PUBLIC LIBRARY
WEST ORANGE AVENUE

W9-BZO-154

S.S.F. PUBLIC LIBRARY
WEST ORANGE AVENUE

NOV   2000

S.S.F. PUBLIC LIBRARY
WEST ORANGE AVENUE

THE MAN WHO WAS
DORIAN GRAY

Jerusha Hull McCormack

St. Martin's Press
New York

THE MAN WHO WAS DORIAN GRAY
Copyright © Jerusha McCormack, 2000. All rights reserved. Printed in the United States of America. No part of this book may be used or reproduced in any manner whatsoever without written permission except in the case of brief quotations embodied in critical articles or reviews. For information, address St. Martin's Press, 175 Fifth Avenue, New York, N.Y. 10010.

ISBN 0-312-23278-0

Library of Congress Cataloging-in-Publication Data
is available from the Library of Congress.

Design by Acme Art, Inc.

First edition: November, 2000
10 9 8 7 6 5 4 3 2 1

PERMISSIONS

TEXT

Unpublished material concerning John Gray and André Raffalovich from the Department of Manuscripts at the National Library of Scotland, including Gray/Raffalovich correspondence; letters to and from Gray and Raffalovich from various correspondents, including those from "Michael Field" (Edith Cooper and Katherine Bradley); correspondence from Raffalovich to Charles Ballantyne and Norman Wright; and manuscripts of Gray's original, unpublished work reproduced by permission of the Department of Special Collections, the National Library of Scotland.

John Gray letters to Mrs MacLagan, 9 Feb. 1906, to John Lane, 4 January 1893, and to A.J.A. Symons, 6 May 1925, as well as selections from Oscar Wilde, *Notebook,* and Oscar Wilde and John Lane, contract for *Silverpoints,* 17 June 1892, published by permission of the Princeton University Library.

Letter from John Gray to Oscar Wilde by permission of The Hyde Collection, U.S.A.

Typescript reminiscences of Frank Liebich courtesy of William Andrews Clark Memorial Library, University of California, Los Angeles.

Letters from Charles Ricketts to John Lane, Max Beerbohm to Reggie Turner, and John Gray to William Rothenstein reproduced by permission of the Houghton Library, Harvard University.

Letters from John Gray to Gordon Bottomley reproduced by permission of the estate of Gordon Bottomley.

Letters from John Gray to Félix Fénéon reproduced by permission of Archives Félix Fénéon, Fonds Jean Paulhan/IMEC.

Letters from Charles Ricketts to John Lane and to John Gray; from "Michael Field" (Katherine Bradley and Edith Cooper) to John Gray; and from T. Sturge Moore to "John Gawsworth" (Terence Ian Fytton) reproduced by permission of L. Sturge Moore.

Letters from Heather Coltman about John Gray and his family, courtesy of Heather Coltman.

Papers from the estate of John Gray and André Raffalovich bequeathed to the Dominican Chaplaincy, Edinburgh, are reproduced by permission of the Prior Provincial of the Order of Preachers, St. Dominic's Priory, London, England.

Arthur Symons' "Prologue: In the Stalls," from *London Nights* (1895) reproduced by permission of B Read.

Letters from Félix Fénéon to John Gray and from John Gray to Charles Ricketts, to Walter Shewing, and to his niece, Coralie Tinklar reproduced by permission of The John Rylands University Library of Manchester.

Letters of John Gray to Katherine Bradley and Edith Cooper ("Michael Field") for 17 April 1907, 24 July 1907, 20 January 1908, 1 July 1908, 3 August 1908, 24 October 1908, 24 November 1908, 29 November 1908, 29 January 1909, 10 June 1909, 14 November 1909, 7 November 1910, as well as other letters dated and undated reproduced by permission of The Henry W. and Albert A. Berg Collection of English and American Literature, The New York Public Library, Astor, Lenox and Tilden Foundations.

Letter of T. Sturge Moore to John Gawsworth, 21 March 1940, reproduced by permission of the Reading University Library.

Four typescript pages of a diary entry recording Desmond Flower's meeting with John Gray in 1931 reproduced by permission of Mr Jad Adams.

Selection from "Upon a Dying Lady," reprinted with the permission of Scribner, a Division of Simon & Schuster from *The Collected Poems of W. B. Yeats,* revised Second Edition edited by Richard J. Finneran (New York: Scribner, 1996) and with the permission of A. P. Watt Ltd on behalf of Michael B Yeats.

Three letters from John Gray to Edmund Blunden, 21 July 1929, 20 February 1933, and undated, reproduced by permission of the Harry Ransom Humanities Research Center, The University of Texas at Austin.

Lord Alfred Douglas' "In Praise of Shame" and "Two Loves" from *Lyrics 1935* reproduced by permission of Mrs Sheila Colman.

ILLUSTRATIONS

1. John Gray, Senior; Gray's father, reproduced by permission of Heather Coltman.

2. Beatrice ("Trixl") and Sarah Gray, Gray's sisters, c.1896, reproduced by permission of Heather Coltman.

3. Beresford Square, showing the gates to the Royal Arsenal, Woolwich (1913?), reproduced by permission of the Greenwich Local History Library.

4. Furnace and steam-hammer in the foundry of the Royal Arsenal (c. 1910), reproduced by permission of the Greenwich Local History Library.

5. *Ricketts and Shannon.* lithograph by William Rothenstein, 1897, Fitzwilliam Museum, Cambridge, and © courtesy of the artist's estate / Bridgeman Art Library.

6. John Gray, from a drawing by Reginald Savage (c. 1890), reproduced by permission of the National Portrait Gallery.

7. "Dorian" Gray (1893), reproduced by permission by the Prior Provincial of the Order of Preachers, St. Dominic's Priory, London, England.

9. *Silverpoints,* 1893, reproduced by permission of the British Library (c. 109 c. 6 or c. 134 c. 14)..

10. Oscar Wilde and Lord Alfred Douglas ("Bosie"), © Merlin Holland, reproduced by permission.

11. André Raffalovich, from a painting by A. Dampier May (1886), reproduced by permission by the Prior Provincial of the Order of Preachers, St. Dominic's Priory, London, England.

12. André Raffalovich by Max Beerbohm, © Estate of Max Beerbohm, reproduced by permission of the Estate and by Michael Maclagan.

13. André Raffalovich in the garden of his summer house at Weybridge, Surrey, reproduced by permission by the Prior Provincial of the Order of Preachers, St. Dominic's Priory, London, England.

14. John Gray, Sophie Raffalovich, André Raffalovich, Florence Gribbell, and Georges Raffalovich (?) c. 1896, reproduced by permission by the Prior Provincial of the Order of Preachers, St. Dominic's Priory, London, England.

15. The Cowgate, Edinburgh, during Gray's lifetime, Crown copyright: Royal Commission on the Ancient and Historical Monuments of Scotland, reproduced by permission.

16. Katherine Bradley and Edith Cooper ("Michael Field"), reproduced by permission of L. Sturge Moore.

17. St. Peter's Church, Edinburgh, Crown copyright: Royal Commission on the Ancient and Historical Monuments of Scotland, reproduced by permission.

18. Interior of St. Peter's church as it was in Gray's lifetime, Crown copyright: Royal Commission on the Ancient and Historical Monuments of Scotland, reproduced by permission.

19. John Gray on Skye (c. 1930), reproduced by permission by the Prior Provincial of the Order of Preachers, St. Dominic's Priory, London, England.

20. Eric Gill in the engraving shop at Pigotts (c. 1940), photograph by Howard Coster, reproduced by permission of the Eric Gill Estate.

21. Eric Gill, *Canon John Gray,* collotype of pencil drawing (1928), reproduced by permission of the Eric Gill Estate.

22. Canon John Gray, reproduced by permission by the Prior Provincial of the Order of Preachers, St. Dominic's Priory, London, England.

CONTENTS

for
David and Thomas
who are
becoming themselves

PREFACE

IT IS NOW MORE THAN THIRTY YEARS since the name "John Gray" first meant something to me. Handing me an anthology of 1890s poets, an ingenious mentor had said: "Why don't you write something on one of these guys? No one seems to know much about them." I was dubious. After all, a doctoral thesis on yet one more obscure poet suggested almost a parody of the genre.

Within the week I had done what research there was to be done; it culminated in finding a copy of Brocard Sewell's *Two Friends: John Gray and André Raffalovich* in the bowels of Widener Library. From the moment I opened it, I was hooked. The essays were elegant, evocative—and elusive. The story of the working-class lad who became a decadent dandy, then a Roman Catholic priest, was punctuated by large, eloquent silences. There was mention of missing papers, black holes in correspondences, and, haunting all the accounts, a mysterious relationship with Oscar Wilde. Nor was the lifelong attachment to André Raffalovich ever sufficiently explained.

For a doctoral student, the obstacles to research were daunting. There was only the most rudimentary bibliography. Most of Gray's writing was published in small, offbeat periodicals or in severely limited editions. His papers were said to be locked in a safe in the Edinburgh chaplaincy belonging to the Dominican Order, which Father Gray had appointed executor for both his and Raffalovich's estate. No reply to my letters was forthcoming. In the end, I simply acquired a university research grant and arrived at the doorstep. It was the beginning of a great adventure; after several interviews with the then director of the Dominican chaplaincy, Father Anthony Ross, I became the first scholar to be granted unrestricted access to the Gray and Raffalovich papers, now lodged in the archives of the National Library of Scotland, Edinburgh.

The research literally took years and involved many of the major collections of 1890s material in the United States and Great Britain. Eventually the doctoral thesis fattened into a book, *John Gray: Poet, Dandy, & Priest* (1991). Reading it now, it seems almost like an archeological exercise: a record of finds, mostly fragments, which had to be dusted off and pieced carefully together. There is an almost obsessive concern in the book about the "fit" of these fragments, which have been painstakingly used to recreate a narrative from the available shreds of evidence. Inevitably, a great deal of the action takes place in the footnotes.

With so much of John Gray's life absorbed in its reconstruction, I felt acutely that the story itself had been lost. The publication, a year later, of my edition of John Gray's *Selected Prose* (1992) rendered this sense of loss even more keen. If Gray himself could write so hauntingly of his own life in a story such as "The Person in Question," if he could give such a sharp sense of what it meant to be John Gray in the spectacularly weird fantasy *Park*, how could the biography have missed?

Hence: when offered an opportunity to write the biography again—as the story of a life lived, in all its resonance—I decided against the obvious route. *The Man Who Was Dorian Gray* uses all the resources of the original biography. It also draws on substantive new work on the period by cultural historians such as Linda Dowling and Ellis Hanson, as well as work on individual artists, such as that on Charles Ricketts by Paul Delaney, on Michael Field by Emma Donoghue, and on Eric Gill by Fiona MacCarthy. The new and adventurous work on Oscar Wilde and his milieu has also suggested fresh angles from which to view Gray's story; as editor of and contributor to *Wilde the Irishman* (1998), I am conscious of how much original work there is at present on Oscar Wilde—and how much more there is still to be done.

In order to incorporate as much as possible of this new scholarship, I resolved to try another method of narration: to place the fragments of Gray's life before the reader, as the true, authenticated scraps they are, and to piece them together with a kind of fictive glue, as authentic as possible but still palpably "fake." The idea was to reconstruct the life in the whole, in such a way that the reader can easily distinguish "fact" from "fiction." Perhaps the nearest analogy to this method might be the process used in reconstructing, say, a Greek vase, using a slightly different shade of paint from the original for the reconstituted bits, thus giving the viewer both the sense of the whole while allowing him to identify the original from the modern additions.

In essence what this comes to is that all "facts" are verifiable and certified by footnotes; that material which is without a footnote is not necessarily not an established "fact," but constitutes a fictive account as authentic in tone and detail as is likely under the circumstances. I have also taken the liberty of interweaving present and future events—indicating (in most instances) a shift of time or perspective by means of parentheses and line spaces. Such a method allows the writer to draw on a multiplicity of sources in reconstructing Gray's milieu, particularly in those private, elusive writings that constitute journals, letters, reminiscences. Recording these allows the very voice of John Gray to be reconstituted in his own words. They also give something more important: the talismanic phrase or the unexpected detail which opens up the very heart of the subject and lays it in our hands.

What is fictive, in other words, seeks only to quicken the known facts, to place them in a context which allows them to disclose themselves. And yet, in this increasingly literal world, I am aware there will be those who will object to this method as "faction"—a kind of sloppy compromise between fact and fiction. I would ask such a reader to turn first to the footnotes and bibliography to satisfy himself as to the nature and extent of the research on which the narration rests. Then I would ask the reader to reflect on the actual status of "fact" and "fiction" in this particular narrative. It struck me while writing that many of the "facts" I reported were themselves reports of rumor or gossip—a powerful force in the closed society of late-Victorian London or Edwardian Edinburgh. Are these then "facts"—or "fiction"? And how do you distinguish "fact" from "fiction" in the life story of a man who made his name, literally, in the pages of a novel?

Oscar Wilde is eloquent about the dangers of literalism—a "monstrous worship of Fact" which he saw as reducing the modern public to a savage stupor. After all, Wilde asks, what is a Fact? He cites the effect of the penny-dreadful magazines on little boys, who, having read about Jack Sheppard or Dick Turpin, "pillage the stalls of unfortunate apple-women, break into sweet-shops at night, and alarm old gentlemen who are returning home from the city by leaping out on them in a suburban lane." Does this not prove that the fictive boy is actually a more potent agent than his living readers? That the actual boys are simply poor imitations of their hero? Can we not dismiss the actual boy burglar simply as "A Fact, occupied as Fact usually is, with trying to reproduce Fiction"? In other words, fact and fiction have become so hopelessly intertwined in everyday life that, as Oscar Wilde announced with alarming finality: "A fact simply has no intellectual value at all."

Most biographers would consider endorsing Wilde's position. They are in a position to know that fact—or whatever is meant by fact—possesses a very uncertain status. What does it mean to be born on a certain date? To certain parents? Class and milieu are important, but not insurmountable. In the 1880s, John Gray was entering the age of the invented man. The old class lines, long eroding, were in his generation being significantly breached. A new capitalism lent a hard edge to the performances of the dandy, as a self representing a new aristocracy of taste, an object lesson—and a reproach—to the middle classes. The self-advertising publicity of the artist today finds its genesis in the performances of Oscar Wilde and his circle over a century ago.

From the perspective of the biographer, it appears as if almost everything that is most "real" about John Gray comes mediated through his own performance. Like the hero of *The Importance of Being Ernest*, Gray discovers in his name a kind of fate. For John Gray, from the very first, denomination determines destiny—whether one is talking about his earliest identification with Peter Gray (scalped by the Indians) or Dorian Gray (a suicide) or the Blessed Jacopone or Saint John of the Cross or, finally, with the implicit hero of his novel *Park*, Prester John, the fabled emperor-priest of ancient Abyssinia.

Consequently, as the writer of Gray's life, I have tried to allow it, as much as possible, to tell itself in his own words and through his own fictions. Where these have failed to provide a coherent narrative, I have turned to the words of those who knew him or (in some sense) gave him his script, as Wilde apparently did in *The Picture of Dorian Gray*. My aim in doing so has been to give the reader a lively sense of what it felt like to be a minor poet of the cultural revolution that was the early 1890s in England—and to draw the reader into a vivid sense of what it meant to be that certain man who was Dorian Gray. If the "feel" of the biography is that of fiction, it is not because the facts have been abandoned in favor of fiction, but because, for Gray, the facts *are* the fiction.

In writing this book, I have been assisted by an embarrassment of Johns, each of whom I wish to thank. First of all, Dr. John Flood, to whom I owe a few dazzling feats of research and more than a few simple words of encouragement. His enthusiasm and exemplary scholarship have more than once turned me back to a difficult piece of writing I would otherwise cheerfully have avoided. Secondly, Professor John Blair, who attentively read the manuscript at least once over; his wise patience with the whole enterprise has sustained me. Thirdly, Jonathan Williams, who strengthened my resolve to write this book and to write it in the way that seemed the most appropriate.

There are many others who helped me directly or indirectly. For permission to use the Gray and Raffalovich papers, thanks are due to Father Malcolm McMahon, Prior Provincial of the Dominican Order in England. I also wish to thank the Right Reverend Christopher McElroy for information about Gray's career at Scots College and access to the correspondence held in its archives. In the wake of his biography of Ernest Dowson, Jad Adams sent me invaluable archival notes of a conversation with Father Gray about his early years in London. Among my immediate colleagues I wish to acknowledge the generous support of Professor Declan Kiberd and Dr. Ron Callan of the English Department at University College Dublin, as well as of Kate Stephany of the Boston University Dublin Program. And among those who provided invaluable practical assistance I wish to name my anchorwoman at home, Carmel Douglas.

Finally, to my two sons, David and Thomas, I would like to dedicate this book. I am proud to observe that, in becoming men, you are becoming yourselves. Thank you for seeing me through.

Jerusha McCormack
Dublin, November 2000

OVERTURE
THE MAN WHO WAS DORIAN GRAY

THE FIRE FLARES AND DIES BACK. In the gloom of the long and narrow shop the voices of the men sound hoarse and soft, as if muttered through hollow wood. Faint daylight flickers, then grows large in the smoke-begrimed skylight overhead, picking out shapes as they move about, scalding tea and setting strips of bacon on the anvil to spatter for the first break of the day. Beside the black metal block the smith sleeps, a frown on his face; dead to the world after only two hours.

A hush. Then the blast rekindles. A rumor, a mutter, a hum, an explosion of light. Shadows start and die. The light leaps higher than the flame-flesh-shapes, sweat-swamped, men swathed in cotton shrouds. They strike. The steel complains, all bruised and scathed, from thud to bark, from bark to metal scream. Then hisses venomously as it is plunged into the water trough, drifts of steam rising through the half-dark of this Chinese hell.

Father Gray awakes in the belief that he is dead.

The agony of the dead: to be forced to visit again their own life. He watches the boy, barely man, jump back at the flames and shield his eyes. Hellfire. Not now; but then the fires that burned him in life. The lust for fame. Ambition. To elbow me a place. To be more than the bruised apprentice at the Arsenal, the butt of every joke, the thorn in his father's side. Too good to work with his hands, is it? Too good for his own folk? Reading and music and God knows what la-dee-da stuff. At thirteen, his father orders him from school: teach him a lesson or two. Teach him to work proper, with his hands. His mother had cried.

He nursed the flame. At Arsenal, he had tired of the whirring lathe and rank machine-oil's smell; wit like his should cut harder stuff than steel. He talked himself into the drawing room. There he could write secretly, smuggling pens and paper home after work. Fire in the hand; fire on the tongue. Ah, yes, the reading from the Divine Office of the day. James 3:6. *Et lingua ignis est universitas iniquitatis . . .* The words always come to him in the King James version, the gift of a heretic past: *And the tongue is a fire, a world of iniquity: so is the tongue among our members, that it defileth the whole body, and setteth on fire the course of nature; and it is set on fire of hell.*

Set on fire by a book. Defiled by a book. Among the flaming tongues, the soft suasions of Oscar. Edged wit, but gentle words. *You are beautiful. Come with me. I will introduce you. Dinner. Wait for me at the Café Royal.* Endless cigarettes, their points glowing in the dusk, the smoke curling lazily with the talk, to heaven. The way the disciples would light a cigarette in their mouths and then hand it, cupped, to the other. *Men, women, call thee so and so.* He called me Dorian and Dorian I became. *But in my heart a flame / Burns tireless neath a silver vine.* Poor Oscar. Does he burn now in hellfire—dabbing gently at his large white face with a stained silk handkerchief? I denied him thrice. When he was at trial I swore: *I never knew the man.* Which one of us is the damned?

Father Gray turns over and sleeps again.

It was summer. Through the thick air came a sound, low and sweet, as of a flute. The blaze of noon had given way to a twilight haze and in the violet dusk the bees still murmured from flower to flower. The heavy scent of jasmine and musk rose engorged the night, quivering softly in the faint whisper of a breeze. A few stars sparkled faintly. We met underneath the tangled shadow of the apple-trees. We lingered, talking softly; we touched, gently. The world lay hushed; centuries passed; empires flourished and then vanished into dust. No priest or ceremony bound us, bounden only by our love, mine honey in the honeycomb. And now—now you wind about her—those dear arms, once holden in mine. You call her your lily, your slim gilt girl. But remembering, I think: when the pale stars shimmer, do not our shadows gleam again in the twilight, among the heavy scent of the apple blossoms? No: you will not forget.

We went everywhere together. *Let me introduce you to a friend of mine. A poet. He is translating Verlaine. A young poet, a poet of great* promise. *Is he not beautiful? He is my Dorian Gray. Dorian, sing for them, recite one of your gilded songs. My voice sounds low, almost a murmur, as of someone half-asleep or almost drunk. I begin not to know myself or think perhaps I have become someone else. Reflected in the mirrored room of the Café Royal, my face now seems that of an angel, pure and translucent, now wan and suddenly aged. We meet now always at night, at dinner or at hotels. There are loans of money, discreet loans. But shame, shame. The touching becomes urgent, exact, unkind. Now I see Oscar looming towards me in the darkness of the Underground (the Circle Line), but, oh, how changed. Can this be he who was once lord of language, the splendid, the magnanimous, the inimitable Oscar? The rich laugh has turned raucous. He is bursting out of his clothes; his collar is too tight, his face deathly pale. A large white caterpillar, the huge hands greasy with sweat; familiar, awful. How can revulsion be so strong for someone once loved, nay, adored? Oscar strides in among the company of the dead; they part for him, their ashen faces raddled and rodentlike. Living like rats in the dark, under ground, in the night world of music halls and brothels and bars. Dowson and Johnson, Beardsley and Bosie, Reggie and Robbie. Decadents. Degenerates. Dead men in the realm of the dead. I too have inherited this rich terrain.*

Father Gray jolts awake. The light persuades its way through the thick leaded panes of the bedroom window, dim and dimmer. It is Edinburgh. It is Sunday. Father Gray rises from his bed, turning back the black linen sheets. He rises as if from a coffin. He is older than the stones within which he lives; like the vampire, he has been dead many times, and learned the secrets of the grave; and has been a diver in deep seas, and keeps their fallen day about him.

The fancy of a perpetual life, sweeping together ten thousand experiences, is an old one, but here it is embodied forever in one of the living dead: a man who made himself into a book; a book that made him into a man. One who died and rose to die again to the perpetual life of a priest: John Gray turned to Dorian Gray; Dorian Gray to Father Gray; from boy to poet, poet to prodigal, prodigal to priest.

What he did not burn lives after him to tell the story.

1 | IN THE STUDIO

(AUTUMN 1889–NOVEMBER 1890)

THE PATH LEADS INTO A CUL-DE-SAC off the King's Road, Chelsea, winding towards the three old houses of the Vale; "a muddy retreat from the highway, edged by gardens in which snow-ball trees grow from the soil like wands, . . . full of sighing—one expects to see dead cats mouldering under them"[1] Is it autumn? In London in the rain, it is hard to know; the biographer can never pinpoint the exact date. The snowball shrubs drip into small stagnant pools; the odor of leaf mold and leaf slime frets the heavy air. As the late afternoon mist begins to gather, the last of the summer bees shoulder their way through the late blossoms of rose and nasturtium, entangled and overgrown; the sharp tang of rotten apples, windfalls, cuts through all the other smells of fermentation and decay. The dim roar of the London traffic is like a bourdon note of a distant organ.

John Gray pushes his way through the heavy door of one of the houses; it is ajar; his knock has not been answered. From above, he hears a brief shout, a swift riposte, then laughter. He makes his way through the hallway, the walls still the same bilious yellow painted by the last occupant, James McNeil Whistler, and up the wide staircase to the formal sitting room; knocks swiftly, and enters. Ah, Gray. You're most welcome. One man moves to greet him; small and wiry, his thin face tipped with a pointed, golden beard, his long hands fluttering, his long, aristocratic face that of a decadent Christ.[2] My disciple, he announces.[3] Across the room, another, but tall and well made, "exactly like one of the comely angels of Della

Francesca,"[4] watches with his eyes, the eyes that follow his Beloved everywhere. The two Charleses—Ricketts and Shannon—inseparable, enigmatic. Bound by their art; a sterner bond than any fleshly one. Have you met this man, Ricketts half declares, half asks. You surely know him: Oscar Wilde. A large figure looms against the window, cloaked, courtly, smiling with his mouth closed. As his eyes take in Gray, they narrow, as if looking at the sun. Then he laughs, extravagantly, throwing his head back, like a man who has suddenly noticed a treasure, a loud, careless laugh with the mouth wide, showing blackened teeth.

Ah, yes, Mr. Gray. We have met, have we not? Several times? It has been so long, I have almost forgotten. (If Wilde has forgotten, the biographer never has been able to establish the date.) Was the last not just before you left for France? Early summer? (Yes, the biographer concurs, early summer. It was "at one of those Soho restaurants that furnish private rooms for supper parties," Frank Liebich, a popular concert pianist of the day, recalled; he had been invited by a young poet-anarchist, John Barlas. Wilde had bantered with Barlas, "full of lively trivialities"; but, Liebich remembers, Gray seemed bored and tired. "I thought him a thoroughly blasé worldling,—a type which I could neither understand nor admire." Barlas "had hinted rather vaguely, of the [alleged] intimacy between Wilde and Gray, so that I was really rather more curious about the latter, an extraordinarily good-looking youth . . . but severely conventional in both speech and behaviour."[5])

Ah, but Oscar says, I have just learned that you are one of the Valists. You see, The Artists have sent me a copy of your wonderful first *Dial*. The occasion of this, my first formal visit. You have told me of them, but you did not tell me that you were among their small band—nor that they were so cultivated and interesting.[6] You have your secrets, I can see. This *Dial*, now. They will call it "that mad journal the *Dial*, with some good line work in it, & rubbish for prose."[7] But they do not know. The drawings are exquisite; and your prose, Mr. Gray, your prose is immortal. That delightful fairy story of the Worm in Love—pure rococo.[8] I must recite to you my own fairy stories some day soon. And that masterpiece on the Goncourts, written in exquisite imitation of their own decomposing style, all nervous detail, like some mad *pointillisme* in prose. You are right to argue that "where there is unusual insistance [*sic*] over trivialities, it is merely nature seen by two exceptional organisms of peculiarly rare culture." Of course the artist is "always an abnormal creature, a being with an overdeveloped brain, or diseased nerves . . . "[9] Is this not the predictable result of the savage stupor in which we live? Does it not reduce us to exquisite doomed wrecks who can only register the degeneration of the world about them, taking refuge in the beautiful sterile redoubts of Art? I despair of English art, but perhaps you are right, that it will be freed from the trammels of tradition. Perhaps, like the French, the English will reinvent Japan or the exquisite frivolities of our last, lamented century, when English art flourished in the moment before it died an official death. As you say, the Goncourts point the way. It is right, too, to insist that they are more than literary men: that they have changed forever "the manner of seeing, not thinking, of contemporary painters."[10] In an age of barbarism, the arts borrow not from life, but from each other. English art has not learned this; it has denied the ancestors. Will they ever understand that they must become, in all things, Pre-Raphaelite? My dear Mr. Gray, you must finish your essay on Rossetti.

Gray nods quietly. He has tried to keep his life compartmentalized but the compartments keep collapsing into each other. He had told Oscar about his trip to Brittany but nothing about what had happened there; he scarcely had had time to get back to the Foreign Office and resume work there before horrid family troubles began to multiply.[11] Oscar knows nothing about them either; Gray let him assume his background was very simple;[12] he worked hard to disguise his cockney accent, but it would break through.[13] He is learning; the Artists are his first teachers. He walks to the high window and looks out at the orchard.

You are an artist, you know, the true thing. Once the gates are open, Wilde's course of talk swells to a flood. The disciple remains impassive, letting it flow over him as Oscar plunges ahead. I came to thank the noble Artists for their exquisite picture of Willie Hughes, sent to me to vindicate my theory. I was just telling Ricketts, "it is not a forgery at all; it is an authentic Clouet of the highest authentic value. It is absurd of you and Shannon to try and take me in! As if I did not know the master's touch, or was no judge of frames! Seriously, my dear fellow, it is quite wonderful."[14] And now he has just shown me a sketch he made of you, so alike, I would not have known which was which. Ricketts tells me he is to do your portrait in lithograph.[15] He tells me he is putting his life into it, that he will never part with it. That he is inventing you as he is inventing for England a new kind of book, a kind of total and final object, where all the arts of typography and binding and print and prose and poetry will play into each other, like some divine polyphony from the Renaissance. This *Dial* will be the ancestor of many such books, perhaps the ancestor of my own beautiful as yet unwritten book, full of beautiful yet unwritten thoughts, a book so perfect that every reader will find his own life in it and the face it paints will be the face of the reader. Ah, my dear Artists, you must print no further edition of *The Dial*—it is quite perfect and all perfect things should be unique.[16]

Wilde half turns, aware of the averted gaze. My dear Gray, I do not think you comprehend what I am saying. Ricketts tells me that you are to be his next work of art. That you came here with a portfolio of mediocre drawings and that you left here a poet. That he has set you the task of translating Verlaine and desires you to go to Paris to meet with him. Ah, Ricketts I see knows everything about Paris and speaks French as his mother tongue. And such an eye! It takes in everything! "What a charming old house you have! And what delightful Japanese prints!"[17] Oscar gestures towards the sage-green walls onto which the Artists had tacked a few exquisite Hiroshige prints alongside various reproductions, both in their own hand and by photograph, of every kind of artwork they admired: here a drawing of a Greek or Egyptian sculpture; there a copy of an early Florentine Madonna; elsewhere an early Rubens set off by a late Rossetti thing. In one corner, a Chinese screen with three exquisitely delineated baboons; in another, a few lithographs by Shannon and a gilded fan left by Whistler. Rare shells shimmer within bowls of water and there are cut flowers everywhere, in vases of every imaginable shape and size, filling the room with the heavy scent of a greenhouse. On one wall, "hideous toys purchased in odds & ends shops strike the necessary discord."[18]

Oscar draws himself up to full height. It is clear, he announces to the room, that Ricketts is "one of the first to recognise what is, indeed, the very keynote of aesthetic eclecticism, I mean the true harmony of all really beautiful things irrespective of age or place, of school or manner. He saw that in decorating a room, which is to be not a room for show, but a room to live in, we should never aim at any archaeological reconstruction of the past, nor burden ourselves with any fanciful necessity for historical accuracy. In this artistic perception he was entirely right. All beautiful things belong to the same age."[19] Because they know this, it is fated that the Valists will become the great collectors, the great connoisseurs, of our age.

Gray glances skeptically at the scrubbed, simple wooden furniture; Ricketts and Shannon live like monks. With adequate means they could do anything; but where do poor artists in these days find patrons?

Oscar comes to an abrupt halt and completes his turn, pauses for a moment, then launches into a theatrical address aimed towards Gray at the window. Unfortunately, sir, I too am a collector. I have asked Ricketts if I might buy this sketch, but he will not part with it. So I will simply have to collect you in person and take you with me everywhere. You will not be as permanent as the sketch; but we will make the most of you before you are grown old.

I never wish to grow old, Gray finds himself murmuring.

Naturally, my dear man, Wilde purrs. Youth is the inspiration of genius. You have the profile of a poet. Become the poet and the profile will never desert you. It will become your mask. Of your intellectual and emotional life, history will know nothing; you will simply represent the dominance of form.

The words seem to ring, then fade. Through the windowpane, Gray looks through the twilight towards the Thames, downriver and through the mist, to where his own miserable island history had its origins.[20] From its very beginning, the notion of history had been mocked; the facts, which should have been solid and incontestable, had become one way or another flimsy and factitious. Even his birth date. Does not everyone own the day of their birth, written in firm black pen on certificate, ratified by midwife and all the attendant trivia of time and place? According to the Register Office, John Gray was born on 10 March 1866.[21] His mother was twenty-one; his father, twenty-three. But his parents, as Gray reflects bitterly, being "weak in astronomy and novices in their character," registered the birth of their firstborn a day later than the actual event.[22] It set the course for all subsequent events. With the common sense of a young child, Gray abandoned history, preferred to piece together his lineage from fragments of family lore. His father claimed Scots ancestry, even though there were no visible Scots ancestors to verify this. Nevertheless there is a certain satisfaction in feeling foreign, in not being totally accountable to his time and place. England is a miserable island; the center of a self-satisfied, satiated society, glutted with the spoils of empire. It is not a time or place to which he wishes to belong. To be a Scot, or a least a Celt, indicates some sort of resistance. Now that he is discovering France, he is beginning to refer to England as "my adopted country."[23]

His mother, on the other hand, is a native Londoner, and in all their wanderings from one set of rented rooms to another, they keep loosely within her known world: he was born in Islington, as was his sister Ada two years later; Frederick, again two years later, in Lambeth. Is it the gypsy blood from his mother's mother, or perhaps even from his father's father, that leads to this restlessness?[24] He does not know, but as a lad he had felt drawn to the gypsy bands in the fields just beyond; he was, as now, fond of wandering. When older, he would "often get up very early during the holidays, take some food from the larder, and leave a note" for his mother saying he would be out all day. His mother indulged him in this as in everything, telling his father loudly, if he protested, that she "never worried" about young John, that "in her eyes he could do nothing wrong or foolish."[25]

She raised her boys to be gentlemen. Hannah Mary née Williamson "adored and spoilt her sons, particularly John."[26] Even now, Gray can feel her willing him to success; she is ambitious for him, a strong-minded and sometimes overbearing woman. She is at times baffled by his mixture of ferocious independence and equally fierce dependence. What was the remark she used to make after cutting up his apple? "Perhaps you would like me to eat it for you?"[27] She sang him songs. "The first song I ever knew was Peter Gray," he had recalled to Sarah, one of his younger sisters. "He finished in the company of Indians (who scalped him)."[28] He was alien—a Scot, a gypsy. The song with his name in it told him he was also doomed.

An urge to escape seizes Gray, perhaps to jump; he looks down from the tall windows of the studio into the tangled orchard below, damp and gloomy, and then reflects that, after all, he is on the right side of the window. He gazes again through the darkening day towards Greenwich.

His mother has been his ally; most of all, she has stood between him and the father. Dismay seizes Gray momentarily as he glances back into the room towards Wilde and Ricketts. How had fate contrived to give him such a father? They share the same name but they are worlds apart. He knows only a small part of his own father's history. His grandfather had been a soldier and had been somewhat unprepared for the slightly foppish man into which his son had transmuted. By the time of his marriage, John Gray senior had risen to the position of merchant's clerk.[29] His wedding picture makes him look almost genteel: a slight, very youthful figure standing, leaning on one elbow, his wavy hair falling below the ears. Under the wing neck of his collar he wears an over-large black bow tie; in the left hand, he grasps firmly a slim malacca cane. Gray winces at the memory of the photo, which might be of a boy at seventeen; now nearly the same age, he knows himself to look just as boyish. But Gray has learned to his cost how his father's air of assurance, even coldness, belies itself in the weakness written in mouth and chin. Properly read, that photograph might have predicted his whole miserable island history.

Like the procession of rented houses in which they live, his father's work comes and goes. For a while he labored as a wheelwright and journeyman carpenter in the Woolwich dockyard; visiting him in yard, young Gray learned more than he wished to about the intricate art of making a wheel.[30] It was only later that he began to value the old handcraft work, dying with the horse-drawn carriage, as its own kind of poetry. His father never lost a truculent respect for those who work with their hands, even when he rose to glory as Inspector of Stores at the Woolwich Arsenal.[31] Straining to look through the darkening mist, Gray can almost see him now, on his way home from the pub through the filth and smoke of the roads near the Thames dockland. He can almost hear, as he finally arrives at home, the opening salvo of the ongoing battle; mother chiding father grimly: for drink taken, for the wages drunk once again; a clatter of children, one born every two to three years, the last of the nine, Beatrice, now only two, and no money in the house again. "You never disguised from us your dislike of our father," he finds himself addressing her. "You drew our attention to his bullying vulgar voice, his heavy tread, his untidy mustache, his physical delinquencies, his moral deficiencies. You sapped his power, and our love at the same time, and when we were older, and you needed his authority as a weapon against us, you called us unnatural because we despised him."[32] (Years later—a lifetime later—Father Gray was to grow more eloquent about "this man" in notes for a sermon which addressed this type of the "unskilled, uneducated, irreligious, labouring man." Of all the classes in English society, he would observe, this man is alone in being a pariah—not even having the claims on society of a criminal. The marriage he makes is

> a daily debasement of two bodies. The prospect of family is at first kept out of thought, then hated. The wife is hated, for this man does not accuse himself on the cause of his wretchedness. It is not lack of affection, incapability of feelings of fellowship. This man is never so sullen but he has some vibration of warmth, however low, towards the men he sees every day, by the mere fact of seeing them; but with his wife, not at all . . . It is conduct minutely parallel to his sexual conduct if this man should drink one third of his earnings; it is the same conduct expressed in two different sets of terms.[33])

He hears his name mentioned. Ricketts, full of mischief, is relating to Oscar how Gray had been flattered when a woman said, "You are d—d handsome, but you're deadly dull."[34] The burst of laughter to his back dislodges Gray momentarily from his bitterness, but it careens relentlessly on towards that black day when he, decisively and forever, disowned his father. School. His father hated him going to school. Did he know instinctively that his first son's defection was implicitly a rejection of him, of his class, his manners, his ambitions? He is his mother's child. She is a printer's daughter, with books in her blood. From the time she had taught him the alphabet, he knew, before she even voiced it, that school was the only door out of the jail of iron circumstance and low birth. No fuss had been made when they moved again, to Plumstead, and he had been placed in Mr. Nichols's Wesleyan day school; the younger lads all dropped by for help with their schoolwork from their "clever" classmate.[35] No, his father chose the moment of his triumph. Young Gray had won a scholarship to the Roan School in Eastney Street, Greenwich. That year was drunken with promise: he had gained a prize from the Royal Humane Society for an essay on cruelty to animals; at the end of the first year, his character and conduct had been recorded as "excellent." And then, with no warning—he could scarcely write about it years later, in a rough draft of a poem (the only form in which it would bear thinking about)

{My father then commands
That I must learn to use my hands
Thinking that use is everything.}
Then and still being young
Ill liking it I went among
Whose art it is to make a useful thing.
There many a long year I learnt
To make a thing; where living is well earned,
Where men set up the engines of their suffering.[36]

They had had words, but the words were carried on a current of ferocity that pushed young Gray under; he felt he was drowning. You're the eldest lad; the younger ones will be needing to be looked after; you know there's lack of food and shoes and all. You can work now for good money at Arsenal, and the superintendent there's willing to give you your chance. So you're off now, lad, and bugger the books.

In pain, he turns from the window momentarily back to the room, watching Ricketts, prancing across the wide room, which ran the entire length of the house, "a short, ramshackle youth in a cloud of extremely fine, tow-coloured hair which stood around his head like a dandelion puff." He had only recently turned out of bed and had disappeared and reentered the room "imitating an orchestra with gestures as well as sounds, a characteristic mode of progression from room to room all his life." Somebody began describing a picture of a young girl with hay-rakes: he pretended to be shocked. "'Young girls with rakes!' and danced about hiding his face in his hands and laughed even more" than the others in the room.[37] Now he grew solemn again; his composed face, with its small, pointed beard, reminds Gray of one visitor who described Ricketts as "Shakespeare in a fit."[38] Was it Roland Holst, a Dutch artist he had brought to the Vale?[39] Or was it another, the wit who pictured Ricketts as "a little tin Jesus"?[40] Gray smiles wryly, recalling how, when Ricketts was posing for Frederick Shields's picture "Christ and the Woman of Samaria," one of the helpers boiled the water and filled the pot, then discovered he had forgotten to add the tea. "Wait, I'll get it," he exclaimed. "No," Ricketts had raised one majestic hand: "my miracle."[41]

Now Ricketts perches on the edge of the table, sweeping away the wood blocks and burins, flinging himself into another discourse of inspired rot,[42] playing with ideas as if they were toys, throwing them up into the air and catching them again.[43] Gray follows not so much the words as the swift movement of mind, as Ricketts pounces on essentials, flushing and quivering, now in admiration, now in anger; his laughter frequent and tempestuous.[44] Ah but Oscar: we meet on Flaubert and Baudelaire; here we are on common ground. I have never read Pater; so we will come to an understanding. I will read your Oxford don if you will read my riff-raff Verlaine. Oscar protests. He has read Verlaine; he has met Verlaine. Verlaine, Wilde pronounces, has led one "of the most perfect lives I have come across in my experience . . . [He is] the one Christian poet since Dante."[45] Ricketts pounces: How can you say that? This man abandons his wife and child for a debauched adolescent whom he considers a genius and with whom he is madly infatuated. When he thinks Rimbaud might break away, Verlaine tries to shoot him and winds up in prison. What a lover! Of course, it makes for wonderful poetry; and the conversion just translates all that fleshly love into lurid religion. "What's the use of saying that?" Shannon queries mildly. "You know you don't think it."[46]

The outburst of laughter from the room makes Gray wince. As he turns back to the window, he feels the blackness of the evening move inside him. He allows himself to become lost in it, walking through the early morning gloom towards the Arsenal, hungry, still asleep, a boy joining the growing throng of men making their way through darkened streets to work. (It will be years from now—how many? five? six?—before he can exorcise the hellish vision that awaits him behind the high gates, until art renders even that suffering into a shape, in a poem called "The Forge":

> A long and narrow shop, magenta black
> Mottled with rose; ten fires along one wall.
> Faint day comes through the skylight overhead
> Smoke-grimed to orange, when it comes at all.
> The blast shut off for breakfast, fires are slack.
>
> The buzzing neighbouring engine quieted,
> You hear the mates talking from berth to berth;
> The silence is complete. The seldom noises
> Reverberate as, quaintly, under earth
> The graves repeat the sayings of the dead.
> . . . .
> A rumour stirs, a hum, the blast comes back;
> Shadows on wall and roof start forth and die.
> Rattle of tongs, slosh, fume; unlovely night
> Grown Chinese hell, to seeming, suddenly,
> Where strange gods heap the fire and trim the rack.
>
> Half shapes of light leap higher than man's height
> Out from the blackness and as soon subside,
> Flame-flesh-shapes, sweat-swamped clinging cotton swathed,

In violent action, following the guide
Of the smith's gesture bidding where to smite.

The smitten steel complains, all bruised and scathed,
From thud to bark, from bark to metal scream;
Through ordeal of the fire and scaling trough,
To wake it from its long-embowelled dream,
To uses brought, flame-licked and torture-bathed.

This the arena wherein stubborn stuff
With man locks strength; where elements dispute
The mastery, where breath and fire bear blaze,

Where sullen water aids, to quell the brute
Earth into shape, to make it meek enough.

And this day is the type of many days.[47])

For almost three years, this had been the prison of his soul. In desperation, Gray had talked himself out of the machine shop into the design room, away from the blast; he had some modest drawing talent. But he was looking for a door out; was it his mother who told him that Civil Service positions now went by exam, so that even a boy of his circumstance could have a chance at them? He had prepared himself for the Civil Service Certificate exam as best he could, studying in the slack hours of work; certainly the drawing room was more congenial than the forge. (He was, as he later confessed in the half-baked poem about these years, "tired

Of whirring {lathe} and rank machine-oil's smell.
  I lied. I loved them one & both;
  Truth being vanity in me was loth
That wit like mine should cut no harder stuff than steel.[48])

Vanity goaded him on. On 29 September 1882, at age sixteen, he sat for the Civil Service Certificate exam, qualifying as a boy clerk in the Post Office Savings Bank. Again that autobiographical fragment provides a gloss:

> {I left the shop; & thence
> Addicted me to pens & pence.}
> Ah, that I thought to face
> The world! To elbow me a place
> Ah Lord! I thank thee for that chastening.)

The lord and His chastening were yet years in the future. Now Gray was driven only by the desire to make his name. At sixteen, he wrote his first poem, a drugged Keatsian reverie, heavy with weariness.[49] At the speed he was moving, Gray had reason to be weary. Within a year, he moved to the Confidential Enquiry Branch, to work that dealt with questions of crime against the Post Office, such as theft or fraud.[50] This appealed more to the imagination, as did Arthur Edmonds. Edmonds was the first older man known to take an interest in him. "My dear Boy," he would call him, as they exchanged critiques, and later notes, about their explorations, particularly into Zola. Gray had jokingly called him "Parent" and parent he had become, at least to his waking soul.[51]

Two years after entering as a boy clerk, in December 1884, Gray scrambled up the next rung of the Civil Service ladder by winning another competition, to qualify as a lower division clerk. The qualifying exam stressed the importance of handwriting and orthography as well as competence in the obligatory subjects: English composition, précis writing, French and German, geography, and the history of Europe, 1789-1871. And general intelligence.[52] On qualifying, Gray immediately transferred back to the Post Office Savings Bank. He had his plans. The study was paying off. He had learned that the new redbrick University of London had established itself not as a teaching university but as an examining body which set a daunting standard for its matriculation examination—which in his generation was open to women as well as to men, regardless of class origin or religious affiliation. Gray decided to take the exams in order to establish his suitability for promotion. Among the exams, he had to gain passes in Latin and either Greek,

French, German, Sanskrit, or Arabic; in English language and history; mathematics; mechanics; and one science subject, either chemistry, heat and light, or magnetism and electricity. After two years of hard grind, of hours snatched behind the desk or in his corner at home, he passed the matriculation exam in June 1887.[53] He had just turned twenty-one. He was, at last, a man, in charge of his own destiny. He applied for a transfer to the Foreign Office, but to a post in which the work was familiar, that of its Post Office. It was time to level off, to take stock. One could continue the vertical scramble, it seems, ad infinitum; for once, Gray had had enough. After all, he had, by his own efforts, risen from metal-turner's apprentice to Civil Service clerk, doing in six years what it often takes a generation to achieve, if it is achieved at all: to cross the great Victorian divide between those who work with their hands and those who work by their head. John Gray declared himself a success. He made plans to move from home and to buy some decent clothes. The career of a complacent nobody awaited him.

Then he met Shannon and Ricketts. And Oscar Wilde. Until now, Gray muses, turning back from the window, he had kept these, his masters, apart, just as he had kept his family and his career, his career and his artist friends, all in separate compartments. They were each worlds asunder, and the strain of keeping them all going at the same time was beginning to tell when he decided, on impulse, to simplify matters by going off during the summer with a friend of a friend to his home in Brittany.

Gray stares into the fire, then begins a cursory tour of the Japanese prints on the wall, listening with one ear to the banter between Ricketts and Wilde. He had felt the need to clear his head. He applied for a few weeks' leave from the Foreign Office to accompany Marmaduke Langdale on the boat train to his family home in the Breton fishing village of St. Quay-Portrieux.[54] It was the early summer of 1889. Marmy had told him something of his circumstances. Gray had guessed that with so grandiloquent a name, Marmaduke was of ancient lineage; from his occupation, as travelling actor, that he had fallen on hard times. His father's recent death, Marmy explained, had left his mother almost destitute with five children to rear, several in poor health. Yet

Marmy was confident Gray would be welcome. His mother was an extraordinary woman who drew her strength from the Old Faith. In Brittany she was sustained by what Marmy described as its charm, dwelling on how the peasants showed their piety in the most direct, childlike ways: praying in the fields at the angelus, reciting the rosary around the hearth at bedtime. When Gray saw Gauguin's paintings of this place and time years later, it all came back to him: the sun, the poppy fields, the dusty roads, the men and women bent at their work or resting in the fields at the harvest. Simple and pure. The last refuge of the complex. An antidote to Oscar's glittering allure.

Fanny, one of Marmy's sisters, had met them at the door, with a reproving look to her brother. ("I was very lonely and not particularly happy when I had the good fortune to spend that time with you at St. Quay," Gray later wrote to Fanny, after he had become a priest; "consequently it has left a deep mark upon my affections.")[55] She must have been only eighteen, but there was "no trace of frivolity (one might almost say of femininity) about her nature."[56] She seemed quite indifferent to the stunning youth who had accompanied her brother from London or even to the matter of her own dress, which was clean but merely functional. Fanny—austere, strict, capable, "with the sort of faith that will move mountains"—welcomed them. The household routine was precise: prayers before breakfast and after supper; dinner at three. You may come and go as you please, she smiled. It is summer and the fields are blooming.

Gray rose at dawn, took a handful of bread and cheese, a small canteen of water, and left in time to greet the light. Day after day he turned his back to the sea to wander in the countryside of rock and pasture, passing fields of grain, watching the early harvesters mow and gather and build the small, round haystacks smoldering in the sun, thatched against the rain. The mist rose off them at dawn, haloing them in steam; they simmered at noon; they returned the light to the sky at dusk in a purple glow. A single magical spell kept their shadows anchored at the base, while its bulk moved around them as if in a dance with the sun, a dance wherein entered the smell of new-mown grass and the soft palette of violets, greens, and gold, all blurred in the blaze of the melting sun and subdued by the hush of a summer noon.

Early one morning, Gray "found himself at Mass in a small, wayside chapel, with half-a-dozen peasant women." (As Gray will recount the story to a fellow priest more than forty years later,

> it was an untidy, neglected place, and the priest an unshaven figure at the altar, slovenly, and in a hurry. Vividly and slowly, as if savouring afresh each tiny detail, Canon Gray reconstructed the scene, without a hint of criticism, leaning forward in his chair, hands on knees, and, in his grave eyes, a look of brooding wonder even after so many years. "Yes, Father," he said, with a slow turn of his head in my direction, "it was then that it came to me. I said to myself, 'John Gray, here is the real thing.'"[57])

The real thing, Gray reflects, having stopped in his circuit of the studio in front of one of the Artist's copies.[58] It is of a tempera panel from the early Florentine school: the Madonna, almost Oriental in the exquisite fineness of her features, caressing the naked babe; the refinement of gesture, the smaller angels playing lute and lyre at her feet, the faded pattern of rose and leaf behind her rich robes, even the slight greenish tinge to her face against the halo's gold, makes Gray desire something so infinitely gentle and tender that he can hardly name it. He feels desire take hold, like the first small licks of fire.

For a moment, the growing flame engrosses his attention. Behind him, the voices begin to fade as the light from the window deepens into that of another season. It is now March of a new year; in the steady gloom, the apple trees wave their budding branches beneath low clouds, driven by a wind which whistles through the rattling casements of the big old house. Oscar has disappeared. In his place, others are settled around the low fire; one, Sturge Moore, an intelligent but vague young man,[59] works intermittently on a draft of a translation from Rimbaud. Ricketts periodically wanders over to offer suggestions for possible English equivalents. But no one word has its equivalent in another, Moore protests, putting down his pen. Moore, you have a muddled brain,[60] Ricketts shoots back. Maybe the muddle is what makes you the poet. I am sure that some day I will be able to say, perhaps a bit pompously: I consider his poetry "the best work of his generation and perhaps of the present time." But when you work with your hands, you are "an Ass, but a Golden Ass."[61] Your hands are not intelligent; they are not the hands of a craftsman. Moore lays down the pen, glancing up at the Artist; the lines under Ricketts's eyes have deepened. He has, as he confesses, been up all the night before, engraving. "And how do you see, my dear man?" Moore peers at him sympathetically. "With a paraffin lamp to light the work and a decanter in front of it to concentrate the beam. Reginald Savage played Wagner" very loudly on the piano to keep me awake. "When his right hand got tired, he would go on with his left," Ricketts announces rhetorically, as if pronouncing on a great man. Ricketts "rose late," but had "worked every waking hour."[62] There is a pause. This evening I feel the toll, Ricketts mutters quietly and then, uncharacteristically, falls silent.

In the gloom Savage lingers in the corner, waiting for the moment when Shannon would offer a small supper of eggs and cocoa; on the last occasion, he recalls, the eggs were less than fresh.

Gray pauses near the window. The expedition on the raw March evening via the Fulham bus has left him weary and damp; the fire is small, and near the window the room seems distinctly drafty. He moves toward the table, seating himself gingerly in one of the sturdy, scrubbed wooden chairs, takes up the Rimbaud on which Moore had been working, unconscious that Savage has, in turn, picked up his pencil and begun to sketch.[63]

Rimbaud does not dispel the mood of gloom nor incipient sense of dislocation. It is hard to tell, Gray meditates, whether March is an end or a beginning. It has seen his birthday; he is now twenty-four. Last autumn he had decided to set the seal on whatever had happened in Brittany, arranging for formal instruction in the Roman Catholic faith. Then, on the dark day of St. Valentine, 14 February 1890, he had been formally received into the Roman Catholic Church as a convert, with conditional baptism, at Saints Anselm's and Cecilia's, Lincoln's Inn Fields. A few weeks later he was confirmed at St. Mary's, Cadogan Gardens.[64] After the summer, the heat, the sun, the moment of revelation among the fields of Brittany, the fire guttered and died. Was it only the London damp, or some native perversity, that made the blaze freeze into a cool indifference? (Nine years later he would write from seminary that "I went through instruction as blindly and indifferently as ever anyone did and immediately I began a course of sin compared with which my previous life was innocence."[65])

Innocence dies hard, Gray mutters, returning his gaze to the poems of Rimbaud. He had heard from Ricketts of Verlaine's love for this astonishing boy: how Rimbaud had become the occasion of his "grand and radiant sin" and how sin itself had led to conversion.[66] Certain of Verlaine's Catholic poems stirred Gray as no others had. One, from that effulgent book *Sagesse,* had stolen his tongue. With an incantatory moan, Verlaine directed the attention of Christ to his own wounds of love: "O my God, you have wounded me with love, / The wound is there and it is throbbing still, / O my God, you have wounded me with love."[67] How could he in his mind untie the love that bound Verlaine for his adopted, prodigious son from the love that now bound him to God? Had not this fallen archangel, by provoking him to violence, become the very instrument of Verlaine's salvation? The wounds of love had become literal when Verlaine, fearing Rimbaud would leave, had shot him twice during a violent quarrel. It was not so much the violence itself as rumors of their relationship that had led to Verlaine's two-year jail sentence. And yet in jail, he found his soul, and his soul found its true voice. Who can unweave the good from the evil, sin from salvation? Who can sever the love of God from the love for man, or, in this world, the world in which flesh must reign, carnal love from the love in the spirit? Gray rises abruptly, and reverts again to his stance beside the window, watching the gathering storm outside.

It is typically English weather, a shaft of sunshine through heavy clouds, portending only the next deluge. Gray thinks suddenly: Why do the English never learn from their weather how dark and light are inextricably bound to each other? Why is it so characteristic of the English to separate everything into dual categories, each mutually exclusive, each policed as relentlessly as the borders of the Empire? Good and bad, sin and salvation, manly and womanly, even English and un-English? Perhaps it was no accident that his faith came to him in Brittany and found its voice in the tortured cadences of a French poet. Catholicism, even in its attenuated Anglo-Catholic form, is feared here, even loathed, as un-English and unmanly. Verlaine is not English and loved a boy. But it takes a Verlaine to comprehend that the true faith can be ratified only by the necessary, the therapeutic sin.

Now as a Catholic, he reflects, moving along the wall to a reproduction of a Rubens male nude, I can sin as no Methodist is able to sin. Ah, sweet apostasy. Was it Oscar's new friend, Lionel Johnson, who had come down to London from Oxford a few weeks before, who set him on this track? Oscar, delighted with their meeting, had, as Johnson had reported, "discoursed, with infinite flippancy, of everyone; lauded the *Dial;* laughed at Pater; and consumed all my cigarettes."[68] By some alchemy, the earnest faith of Brittany had become sophisticated into the half-tender mockeries of London. Johnson regarded himself as having been seduced by the Old Faith, a seduction to which even Oscar (or, to hear him tell it, his impeccably Protestant mother) had succumbed. According to Oscar, she had taken her son to be baptized by a Roman Catholic priest, to the scandal of Protestant Dublin. Nor had Oscar been immune to the blandishments of Anglo-Catholic Oxford, from whence Lionel Johnson now issued. Oscar amuses Gray with Johnson's infectious mockery, his account of how the "exquisite thrills of anguish, exquisite adoration of suffering" are engendered by "a tender patronage of Catholicism": the

> white tapers upon the high altar, an ascetic and beautiful young priest, the great gilt monstrance, the subtile-scented and mystical incense, the old world accents of the Vulgate, of the Holy Offices; the splendour of sacred vestments! We kneel at some hour, not too early for our convenience, repeating that solemn Latin, drinking in those Gregorian tones, with plenty of modern French sonnets in memory, should the sermon be dull. But to join the Church! Ah, no! better to dally with the

enchanting mysteries, to pass from our dreams of delirium to our dreams of sanctity with no coarse facts to jar upon us. And so these refined persons cherish a double "passion": the sentiment of repentant yearning and the sentiment of rebellious sin.[69]

Ah, yes, Gray remarks to himself, passing from the window to Ricketts's prized copy of the Rembrandt etching of Christ at Emmaus; ah, yes, the charms of rebellious sin. Recognition: that is the secret. How the light had blazed for him when Oscar had taken the word "sin" and played with it, until it became something sparkling, jewel-like in its facets, held up to the light. Sin, Oscar pronounced, is "an essential element of progress . . . In its rejection of the current notions about morality, it is one with the higher ethics."[70] To transgress is to venture into forbidden worlds. To revolt against the bloodless rules of authority; to utter the unspoken words of his body in a world which is the world of flesh, of the word made incarnate.

(Years later, reading another Irishman, James Joyce, Gray will recognize in *A Portrait of the Artist as a Young Man* this idea's exact expression when Stephen proclaims: "It was his own soul going forth to experience, unfolding itself sin by sin, spreading abroad the balefire of its burning stars and folding back upon itself, fading slowly, quenching its own lights and fires."[71] Nothing else so caught that first beat of the soul's heart, expanding and contracting, opening and closing, as it takes its first breath in the world, alone. What was it that Joyce had said of his fellow countryman? That Oscar Wilde—that notable Anglo-Irish Protestant—exemplified "the truth inherent in the soul of Catholicism: that man cannot reach the divine heart except through that sense of separation and loss called sin."[72])

All that lurid paradox, lately turned to something near self-parody by Oscar's witty new friend, Lionel Johnson. Gray so far knew about Lionel Johnson only from Oscar, who was apt to muse aloud as to whether the diminutive Lionel was really a boy disguised as a man. And Gray had met another of Johnson's acquaintances through Marmy—Ernest Dowson. Dowson had come to know Johnson slightly at Oxford but, unlike Johnson, had abandoned his formal education for what he could learn in the music halls, the bars, and streets of London. Since coming down from Oxford in this Year of Our Lord 1890, Dowson had been to the Vale twice, accompanied by Gray. But it was all a dismal failure; the last time he had come, the Artists had cleared the table and were printing lithographs and "the atmosphere was probably too strenuous & too technical for visitors."[73] Gray had taken Dowson off to the Empire to look at the actresses. Dowson was taking up work now—in a fashion—at his father's business, a decaying dry dock in East London, making his way into the city each evening and returning to the dock most nights to sleep. Except the nights when he got drunk.

Gray momentarily recalls the poet, "round-shouldered, [with] irrepressibly curly hair, blue-grey eyes, terrible teeth" which "protruded horribly."[74] Poor Dowson. There was something so infinitely gentle and resigned about his manner, which was always precise, always polite, even under provocation. Glancing one further time at the explosion of light in the Rembrandt etching, Gray muses that Dowson, too, had not escaped the seduction of Catholicism.

What had he said when they first met? I too have become a Catholic, as every artist must.[75] Was there some infection at Oxford, a diseased longing for ritual and candles and beautiful young priests? (Years later, the poet Yeats would describe Dowson's religion as having "certainly no dogmatic outline, being but a desire for a condition of virginal ecstasy."[76]) Gray stops in front of a photograph of a statue: one of those slim Greek tanagra figurines, the girl graceful, young, looking as untouched as the day it passed through the fire. Yes, Dowson yearns for that which, in the girl, he despises in the grown woman. He had told Gray how, all the previous summer, he had been mired in writing a novel about a cold, high-minded grande dame, married unfortunately and to her great unhappiness. Madame de Voile was to be his ideal, a woman who actually had a brain, who distanced herself from the sensuousness, the frivolity, the manipulative destructiveness of the usual bourgeois woman. But his vision of his heroine, for all her cool and sad serenity, faded just as her small daughter—playful, wise, innocent—made her entry. The novel was still not finished. Perhaps, Dowson sighed, it never can be.

For at that moment when he recognized the shift in his interest from the noble matron to the *jeune fille,* Dowson was truly lost. He felt that only in the Church of Rome could one still find a world in which the pure, the virginal, are placed apart from the soiled crowd. "I am afraid, my dear, I am being driven to Rome in self defence," he wrote to his closest friend. "Vulgarity, sentimentality, crudity: isn't *there* an effectual, the *most* effectual protest against it all?"[77] To the poet, Rome in all its aspects constituted dissent from what he saw in London. For this reason, he and Lionel Johnson were drawn to the Church as artists. Not one he knew "adores Catholicism more than Johnson and myself," he wrote this friend again.

> You ought to have come to N[otre] D[ame] de France tonight. There was a procession after Vespers of the Enfants de Marie & I just managed to discern my special Enfant in spite of her veil, carrying a very big banner & looking as usual extremely self possessed & mistress of the situation. It was a wonderful & beautiful situation: the church—rather dark the smell of incense—the long line of graceful little girls all with their white veils over their heads—banners—: a few sad faced nuns—and last of all the priest carrying the Host, vested in white—censed by an acolyte who walked backwards—tossing his censer up "like a great gilt flower": and to come outside afterwards—London again—the sullen streets and the sordid people & Leicester Square.[78]

Dowson, too, had had his conversion, and clung to this bit of Paris within the heart of dreary London. Paris as a rebuke to London.

And what is sin, Gray murmurs, if it is not also protest? Protest against the narrowness of imagination, the iron conventions of the world into which he has been hurled. Is not sin for the Catholic merely the second act of his redemption; simply part of the drama? Moving back towards the window, his eye is caught momentarily by a magnificent copy of a pencil drawing by Puvis de Chavannes: of two young, godlike workmen stripped of all externals, as Ricketts had commented, engrossed in the drama of work and repose, composed "under the spell of passion, tenderness, and meditation."[79] Gray follows the line of the turned back, then moves towards the window. When he thinks to look out again, the apple trees are in bloom.

Oscar is in his usual dazzling form. There is a duel afoot. Whatever topic comes up, Wilde and Ricketts set to: thrust and parry and riposte, the wit flashing or sparking as the hard steel touches, then retreating for a fresh sally. Everything is game: the anarchists, the artists, the frauds; French elegance, English stupidity; the sterility of art, the fecundity of life. At the height of the exchange, "Oh, nonsense, Oscar," Ricketts shouts, with a great laugh. Then they take up their swords again, with Shannon joining the fray, Ricketts "following him about with rippling laughter & eyes that deprecate the Beloved's willfulness."[80] The names blaze, names that are new to Gray: those of Cézanne, Pissarro, van Gogh, Seurat, Signac, *Le Chat Noir, La Vogue*. Others they were tender about: Simeon Solomon, a great artist of the school to which Verlaine belonged, now a recluse in his old age, whispered about in the streets. Rossetti and Rossetti again, the flame that will blaze the way to a new tradition in art. They are the last of a little band of artists, painters, and men of letters who care about nothing except art. The talk lapses, flares briefly again, then dazzles and dies. Gray takes his leave with Oscar.

Coming out of the door, silently, without a word between them, they turn in the heavy dusk towards the deserted orchard, now overgrown. They stand under the boughs heavy with blossom, drooping, burdened, and as they pause Oscar touches him, a touch as soft as breath. You are beautiful. Your beauty is a form of genius. How clever of you to be so beautiful. Because you are made of ivory and gold, the world is changed; the curves of your lips will rewrite history. The sweet tremble of his voice, low, flutelike, melodious; the sweet tremble of his body. Burning. Then the hot breath, the sighs, the fumbled caresses, the mumbled endearments: mine honeycomb. My heart like wax receives the seal love setteth there.

Love flaming, running like molten metal, a river of fire in the dusk. Then afterwards, cooled by the dew; sighs, tears, explanations that explain nothing. Promises. Come with me. I will teach you. We will set the world ablaze, together.

(The memorial of that evening survives in Gray's hand, under the title "Passing the Love of Women":

> In the twilight darkling
>> When the sky was violet
> And the stars were faintly sparkling,
>> Thus it was we met,
>
> In a lonely meadow
>> Carpeted with crocuses
> Underneath the tangled shadow
>> Of the apple-trees.
>
> Long and fain we lingered
>> Whilst the world lay hushed in sleep.
> Till the dawning rosy-fingered
>> Clomb the eastern steep.
>
> Priest nor ceremony
>> Or of Orient or Rome
> Bound to me my love, mine honey
>> In the honey-comb.
>
> Who, albeit of human
>> Things the most sublime he knew,
> Left me, to espouse a woman
>> As the people do.

About the "overwhelming, superabounding-and-all-that-superlative-importance of the first sexual act," the older Gray was to remark: "All the passion of making the discovery that man is naturally chaste comes to me."[81] He did not "credit women with any of the virtues."[82]

Though he wind about her
  Those dear arms were holden in mine
He shall only reach the outer
  Precinct of the shrine;

For, when the pale stars shimmer
  In the vault of violet,
As far gleams of memory glimmer
  He will not forget.[83]

Near the end of his life, approached about the authorship of the poem, Canon Gray's chilly response was: "I cannot remember ever having written a poem with the title 'Passing the Love of Women.'"[84] But he did not forget.)

Now Oscar has to go home; Constance will be worried. The boys are still very young; Cyril is four and Vyvyan only three. Indeed, Constance has become increasingly anxious about Oscar's other boys, the young, adoring disciples who seem to appear from nowhere, to accompany him to private views and parties, or collect around him at Fitzroy Street or the Café Royal. Oscar moves like an emperor among them, dispensing quips and *aperçus* with the aplomb of a man born to be adored. Constance has become aware that he finds adoration short at home; that Oscar has had enough dinner conversations about babies and bills and Cyril's boots; that Oscar is moving into a world where she can no longer follow him.

She has tried hard to be agreeable when Oscar brings his young men home. There was a young Jewish disciple, for instance: André Raffalovich. She had gathered from Oscar only a sketch of how he had come to be in London. Apparently he had arrived some eight years ago, in 1882.[85] He is immensely rich, Oscar said, the younger son of a banker who had left Odessa for Paris. His mother keeps a fashionable salon on the Avenue Hoche; she is known to be both beautiful and brilliant. But with this third and last child, it seems there has been some painful constraint. Marc-André, or André as he is known, resolved the tension between them by deciding to continue his education at Oxford. He stayed there long enough to be warned by a watchful professor "to avoid the acquaintance of Pater and Symonds." But "I, of course, made a point of knowing Pater," as André confessed later.[86] To know Pater was to become infected with the Oxford taint of romantic love between men; Pater had been under dire suspicion since the publication of *The Renaissance*. In 1874, "at the very moment Pater's infamous 'Conclusion' was being denounced from the university pulpit of St. Mary's,"[87] Wilde had taken up this fatal book, "which has had such a strange influence over my life"[88]—and committed to heart its intoxicating command to end the crucifixion of the senses and initiate the renaissance of joy.[89]

Constance recalls Wilde claiming Raffalovich as an old friend. Shortly after Raffalovich had left Oxford, some seven years previous, he and Wilde took lunch together; as Raffalovich remembered it, Wilde "bullied the waiter and then took me to call on Speranza, his tall mother, in her darkened rooms in Park Street."[90] Raffalovich reciprocated with a dinner invitation; they later went to a play. Years passed: Wilde went to America, married, became a father. He had become known as a poet and man about town, most recently as the editor of *Woman's World*. When they were brought together again (in later years, Raffalovich could not recall how they had been reintroduced—perhaps by Whistler), Wilde had changed. He was flirtatious, dangerous. "You could give me a new thrill . . . ," Raffalovich recalls his saying, "you have the right measure of romance and cynicism." But that must have been "towards the close of our friendship." Wilde would tease "Sandy," as he nicknamed André, about the questionable company in which they would now find themselves. On the way to a musical club, Wilde had whispered, "My dear Sandy, come with me, and I will look after you there, and see you do not get introduced to any dangerous characters: the place is full of them." On another occasion, having just finished reading *Monsieur Vénus* by Rachilde, Oscar was in a visible state of excitement, talking "to me for several hours about the more dangerous affections." It must have been soon afterwards, Raffalovich recalls, "that his wife Constance, who had always befriended me, estranged us. She said to me: 'Oscar says he likes you so much—that you have such nice improper talks together . . .' I was furious: never again did I speak with him without witnesses."

(And later, after Raffalovich had stolen one of the disciples, a beautiful young man by the name of John Gray, he never spoke to Wilde again with or without witnesses.)

But in the spring of 1890, Wilde moves among the company of young men like a young Socrates: Constance might as well be Xanthippe. His disciples drink in his words as wine: coruscating, subversive; the voice flutelike, carrying into their hearts on its low and sweet music the exquisitely phrased cadences, the cadences of Socrates and of Plato after him, of Plotinus and Ficino and Michelangelo and Shakespeare; to the disciples, the cadences sound like the music of the soul. Those of the charmed circle from Oxford—Barlas and Johnson and Dowson (and later, Douglas)—to which Gray does not belong, had learned the music in the original Greek and heard its subtle modulation in the reveries of Pater; but it was Oscar who, in *The Portrait of Mr. W.H.,* traced the common genealogy from his "passion for Greek life and thought" to a "book of Sonnets, published nearly three hundred years ago, written by a dead hand in honour of a dead youth" which "suddenly explained to me the whole story of my soul's romance."[91] In the fictive youth of Willie Hughes, boy actor, Beloved of the Bard, Oscar claimed to have discovered the "real tragedy of his life. The moods of his own soul seemed to have taken shape and substance, and to be moving before him."[92] He espoused the notion that consciousness is "quite inadequate to explain the contents of personality. It is Art, and Art only, that reveals us to ourselves."[93] In Shakespeare's sonnets "I was deciphering the story of a life that had once been mine," [94] of an artist who fell in love with a boy and made him immortal through his art. And in the great love that he bore him, the "essentially male culture of the English Renaissance found its fullest and most perfect expression," [95] which was also the fullest "realisation of the Greek ideal,"[96] that the love of the beauty of the beloved inspires a "mystic transference of the expressions of the physical world to a sphere that was spiritual, that was removed from gross bodily appetite."[97] The children of this love, engendered in the soul, would be brought forth as the great creations of Art, the radiant Ideas of Thought.

(Looking back forty years later, Gray would realize that there was a moment—for it seemed brief, although it lingered for a generation—when the love of one man for another was an innocent love, innocent even when its impulse was desire and the desire only half expressed in the caresses and endearments of the beloved. It was in essence still almost childish, like discovering a small, low gateway back to the freshness and joy of boyhood. Even six years later, Raffalovich wondered about the naiveté of the late eighties, when he, as an artist, struggled to express a love that didn't even have a name. Some called themselves "Uranians," after the "heavenly" love between men, influenced by the planet Uranus, described in Plato's *Symposium*. Others referred to "Greek love," drawing on the ideal of Dorian comradeship first discovered in K. O. Müller's *Dorians*, "the ideal that so powerfully contested the ancient slur of 'effeminacy' invariably raised in England and America against men who loved men."[98] Still others were to refer to themselves as "inverts," on the grounds that they inverted normal relations between the sexes. The word "homosexual" had not even been invented. And this lack of a name was in a sense its liberation—for the movement found its uncategorized state gave it a freedom to conceive of itself as innocent and spiritual, the stirrings of a new artistic and spiritual brotherhood that would revivify an exhausted civilization.

The love that dared not speak its name thus had, in effect, no name to speak and lived in a half-articulated state, somewhere between innocence and danger. After all, it was only in 1885, five years previously, that the Criminal Law Amendment Act—making indecent acts between males (even consensual and in private) a matter for the criminal courts—that condemnation of this nascent culture was beginning to take a public form. And even then, this condemnation was of the act of sodomy: a true "Uranian" would have regarded such an act with disgust. Their love was of a higher kind: spiritual and emotional; its locus was Art, which it regarded as the home of the spirit; its children the progeny of the soul. Nevertheless, the new movement was cautious and discreet.)

Raffalovich knew the game. Two years after his arrival in London, in 1884, he had published *Cyril and Lionel and Other Poems: A Volume of Sentimental Studies*. One critic called its first poem an "almost flawless Uranian piece." Nor were its questionable emotions missed by a reviewer for the *Academy*, who commented that "it is hard to say from internal evidence whether the poems are the work of a man or of a woman, the male and female attitudes of minds towards love and nature being exhibited on all but alternative pages."[99] A year later, Raffalovich's second book of poetry, *Tuberose & Meadowsweet*, appeared and, in common with its sequel, *It Is Thyself*, managed to write a poetry in which "no third person possessive pronoun occurs at all and nowhere is the sex of the object of the author's deep passion mentioned."[100]

The hide-and-seek tactics of Uranian poetry were extended to their modes of publication. In the spring of 1890 Gray has just published his first translation in *The Artist and Journal of Home Culture*, a version of a Verlaine poem to his estranged wife.[101] As he knows, Gray is secure in the hands of his publisher, for Kains Jackson is a London lawyer by profession who understands the value of discretion. From 1888 onwards Kains Jackson has been using the *Journal* as a front for purveying "Uranian" material; yet "only among the initiated" would the magazine be recognized for its advocacy of boylove. As editor, Kains Jackson is known to be "tactful in the extreme, closely respecting pseudonyms and refusing to allow more than a thin scarlet thread of questionable literature to weave its way through the homespun of the monthly columns." During the spring, at about the time his translation—and first poem—is published, Gray makes plans to move away from his rooms at the Inner Temple to 62, Chancery Lane, a few doors from Kains Jackson's residence; Gray, too, is learning discretion.

Just exactly how discreet does one need to be? Gray wonders, looking again through the window into the glow of a June evening that has transmuted the overgrown tangle of the orchard into an Eden of scent and color. The crocuses and apple blossom are blown; now it is the turn of the flowering hawthorn, the laburnum, the lilac, and the early rose to fill the room with their heavy odor and the last silver notes of the twilight thrush.

Oscar is teasing the Artists again: Ricketts, he declares, is like an orchid—delicate, fair, pale, flamboyant, rare; Shannon, like a marigold—ruddy, boyish, blue eyed, decorative and quiet. Gray notes how Ricketts, giving his opinions, always speaks as "we." The partnership, Savage murmurs in his ear, *sotto voce,* always seems so perfect, as if they were twinborn in their art; there is never a sign of difference or discord; each sets the other off, in looks as in mind. Their simple and austere ways, their fine taste and fine manners, make them seem, for that moment, like two medieval saints, outlined in the shaft of late evening sun which beams dustily through the tall windows. Here, to Gray, is the ideal of manlove incarnate: each dedicated to his Beloved; each dedicated to the high religion of Art. Does Oscar have any idea how gross, how soiled by the world he appears, sitting in one of the white, scrubbed kitchen chairs next to Ricketts and Shannon? Gray surveys the rest of the company—Savage again, and a new man, Walter Sickert, witty and captivating in his talk, warmly responsive to both his hosts. Is there anyone Gray would not eventually meet through the Vale? (Only later in life would he appreciate that "everyone then lived in a very small circle: in Piccadilly, in the haunts [of the Cock, the Crown, the Empire and the Alhambra], at the art exhibitions; you knew exactly who you would see.")[102] At the studio of the Vale almost everyone who was trying to remake the old traditions would make an appearance during one week or another to pay homage to Ricketts. Now Prince Charles (the nickname is Gray's) urged his disciples to extend his contacts by travelling to France.

"Ricketts had a passion for influencing others," a fellow artist, William Rothenstein, later remarked.[103] And with Gray, as with others, the Artist is to fulfill his role according to the Platonic ideal—as that of an older man "inspiring" a younger "hearer" with "his own strength and noble taste in things."[104] Of course this was simply an enabling fiction; Ricketts, as Gray knows, is almost exactly his own age; but Ricketts possesses a knowledge of art and galleries befitting a man twice his years, and a taste as true as natural musical pitch; "He had been nowhere except to the Louvre," Rothenstein recalled in his memoirs, yet Ricketts "seemed to know everything, to have been everywhere. And he knew the names of rare flowers, of shells and of precious stones."[105] (Twenty years later, Gray was to confess: "It has struck me often that Ricketts is able to show things as wonderful now as things were in childhood. How many a time did I walk home to the Temple in the small hours, dreaming sunnily all the way from the palace of enchantment which the old unhygienic Vale already was."[106]) Ricketts had taught him what to read and how to see. And now, Gray muses, picking up a crudely printed manifesto in French, Ricketts has brought his disciple to the point where he is about to go to Paris, to form an alliance with the anarchists in art who are the only true revolutionaries.

It is not to be Gray's first trip. Looking around at the company, he reflects that the "'closed circle' atmosphere of the Vale had its prototype in Paris, where, at the age of twenty, [he] was told in Montparnasse that he was expected not to go to the right bank. With its own cafés and entertainments *and* the Luxembourg Gallery, the left bank was complete and enough for any man."[107] But this time Gray is determined to look up Félix Fénéon, a leading connoisseur of the *symboliste,* impressionist, and neo-impressionist artists working in France. A few stray issues of *La Vogue*—a journal edited by Fénéon—had made their way to the Vale, causing great excitement. The Valists had been set ablaze by new names—Seurat, Signac, Pissarro among the painters; in literature, by an enigma under the name of Arthur Rimbaud. Ricketts establishes through his Paris contacts that Fénéon, having rescued the manuscripts of poems called "Les Illuminations," is to edit and publish them—it seems posthumously, for Rimbaud has disappeared mysteriously from France and is rumored to have perished somewhere in the wilds of Abyssinia. Fénéon seems to champion many lost causes, Gray reflects, thinking of his own attempts to render the Rimbaud lines taken from *La Vogue* into English—and his less bumbling attempts at the lines of one Jules Laforgue, another poet saved from obscurity by Fénéon's advocacy.

Arriving on the Paris boat train in mid-July 1890, Gray enquires, as instructed, at Leon Varnier's bookstore as to how he might contact Félix Fénéon. He is given Fénéon's work address at the War Ministry—the right address, Gray reflects, for a committed anarchist. Discovering that Fénéon is out, Gray returns to the Hotel Continental on the Rue Castiglione to compose a note introducing himself. "You don't know me," he writes, " I am the least of a little band of artists, painters and men of letters in London which, like yourself, care about nothing except art. I intend to return to the Ministry of War tomorrow morning and beg you to give me a few moments of your conversation."[108]

Fénéon responds immediately, setting a time for Gray to meet him at his office; then, after the short, satisfactory meeting, he invites the young Englishman home for more leisurely talk over dinner. It is clear he is taken by the passion of Gray's search, for he arranges introductions to all the "notables" among the *symbolistes,* even dispatching Gray to visit Verlaine in hospital. Learning that Gray's Civil Service job allows him only a few days abroad, Fénéon also prepares a package of books and reviews for Gray to take home with him. Gray is charmed by the tall, lanky dandy, who removes his top hat only inside the office or at the dinner table; his monocle, glinting down from a height, makes Gray feel even more that he has found a true original, an aristocrat of the spirit. He asks Fénéon to give him a lithograph he has done of himself, a self-portrait in which Fénéon pictures himself as Mephistopheles. Fénéon is fond of depicting himself in this guise, cultivating a goatee, an intense gaze, a questioning frown; he himself describes his mask as that of an "icy Anglo-American comic."[109] But his friends detect the fire of a true heretic behind the impassive face and the marked silences.

Nothing, in the event, turns out as planned. Two days after the first letter to Fénéon, Gray finds himself writing again on 20 July, thanking him for his kindness and "this big pile of decadent litera-ture" in which he takes great pleasure. But Gray must now confess that he has stopped over in Switzerland because of a "bout of fever. The result, I think, of the insomnia from which I've been suffering for a while . . . I am very ill unfortunately." When I am a bit better, Gray writes, I propose to join some friends at Interlaken, then return to London to find my usual doctor. I plan to stop in Paris on a return trip and, if possible, I wish to see you again. I particularly wish you to accompany me again to the hospital where Verlaine lies ill—my attempt to see him proved a disaster; the servants there so irritated me with their "ridiculous questions that I abandoned my quest out of fear of becoming violent. (It is so annoying to think that this great poet is in the hands of such pigs.) But I'm going to make another attempt when I go by there on my return."[110]

In London once again, Gray realizes that in the confusion of his sudden departure, a tragedy has occurred: he has lost the wonderful self-portrait of Fénéon as Mephistopheles: Gray begs for a signed replacement, dedicated to himself.[111] Their correspondence is from disciple to master; Gray alternatively apologizing for his execrable French (apologies are certainly in order) and pressing Fénéon urgently for news of the revolution, of the new artists and writers battling for recognition in the salons and academies. Occasionally, Gray asks for actual books and articles and poses specific questions. Fénéon—affectionate, avuncular, satanic—undertakes to educate the former mechanic, providing information on Verlaine and Laforgue, advancing him copies of their latest books, sending on addresses of the editors of esoteric reviews in Paris and Brussels. He encourages the Englishman to try his hand at translating Verlaine and, later, the poetry of Rimbaud and Mallarmé.

At the Vale, the Artists appoint Gray emissary to Fénéon's Paris office. The disciple forwards lithographs by Whistler and Ricketts; Fénéon arranges for Ricketts to illustrate several of the new avant-garde journals which he edits. From Gray, Fénéon solicits articles and short notes on the new art of London and Paris, which he proposes to intercalate in his own pieces for *Le Chat Noir*.[112] To write these notes, Gray eagerly devours whatever material he can beg from Fénéon. His subsequent obituary for Dubois-Pillet, a neo-impressionist of the group which comprised Signac and Pissarro, demonstrates just what a command of technical idiom he had absorbed under the tutelage of Fénéon and of his master Ricketts.[113]

Above all, Gray writes fervently that Fénéon must come to London, to meet his friends, to stay with Ricketts and Shannon. To one such invitation, Fénéon replies that, while he cannot come immediately, he will certainly try for the next year, 1891. Immediately, Gray begins to make enthusiastic plans: when you come, he writes,

> We will see everything there is to be seen in London; we shall seek out drawings by a fellow named Simeon Solomon, a pre-Raphaelite, but also something else—somewhat like Verlaine, if what they say is true. [He does not add: Solomon's erotic

drawings of boys are known among a certain set and collected by Oscar; nor that Solomon had been arrested sixteen years previously for soliciting in a public urinal.] People no longer speak of him, except in whispers, but he was one of the great artists of the School (sometimes)—we shall go to Hampton Court, all the art galleries, and drive from one end of London to the other. Ricketts will decorate a room for you in Whistler's old house with mystical, sweet arabesques and decadent colours, the faint glimmer of gems on a tray of jade.[114]

Fénéon does not come that summer or autumn to the Vale, but keeps up a warm correspondence with his "dear," his "lovely friend," sometimes hinting at an erotic interest: "You have told me that Ricketts intends to do your portrait in lithograph. That is a very seductive project. Has he carried it out?"[115] And, being the true impresario, a man who brings all who believe in the cause of the new art together, Fénéon introduces Gray to his own friend, Francis Vielé-Griffin, who translates one of Gray's poems into French and solicits articles from Gray—in the first instance, on Rossetti—for his new magazine, *Entretiens politiques et littéraires*. Fénéon also presses Gray to translate Rimbaud's *Illuminations* as a matter of urgency; but Gray finds his skills routed in the attempt; there are as yet no equivalent models that would allow for its rendering into English.[116]

Yet, for all these gaps in transmission, Gray and Fénéon remain warmly appreciative of each other; the correspondence continues until the time Gray leaves for Rome. (In the mid-nineties, when Fénéon becomes editorial secretary of the remarkable *Revue Blanche,* he will get in touch with his friend John Gray to ask him to contribute.) Gray for his part is smitten. Something more than Fénéon's artistic perspicuity, more than the "finely penetrating mind" praised by Mallarmé, more even than his affectionate avuncular manner towards the young ambitious poet makes him beloved by Gray, in a manner he could express only in a poem dedicated to Fénéon:

Men, women, call thee so or so;
  I do not know.

Thou hast no name
For me, but in my heart a flame

Burns tireless, neath a silver vine.
   And round entwine
   Its purple girth
All things of fragrance and of worth.

Thou shout! thou burst of light! thou throb
   Of pain! thou sob!
   Thou like a bar
Of some sonata, heard from far

Through blue-hue'd veils! When in these wise,
   To my soul's eyes,
   Thy shape appears,
My aching hands are full of tears.[117]

Men and women did call Fénéon so or so—he himself adopted both feminine as well as masculine sobriquets, according to his mood, and published under various pseudonyms. Nor is there, this particular decade, any name for the hysterical ardor Gray feels towards Fénéon; the same flame burns through the poem of Lionel Johnson for Oscar Wilde, the same stutter about designation in Alfred Douglas's line about "the love that dare not speak its name." Fénéon plays with Gray's devotion, tenderly, when the young poet proposes another visit to Paris in early 1891, despite his straightened circumstances. Regretting that he could not help him materially, Fénéon adds, half wistfully, "I would like very much to receive you in an intimate apotheosis, esoteric and enchanting."[118]

Instead, Fénéon sends Gray a young French artist bound for London: Lucien Pissarro, the son of the painter Camille Pissarro, for whom Fénéon had mounted the critical barricades many times. On his leaving Paris in November 1890, Fénéon gave Lucien letters of introduction to Shannon and Ricketts along with instructions to look up Gray at his then lodgings in Number 1, The Cloisters, Inner Temple.[119] Lucien finds Gray "un charmant jeune homme, tout jeune," as he reports to his father.[120] A few days later, Gray makes his way on the Fulham bus with Lucien, through the bilious yellow hallway of the house in the Vale and up the stairs to make the necessary introduction to the Artists. Ricketts, forewarned by a note, is at first on his guard. Gray makes his way to the window, where, leaning with his back to the cold gloom of the November evening, oversees the proceedings. Lucien unties his portfolio and, woodcut by woodcut, spreads his recent work on the drafting table. Ricketts begins to exclaim, alternating his rapid and idiomatic French with English for emphasis, to point out to Savage and Shannon and Gray the importance of this, his most recent discovery. Shannon abandons his station near the fire to warm himself in Ricketts's enthusiasm; Lucien starts to thaw from his French formality, even to glow. And as the talk kindles the Artists begin to quiz him: about his father, about Signac, about Verlaine and Rimbaud and Mallarmé, about the various enterprises in which Fénéon has become embroiled. Lucien is disconcerted, then delighted. "There is a whole troupe of young people here," he writes his father, "who follow this new movement [of symbolism] ardently. Parisians have no idea of the influence abroad of certain writers they despise."[121]

(A few years after the death of Charles Ricketts and a year before his own, Gray recalled that evening and the long partnership it was to inspire—Lucien was to make his mark in the later *Dial* of 1893 and to contribute to the *Pageant*, another Valiste production. As Father Gray would recall, that partnership was only one instance of the richness of spirit sustained within the "old, unhygienic Vale":

> In the midst of want, I mean of the necessities of life, there were the richest projects abounding; series were without hesitation planned which it would have taken a life-time to carry into being: volumes, palaces, statuary. There used to be word of a volume of Songs of the Flesh (which, need I say, were never sung); and the Spirit may have received a like attention. Prince Charles was fully capable of designing what would never be, as he was of drawing copies of Hokusai prints and Dürer engravings. I have heard him curse fir trees, and I handled the Melancholia.

Of Ricketts, Gray concluded, "Knowledge was what he had. But how he had it. It made him like the giants of the Renaissance."[122] Gray was not to be surprised when, as the old century drew to its close and the new century gathered its own momentum, that the Artists were to be named as those who brought startling innovations both in book and stage design. He also knew that Ricketts's reputation as connoisseur and collector had prompted an offer of the position of director of the National Gallery in London—a position, which, to his later regret, Ricketts's turned down. And, after Ricketts's death, Father Gray was satisfied to learn that the pictures and prints he had once appraised, and even handled, in the Vale were to be bequeathed— as a rich legacy—to both the British Museum and to the Fitzwilliam Museum in Cambridge. Gray made a point of never going to see them there; it seemed too hard a reminder of what had changed; too public an exhibition of what had been hidden and, for many years, denied adequate recognition. Gray reflected that at least he had the satisfaction of having found, while still young, a master worthy of his admiration.)

Now in late middle age, Canon Gray meditates on the silvery engravings of the Artists on his own walls, washed in the dim light of an Edinburgh evening. And from that long perspective in time— and the even longer one of his own varied lives—Canon Gray confesses to a fellow poet, Gordon Bottomley: "I am able to say to you alone that, with my little talent, I was an invention of Ricketts. He used to set me tasks to perform; he was infinitely patient with the performer and very hard upon the performance." Ricketts, he writes, "was to me the kind of tyrant I have always approved of— and meet in my present profession. No more than the Pope would he ever have told me what he intended."[123] Ricketts had made him. Gray now knows himself to have been as much a part of the treasured collection of the Vale as any etching in silverpoint or masterly design that had been made there. Ricketts's friendship, "so rarely given,"[124] had been granted him; Ricketts was the begetter of the beautiful young man with flawless taste who was to be appropriated as "Dorian" Gray. Yes, Ricketts had made him.

Oscar was to be his undoing.

2 | THE FATAL BOOK
(DECEMBER 1890–NOVEMBER 1892)

CIVILIZATION HAS NEVER BEEN AN INDIVIDUAL THING; even if one were completely alone on a desert island, one would have to cultivate a multiplicity of selves to allow for the necessary friction of minds, the contact of personalities, the interchange of ideas. Alone momentarily, John Gray toys with the thought as he awaits Oscar Wilde in the Café Royal. Conviviality is the catalyst of true creativity. After all, even Plato began with a party; without food and drink, the divine talk would never have flowed through the *Symposium*. Here among the smoky acres of painted goddesses and cupids and tarnished gilding, beneath the golden caryatids and the dusky lighting which filters through the drifts of tobacco smoke, the flames from the chafing dishes, and the fumes from food, Oscar holds court. Secure from the fog and the outside world, the stiff conventions of the office and the jostle of the street, here Gray becomes "the poet," perhaps even the pet, of the large and flamboyant man who has, for years, been intent on making his name—as well as that of others—if not by fame, then by a sudden, astonishing notoriety.[1]

Gray glances at the opposing mirrors. He no longer recognizes himself. Through the haze he discerns a face, young and pure, at one moment as transparent as an angel's, at another, as pale as the shadow of death. Within a matter of months—six to be exact—he has become a creature of another's fantasy, a character from a book. At the beginning of summer, near the end of June and just before he embarked for France, Gray had been audaciously translated into fiction, to live among the pages of Oscar's first great literary scandal as the hero of "The Picture of Dorian Gray."[2]

How had this come about? He glances sideways at his profile through the immense, artificial gloaming. For months, Oscar and he had gone everywhere together: to private views, to first nights, to the opera, to plays, to pubs, to upstairs private dining rooms for dinners; to crushes; to at-homes and teas. They met regularly in the Café Royal, which quickly became his Eton and his Oxford. All the artists that mattered seemed to make their way there one week or another. He and Oscar were noticed together; his name was picked up. As a playful comment on their friendship, which in his literary mode Oscar compared to that of Socrates and Phaedrus or to Shakespeare and Willie Hughes, Oscar began laughingly to call him "Dorian."[3] With all the grandiloquent panoply of his Oxford education, Oscar explained that the name was given in honor of the strenuous love celebrated in Greek culture. It was a half-private joke, a nickname among the circles of artists among whom they moved. But since the moment that he had picked up the June edition of *Lippincott's Magazine,* the disciple felt his own solidity decomposing word by word, sentence by sentence, into the falling cadences of its seductive prose: John Gray disintegrating like a figure in a painting of Signac which, when viewed too closely, reads as an illusory mass of collated dots.

It came first as shock. Still ill and recovering from the misadventures of France, Gray took the novella to his bed, devouring it in one fevered morning. "It was the strangest book that he had ever read. It seemed to him that in exquisite raiment, and to the delicate sound of flutes, the sins of the world were passing in dumb show before him. Things that he had only dimly dreamed of were suddenly made real to him. Things of which he had never dreamed were gradually revealed."

"It was a novel without a plot," and with only one main character, being, indeed, simply a psychological study of a certain young London aristocrat, "who spent his life trying to realise in the nineteenth century all the passions and modes of thought that belonged to every century except his own, and to sum up, as it were, in himself the various moods through which the world-spirit had ever passed, loving for their mere artificiality those renunciations that men have unwisely called virtue, as much as those natural rebellions that wise men still call sin. The style in which it was written was that curious jeweled style, vivid and obscure at once, full of argot and of archaisms, of technical expressions and of elaborate paraphrases, that characterises the work of some of the finest artists of the French school of *symbolistes*. There were in it metaphors as monstrous as orchids, and as subtle in color. The life of the senses was described in the terms of mystical philosophy. One hardly knew at times whether one was reading the spiritual ecstasies of some medieval saint or the morbid confessions of a modern sinner. It was a poisonous book."

Gray knew even as he read that he would be changed forever; the "heavy odour of incense seemed to cling about its pages and to trouble the brain. The mere cadence of the sentences, the subtle monotony of their music, so full as it was of complex refrains and movements elaborately repeated," produced in his mind, as he passed from chapter to chapter, "a form of reverie, a malady of dreaming,"[4] that even now, reverting to it, makes him unconscious of the large figure looming over him, coming between the mirrors and the light.

He turns to the shadow. Ah, Oscar, you are returned. Please do sit down. I did not wish to join you in greeting those tedious creatures at the back table. They have fallen into bad habits, loudly calling me "Dorian" and reciting passages from your fascinating book.

You do not like the book? Oscar sits heavily, signaling to the waiter as he does so.

I said it fascinated me. I didn't say I liked it. There is a great difference.

Ah, if you have discovered that, you have discovered a great deal, Oscar murmurs. He turns to Bismark, the waiter, making his order for hock and seltzer as he opens his silver cigarette case.

What I have discovered is how little your book owes to Art. You have simply stolen everything and everyone. It is like a monstrous collation of everything you have done and said and everyone you have met over the past few years. A catalogue of thefts. I wouldn't know even where to begin. With the other books with which you have infected me? With the wonderful paraphrases of Pater, used by Lord Henry to translate the gospel of *The Renaissance* to Dorian, saying: "I believe that if one man were to live out his life fully and completely, were to give form to every feeling, expression to every thought, reality to every dream—I believe that the world would gain such a fresh impulse of joy that we would forget all the maladies of mediaevalism, and return to the Hellenic ideal—to something finer, richer, than the Hellenic ideal, it may be."[5] These subtle and fine words from Pater you steal and twist into a new gospel of sin.

Oscar smiles, and begins to recite in a low, languid voice; his cool, white, flowerlike hands waving his cigarette before him: "But the bravest man amongst us is afraid of himself. The mutilation of the savage has its tragic survival in the self-denial that mars our lives. We are punished for our refusals. Every impulse that we strive to strangle broods in the mind, and poisons us. The body sins once, and has done with its sin, for action is a mode of purification. Nothing remains then but the recollection of a pleasure, or the luxury of a regret. The only way to get rid of a temptation is to yield to it. Resist it, and your soul grows sick with longing for the things it has forbidden to itself, with desire for what its monstrous laws have made monstrous and unlawful. It has been said that the great events of the world take place in the brain. It is in the brain, and the brain only, that the great sins of the world take place also. You, Mr. Gray, you yourself, with your rose-red youth and your rose-white boyhood, you have had passions that have made you afraid, thoughts that have filled you with terror, day-dreams and sleeping dreams whose mere memory might stain your cheek with shame—"[6]

Stop, murmurs "Dorian" Gray. It is true: you have stirred me with your music, even if the music is borrowed. When I read, I know that Lord Henry himself, with his low, musical voice and his insidious creed, even Lord Henry owes so much to yourself. How could you take such chances? A year ago London was on fire with scandal when Lord Henry Somerset fled to France after the dreadful accusations of his conduct with perverted telegraph boys; the way people talked, it looked as if even the prime minister and the Monarchy itself might be sullied.[7] How could you write yourself into such a melodrama? Do you not think you are courting danger? Do you have no idea of how literally the public takes a book? Think of the reaction to the novels of the Goncourts: do you remember how I parodied it?

> And what shall we, we English say? we the chosen? we who understand so well that a book, to be good, must recount a series of good actions? . . . Germinie Lacerteux stayed out late at night? stole from her mistress? Manette Salomon was not married to Coriolis? Put it away! put it away! Dear me! if Freddy should get hold of it! Socking blemishes, happily so soon discovered. Let us beware of the glittering poison.[8]

My dear Oscar, I know how highly you regard poisoning; you laud it as a subtle art.[9] It is not the art of poisoning or even the poison of art which makes me anxious. What about the betrayal of our friends the Artists? They marveled at your cleverness in becoming Shakespeare. But do you think they are enjoying their debut in your new novella? Even Dowson thinks that Ricketts is the "prototype of the artist in 'Dorian.'"[10] Does Ricketts now bask in a new infamy as a result of your purple prose? Or does he wince at the thought of his fate in the melodrama, of its blood-red climax in which he is cruelly murdered?

Oscar, you will be accused of being a murderer, a poisoner of souls. But you are really only a pirate. I do not allude to your outright and outrageous theft of the list of rare musical instruments from the catalogue of the Kensington Museum—nor even of your appropriation of my own poem "Sound," which our visit there inspired.[11] This is trivial, my dear fellow, compared to the theft of my name. Not even my good name; simply my nickname, our joke, our revenge on the serious world. But now it might take its own revenge on us. You know perfectly well what trouble "Dorian" has gotten us into already, even though no one in our circle takes it seriously. But please to remember, dear fellow, that I am a civil servant and that my name does count for something in that world. Can you imagine what they will make of it in the Foreign Office? Foreign indeed!

Oscar looks at him slowly. "You have a wonderfully beautiful face, Mr. Gray. Don't frown. You have. And Beauty is a form of Genius—is higher indeed, than Genius, as it needs no explanation. It is one of the great facts of the world, like sunlight, or spring-time, or the reflection in dark waters of that silver shell we call the moon. It cannot be questioned. It has its divine right of sovereignty. It makes princes of those who have it. You smile? Ah! when you have lost it you won't smile."[12] But I have made that beauty immortal; in my words your face will live forever, with all the freshness of youth, with all the charm of its beauty, it will become an icon of the ages to come.

"'Stop!'" falters Dorian Gray, "stop! you bewilder me. I don't know what to say. There is some answer to you, but I cannot find it. Don't speak. Let me think. Or, rather, let me try not to think."[13]

For nearly ten minutes Gray sits there motionless, looking into the artificial gloaming as Oscar lights another of a succession of cigarettes, leans back in his chair, and studies carefully the effect of the rings of smoke turning from perfect circles to ovals, their shape gradually dissipating into the hazy gloom. His cigarette weaves a graceful firedance to the motion of his hands, as if he were tracing the thoughts that dance their way through his mind. Dorian glances sideways at the two figures reflected dimly in the large opposing mirror, his gaze brightening as his imagination quickens at the effect of Oscar's words. He is dimly conscious that entirely fresh impulses are at work within him, and they seem to have come really from himself. Oscar's words had touched some secret chord that had never been touched before, and he now felt he was vibrating and throbbing to new and curious pulses.

The slow, musical voice begins again, threading its way through his reverie: "'Ah! realise your youth while you have it. Don't squander the gold of your days, listening to the tedious, trying to improve the hopeless failure, or giving away your life to the ignorant, the common, and the vulgar. These are the sickly aims, the false ideals, of our age. Live! Live the wonderful life that is in you! Let nothing be lost upon you. Be always searching for new sensations. Be afraid of nothing . . . A new Hedonism,—that is what our century wants. You might be its visible symbol. With your personality there is nothing you could not do. The world belongs to you for a season . . . The moment I met you I saw that you were unconscious of what you really are, what you really might be. There was so much in you that charmed me that I felt I must tell you something about yourself. I thought how tragic it would be if you were wasted. For there is such a little time that your youth will last—such a little time.'"[14]

Dorian Gray listened, open-eyed and wondering. Looking through the dim haze of the café out towards the gray fog of the London November evening, the moment in the garden of the Vale came back to him as a moment of revelation. He remembered watching, with all the "strange interest in trivial things that we try to develop when things of high import make us afraid," how a bee buzzed around for a moment, then began to scramble all over the fretted white and rose of the apple blossoms. "After a time the bee flew away. He saw it creeping into the stained trumpet of a Tyrian convolvus. The flower seemed to quiver, and then swayed to and fro."[15]

He turns to Oscar, who stumps out his cigarette in a small burst of sparks and ash, and rises as if to go. My dear fellow, I am late. Is the poet to accompany me tonight to Horne's? Or do I go alone?

The poet nods silently to the last and watches as the large figure threads its way through the tables towards the door and the November night. Catching again the profile of his face in the mirror opposite, the purity of his face seems to rebuke him. How had he changed? What indeed had changed? There were places and things done and things resiled from; but above all, it was the words that had changed him. "Words! Mere words! How terrible they were! How clear, and vivid, and cruel! One could not escape from them. And yet what a subtle magic there was in them! . . . Mere words! Was there anything so real as words?"[16] And yet mere words had given him a shape and a name: the beautiful boy who was Wilde's— disciple?[17] Mere words had created him and, in doing so, revealed him to himself. Was there anything more terrible than becoming the spectator of one's own life, to have every impulse, every enthusiasm, every passion chronicled and analyzed—no, not ana- lyzed, vivisected? In the words of that terrible book, his newfound faith had been transmuted into a sensuous ritual, a mere exercise in the hedonism of Dorian Gray; in the terrible words of that book, his discovery of the *décadents* transformed into an experiment in dissolution. John Gray felt his safe and solid exterior dissipating into the words of Wilde's novel, as if dissolving, bit by bit, into its liquid cadences.

But gradually over the next few months, Gray became accustomed to his fate. The first reaction—a wave of public denunciation—had washed over Wilde in a tide of vituperation. The book was spittle, slime, wound ooze, the seepage of decay. A leprous book. Corrupting the young. He had read the reviews when he returned from France, carefully saved for him by the Artists. For Oscar, it had all seemed like an inverted form of glory. He luxuriated in the public contempt; Oscar, in his element, lacerated the fools gladly. Brilliant paradox after paradox upset the public's simple desire to be good, to be serious. Responding to it, Oscar conducted himself like one of those curious Japanese fighters who had learned, by a single elegant gesture, to turn the force of his opponent against itself. He turned the public platitudes back on themselves, converting them into incontrovertible countertruths; the Irish temper, the Irish wit, lancing the boil of public stupidity.

Gray could only admire, thinking: Oscar, you have appointed me your prince, your gilt god, your poet among poets. You have made it so interesting to be wonderful, to be young, with a fine pale skin and blue eyes, and a face in which the shadows of fleeting expressions come and go, with a mouth with the ivory curves of a Narcissus. It is so interesting to become oneself in another's eyes, painted out in the purple words of desire for all the world to read. Ah, Oscar, I will be your creature, your boy, your poet; I have even dreamed of how I will become your bear, eager for honey, basking in the sun of your admiration.

In January, he had sent Oscar a poem, signing it, "Yours ever, Dorian":

MISHKA

Mishka is poet among the beasts.
When roots are rotten, and rivers weep,
The bear at play in the land of sleep.

Though his head be heavy between his fists.
The bear is poet among the beasts.

THE DREAM:

Wide and large are the monster's eyes,
Nought saying, save one word alone:
Mishka! Mishka, as turned to stone,
Hears no word else, nor in anywise
Can see aught save the monster's eyes.

Honey is under the monster's lips;
And Mishka follows into her lair,
Dragged in the net of her yellow hair,
Knowing all things when honey drips
On his tongue like rain, the song of the hips

Of the honey-child, and of each twin mound.
Mishka! there screamed a far bird-note,
Deep in the sky, when round his throat
The triple coil of her hair she wound.
And stroked his limbs with a humming sound.

Mishka is white like a hunter's son;
For he knows no more of the ancient south
When the honey-child's lips are on his mouth,
When all her kisses are joined in one,
And his body is bathed in grass and sun.

The shadows lie mauven beneath the trees,
And purple stains, where the finches pass,
Leap in the stalks of the deep, rank grass.
Flutter of wing, and the buzz of bees,
Deepen the silence, and sweeten ease.

The honey-child is an olive tree,
The voice of birds and the voice of flowers,

> Each of them all and all the hours,
> The honey-child is a wingèd bee,
> Her touch is a perfume, a melody.[18]

Gray had explained to Oscar that "Mishka"—a diminutive of Michael in Russian—is a homonym applied both to a man and to a little bear. The honey of romance, Oscar murmured. Then smiled: You remember the bees in the garden of the Vale? The poem is pure Keats: Oh for a life of Sensations rather than of Thoughts! How well you show how the poet, falling into the sweet trance of sensuality, becomes the beast—and how the beast, under its spell, is transmogrified into the poet.[19] You sing, almost as sweetly as myself, of how the senses shall feed the soul and how the soul feeds upon the senses. Poet! You must chant your lines to the Rhymers, who meet in two weeks at Horne's. I am sure to be of the company there.

Gray had heard about Herbert Horne's from the Artists—as well as from Dowson. Herbert Horne and two other artists, Selwyn Image and A. H. Mackmurdo, constituted themselves as a little colony in Fitzroy Street, a colony much like the Vale; and like the Vale, it had produced one glorious journal as a benchmark of the new bookmaking, called (improbably) the *Century Guild Hobby Horse*.

Gray arrives to be greeted at the door by another resident; Gray knows his name—Lionel Johnson—from Oscar, and then again from Dowson, who before Christmas had impressed on Gray the importance of meeting someone so "wonderful & adorable" and with an "extraordinary width of knowledge."[20] Johnson seems almost dwarfed by the door and by Gray himself, with whom he shares a boyish air. His subsequent account of the evening is typically wicked: "We entertained the other night eighteen minor poets of our acquaintance: from Oscar Wilde to Walter Crane, with Arthur Symons and Willie Yeats between. They all inflicted their poems on each other, and were inimitably tedious, except dear Oscar." But the evening was not entirely lost, for almost in the same breath, Johnson records: "I have made great friends with the original of Dorian: one John Gray, a youth in the Temple, aged thirty, with the face of fifteen."[21] (Gray was actually only twenty-five at the time. They were indeed to be great friends; but the biographer notes that the record of their friendship, some twenty letters from Johnson to Gray, has now disappeared.)

Dowson's account of the evening was more engaged; he already regards the assemblage as a coterie—the circle later to be officially organized by Johnson and Yeats into the Rhymers' Club:

> Thursday at Horne's was very entertaining: a more queer assembly of "Rhymers"; and a quaint collection of rhymes. Crane (Walter) read a ballad: dull! One Ernest Radford, some triolets & rondels of merit: "Dorian" Gray some very beautiful & obscure versicles in the latest manner of French Symbolism; and the tedious Todhunter was tedious after his kind. Plarr and Johnson also read verses of great excellence; and the latter, also read for me my "Amor Umbratilis": And Oscar arrived late . . . [22]

(As poets damned, this was clearly hopeless; more like afternoon tea. In later life, Father Gray claimed he "never went to the Rhymers"—which could only mean that he never went to the formal sessions arranged in the upstairs of the Cheshire Cheese, where Johnson and Yeats, Symons and Dowson sat in long and gloomy silence, punctuated only by recitations and occasional attempts to establish some sense of literary purpose, quite doomed by English reticence and a downright hostility to ideas.[23] Meditating on their failure to cohere, Yeats would later proclaim: "England is the land of literary Ishmaels."[24] Looking back, Father Gray had an even harsher view of the Rhymers, remarking that except for Johnson and Symons, Yeats and [probably] Dowson, "the rest were preposterous."[25]

But greater than the effort to invent a new poetry was the effort to reinvent oneself. Being a minor poet in the 1890s was itself an art form: one had to be colorful, and dress meticulously, and be outrageously poor while acting as if one had all the money in the world. One had to drink to excess, but only in public; frequent well-known brothels, but only in company; sit in workingmen's pubs with sawdust on the floors, but only in the presence of young poets straight down from Oxford. Occasionally one was obliged to commit an outrageous scandal, climbing a lamppost in one's silk top hat, like the pompous Teixeira de Mattos,[26] or firing off a revolver in front of the Houses of Parliament to express one's contempt for that body, like poor, mad John Barlas. Or one could simply, like Gray himself, be seen in company with Oscar and his boys at the Café Royal. Meanwhile, as part of one's vocation, one had to impose one's poetry on the only audience that would listen to it: one's fellow poets.)

More stimulating than the evenings at Horne's are Gray's long walks into the grimy back lanes of London with a true poet, Dowson, to seek out his little lady, Missy. Adelaide Foltinowicz helps to serve the meals at her parents' restaurant in Soho; the food, like her accent, is a strange amalgam of English and Polish. (The routine was always the same, as Father Gray remembered: "ECD [Dowson] used to arrive from Bridge Dock at about 6, dressed in a black cut away coat and top hat, with dirty shirt and dirty hands. He would commence to do the rounds of the frequented haunts to find his friends. Then he would take his evening meal at 'Poland'. This lasted a very long time. He sat at the street end of the restaurant, beyond sat unmentionable types of people, mostly Polish."[27] Father Gray "describe[d] the restaurant as worse than a cabman's shelter. After the meal, and when everyone else had been served, ECD gradually coaxed Adelaide to come and sit and talk to him. Her mother watched the people in the restaurant over a partition and, if she saw any she did not like the look of, she would shout to Adelaide to come away."[28]

Gray recalled that "Adelaide was a very attractive child of gypsy type, black hair hanging down on either side of her face. She spoke to the patrons in French or Polish. She would sit down at the table and behave like a wayward child—teasing ECD and deliberately driving him into paroxysms of jealousy. After a time—about 10—she had to go off to bed and ECD then left. He then went the rounds taking more than was good for him." Father Gray opined that Dowson "picked up a woman almost every night" and said "that later in life he was run in drunk and disorderly so often as to be greeted by the magistrate with 'What, you here again, Mr. Dowson?'"[29]

> Last night, ah, yesternight, betwixt her lips and mine
> There fell thy shadow, Cynara! Thy breath was shed
> Upon my soul between the kisses and the wine;
> And I was desolate and sick of an old passion,
>   Yea, I was desolate and bowed my head:
> I have been faithful to thee, Cynara! in my fashion.
>
> All night upon mine heart I felt her warm heart beat,
> Night-long within mine arms in love and sleep she lay;
> Surely the kisses of her bought red mouth were sweet;
> But I was desolate and sick of an old passion,
>   When I awoke and found the dawn was gray:
> I have been faithful to thee, Cynara! in my fashion.[30]

Father Gray did not believe that "Cynara" had anything to do with Adelaide.)

Missy's parents, for obvious reasons, are not convinced that Dowson is a suitable match. The impossibility of his love only makes Dowson more persistent. To be a poet, he had proclaimed, one must be a Catholic. One must also live to excess; and one must suffer. The Dowson "Dorian" knew was the Dowson of legend. (In later life, Father Gray "would describe, but only when the humour took him, how Dowson scribbled on the tablecloth in a Soho restaurant, wooing his Cynara as she served the spaghetti:"[31]

> Little lady of my heart!
>   Just a little longer,
> Love me: we will pass and part,
>   Ere this love grow stronger.[32])

Dowson's love grows, one-sided, rooted in desperation. Gray had become a confidant, and Dowson began to depend on his company, writing to a friend in July 1891, "And Dorian, who is charming, returns frequently to the veal cutlet and the dingy green walls of my Eden: in fact he promises to be one of my most enthusiastic Polonais."[33] Again, in March of 1892, Dowson confesses: "I have seen scarcely anyone lately but Gray & Hall . . . In effect I am become far too absorbed to do anything but sit, in Poland, & gather the exquisite moments."[34] Gray is less disconcerted than most of Dowson's friends by the rough and ready environment of "Poland"; in a strange way, he is almost at home there, being writers together, finding a bohemia in a city that distrusted artists. Dowson admires Gray's attempts at writing a new kind of poetry, addressing him as "Poeta Optime"; Gray in turn attends Dowson's one doomed attempt at the theater, his verse play, *The Pierrot of the Minute*—not only once, but twice. Yet "Dorian" can only look on hopelessly as Dowson commits "all the accompaniments of poetry."[35] (According to Father Gray, these involved not only drink and harlots but also hashish. Dowson's story ended badly, as it was meant to do; Father Gray recalled "what wailing and lamentation went up one day when Dowson was told that she [Adelaide] had eloped with the chef."[36] Poetic license, in fact; Adelaide was married sedately, with her parents' consent, to the waiter; she is then lost to history, some reporting that she tired of her husband and left him; others, that she died young.[37] No one, according to Father Gray, "accompanied ECD through the last stages";[38] the role of his by then former friend Robert Sherard in nursing Dowson through the last weeks of his early and tragic death obviously never became known to Gray perhaps because, by that time, he was safely installed in seminary at Scots College, Rome.)

"Dorian" Gray's friendship with Dowson is as near as he comes to being a *poète maudit*. It is true that his generation of artists, seeing themselves in a dramatic light, think that their particular form of drama is tragedy. Did the book of his name not condemn him to be fated and doomed? And yet, it is hard to be tragic if you have to hold down a Civil Service job every day. And almost impossible if you have, as John Gray does, aspirations to becoming securely middle class. Raffish friends like Dowson are fine; but most of the poets of his acquaintance who are struggling to make their names as writers are already middle class and with middle-class aspirations: what does Yeats say? "The typical young poet of our day is an aesthete with a surfeit, searching sadly for his lost Philistinism, his heart full of an unsatisfied hunger for the commonplace. He is an Alastor tired of his woods and longing for beer and skittles."[39]

Also, there are a great many of them. In the early nineties the pubs on Fleet Street have poets in the way barns have mice. Is it the Time Spirit or simply the demise of the giants that is responsible for the glut of minor poets in London? Perhaps nothing great is possible anymore: Arnold is dead; Browning is dead; Tennyson is dying. All that can be done is no longer on a major, but a minor scale, by obscure struggling groups such as the Rhymers, trying to reinvent English poetry. And even they are at odds with themselves, torn between the pull of the traditional English lyric and the wild, audacious experiments of the *symbolistes* in France; between the secret and obscure writings of a Blake or the musical blur of Swinburne and the forthright "manly" songs to be sung by those who uphold Englishness and the Empire.

The poet sits again in the Café Royal, awaiting Oscar. The opposing mirror tells him all he needs to know: that he has already been made in another's image; that his relation to that image has become an important way of making a relation to himself. For several years now, Oscar has served as a model. Was it not Oscar who had him read Baudelaire's essay on the dandy? Oscar who impressed on the young Gray that dandyism, in the words of the master is, "above all, the burning desire to create a personal form of originality," a revolt of the spirit against the mediocrity of the times, a kind of supreme contempt that turned the rules of social convention against themselves?[40] Revolt was not rebellion; revolt was a way of holding the mirror up to society so as to reflect its flaws, so that it became an image of, what did Oscar say?—"Caliban seeing his own face in a glass."[41] It is a revenge, Dorian reflects, to dress with perfection, severely, fastidiously: a revenge on his low birth, which would not justify his taste; a revenge on his low income, which would not justify its expense; a revenge on all the ordinary conditions of life, which would not sanction his escape. He gazes at the face in the mirror, its pure outline a rebuke to this black anger. Was not his very existence as Dorian Gray a revenge on the world which would bury him alive as common, ignorant—invisible?

As part of that revenge, Dorian Gray seeks to enter the visible world. He has just had his photograph taken: he takes it out to look at it again, noting the chaste profile, the otherworldly gaze. The young, beautiful man looks distant, over a soft silk tie, a stiff wing collar, an expensively lined jacket. He looks as pure and unobtainable as a work of art. As Gray tucks it back into the inside of his jacket, he catches from a corner of his eye another figure approaching rapidly: Frank Harris, his loud American greeting matched by his large mustache;

Oscar not here yet? bellows Harris.

He is late. He is often late. He regards it as a privilege of his Irishness.

Irishness be damned. Harris growls, then smiles. The Princess will not be pleased. Nobody is late for the Princess. I am willing to lay odds the other Irishman arrives on time? Yes, yes, I know it's a risk; George Moore has quarreled with almost everyone in London and Paris. He has quarreled with Oscar. He says they haven't spoken in seven years.[42] Artists! In this corner, Oscar defending the Artificial and pronouncing that Art is primary and everything else its imitation; and in the other corner, Moore warming up for the Realists, insisting that the Sordid Detail of Fact comes above everything else in art. Sometimes I think it would be simpler if they just brought back dueling—you know, the sort of thing I saw when I was a student in Heidelberg. But one never knows how much of it is principle and how much personal with two Irishman! The odds are going up; but I will take my chances. I insist they both meet the Princess. She considers herself a patron—or would it be a matron in her case? Anyway, I've told her about you, Dorian; I've told her that you have "not only great personal distinction, but charming manners and a marked poetic gift, a much greater gift than Oscar possessed"—when he was still a poet. I told her that you have an "eager, curious mind" and recite the most wonderful poems.[43] Don't be surprised if she asks you to perform. She has an eye for young and handsome poets.

Speaking of which, my dear boy, you must do something about that French poem—who is it by? Rimbaud? It simply won't do. Those lines in your translation—what were they?—here they are, I have scribbled them down: "'I have stripped off the boots the stockings now / Naked they stand my eyes embrace their hips'"— my dear fellow, this won't go down well with the public at all. "I've thought much of it and feel sure that 'I struggle to define / The subtle torso's hesitating line' should end the sensual note. Then the girls stop to give him an opportunity to speak—laugh with embarrassment and think him an idiot when he doesn't avail himself of the chance and then he passing on 'feels faint kisses creeping on his lips.' If I thought the stripping naked helped the poem I'd not ask you to alter it."[44] But being editor of the *Fortnightly Review* has its responsibilities. I'll stand behind Oscar despite the cowardly attacks on him. I have just published "The Soul of Man under Socialism" in the *Fortnightly*. It is a mighty piece, splendid! If I did not know Oscar was Irish, I would have thought him American, a strenuous manly fighter for the freedom of the individual. But even Oscar is taking the public into account and taming down "The Picture of Dorian Gray" for its forthcoming publication in book form. And you, my dear Gray, must also take account of our very disgruntled Mrs. Grundy. Please, recite the last verses of the poem now as I suggest it; you will see the improvement.

With a covert glance towards the mirror, Gray begins to murmur the last verses of his translation:

> The loutish roughs are larking on the grass.
> The sentimental trooper, with a rose
> Between his teeth, seeing a baby, grows
> More tender, with an eye upon the nurse.
>
> Unbuttoned, like a student, I follow
> A couple of girls along the chestnut row.
> They know I am following, for they turn and laugh,
> Half impudent, half shy, inviting chaff.
>
> I do not say a word. I only stare

At their round, fluffy necks. I follow where
The shoulders drop; I struggle to define
The subtle torso's hesitating line.

Only my rustling tread, deliberate, slow;
The rippled silence from the still leaves drips.
They think I am an idiot, they speak low;
—I feel faint kisses creeping on my lips.

Excellent, my dear boy. Excellent. It catches all of Rimbaud's
contempt for the tedium of the petit-bourgeois life without any
unnecessary transgressions on its taste. You must understand, I
offer these suggestions only out of concern for your own future.
You must send me the "Beautiful Ladies" piece as well—and the
Flower piece—and you must recite both for the Princess tonight.[45]
She will be charmed. "Then after the French scene is perfect don't
forget *prose*—an article or two or twenty in the *F.R.* can only do you
good. So far as I can make the *entrée* easy to you I will. In all things
believe me—not a monitor—my own conduct of life's anything but
exemplary—but a sincere friend who feels greatly drawn to you."[46]
    Gray swallows a smile. The rumors about Harris's lurid life
have been retailed by many at the Café Royal—not least by Oscar—
and it is now said that Harris is writing them all up under the
flamboyant title *My Life and Loves*. As he recalls, the stories mostly
seem to have to do with little girls. Harris's mustache has finally
stopped quivering and he begins to look about fiercely, a look that
might foretell trouble. At that moment, Oscar heaves into view, a
dim bulky figure crossing towards them through the gloom.
    Oscar! You're late. You're not late, you're very late.
    Ah, the Poet. And the pugilist. Have you been attacking
Dorian, Harris? He looks quite unearthly tonight, as pale as the
shadow of the moon. What have you been doing to him? Advising?
Hah! More like a lion being advised by a lion tamer. Why do I always
find a conversation with you like a battle—or a rugby scrum? Yes,
my dear Harris, I am rebuked by your look. You are right to rebuke
me. I owe you much. I owe you too much to be late for our
rendezvous without an apology. Did you not publish my immortal

defense of "The Picture of Dorian Gray" in the *Fortnightly*, even though you advised against the strongest lines?[47] And have you not agreed to publish my article "A New Poet" as soon as the wonderful Dorian Gray produces enough poems to allow me to herald him as the most decadent of decadents, the poet who will mark a certain moment in the artistic development of the age?[48] I apologize profusely; even geniuses are late; in fact, it is probably a sign of genius that they refuse to be dictated to by the clock. Now that that is over, Harris, and if you are at last ready, we will be off.

At Claridge's most of the guests have already arrived and been shown to the private dining suite. It is typical of Harris, Gray thinks, to ask a woman to dine in a public hotel rather than at his house in Park Lane. It is simply not done; but then, Harris usually does what is simply not done. And perhaps being a princess—as well as the niece of the poet Heine, the widow of the Duc de Richelieu and newly married to Prince Albert Honoré Charles of Monaco—and being indescribably rich, the Princess may do any-thing she pleases, unconventional or not. A string quartet is playing in the corner, the guests chattering in muted tones under the flaring gaslight; the Princess arrives last, announced at the door by a footman. They bow as a group, like a small wave that ripples across the room, as she makes her way towards Harris and Wilde. She looks wonderful; like a woman who has dispensed with her history, Oscar murmurs. She sails into the room, somehow appearing both formidable and fresh; a youngish woman, her bosom bare, laid out like a table bedecked with fringes of lace and ribbons; her waist boned to a mere hands' span and cinched with a belt of diamonds and pearls; her tiara trembling among a conceit of curls and ribbons. After a brief circle among the room, Harris takes her arm and they go in to dinner.

The party is seated and subdued; three-quarters iced over. At one end of the table, the Princess bends towards the booming voice of Harris, always an excellent, if somewhat hyperbolic, teller of stories. At the other, the cadenced music of Oscar, first rising, then falling, is greeted with the laughter of his audience. All except George Moore, who sits stiff and thin and still, sniffing disapprov-ingly at Oscar's best lines. Sensing the disapproval, Oscar turns towards him; he begins, slowly, quietly, one of his finest parables. Moore studies the tablecloth as the waiters begin to circulate with the wine and hors d'oeuvres. Wilde directs his words more carefully towards the downturned face; the musical phrases, finely tuned and phrased, repeated and interwoven with each other like the lines of an early Celtic manuscript, turn and return, weave and interweave in a dance of seduction. Moore glances up; takes some wine; glances down; a slow smile creeps over the wintry face. Others at his side begin to turn towards the warm voice, like flowers opening to the sun. Moore's ashen face begins slowly to flush; he helps himself to more wine. The next course is served; at one end of the table, Harris's boom sounds against Oscar's slow music at the other end, but as the meal goes on, Wilde's infectious laugh and modulated voice seem to ring more and more clearly as gradually his neighbors, and then in turn those next to Moore, fall silent to listen. In the hush, Oscar slowly recites a poem in prose. Then he turns, deliberately, majestically, in full command of the table, to call upon the Poet to recite. Gray flushes, hesitates, toys with his fork; but pressed, at last rises diffidently to recite in a low murmur his "Demoiselles de Sauvre":

> Beautiful ladies through the orchard pass;
> Bend under crutched-up branches, forked and low;
> Trailing their samet palls o'er dew-drenched grass.
>
> Pale blossoms, looking on pale Jacqueline,
> Blush to the colour of her finger tips,
> And rosy knuckles, laced with yellow lace.
>
> High-crested Berthe discerns, with slant, clinched eyes
> Amid the leaves pink faces of the skies;
> She locks her plaintive hands Sainte-Margot-wise.
>
> Ysabeau follows last, with languorous pace;
> Presses, voluptuous, to her bursting lips,
> With backward stoop, a bunch of eglantine.

Courtly ladies through the orchard pass;
Bow low, as in lords' halls; and springtime grass
Tangles a snare to catch the tapering toe.[49]

Silence. Poor men, moans the Princess melodramatically, helpless in the toils of such artifice. And "such strange, weird, fascinating verses"—quite like a Burne-Jones *à la Japonaise*.[50] They already "sing in my ears" and are likely to do so for a long time after. Their soft music "carried me quite far away."[51] Dear Dorian, you are a true poet she gushes. Gray bows slightly in acknowledgement, but the bow is tinged with irony. Dear Princess, he murmurs, when it is printed it shall be dedicated to you.

There is a moment's silence before the Princess turns ostentatiously to Wilde. Now Oscar, she asks imperiously, can you top that? Or will your disciple outdo you? Ah yes, dear lady, for you alone I will recite my parable of the fisherman and his soul. And Oscar begins his tale; it is a chant intoned in long, sinuous sentences, winding about the listeners' hearts, resonating with a thousand echoes; it sounds like a gong, its cadences rippling outwards into an opera of words. At its conclusion, the hearers sit like statues, hushed, enthralled; all the vague distrust created by Oscar's heavy fleshiness and ostentatious dress vanishes like the lady in the circus by the magic of his verbal legerdemain. No one resists the spell; Harris is profuse, booming his thanks; the Princess presses Oscar to repeat their meeting; and even the recalcitrant Moore wonders at the excess of folly by which he had cut himself off for so long, with so little reason, from such delightful company.

For Oscar, it is the usual triumph. "The man who rules a London dinner party rules the world," Wilde is fond of saying. As for Dorian, he is discovering the secret of inventing himself—or, to be exact, discovering the secret of how to perform Oscar's invention of himself. Dorian determines to become not merely a writer, but a poet; because poetry is a craft, and he reveres the craftsman's work; because poetry is an art, and the aesthetic is itself holy. But also because becoming a poet will mark him out for distinction. Poetry will give Dorian a role, a mode, a manner; it too, as Dorian discovers, may be employed as a social instrument, almost a form of etiquette; and as a game that will permit him, an obscure civil servant, to elbow a place in the world.

How adept Dorian becomes at such strategies may be judged by the clever *vers de société* published in the fashionable magazine *Black and White* in early 1891:

VAUXHALL. 17—

Peerless ZELINDA, Can I fitly write
The joy still lingering of Yesternight?
You dined with LADY CAROLINE, and I
In the adjacent Bower. Though so nigh
To all I worship that the World can give—
But for your Charms, ZELINDA, need I live?
You seemed, for me, more distant than the Stars.
I hazarded and lost, while you waged Wars
of Ombre. Later, on the Promenade,
Among the Throng we passed. Your fan kept guard
Upon your Glances; then you dropped your Mask.
ZELINDA, it was mine, oh, grateful task!
To snatch it from the Ground, ere PETERHAM stoops—
And tangles his red Heels with CELIA'S Hoops—
And kiss the Hand that takes it. Not your Glove
You dropped, nor Fan, nor Kerchief. For my Love
Your Mask you dropped, that all Vauxhall might see
It was ZELINDA threw her Gage to me.
What I have else to tell you, will be soon;
I'll see you at the Play this afternoon,
Or in the Park.
        ZELINDA, credit me,
        Your humble Servant, and Eternally,
                JOHN GRAY[52]

A poetry that is politic: that flirts and seduces a fickle world: that is what John Gray is learning. The poetry of Dorian will be as much a part of his artifice as his borrowed name or his carefully chosen cravats; the poetry too will become part of the performance scripted for the metal-turner's apprentice turned dandy. Away from the terrible cenacles of poets, Dorian recites his poems for honored guests, such as the Princess of Monaco, who summoned him to her presence on a second occasion and, on one memorable evening, he stood diffidently before Walter Pater. ("I remember meeting Pater at your house," Arthur Symons wrote André Raffalovich after the turn of the century; "He who was then John Gray repeated one of his poems. A certain expression passed over Pater's face and he asked Gray to say it over again. 'The rest was silence.'"[53])

Dorian's audience is not limited to those in London. In the spring of 1891, Dorian Gray proposed to make an appearance also in France. In mid-March, Oscar had returned from Paris (as Gray reports to Fénéon) full of the news of his encounters—with Mallarmé, Verlaine, Jean Moreas, and Henri de Régnier. Gray confesses to Fénéon that he hopes "to visit Paris with [Wilde] in a little while."[54] But since early March Gray has been suffering from serious bronchitis, which now takes the form of a recurrent fever, erupting every third day for a few hours. Gray is forced to apply for sick leave from work and to leave London to seek relief in the watering places of the south coast of England. His doctor has diagnosed the malady as a nervous fever; it is to rack Dorian at various intervals for the coming year.

Thus it is not until February 1892 that Gray finally arrives in France. By this time, Gray has made the acquaintance of Marcel Schwob, a writer of considerable talent and collaborator on several *symboliste* reviews. Gray writes Schwob in early 1892 about "Oscar, who will be in Paris at the same time as this letter."[55] Indeed Wilde's visit becomes "the 'great event' of the Parisian literary salons" of the season. Schwob reports first conceiving for the visiting aesthete "a rapturous admiration," and takes on the responsibility of being, in the words of Jean Lorrain, Wilde's pilot and "cornac," that is, elephant keeper. However, Schwob quickly becomes disillusioned with Oscar, if remaining a firm admirer of his disciple. In the course of his visit to Paris—possibly through Fénéon—Gray is initiated into that hallowed gathering that takes place at Mallarmé's apartment on the

Rue de Rome every Tuesday. (Later, it is said of Mallarmé that he had "a specially warm place in his heart" for Gray and Dowson.[56])

At the same time as this visit, in the winter of 1891-92, somehow, inconceivably, Dorian also gets mixed up in shady dealings with a newspaper in Tours. A friend of Wilde, Robert Sherard, whom Gray describes to Fénéon as "a kind of god with straw-coloured hair, tired of his divinity," has made his home in Paris.[57] Sherard writes to Gray about a set of discreditable circumstances which will lead to a libel suit and to even more trouble, perhaps even bribery and blackmail, but adds: "we did not know this when we took it up & so neither of us is to blame."[58]

Meanwhile, back in London, Dorian is getting into further trouble, willfully and with aforethought. Over the winter, Gray is drawn into the orbit of one J. T. Grein, an émigré from Holland, who in 1891 sets up an experimental theater in London along the lines of Antoine's Théâtre Libre in Paris. The Independent Theatre proclaims two aims: to produce Continental drama on the English stage, and to produce plays by new writers which are too risky for the conventional stage. In March 1891, Grein launches the new theater with a production of Ibsen's *Ghosts*. (Following as it did on the heels of *A Doll's House* in 1889, the impact of Grein's production has been compared to "the first performance of Wagner's opera, and the appearance of the Impressionist painters.")[59] To the conventional public, *Ghosts* is a calculated outrage, an affront to all it holds civilized, an embodiment of the "decadence" of society. Only thus can one account for the wild display of invective epitomized by the lead article in the *Daily Telegraph* of 14 March 1891, which compares the play to an open drain, a loathsome sore unbandaged, a dirty act done publicly, a lazar house with all its doors and windows open. Bestial, cynical, disgusting, poisonous, sickly delirious, indecent, fetid, literary carrion, crapulous, clinical stuff: "It is difficult to expose in decorous words," the writer concludes, "the gross and almost putrid indecorum of this play." I must meet this man, Gray thinks. How could any decadent poet worth his reputation resist?

Predictably, with such a reception, the Independent Theatre is in debt and at odds with the censorship regulations. Grein cleverly circumvents both difficulties by redefining the theater as a "private club" and putting it on a subscription basis. Known officially as the Independent Theatre Society, it rents various venues for its productions. Slowly, Grein builds up a stable of young, adventurous playwrights—among them Bernard Shaw, Arthur Symons, George Moore, and Frank Harris—who risk their plays in this, the second season of 1891-92.

Not without a sense of humor, Grein decides to avenge himself on his critics with a "little joke": a spoof on the most advanced of "decadent" dramas. Entitled *In the Garden of Citrons,* the play is published under Grein's pen name, "Emilio Montanaro," and solemnly reviewed by another conspirator, Teixeira de Mattos, "from the proof sheets." Not to be left out, John Gray has fabricated a preface in the most archly precious, tangential style at his disposal. His "too-too" introduction (as *The Star* is to call it) proceeds thus: "Whoso cares to do so will find in the *Garden of Citrons* naivety so naïve that it is always blushing—at nothing—side by side with the most astounding precocity." To this, Gray adds a catalogue of nonexistent plays by the same author and a mock biography: "Once in the West Indies, in some moment of weary leisure and physical relaxation, the stifling air of Cuba, the fetid mist creeping up from the tobacco garden, ravished the soul of the young Italian planter, and the simple agriculturalist became the fantastic and complex poet."[60] Thus Gray parodies the new style of Maeterlinck, whose trivial dialogue, mysterious occurrences, and elaborate synaesthesia already seems, to most playgoers, to be parodying itself.

Predictably, the respectable journal *Theatre* takes the piece at face value and rages at the "variest and tritest twaddle that ever came from the invention of anyone not a sentimental schoolgirl." (Mrs. Grein later recalled that, on the night of the play's first and final performance, the parrot, raising its voice in Italian, gave the hoax away: but "not before J. T. [Grein] had his laugh and [the play] had enjoyed serious consideration in many quarters.")[61]

None of this is calculated to allay the suspicions of the public. Is Grein serious or is he not? How can they attack an enterprise that insists on parodying itself? Public disquiet is not allayed by the next event. Scarcely a month after his elaborate hoax, on 7 February 1892, Grein invites another *agent provocateur,* Oscar Wilde, to chair a meeting at the Playgoers' Club—a group Grein has organized to attend first nights and to hold a program of discussions. Gray and Wilde are both members, and Oscar has arranged a rendezvous in the Café Royal with the hope of persuading Dorian to accompany his own invited paper with another on the subject of the modern actor.

I do not think I can do it, Oscar, Gray demurs. Oscar's face looms across the table through a haze of smoke, the cigarette tip describing a circle in the air as he waves his hand vaguely in Gray's direction. Why in God's name not, Dorian? You have the profile, you have the presence, you even have the wardrobe; dear boy, you look more wonderful every day. It is my voice, Gray murmurs. "A clumsy or ignorant person might have thought the voice was of a drunken man, or one half asleep."[62] My dear Dorian, Wilde laughs; it does not matter; those that attend will not hear you; they will overhear, which is better. It will all seem that you are imparting a secret; you will initiate them into the secret society of your fierce beliefs. How ferocious they are, Dorian, and how you blaze when you utter them— like a prophet whose tongue is lit by a burning coal.

Come, Dorian; we will conspire together. We will be like Barlas, firing off revolvers to express our disgust with those who rule us from Westminster; we will be like Félix Fénéon, the anarchist who understands that the propaganda of the deed must always be delivered with impeccable style. From the Ministry of War he wages battle on his own grasping and mediocre society. Or shall we imitate Francis Vielé-Griffin, who has recruited you to write for his subversive publication? What is it? *Entretiens politiques et littéraires?*[63] Frankly, like your French friend, I myself believe there is no distinction between politics and literature—between the Propaganda of the Word and the Propaganda of the Deed. In "The Soul of Man under Socialism" I tried to show how anarchism is born "of a moral revolt against social injustice." Anarchism was created by men who "felt as if suffocated by the social climate in which they were obliged to live; who felt the pain of others as if it were their own; who were also convinced that a large part of human suffering is not the inevitable consequence of inexorable natural or supernatural laws, but instead stems from social realities depending on human will and can be eliminated through human effort"—once people become convinced of these truths, "then the way is open that leads to anarchism."[64]

Remember, dear Dorian, that talk also is a form of action—indeed it is my only action; my detonators will be my words. Oscar waves his cigarette in several large circles, examining the effect of the trail of smoke. So, Dorian, let us lob our bombs at that most deathly of English institutions: the legitimate theater—legitimized by smugness, legitimized by official hypocrisy. We will not throw real dynamite, like that recent bomb in the Barcelona theater which dispatched so many of the best society. An act, to be good, must be elegant. You, Dorian, despise the legitimate theater, which you consider dead from respectability.

After weeks of rehearsals of *Lady Windermere's Fan,* I myself have devised a plan to do away with actors altogether, having reached the conclusion that "the personality of the actor is often a source of danger in the perfect presentation of a work of art. It may distort. It may lead astray. It may be a discord in the tone or symphony. For anybody can act. Most people in England do nothing else." Such friction! Such anxieties! I have spent *weeks* persuading impossible actors to intone their words such and such a way; *whole days* rewriting speeches to keep the speed, the interplay, of the dialogue, so that a scene can come as a tornado— or a nocturne—depending on its place and timing. But I have come to the melancholy conclusion that actors must simply be replaced— with puppets. "There are many advantages in puppets. They never argue. They have no crude views about art. They have no private lives . . . They recognise the presiding intellect of the dramatist, and have never been known to ask for their parts to be written up. They are admirably docile, and have no personalities at all."[65]

What I mean about my voice, Dorian murmurs, is *precisely* that it is unsuited for such a verbal assault. You can do it, Oscar; your voice carries; sometimes I think you must be taking lessons from Harris. And you will probably insult them all by lighting a cigarette at the beginning; at least it is one way of getting their attention. But I think I must put them to sleep. Listen to this, Oscar.

Gray removes a neatly folded newspaper clipping from his inner breast pocket, unfolds, and reads:

> Mr John Gray, who writes the "too-too" introduction to the latest dramatic novelty, Emilio Montanaro's *In the Garden of Citrons,* is said to be the original Dorian of the same name. Mr Gray, who has cultivated his manner to the highest pitch of languor yet attained, is a well-known figure of the Playgoers' Club, where, though he often speaks, he is seldom heard.[66]

This is from this morning, Oscar. See: *The Star,* 6 February 1892.

Which are you worried about? Not being heard or being seen with me?

I told Dowson earlier this evening I am thinking of suing—for libel—in asserting me to be "the original Dorian of the same name."[67]

What did he say?

Only: "This will be droll."[68]

So you see, Dorian, Wilde laughed, leaning over to clap him on his back; no one takes it seriously. I myself will defend you when our evening is over. I will write personally to *The Star*—through my solicitors if need be. The important thing, dear boy, is to do it anyway—have your moment—despite the bullying of the press. The press considers itself the Tyrant of our Day; but we will together put the press to rout. But first: the Playgoers. He gives Gray a hard look. You are not seriously considering backing down now, are you?

Gray avoids his glance as being possibly too meaningful. To appear with Oscar so publicly would again underwrite his position as disciple, as the creature of this powerful Prospero. But this is his chance, at last, of a manifesto; perhaps his only chance.

In the event, on the following evening of the seventh of February, Gray speaks first, as if to introduce Wilde. But this is more than prelude. The first sentence of his speech, entitled "The Modern Actor," jolts the audience: "To spare any possibility of mystification," he murmurs, "let me announce at once that by the modern actor I mean the Music Hall singer, the 'artiste' many estimable and rightly inquisitive people have never seen, the 'professional' thought of by some only with horror and disgust."[69] As the words fall from his lips, Dorian senses a recoil in the audience: actors and even actresses are fine, they may even be idolized—as Lily Langtry knows—as long as they are Respectable. But the artiste of the music halls is not only a degraded, but vulgar thing. "Most, I suppose, look upon this person as more or less of a pariah," Gray drives his point home: "Those who so look upon him are perfectly right."

As he proceeds, Gray feels the listeners before him contract into a knot of discomfort and dismay. But his purpose is upon him; it has been held back for years, this moment, the moment in which he exposes his ancient wound: the wound of being rejected, despised, an outsider, an object of scorn, except to the few who had some surmise of the value he had set upon himself and some knowledge of how hard, how very hard, he had toiled to win acceptance. Now the words break out, roughening the modulated voice, which almost crumbles under the strain, uttering the credo of his art word by word. Not only the music hall artiste but "every actor, and indeed, every artist, is properly an outcast and unclassed person." What would they know of this? He looks directly at the rows in front of him of respectably dressed people, mostly men in evening suits. They pose as friends; but these are the enemy. "England has been rich in singers; the best of these have been done to death. Give her the advantage of one or two doubtful exceptions; all the rest she has driven to exile and suicide and misery." They do not—cannot—know how the artist, pure and childlike, is tortured; not only by the Philistine but even by "those he would love," who "look upon him with dread and hate, or, taking courage from his harmlessness, try which of them can first draw from him a sob of pain. They mix ashes and offal with his food and his drink, and pretend themselves defiled by touching the thing that had left his hand, or by treading in one of his footprints."

Having noted the hyperbole, Gray defends it as a true description (it was typical, a friend of his later years remarked, for him to express himself exaggeratedly.[70]) Yet, if the rhetoric is upholstered, the logic is clear: the artist is an actor and the actor is, in some sense, a martyr. He is a martyr to the outrage of the audience, who revenge themselves on the artist for representing it to itself; Oscar would call it Caliban seeing his own face in a glass. In this case, Dorian argues, those holding up the mirror are not the army of beautiful "mercenaries" of the legitimate theater, but the juggler, the contortionist, the mime, the petticoat dancer, the cloggie, and the magician: those who consciously work in the world of trickery and suspect illusion. And they are working class—drawn from the very streets and neighborhoods in which Gray grew up. Being working class alone does not make them more authentic even though the working class is suddenly becoming "smart." Gray argues that they are the true artists precisely because they must create everything themselves—they have no wardrobe, no make-up, no props; even the music hall's "trashiest artiste has to face a difficult, a master feat—he must *act,* in the absolute sense of the word." By so doing, he is able "to make something out of nothing, to so utter the words of his song as to give an illusion, to so dance that mechanical movements are rightly combined to a complete, a satisfying result in art."

The applause is polite, but merely polite. Oscar rises and looms over them; his speech on the superiority of puppets over actors, predictably perverse and amusing, is greeted as such.

Then the evening is suddenly over as Wilde turns to congratulate Gray on being misunderstood, "a distinction he himself shared."[71] The next day Dowson writes to Gray: "*Mes compliments* upon your Paradox of Café concerts, which was altogether admirable and charming: and my thanks for the ticket . . . I am quite of your advice, and hold that the artist should be too much absorbed in God, the Flesh and the Devil, to consider the World, quâ World, at all . . . I drink to you, & to the memory of Master François Villon: and hope that you will pay me a visit some day, when you have time . . ."[72] Such comprehension escapes the critics. On 9 February the journal *Players* dismisses the lecture altogether in order to concentrate on the mannerisms of Gray's delivery: "Delicacy is developed to an extent almost abnormal in Mr John Gray. He had nothing that was pleasant to say about the modern actor; and so he was one of the few persons he did not mention in the series of matchlessly consorted epigrams which formed his address. Mr John Gray is the poet of the music-halls . . . Spangles and muscles, 'wilful pyramids,' skirts, cat-calls and coster's cries—of these Mr John Gray has builded himself a world of strange féerie, wherein he dwells, anticipating the re-birth of the native drama within its limits . . . His language is irridescent, or perhaps scented . . . His method of delivery is very gentle. He ceased; he did not conclude."[73]

It is Chevalier, isn't it? Arthur Symons puts the question to Gray several evenings later at the Café Royal. Gray did not particularly like Symons, even though he had become a neighbor of his when he moved, less than a year ago, into rooms in the Temple. Symons seems so hysterical, so demanding, Gray reflects; but Oscar admires him and they all share his enthusiasm for the French *symboliste* poets, and for Verlaine in particular, whom Symons was trying to persuade to come to London.

Oscar, strangely distracted—perhaps waiting for someone, Gray thinks—lights a cigarette; then offers one to Symons, reaching across the table to light it with his own.

Gray hesitates, regarding Symons's scraggy mustache with distaste. He addresses the end of the lighted cigarette, looking behind Symons towards the mirror, to be forewarned of Oscar's guest. Someone appears at the door, a young, elegant, boyish figure; he gestures languidly, as if half asleep. Wilde excuses himself hastily and leaves. Gray regards his large retreating back, then turns to Symons:

Yes, of course it is Albert Chevalier. I have written to the *Players* about him; I thought it might clarify some of the things they said about my lecture. The legitimate theater is "dead"—dead beyond resuscitation. The future belongs to the people—the people of the street—and the artists they choose to celebrate. The artiste is a celebrity; he believes that the true artist is one who believes in the development of his own personality—what did that review in *The Artist and Journal of Home Culture* say?—one who uses the devices of art to intensify his own eccentricities.[74] The Artist of the

Future is the *artiste* of the music hall. You can see it all in Chevalier. He comes from the working class. We have the same accent, although—a wintry smile from Gray—I am trying to lose mine and he exaggerates his. He left the legitimate theater to work the halls—a reversal of most actors' ambitions. On stage, he is master, able to reveal in a "single moment in the life of a single individual . . . all its human significance." Chevalier has that spontaneous mastery of illusion which I regard as "a key to all life and all emotion"; his "sure and supple intelligence as an artist" makes him a "prince in the world of masks."[75]

Ha, says Symons, slamming down his absinthe and throwing back his head, he begins to recite:

My life is like a music hall,
Where, in the impotence of rage,
Chained by enchantment to my stall,
I see myself upon the stage
Dance to amuse a music-hall.

'Tis I that smoke this cigarette,
Lounge here, and laugh for vacancy,
And watch the dancers turn; and yet
It is my very self I see
Across the cloudy cigarette.

My very self that turns and trips,
Painted, pathetically gay,
An empty song upon the lips
In make-believe of holiday:
I, I, this thing that turns and trips!

The light flares in the music-hall,
The light, the sound, that weary us;
Hour follows hour, I count them all,
Lagging, and loud, and riotous:
My life is like a music-hall.[76]

Is it yourself you see there, Mr. Gray, as you imply? Well then, you know this is not the work of magic; this is the effect of power. Power, Mr. Gray, power! The actor must hold the audience down. You know what they are like—I've seen you often enough at the Alhambra and the Empire with Dowson. The crowds are rowdy, rough, usually drunk; you have observed how they cheer and boo or talk or simply walk out if they do not care for any particular "turn." I know how you feel about Chevalier; I share it. Your review captures his quality exactly. Chevalier is entirely conscious that his power depends solely on his ability to manipulate his audience. He is a Machiavelli of the boards—as you say, a "prince in the world of masks"—but only for that "single moment" he can sustain the illusion. His spell springs from the very labor of its contrivance; it has a wonderful speciousness which, like *trompe l'oeil,* gives the spectator a sense of intense, consummate reality—until the second look. In the end, it is really the whole elaborate sham that excites me.

Symons leans over the table, his voice lowering almost conspiratorially. And then, of course, Mr. Gray, there is the whole question of the atmosphere of the halls, is there not? There was a time in which "I lived in them for the mere delight and the sheer animal excitement they gave me. I liked that glitter, barbarous, intoxicating," and I loved "the violent animality, the entire spectacle, with absurd faces, gestures, words, and the very odour and suffocating heat."[77] And the women—fast, explicit, available. Did you know your favorite haunt, the Empire, has been described as "the most popular whore market in London"?[78]

Gray demurs. He leans away from Symons's hot breath, which has by now enough alcohol in it to ignite by spontaneous combustion. Symons, he knows, is working on a manifesto, "The Decadent Movement in Literature," by which he hopes to introduce the literate English reader to the new *symboliste* literature in France. Decadence is becoming, alas, fashionable, whatever the English public thinks of it: being the English public, they think about it as little as possible, but when they do, Gray reflects, it has nothing to do with French literature and everything to do with French vice, which, by definition, is anything French at all. Gray coughs in the smoky atmosphere; he is not feeling entirely well; Oscar's abrupt departure has upset his equilibrium; but even on his best days now he feels he is suffocating in the very air of London.

It is getting more difficult to meet Oscar on his own. The rehearsals of *Lady Windermere's Fan* are consuming him; and then there are new, younger disciples who surround him everywhere he goes—or appear abruptly to claim him at the Café Royal. But there is now an emergency; the rumors that John Gray is the original of "Dorian" Gray have taken on a life of their own.

Oscar arrives, flushed, in a long coat with a fur collar which he peels off conspicuously at the door before heading through the gloom towards Dorian's table. My dear fellow; I can only guess. First *The Star;* now the *Daily Telegraph*. Where is it? Ah. Wilde fishes out a crumpled piece of newsprint from the breast pocket of his large, double-breasted jacket, the white, fat fingers leaving small stains on the porous sheet. Ah, yes, here it is; they have referred to my last appearance at the Playgoers' Club as being in the role of the "literary and dramatic godfather of a youth, who, with sublime assurance leaves Ibsen, Maeterlinck and Montanaro far in the shade of obscure Philistinism."[79] Terrible prose, dear boy; troublesome allegation. Obviously impossible to hold down a Civil Service job with this sort of nonsense going about. In any case, the press have taken to exercising an authority that is quite degrading. "In the old days men had the rack. Now they have the Press. That is an improvement certainly. But it is still very bad, and wrong, and demoralising . . . The tyranny that it proposes to exercise over people's private lives seems to me to be quite extraordinary. The fact is that the public have an insatiable curiosity to know everything, except what is worth knowing." Consider Parnell—our Great Lost Leader; not even a year dead, hounded to his death by the conduct of a degraded press—a press that "will drag before the eyes of the public some incident in the private life of a great statesman, of a man who is a leader of political thought as he is a creator of political force, and invite the public to discuss the incident, to exercise authority in the matter, to give their views, and not merely to give their views, but to carry them into action, to dictate to the man upon all other points, to dictate to his party, to dictate to his country; in fact, to make themselves ridiculous, offensive, and harmful. The private lives of men and women would not be told to the public. The public have nothing to do with them at all."[80]

Wilde stops suddenly, staring wildly for a moment ahead of him, not even noting his reflection in the darkened mirrors; then takes out a large rose silk handkerchief from his pocket and, with trembling hand, mops his brow. I am sorry, dear Dorian; the shock of it all is still with me. We must protect you from these vampires; they will suck the lifeblood from your veins. I will drive a stake through their villainous hearts. You are right to threaten a suit for libel. I have also been busy; through your solicitor I have contacted Ernest Poole and have, in writing, told him a barefaced lie: that we simply did not meet until after the publication of my wonderful novel on Dorian Gray. It is not an imaginative lie as lies go, but it will be an effective line of defense and we must stick to it if you are to be protected. Did you note the swiftness of the retraction? Oscar fishes again in the depths of an inner pocket. Here—did you read it? It sounds very well: *The Star,* 15 February:

> By the bye, we are told that some people have taken quite seriously a suggestion which appeared in this column a few days since that Mr Gray was the prototype of Mr Oscar Wilde's Dorian Gray. The risks of the New Humour could not have a more unfortunate illustration than the acceptance as serious of a statement that a skillful young literary artist of promise like Mr Gray could possibly be the original of the monstrous Epicurean of Mr Wilde's creation, and we greatly regret the erroneous impression that has been produced. Apart from the fact that Mr Wilde's acquaintance with Mr Gray did not commence until after the publication of this novel, Mr Wilde would be as likely to draw a character from life as to call a photograph an artistic production. Character sketching he regards as literary work, but not as literary art.[81]

Quite good, eh? The public are beginning to understand that Art does not imitate Life—although I have not succeeded yet in leading them to an understanding of how Life imitates Art. However, Dorian, we will see whether you will be proof or not of that proposition. Meanwhile, I take pleasure in a letter from Mr. Ernest Poole of *The Star,* which indicates he has forwarded much the same retraction to your solicitor—in his evident "anxiety to repair the wrong." [82] As for the *Daily Telegraph*'s assertion that I am to be regarded as your "literary and dramatic godfather"—you must leave them to me.

Oscar proves as good as his word; or rather, his word proves as good as Oscar. Within days, a letter appears in the *Daily Telegraph*; Gray's breath tightens as he reads it, within hours of its printing: first the coruscating defense of Wilde's own perverse logic on the superiority of puppets over actors; Oscar must be having a rough time at the rehearsals, Gray reflects. Then a final paragraph about Gray himself:

> Suffer me one more correction. Your writer describes the author of the brilliant fantastic lecture on "The Modern Actor" as "a *protegé*" of mine. Allow me to state that my acquaintance with Mr John Gray is, I regret to say, extremely recent, and that I sought it because he had already a perfected mode of expression both in prose and verse. All artists in this vulgar age need protection certainly. Perhaps they have always needed it. But the nineteenth-century artist finds it not in Prince, or Pope, or patron, but in high indifference of temper, in the pleasure of the creation of beautiful things, and the long contemplation of them in disdain of what in life is common and ignoble, and in such felicitous sense of humour as enables one to see how vain and foolish is all popular opinion, and popular judgment, upon the wonderful things of art. These qualities Mr John Gray possesses in a marked degree. He needs no other protection, nor, indeed, would he accept it.
>
> I remain, sir, your obedient servant,
> OSCAR WILDE [83]

Gray cuts out the letter, reads it again later that morning at work, glancing surreptitiously at the other slaves in the galley where life has chained them. No one has as much as looked up at the fire at the far side of the Post Office Section of the Foreign Office, where he now works, only twitched and coughed abruptly as its smoke registered in their lungs; his own, he realizes, are already inflamed. Noble Oscar: to lie to such effect, and to contradict himself so generously, asserting that he himself needed no protection while in the very act of giving it.

The next time he sees Oscar is on the following evening: he is standing in front of the last curtain, responding to calls of "Author! Author!" amidst the thunderous close of his first successful play, *Lady Windermere's Fan*. In Oscar's mauve-gloved fingers is a cigarette; in his buttonhole a green carnation. (What does it mean? they all ask; and nobody seems to know.) "Ladies and gentlemen," Wilde intones, waving the cigarette in a grand, encompassing circle; "I have enjoyed this evening *immensely*. The actors have given us a *charming* rendering of a *delightful* play, and your appreciation has been *most* intelligent. I congratulate you on the *great* success of your performance, which persuades me that you think *almost* as highly of the play as I do myself."[84]

The conservative critics find the cigarette even more outrageous than Oscar's egotism. But the play is a wild success. It is not only the disciples, ranged in the boxes, wearing the new emblem of the green carnation. Not only the new converts, such as Edward Shelley from the offices of the Bodley Head or the new poet from Paris, Pierre Louÿs. Not only the celebrities who come at Wilde's own invitation. After that jubilant first night, the crowds come in a tidal wave of acclaim. The Prince of Wales approves. And the manager, George Alexander, notes that the pit and the galleries are as full as the stalls and the boxes.[85] "How delighted Oscar must be," Sherard writes Gray from Tours. "I devoured the notices. It is a perfect triumph. I am announcing it in the French papers . . . By the way I see the papers have been busy with your name of late. You ought to get your book out soon."[86] Ah yes, the book, Gray thinks; the book of my poems to which Oscar is to stand as godfather—or at least as financial backer. Problematic, like Oscar himself.

When Gray is asked to review *Lady Windermere's Fan* for the *Spectator,* he finds himself admitting that he is not in "any great sympathy with the methods and feats of Mr. Oscar Wilde," since he had "always disclaimed respect for the forms of charlatanism in which it has pleased him [Wilde] to indulge, and which he would, we suspect, be about the first himself to admit." Yet even with this disclaimer, Gray can still judge *Lady Windermere's Fan* comparable to Swift's *Polite Conversation* and Sheridan's *School for Scandal;* and, "as a speciman of true comedy . . . [*Lady Windermere's Fan* is] head and shoulders above any of its contemporaries."[87]

A few weeks later, Gray is on stage and Oscar is in the audience. The venue is once again the Independent Theatre, which is, once again, in crisis. Their previous production, a dramatization of Zola's *Thérèse Raquin,* had been assailed almost as hysterically as had the notorious production of *Ghosts.* In the wake of such vituperation, J. T. Grein had appealed to Gray: would Gray allow him to produce his translation of a slight, but noncontroversial, playlet by Théodore de Banville: *Le Baiser?* Gray could fill out the evening by introducing the play with a repeat performance of his lecture "The Modern Actor."

Thus it is that Gray is to be placed once again *devant le public* on 4 March 1892. Realizing that this is a last-ditch stand, J. T. Grein packs the audience. Fresh from the triumph of *Lady Windermere's Fan,* Oscar Wilde rents a box for himself and a "suite of young gentlemen"; all appear in front of Gray conspicuously wearing in their buttonholes green carnations, now conscious of its significance in Paris as a mark of the Uranian clique. Opposite, not to be outdone, George Moore—another convert to Oscar's charm, Gray reflects—has rented another box; below in the stalls a reporter notes the presence of Henry James and J. M. Barrie.[88]

The charm of deBanville's delicate little piece wins through, as it is meant to do; the reviews of Gray's effort to render it into English are mixed and even contradictory, noting on the one hand the adroitness of the translation and, on the other, a certain clumsiness in the verse; one comments that "some Cockney rhymes occasionally offend the ear."[89] But the evening passes without a riot, either in the gods or in the next morning's press. (In future this evening's modest venture is to gain a reputation as being the strategic turning point in the fortunes of the Independent Theatre.)

About a month after the event, however, a "dramatic critic" from the *Players* decides to have a go at a young man who clearly has gotten above himself. In a piece entitled "The Very Little Vance," the writer opens by recalling "The Great Vance": a celebrated music-hall singer of a few years back, whom he pictures as a flashy and conceited person of atrocious taste; a prop of the music hall at the most degenerate stage of its existence. During his heyday, the huge Vance often appeared clad in startling colors and gaudy accoutrements—a puce, lemon, and bottle-green suit; a gold-knobbed cane; huge diamond studs: in short, in the costume of a type known in the halls as a Heavy Swell. Now, the critic snorts, the music hall has found a new star, "whom by way of contrast I will call 'The Very Little Vance,' otherwise that music-hall champion and illiterate lecturer, Mr. John Gray." He tops the review by sneering at the "execrable English" of this "very silly youth."[90]

Well, Dorian; it was only a matter of time before you were cast as one of your own artistes, Oscar exclaims. Gray notes that Oscar is not looking well after his trip to Paris; it is hard in the gloom to discern the precise outlines of his face, but it seems as if it had begun to soften somehow and blur at the edges, as if a kind of gentle deliquescence had set in; its color had moved towards the putty gray, with a slight yellow tinge. In fact, Wilde does not look in any better health than he, Dorian, does himself. For weeks now, he has begun to feel that he is suffocating; is it that the winter fogs, thickened by coal smoke and other noxious fumes, are conspiring with his own sense that his small world is tightening about him, like clothes which he has already outgrown? Gray is beginning to find the company of the Café Royal tedious; the music halls loud and tiring; work at the Foreign Office insufferable. And the hounding of the press now inflicts acute pain, as if he were kicked on an old bruise not yet fairly healed. The attack from the *Players* hurts more than he would like to admit; it has hit him in a vulnerable spot, his own sense of being an intruder from another, degraded class: an outsider, a parvenu, an *arriviste*. He looks down at his scribbled reply; he would try it out first on Oscar.

I confess, Oscar—he speaks to the flaccid face that turns to him through the gloom—that I "feared offence." I "rightly feared offence" as I have obviously given it. I am bewildered as to why my words, "blameless when they left my lips . . . were afterwards picked up in gutters, soiled and distorted, and turned to all unworthy account, so that I am hissed and brayed against in public places."[91]

That is simply naive, Dorian; not that your innocence is something I don't value. You yourself argued that every artist is a martyr; when the soldiers from the press aim their arrows at your Sebastian, naked and tied to a stake, do you not expect to suffer? It is you who have given them their pretext. Or is it just that you did not expect them to take you seriously? You have caught their attention. They have seen something arresting, an impeccably dressed, beautiful young man reading, in an accent not entirely free from its origins, a paper that praises as art's finest artifice the artiste of the music halls. You have offended their sense of the respect-able—their highest and most solemn value—of which they hold the theater as altar. You have provoked them beyond patience by asking them to imagine an art that is outside their ken—outside their class and their limited notions of decency. As an *agent provocateur* you must expect for crimes against respectability only the most severe of punishments.

Perhaps it has nothing to do with me; perhaps it is you they seek to punish.

Very likely, my dear Dorian; it is true my success with *Lady Windermere's Fan* has given them an excuse; but they will have a better one when they have a chance to see the divinely sulphurous *Salome*. Meanwhile, Dorian, you must be aware that the public response is merely a craven acknowledgement of the truth of my proposition that, in the end, Life imitates Art. The public has done you the immense honor of naming you after one of my finest creations—misunderstood as he may be, Dorian is beautiful, and he comes to the consciousness of his beauty as a kind of power. Once people behold him, they cannot believe that any evil attaches to such a countenance. Ah, Dorian, you can be such as he; yours is the face upon which all the ends of the world are come and that beauty, wrought out from within the flesh, quickens again the old fancy of a perpetual life. You, Dorian, are becoming your own best work of art.

Gray quails; he has trouble catching his breath. Perhaps Oscar's cigarettes have at last poisoned him; his health has been precarious for the last few months, with an alternating fever and a shortness of breath that would, on occasion, alarm him. He takes a gulp of air and looks directly at Oscar, who catches his glance from the corner of his eye while turning his head to light another cigarette; only a woman, Gray thinks, looks at another person in that way.

But Oscar, you have brought it upon me. First you steal my name; then you address me as "Dorian" in public; and, for all your rhetoric about Life imitating Art, you tease your readers by larding the book with incidents drawn from life. Your public has been very quick to identify the infamous Lord Henry Somerset with your Lord Henry—and both of them with you. Those who know of the Vale swear that the artist Basil Hallward is based on Ricketts; some say, on Whistler. You do not help the situation by going about saying that each of the characters, on the contrary, is drawn from your own character: that "Basil Hallward is what I think I am: Lord Henry what the world thinks me: Dorian what I would like to be—in other ages, perhaps."[92] Then Symons has gone about muttering that he was "not aware," when you first introduced me to him in what he calls the "zenith" of my youth at some private view, that I was "supposed to be the future Dorian Gray" of your novel.[93] Not that I was aware either, Oscar, of your plans for me. Then there is what some people call the cruel caricature of your mother in the figure of Lady Brandon—you are not capable of such treachery, are you Oscar? Your own mother? But you have left me to speculate about your loyalty to your friends—forget me, for a moment. How do you think Robert felt about being placed in your novel as "Sir Anthony Sherard"?[94] He has objected, I know. But if you insist on placing your acquaintance in your prose, it is no wonder your public think you are writing a *roman à clef*.

My dear Gray, of course you are right. It was wrong of me to translate you into my novel, even though by doing so I have made you immortal—and thus rendered you more permanent than anyone who lives in that void full of names we call history. "Art . . .

takes no care of fact; she sees . . . that Achilles is even now more actual and real than Wellington, not merely more noble and interesting as a type and figure but more positive and real."[95] Dorian Gray will outlast Napoleon, will outlast Gladstone, will be on everyone's tongue when the long catalogues of the Queens and Kings of England are remembered as some antique remnants of an Elizabethan dumb show surviving unaccountably into our modern age. History will remember the heroes of tragedy when history itself is forgotten. I have written your life for you—I have given you, dear Dorian, the key to yourself. Whatever the alienists and philosophers say, "consciousness . . . is quite inadequate to explain the contents of personality. It is Art, and Art only, that reveals us to ourselves."[96] I have painted your own portrait. You are not a "cool, calculating, conscienceless character," as the less perceptive reviews claim. "On the contrary," you are "extremely impulsive, absurdly romantic," and you are to be haunted all through your life "by an exaggerated sense of conscience" which will mar your pleasures for you and warn you that youth and enjoyment are not everything in the world. "It is finally to get rid of the conscience that had dogged his steps from year to year" that he destroys the picture; and "thus in his attempt to kill conscience Dorian Gray kills himself."[97] Mark me, Dorian: in this book I have given you a prefiguring type of yourself: you will find yourself within its pages. You have only now to observe—and imitate; to prove my axiom that when "a great artist invents a type, . . . Life tries to copy it, to reproduce it in a popular form, like an enterprising publisher."[98]

My dear Oscar—Gray finds himself stiffening and leaning sharply back from the last wave of cigarette smoke—I do not have any ambitions to be held up as proof of your aesthetic theories, or to be hailed as your latest deluxe edition. Even if you have been superbly generous in offering to underwrite the Bodley Head's costs for publishing my poems.

Come, come, Dorian; you are lovely when you are petulant, but it will spoil your wonderful countenance. I have given you your script; all that is left is for you to act it out. You might consider that you are in fact luckier than most men; you have some responsibility in choosing your part. "In real life it is different. Most men and women are forced to perform parts for which they have no qualifications. Our Guildensterns play Hamlet for us, and our Hamlets have to jest like Prince Hal. The world is a stage, but the play is badly cast."[99] In this case, I might say, the part is exquisitely cast; you are becoming Dorian Gray, are you not? in every fiber of your being. And by so doing, you will not lose your life, but discover it. For all art is "to a certain degree a mode of acting," as you have observed in your own wonderful lecture, and as such is "an attempt to realise one's own personality on some imaginative plane out of reach of the trammeling accidents and limitations of real life."[100] But remember, my dear Dorian, that the secret is not to take the role seriously; true wisdom lies in the exquisite modes of folly. Did you not mark my little parable of Sybil Vane, which I saw fit to add to my original tale? Does Sybil's tragedy not convince you of the dangers of your position? All bad art "springs from genuine feeling."[101] The public's naive assumptions about art are disastrous; do not subscribe to them. Forget the bullying of the press. If you start taking your role seriously, you will cease to be an artist, for you will have forgotten that, as an artist, "the first duty in life is to be as artificial as possible."[102]

Gray gazes at Oscar's bloated fingers as they stub out a cigarette in a shower of sparks and ash, then follows his quick glance towards a slim, white-faced boy making his way towards them. Ah, Bosie; Wilde rises abruptly, gathers his walking stick, and, with a flick of it towards Gray and a brief nod, disappears into the dim immensity in the direction of the door, leaving Gray to contemplate in the surrounding mirrors the image of his own tarnished reflection.

Who could intervene between himself and his double? Oscar might succeed in protecting him from the press, but he could not succeed in protecting him from Oscar—or from himself. Once again, Gray senses the need for disengagement. Yet, just as Oscar seems to be drifting away into a crowd of adoring disciples and into the arms of a new and alarming young man—those of the beautiful, spoiled aristocrat Lord Alfred Douglas—Gray finds himself once again entangled in Oscar's seductive presence. This time, in early June of

1892, the snare is laid by a letter. Written in a round, childish hand on blue paper underneath an embossed yellow sphinx and signed by a stranger, the note poses a riddle in the most exquisite French. Gray puzzles it out:

> Sir,
>
> In Paris quite extraordinary things are taking place: naiads have been found seated upon the bed of the Seine, beside an old boat which one wanted to refloat; at the Bois de Boulogne a trampled clearing has been discovered where fauns had certainly danced, for there were prints of goats' hooves everywhere, and where they had been sitting, their little tails had made hollows in the dust. Lastly, Monsieur, the moon, which was last month like a Princess who wears a yellow veil and silver shoes (ask Oscar) is now just like a beautiful nymph who offers an iris to another small nymph who cannot be seen. I find this very frightening, Monsieur, because one must not see goddesses; one must only say that one has seen them, to people who do not believe you. Moreover I am about to leave Paris to go to London, if the fauns are not there already.
>
> I am,
> Pierre Louÿs[103]

So Oscar has already seduced this young man with one of his wonderful stories, that of the storyteller who, when asked daily what he has seen, enchants his village with tales of fauns and naiads and nymphs. Until one day, while walking in the woods, he comes suddenly on a clearing where fauns and nymphs are at play. Dazzled, he returns to the village and, when asked what he has seen, he nods with finality. "Nothing" he explains. Oh, Oscar of the fauns, now Oscar of the silver moon which watches Salome dance her dance of death; while in Paris you have become like the moon, looking coldly on your self-created performance, imaging a dance so seductive that it can only lead to your own nemesis. And now have you sent an emissary before you, a disciple whose cry is, a greater one comes after me, of whom I am only the forerunner?

Gray considers the riddle, then replies to the faun, of whose fame he has already heard from Oscar, only as befits one: in the cadences of an artful medieval French:

Dear Monsieur Pierre Louÿs,

As thou dost me, I know thee beforehand by thy name from the telling of Oscar Wilde. With free and open speech I may tell thee of the denizens of the woods and the rivers of this dismal country. Verily they are stuffed with sheep and fish and other such beasts, the most of these neither fauns nor nymphs, none having need of any such now-a-days. Come shod with light or straw, thou shalt be welcome. The school is at this present hour most shrunk in. Our Kit Marlow is gone down to the shades, dispatcht thither by a scurvie poniard thrust through his eye. The froward Jehan Keats hath nought else in his noodle but to search out the grounds of gold and set there marygolds and greensward. Shelley is become a fisher of corals, and Shakesper doth busy himel about the putting-on of his plays. There thou hast all our intelligence, and no more.

JOHN GRAY[104]

How much, Gray wonders, does the young man already know of this school? He is acquainted with Louÿs only through Wilde's praise of him as a young but rising poet and the founder of an avant-garde review, *La Conque*. He knows that Oscar first met Louÿs in Paris in December, and that Oscar has entrusted to Louÿs the correction of the less-than-grammatical French of his new play, *Salome*. Gray is not sure how much Oscar had conveyed about his London life; this letter would test him. Would Louÿs catch the double-entendre in such phrases as "les habitans des boys"—or pick up the nuances of "Ils sont emplys de moutons et poyssons et aultres bestials"—or even register the resonances of "les fondes d'or"? How much did Louÿs already know about Shelley, whom Oscar had proposed would sit next to Louÿs in his invitation to the first night of *Lady Windermere's Fan*? Did Louÿs, for instance, know that Shelley, one of the new office boys at the Bodley Head (later the publishers of Gray's own wonderful book), had the eyelashes of a poet? Or did Louÿs understand what was meant by fishing for coral? (Later, when Gray was to give Louÿs Shelley's address, he would advise him: "Only, if you seek the experience of Shelley, you must explain to him precisely that he should address himself to your interests and not fool around.")[105] As for Kit Dowson, even Louÿs must know that he was famously struck with the beauty of Missy, his Polish girl love;[106] no great wit was required to unravel that riddle, nor the reference to that great lover of boys himself, Oscar Shakespeare.

Despite every attempt to initiate him, Louÿs arrives in London with his mistress, Lucile Delormel. Ah, the French! Gray meditates; how lacking in imagination to attribute so many of the virtues to women. At a hint, however, Louÿs tactfully abandons Lucile for the pleasures of the school, which, from first meeting, astonishes him. To his close friend, André Gide, another fervent admirer of Oscar, Louÿs confesses he is seduced by the courtesies of the pupils of the "school":

> It is not at all as one thinks it is here . . . These young people are most charming . . . You cannot imagine the elegance of their manners. Well, then, to give you an idea: the first day I was introduced to them, X, to whom I had just been presented, offered me a cigarette; but, instead of simply offering it as we do, he began by lighting it himself and not handing it over until after he had taken the first drag. Isn't that exquisite? And everything is like that. They know how to envelop everything in poetry. They have told me how several days previously, they had arranged a marriage, a true marriage between two of them, with an exchange of rings. No, I tell you, we cannot imagine such a thing; we don't have any idea of what it is all about.[107]

As for Dorian, Louÿs is all delight at their meeting, writing him with an open, affectionate childishness: "I am very pleased with your letter, with your invitation, and with yourself."[108]

Gray replies with an invitation written from the Foreign Office on Wednesday, 15 June. He has abandoned all attempts at French, fake medieval or otherwise:

My dear Pierre Louÿs,

I write to you from the galley where life has chained me. Tomorrow and the next day I purpose absenting myself and if it seems well to you to pass a few hours with me I should be filled with joy. I[t] happens that on Thursday and Friday the National Gallery is filled with students—all hideous. I think we might go into the city: there are some Pre-Raph. pictures at the Guildhall of entrancing loveliness among them the two best things Millais ever painted and probably therefore the finest modern pictures in existence. Or we could go to the British Museum together and see the Greek vases and mediaeval missals[.] Or again, for pleasaunce, we might go for a promenade on a River Steamboat *down* the Thames where all is filth and smoke and the very hub of beautiful scenery[.] If you think this last excursion would be delightful come in your oldest clothes—in any case I shall be more or less débraillé. If you write me a note any time this evening, I shall receive it early tomorrow morning; then I will meet you at any time and place you choose to name[.] It might be well to set out before noon. Above all if you have better things to do, do not hesitate to say so.

Ever yours
John Gray[109]

To this Louÿs replies that he is not free until 17 June, but will call that morning at the Temple. He also suggests they lunch at St. James's Hall—a restaurant where Wilde often dines and which he likes to recommend to his friends; they can then proceed on their expedition.

Thus it is on a Friday afternoon that Louÿs and Gray find themselves at the Guildhall, gazing together at Millais's *Ophelia*.

They comment that she is not beautiful; that the calm of the picture is unnerving; the technique devastating. Like the Sensitivists, Gray observes: its chief virtue is "exact observation . . . Most people, knowing that water is transparent, look *through* it: they see water, green, brown, or whatever may be in its density. Some, with a quicker visual sense, look at its surface, and almost always see beautiful colour."[110] Look how Millais catches the deliquescent flow of the senses, he exclaims softly, holding it at the moment of its dissipation. This should be a picture about madness and death; instead it is about order, pattern, stasis: about a moment when the heart is arrested by the radiant detail of the senses. In the silence, you can practically hear the mad song as she sinks gradually to the depths. Nothing breaks the spell except one furtive gleam of light, breaking up the picture, moving it towards inevitable death.

That evening, he writes a poem on the picture. (When it is published, Gray will dedicate it to Louÿs.)

> Not pale, as one in sleep or holier death,
> Nor illcontent the lady seems, nor loth
> To lie in shadow of shrill river growth,
> So steadfast are the river's arms beneath.
>
> Pale petals follow her in very faith,
> Unmixed with pleasure or regret, and both
> Her maidly hands look up, in noble sloth
> To take the blossoms of her scattered wreath.
>
> No weakest ripple lives to kiss her throat,
> Nor dies in meshes of untangled hair;
> No movement stirs the floor of river moss.
>
> Until some furtive glimmer gleam across
> Voluptuous mouth, where even teeth are bare,
> And gild the broidery of her petticoat . . .[111]

Ah yes, he thinks; we are the Hamlets of our age. We stand aside and watch the play of madness, of disintegration, of death. (Years later, Yeats, standing before the same picture, will recall the "old abounding, nonchalant reverie" of death—the "old emotion" which, for him, this image once again recovers.[112]) Outside the picture, Gray fends off its seductive reverie, framing his response within the formalities of craft, in the cadences of a voice moving into silence, arrested in the divine stasis of print. Gray is vaguely conscious that, for another moment, he has contrived to hold off the hour of his own dissolution. Increasingly, he reflects, his poetry is becoming a measure of desperation, an attempt at detachment in the midst of a life that is beginning to fall apart.

Four days later, on 21 June, he again writes Louÿs:

> My dear Pierre Louÿs,
>
> I have been reading the songs of your Astarté. They fill me with despair; the technique is exquisite and in every way they are so "clever" that they make me afraid and uncomfortable. Also you are a true poet which is far far rarer. I hope I may see you very soon indeed but I am so bothered at a prospect of the huissiers [bailiffs] coming that I do not like to show myself. I expect to be in the Café Royal for a few minutes this evening but the time is uncertain and I will take my chance of meeting you.
>
> Always your
> John Gray [113]

Meanwhile, Oscar has, after ten days of searching, finally tracked down the elusive visiting poet in order to issue an invitation: "Enfin, voulez-vous dîner avec moi ce soir? Rendez-vous Café Royal, Regent Street, 7.45, habit de matin. Je serai charmé naturellement si Madame vous accompagne. Et j'inviterai John Gray."[114] But John Gray does not put in an appearance. He is broke again; this time, not simply broke but gloriously bankrupt; he feels he is obliged to stay in his flat at 3, Plowden Buildings in the Temple in case the bailiffs come to claim the furniture—and anything else of value. Ironically, the one thing he most desires after starving himself for the last three days is a good hot dinner. He meditates on his impossible position; perhaps the cost of living as Dorian is becoming, at last, unsustainable.

Almost three weeks pass before Gray writes Louÿs again. Meanwhile, Oscar has been ill and has finally abandoned a hot and stuffy

London to take the waters at Bad Homburg. He has been on an emotional roller coaster: within weeks of Sarah Bernhardt agreeing to play the lead in his *Salome* and the rehearsals going into full swing, the play was banned by the Lord Chamberlain on the ground that it contained biblical characters. Gray heard that Oscar gave an interview claiming he was leaving for France, where it was still possible to have a work of art produced, and was contemplating becoming a French national in protest: "I will not consent to call myself a citizen of a country that shows such narrowness in artistic judgement. I am not English. I am Irish which is quite another thing."[115] It is part of the play, and so like Oscar; hysterical hyperbole, but hyperbole with a point. So it is now up to him, Dorian, to entertain the faun; and, with a new month's pay in his pocket, he issues an appropriate invitation:

> My dear Pierre,
>
> I think I remember that your free days next week are Tuesday Thursday Friday Saturday. Alexander is writing for seats at the Empire for Tuesday and afterwards if you are agreeable we will go to a place called the Corinthian Club where most of the swell whores in London resort.
>
> Altogether it will make an interesting if not vastly amusing evening.
>
> Ever yours,
> j.g.[116]

On this expedition, madame is emphatically not invited; the Empire, after all, is known as the "most popular whore market in London."[117] The intention of the letter is made explicit by Dorian's enclosure of a photograph of a large and ugly black prostitute, naked, seated in a chair with her heels together and her legs spread for a full view of her genitalia. Gray inscribes it: "The new mistress of Alexander." Alexander is Alexander Teixeira de Mattos, a comrade of Gray's from the Temple, organizer of translating work for starving poets and cotranslator with Gray of the Dutch novelist Couperus's book *Ecstasy*, companion of Gray's and Dowson's at

Poland, an "inveterate at arts and letters," and fellow conspirator from the Independent Theatre. As well as a climber, for laughs, of lampposts in his top hat.

Nothing turns out as imagined. In the event, Louÿs replies the next day that he will have to leave London on Thursday morning in order to sit for his exams in Paris, which are commencing sooner than he had anticipated. Until then his three evenings are taken, but "Sarah has given me two *stalls* to go hear her on *Tuesday* in Frou-Frou; there is one for you, of course. Come with me and afterwards we shall go to the whore-Club."[118] Sarah, of course, is Sarah Bernhardt, whom Louÿs idolizes; the high point of his London visit had been his introduction to her at the end of June. On hearing he is a poet, Sarah had asked him to write a play for her, and, in feverish excitement, Louÿs began the text of what is to become the basis of his notorious lesbian novel, *Aphrodite*—which four years into the future is to bring him international acclaim.

(One biographer claims the rendezvous was kept and that Gray and Louÿs go that night to 46, Fitzroy Street, a notorious house for "rent boys," closed down by a police raid on 12 August 1894, and cited as a clandestine brothel in the Wilde trials of 1895.[119] Whatever occurred, this turns out to be their last meeting.)

Two days later Louÿs departs for Paris to take his exams. Gray writes him one short note in careful French before his departure:

12 July 1892
My dear Pierre,

A little farewell: although I hope to see you again before this beautiful sojourn is over—at least for your departure. There are a few small matters I must mention: in memory perhaps you will sometimes accuse me of indifference: you will recall stretches of three or four days when I did not seek you out and said nothing. But you must not hold it against me; I am melancholy by temperament and careful to hide myself very often on that account.

Also you will promise not to forget me; I do not insist on letters—that is too much—but I would like, when I see you again—be it after a twelve month, to find this friendship still warm, that has been so dear to me—do you not agree?

This is quite the letter of an irritated child, but all the same it represents my true feelings.

That is all my dear friend. I give you my hands.

always

j.g.[120]

Gray had hoped to meet Louÿs once again, however briefly. But four days later, he finds himself writing again—this time to Paris:

16th July [1892]

My dear Pierre

So you have gone and I did not see you again. It was unlucky: a godless cousin of mine arrived in London from Ceylon on Thursday evening without a shilling and almost without a shirt.

Naturally I had no alternative to looking after him and getting the things he most pressingly needed. I am really quite alone now among drunkards only. How kind you were to send me back Pater[.] I do not know if it is the same in France but here the return of a book is a thing phenomenal. But I think perhaps you did not care for it.

Ever yours

John Gray[121]

"Quite alone among drunkards only," Gray mutters to his reflection in the Café Royal. The convivial group of Oscar's young men—among them, now invariably, the petulant and beautiful Bosie—is breaking up. Later, Symons might come in and order an absinthe; or Dowson—before they make their way to Poland, and another long night of drinking and despair. Louÿs had done something to dissipate Gray's emptiness, the realization growing within him that he is living now only with a simulacrum of himself; "Dorian" lives in the imagination of others. But with Louÿs he can share his frustrations, his depressions and despairs; perhaps coming from the outside, Louÿs does not expect him to perform. To Louÿs he can confess his melancholy temperament—and be excused for hiding himself away.

That Louÿs also understands the rare nature of their friendship is confirmed by a letter which reaches Gray just before the poet's departure for Paris:

> My dear John
>
> When I told you last evening about a letter I had received from you, I meant only the first one and I did not know you had written to me such a beautiful second letter. I know now you are quite a *friend,* such a terrible word! how many have you? how many have I? Do we know? You shall go in Paris. We will meet again and often. I wish now one thing: to be for you what you have been for me during that short month.
>
> Give me your hand
> pierre louÿs
> Chelsea 18 July[122]

Gray had promised to visit Louÿs in Paris that autumn, but over the next three months things start to go badly wrong. Gray is often ill; he is chronically short of money; he is not eating properly. He struggles to finish his translation of Paul Bourget's *A Saint and Others,* and when Oscar returns from Bad Homberg and in the interval before he leaves for a rented house in Barracombe Cliff, near Torquay, Gray presents him with a copy, inscribing it: "To my loved master my dear friend Homage."[123] Ah, Dorian, Oscar says, lightly caressing his shoulder, My real life, my higher life, is with you and Louÿs and such as you.[124] But Gray sees that Bosie exercises an increasingly stronger fascination over his master, who no longer now seems master of himself, or of others.

During the heat of August, Gray retreats to the cool haunts of the Café Royal, writing Louÿs that he has handed on the small payment to Bismark which the poet owed from his visit. He recalls gratefully Louÿs's idea of writing something on his own poems when they appear—when indeed, he wonders; between the dawdling of Ricketts in designing the cover and the procrastinations of the Bodley

Head in fixing a contract, the delays seem interminable—and asks him what he thinks of approaching Frank Harris, the editor of the *Fortnightly Review,* for an article on the subject? And, meanwhile, he recalls Edward Shelley, whom he saw two or three days ago: still, as always, with very long eyelashes—almost those of a poet.[125] In a second letter, on 29 September, he gives Shelley's address to Louÿs, along with the admonition that if he seeks the experience of Shelley, it is necessary to explain precisely that Shelley should address himself to Louÿs's interests and not fool around.[126] Perhaps, Gray meditates, it is all in the name of research after all. (A few years later Dowson will comment that Louÿs had become "the greatest living authority on lesbianism"—and perhaps on homoerotic behavior too—except possibly that notorious publisher of Beardsley, Leonard Smithers.)

But something happens. London, emptied after the season, slowly refills. Oscar returns and then departs again. On the second of October, Gray writes Louÿs a strange letter (more than half of it has disappeared, presumed destroyed):

> My dear Pierre,
>   The other day, early in the afternoon, I received a telegram signed in your name: it read: "Good night." This was not a matter of indifference to me, but I instantly decided that, in a moment of agitation, you had committed suicide. And now, after a long silence, this decision is more or less confirmed—and I am writing for news.

Is this a joke, part of the Hamlet performance? Or a reflection of Gray's own morbid preoccupations? For his fears for Louÿs's fate are quickly lost in an account of his holiday in the country:

> It is quite nice, in its way, and thanks to its comfort, I am sorry to inform you that I am completely cured of my nerves and other vices. I am in a droll port: one with dirty sailors and other beasts of which I do not know the names in French. There are always hunts, riding on horseback, experiments in trapping curious fish of which I ignore the names, the sexes and the genders. We wear, the sailors and I, the clothes . . . [127]

(And there the letter breaks off, in the midst of the usual rodomontade about sailors and beasts and fish and clothes; the playful double-entendre of the closet gay.)

Coincidentally, Louÿs writes to John Gray on precisely the same day. He has just returned to Paris from the Bayreuth festival, where he was supposed to meet Wilde, but did not see him. He speaks also of another mutual friend: over the summer, Louÿs has become a drinking companion of Robert Sherard; in this dispatch, Louÿs seems far more worried about Sherard than he is about Gray:

> My dear and good John Gray,
>
> Why aren't you [*vous*] yet in Paris? I am waiting for you, hoping for you, you really ought to be here. Come in any case, for Sherard, if not for me. Martha tried to kill him the day before yesterday with a hat-pin and she has only just bought a revolver to be more successful the next time. If you wish to see him still alive you must hurry yourself a bit.
>
> . . . I am writing you during a sad rainy day which reminds me of St. James's Park. I would like to return to London but my military service obliges me not to leave France during the next year. Above all, I want to see you; come quickly and deliver Sherard from this poor hysteric who is so tiresome.
>
> See you soon, my friend. I send a thousand affectionate wishes to Alexander and I shake your hand heartily.
>
> Pierre Louÿs.
> 2 October 92.[128]

By the time Gray replies, Sherard's difficulties have transmogrified from trouble with his Polish wife into a challenge to a *duel à mort* with a Pole who lives in his village. Somehow in the interim, Sherard, together with Louÿs, has persuaded Gray to act as his second. Thus it is that Gray writes to Louÿs from his desk at the Foreign Office on 10 October:

> My dear Pierre,
> This unlucky affair. Naturally I consent to assist in it. Elective affinities are stronger than those of blood. Now is the hour to

confide in you my plan—which is principally for you alone.
You are not to say anything to Robert as he is able to decide
not to engage me. First of all, my job: I will ask for leave of
four or five days to conduct my sister to Petersborg [*sic*]; and
by this ruse I will obtain a passport without exciting any
suspicion. If things turn out badly in the end, I will probably
be prevented from returning to England which is all the same
to me, almost desirable. As for my mistress, the day before my
departure, I will confess to her that I have fallen in with a
former mistress. Then she will become very cross and will
refuse to see me for several days at least. About the costume
which I must wear to the field of battle: are frock-coat and top
hat such as one wears in French duels necessary? I would be
very grateful if you could give me the information I am looking
for. Goodbye, then, my dear Pierre. I will be very happy to see
you. I must write in French in order to express myself better
but I hope that you understand me. *Au revoir.*

> Always your
> j.g.[129]

(Nothing in the correspondence accounts for this baroque
response. Why should Gray lie to obtain a passport? Why would
he escort his sister to St. Petersbourg—and which sister is he talking
about? Who is the mysterious "mistress" whom he must deceive?
Why should Gray be just as happy not to be able to return to
England? An avalanche was gathering; nothing but an eerie silence
haunts the existing letters, the silence of letters burnt—a silence
that enfolds both correspondents.) Then, on 24 November, Gray
writes Louÿs in more than usually imperfect French. He begins
almost inconsequentially. "Silverpoints (my verses) is about to
appear. I am occupied at the moment correcting the proofs which
is very difficult the poems being printed in italics . . . Besides this,"
he continues more to the point:

I have as guides and peers companions who are a bit bizarre.
Of late, I have consorted with the dead. Nowadays it is DEATH
who loves me now. It is Folly and Calumny who keep me

company. I am an heir. The rich ground which hangs between
Life and Death is almost mine. I am going to enjoy my new
estate presently. Write to me. That is what I need. I will write
to you again about that. I am very unhappy. Some days ago I
almost decided to leave England, to withdraw my poems, in
order to become a French citizen, never again to speak a word
of English . . . I have lost my father. I am well pleased with the
loss. Write me.

> Always your
> j.g.[130]

His father had died three weeks earlier. Gray makes the
announcement with some satisfaction: this was the man who had
bullied him, snatched him from school, degraded his mother. Now
at last he was able to reject him decisively, having escaped him, his
class, his aspirations. In the older John Gray, one double had died;
but now another begins to haunt him. His companion is more than
a little bizarre, and perhaps comes from the realm of the dead. Was
it one of Oscar's stories that has summoned him? Sherard had told
Gray that, when he had asked the name of a man sitting alone in
the Café Royal, Oscar had replied: "That is Frederick Sandys"—
adding sorrowfully that he had been dead for some years.[131] Gray
calls his strangely dispassionate account of the episode "The Person
in Question."[132]

Dorian writes: "As well as I remember, the first time I saw—or to be
quite accurate, the first time I observed—the person in question must
have been in the last days of last August twelvemonth." The season is
over; London is empty and "hot, so hot, and I know not what fevers
were raging." On the dusty Strand, the cab horses sweat and droop; the
air is fretted with animal smells, from the shops, the people, the river.
Oppressed by the heat, the glare of the streets, Dorian seeks refuge in
the benign gloom of the Café Royal. He calls Bismark into conference;
what will tempt his fainting appetite? Together they work out: some
cold roast beef, very underdone; a little sardine on toast, followed by
vegetable marrow, and a small bottle of Niersteiner with soda water.

"Garçon!" said, rather murmured, a soft voice near me. It struck me strangely, it might have been my own. I believe I am singular in hearing the timbre of my own voice, so I was able to see the resemblance. A clumsy or ignorant person might have thought the voice was of a drunken man, or one half asleep. I understood its pitch only too well; so well that I listened for the repetition of the word, which came after the lapse of time I had allowed for it, loud, harsh, and unhesitating in key, as I had mentally predicted it. So that I looked whence it came. I knew the person knew I looked at him, though he seemed not to notice; but I stared steadily. I am not particular on this point; I know when I am at liberty to stare, not to mention the fact that people stare at me enough, people, too, who know better.

He was a man of about my own proportions; he might even once have been like me in face—for he was at least twenty five years older than myself, and bearded stragglingly; so that any existing likeness between us was well obscured.

"Pass me the Handelsblad," he said to the waiter who bent towards him, pointing with a stiff arm and drooping hand, "and some ice and some butter. Bring me my lunch . . . It's that Dutch paper I want," he continued, the waiter seeming stupid, still pointing with his wrist to the pile of newspapers.

My first emotion was fear, as these words followed one another from his lips. Then I gave myself up to observe this so complete illusion; for such I supposed it to be. The coincidences offered me nothing new, unfortunately—in principle, I had for months been accustomed to see my own face suddenly, unexpectedly, younger and better looking, or quite old, looking into my own and very close to me, healthy or haggard, puffed and spotted, or pure and transparent like an angel's.

I looked again at myself in the mirrored wall, then at the person in question reflected there. Did he really exist or was he a figment of my fevered imagination? Coincidences can reach a certain point only within safe and normal limits. There was about this person not one or two points, but, so far as my close observation could detect, complete resemblance to myself, in distinctive gesture and turn of phrase. Otherwise why should so complete an Englishman, in the Café Royal, want a particular Dutch newspaper? I happen to know Dutch, my chance accomplishment is a rare one, and this particular newspaper happens to be interesting to me for the remotest of reasons.

Fear passed into panic. The sweat on my brow crystallized; feverish speculation settled into a dull pain when I saw that my neighbor was eating the things I ate and drinking my own idiosyncratic combination of Niersteiner and soda water. There he sat, fully materialized, for were not a waiter and a boy running hither and thither for him? One person coming in spoke to him and shook hands. Yet, although his voice, his manner and sequence of acts were my very own, his movements did not follow mine seriatim. I took trouble and arranged tests to be sure of this.

Why did I not seek an excuse to speak to him, to touch him? I put to myself this possible, absurd question, for the mere sake of laughing at it. No, and no; I knew a little more, even then, than to have done such a thing. Seriously, was it a warning? What was it—this acute phenomenon? I must be excessively ill, was all I could resolve; and, panic-struck, I was not altogether displeased. I left the café and did not see the person in question for months.

Then it was one Saturday night, at a crush party, at Lady N's. I was thoroughly surprised to see him, for I had come to a very precise conclusion as to his appearance. The day following my first experience I had looked for him at the same hour and place; but I did not see him. Singular thing: all the hallucinations from which I had suffered, and suffered daily, after my prolonged fever, suddenly ceased from that time.

Well, there he was, looking very much as he had looked before, perhaps a little younger and smarter in evening dress, for he was scrupulously clad. I noticed his gloves, which were clean and well fitting, made of suede, of which I am so fond. I did not see him look once towards me, though he had the air of being keenly aware of my presence. Why bandy words? I *know* and *knew* that this was so. Also our resemblance was not less. The back of his head recalled vividly to me the appearance of my own, and he had a comic manner of mine on such occasions—it was troubling me at that very moment—which made me laugh: a half-controlled mania I have to put my hands in my pockets.

I was feeling so well that evening, so indifferent to hallucinations—one gets used to them as to anything else—that I sent boldly to Lady N. at the top of the stairs; and pointing out the person with every precaution against mistake, asked her his name. She looked carefully, and without hesitation told me. I thanked her for the odd-sounding sequence of syllables, resolving to puzzle out the name from the memory of them. But in a moment they were quite gone; I no longer had an idea if it was an English name or a foreign one, or if part of it was a title. Still, one thing I thought important; I was certain Lady N. had seen the person I pointed out, and I felt sure the sounds she had spoken as his name, really made a name. I resolved to put the whole subject out of my mind, to adopt the sanguine hypothesis that the person in question was a real, ordinary man; that when I had first seen him, a certain convergence of unhappy coincidences had engendered this illusion, into which I read much more than there was.

I left the party. But from that moment his presence never seemed to leave me; he was like a figure seen at the edge of the eye; when you turned, he was gone. One Sunday morning, feeling particularly well, I took the train for Brighton. The trip gave me time to consider: at length I summed up something in this way. I am certainly very much better than a few months ago; probably better than ever in my life before; incontestably. A person whose appearance is undoubtedly interesting to me is constantly in my way. This person is to be classed in one of several categories; in some near or remote sense *he is myself*. It will require time, observation and wary calm for me to discover in what sense he is myself. It may be, probably is, that my nerves, quickened and refined by disease, and unable to return to their first insensate condition, put me in a position to appreciate a phenomenon perhaps of the most ordinary description, which those who can detect it do not think themselves bound to disclose to those who cannot.

I had reached roughly this conclusion by the time I had taken my seat in the smoking compartment of the Pullman car for Brighton. I was so well possessed of myself that I was quite prepared to see the person in question enter the carriage, and occupy the one vacant seat. We started without him; I felt sure he was not on the train, even though I made one cursory trip looking for him. I arrived at the Metropole, and there in the hall he lay, asleep in a great armchair, before the fire. I was surprised, later in the day, to remember having felt compassion for him, sleeping there in the morning time. I had accepted him, for whatever he might be.

Well that I had, and so easily, for through the months of winter, dine where I would he was at a table near; in obscure Italian restaurants, at supper in fashionable and fraudulent places. He often had friends with him, a strange assortment too. I used to laugh sometimes, at the expense of the people with whom I supped or went to the theater. "There sit," I would think, looking at the other table, or in the opposite box, "themselves, or their parts or doubles, whatever they are, and *they don't know.*" I would try to *pair* the actual and the phenomenal.

Then came the season. Promenades in Hyde Park, croquet at the Hurlingham Club in the Ranelagh Gardens; opera at Covent Garden. He never failed: impeccably dressed, eloquently gestured, silent. His appearance at the opera I thought the strangest—if strangeness in such a case is susceptible of degree: my visits to the opera rest mainly on chance; I am either invited, or I buy my stall guided by tastes that make the choice on any one night quite complicated. Yet during that whole summer—June, July, August— he was my invariable, my inevitable companion. He was at every restaurant at which I dined, at every public place I went to, though often for not long at a time. He was so omnipresent that the most I could be grateful for was that I had kept him out of my dreams.

Then, on 3 September, I woke very tired in the morning. I could neither eat nor speak, scarcely could I walk. I looked for him at lunch; in fact, before ordering, I waited a little for his arrival. He did not come at all. During the afternoon I made up my mind that the moment I had seen him I would go straight away to bed. By dinner I was desperate. I thought out the matter carefully, and went at length to a new restaurant, placing myself where, by aid of the mirrors on the wall, I commanded a view of the door. He did not come; all through my dinner I watched every swing of the door in vain. As I took my coffee, I knew if I did not find him, I would be cheated of my night's sleep. I must go somewhere—but where? I could think of no place. In the end, I simply took myself off to the Exhibition.

The switchback is one of my secret joys; too childish to confide even to a friend.[133] Suddenly, there he was. There was a moment's awkwardness—you know, usually people go on switchback in couples—but I climbed on near the front by myself. Quite unconcerned, he took a place on the back bench, deferring to me, indulging me and yet not seeming to do so. I wondered to myself who was sitting next to him when a sudden waft across the still dusty air brought the scent of *foin coupé*. You may guess I winced, and turned abruptly away, only thankful I was windward of the hateful odor. A natural, rational woman riding by herself on the switchback! Unheard of! It was a hateful accident—*that* man with such a woman—it was so full of possibilities that I *dared* not dwell upon it. The car rushed away; I felt I wished to gain speed too, to take flight from this sordid betrayal; I felt it might be carrying me away from them, even though surely they were always exactly the same distance from me. So when the car paused, on its return flight, I preferred blundering over a partition to escape, pretending to the angry attendants that I had never been on a switchback before and had taken fright.

From that moment I have not seen him since. Days and evenings and nights I passed, haggard, looking for him. My senses grew painfully keen as I strained sight and hearing for a trace of him. I could not bear to be in a place where there was a door, and a possibility of his entering behind me. I placed myself in cafés where the mirrors would reflect back the room around me, in order to search for him without seeming obvious. I would even snuffle at times, in my despair, for a waft of that dreadful scent that only prostitutes use, that hated *foin coupé*. And wherever I was, my poor skin, with a false sense it should never have had, shuddered and queried for some sign of him near. Hysteria soon set in, as from hour to hour I had this unappeased craving for what had once been so unpleasant to me. Through the nights I tossed in my bed, waking up in a sweat after a short hour's sleep, repeating over and over to myself in an agony: "What shall I do? What shall I do?"

What shall I do, indeed? Gray thinks. That is the tragedy of my life now: what shall I do? He sits over the question once again in the Café Royal. His face in the mirror is thin and haggard and shows the beginnings of fine lines across the brow. What shall I do? he murmurs back to himself in the mirror. Look at me. I am so broken in health that I am frightening myself. I am like a man possessed; call it mania if you will. Maybe it is more like infatuation. Now for more than a week, convinced a glimpse of him would calm me, I have roved from place to place, to every spot where I had ever seen him. Ten disappointments a day had not the slightest effect in deterring me. Vanity of vanities, all is vanity.

Fool that I was to think I could walk alone in the possession of such rare knowledge and experience. The person in whom I found myself has betrayed me to myself. He painted me into a picture, he wrote me into a book. There I do not age; there, not *doing,* but *being* is the ideal, the ideal of the dandy. Oscar initiated me into the world of art, my father into the world of death. And now I see that both those worlds—existing outside the quotidian, but miming it—have become one and the same. It is DEATH that haunts me now.

Oscar, grown fat and appearing everywhere with Douglas, is my ghost, the ghost of my future. He is only twelve years older than I, but looks more. He is bursting out of the frame of the picture, just as he is bursting out of his clothes. He breaks all the rules now, appearing publicly with his rent boys, even bringing them to the Café Royal or to St. James's Restaurant, for the *frisson* of their entry into respectable company.

Worse than prostitutes, it soils what Dorian once considered a beautiful friendship, one passing the love of women. (Gray could not know that, from prison, Oscar would write to Douglas: "When I compare my friendship with you to my friendship with such still younger men as John Gray and Pierre Louÿs I feel ashamed. My real life, my higher life was with them and such as they."[134]) Feasting with panthers is what you call it; the danger is part of the thrill. Beautiful manners deployed on these painted creatures of the underworld; Oscar throwing his pearls to swine.

There is only one person who understands, thinks Gray; I am sure he understands. I must find him. If I remain here, the mirror will soak up my essence and I will finally become only the ghost of myself. What was it that Arthur Symons had said the last time we met Oscar in the Café Royal? Oscar, I sometimes think you do not actually exist. Ah, yes, Oscar—you are become "an apparition; sometimes with John Gray: another apparition."[135]

The mirror gives back Dorian's reflection as he rises to go.

3 | DECADENCE
(NOVEMBER 1892–AUGUST 1893)

A FIRE HAD BEEN LIT at the end of the long room immediately on their arrival, just after eleven in the morning. But as the new man, and a mere second division clerk at that, John Gray is pointed towards the far end of the long oak table on which maps of all sizes and shapes are spread out, studied, then rolled up firmly or laid to rest in the thin horizontal wooden files which fill one wall of the room opposite the tall windows. In winter, the working conditions in the Map Room (the unofficial name for the Foreign Office Library) are simply insufferable, he notes, as if filing a report in his head. The smoke from the fire fills the room; he is still not entirely well; the smoke irritates his lungs and his eyes. But if there were no fire, it would be oppressively cold. At least the distance of the Map Room from the rest of the department will make it difficult to exercise control over his comings and goings; he gathers from the other clerks that arrivals after eleven in the morning, long lunches, and departures before five are seldom reprimanded.[1] The experience of these first few days convinces Gray that there will be enough margin in this new posting to write, to muse, to continue being, as Dowson teased him, "incurably given over to social things."[2]

It is January 1893: the beginning of a new year. Gray unrolls a map of the world and notes the more than a third of it colored red, the color of empire; his Scots ancestors murmur, the color of blood. Directed to check for discrepancies in naming among various designated Foreign Office maps, he has already noted a dozen (most of them in Ireland); then he gazes towards the fire. A line from

Verlaine haunts his head: "Je suis l'Empire à la fin de la décadence."[3] He decided a few months before, while correcting the proofs of his first book of poems, *Silverpoints,* to use one of its subsequent phrases as an epigraph: "en composant des acrostiches indolents." Exactly. A poetry of complicated form, reflecting the pointless word games of indolence; indolence being (contrary to popular opinion) the very finest achievement of his posting to the Foreign Office Library: and for civilization in general, its very aim and raison d'être.

A momentary cold fury seizes him; how could he dare to even contemplate indolence? Since his father's death, he has become the sole financial support of his mother and younger brothers and sisters. Even without his father's drinking, there is scarcely enough to go around. He earns only two hundred pounds a year; the rooms at the Temple alone come to sixty.[4] The rooms have no kitchen, communal or otherwise, so he must eat out or do with bread and milk in his armchair or writing desk. He looks towards the men around the table, considering the backs of his colleagues; bent, humbled, beaten; white hairs and worn suits, shirts on which the collars or cuffs have not been changed often enough; shoes down at heel or cracking uppers. Most of them support a family on their income; but not an expensive double life. Laundry. Lunches. Hot dinners. More than three times a week, unthinkable. John Gray might thus be sustained. The Grays of Woolwich might also be fed and clothed. But Dorian is becoming, increasingly, an unconscionable expense. Elegant clothes are, for him, a necessity, whether dressing for first nights at the opera or to act as a second in a duel in France. There are tickets to the theater and the opera, on those occasions when he is not invited. Some modest travel: an occasional trip to Cornwall, Edinburgh, Paris. Journals and books: simply mandatory. He feels a little ill; then remembers he had no dinner the night before and a negligible breakfast. He does not know what is worse about being in debt: having to starve himself, as he once did, from Monday to Friday; or hiding in his rooms, as he found himself confessing last summer to Louÿs, in case of a visit from the bailiffs or the debt collectors.[5]

Inevitably, hunger, debt, anxiety take their physical toll. The death of his father was the occasion of an entire physical collapse.

At the time, only Pierre Louÿs seemed to understand. "My poor friend," he had written at the end of November:

> What's going on with you? Your letter frightens and worries me. What do all those words of death mean? I no longer recognize you. Why do you give a damn about being recognized at your own worth by imbeciles? Do I worry about them? Forget it and read in Ronsard the admirable sonnet of scorn for the people which ends with this verse: "Tyard, I understand you well, one must let them talk and for ourselves to laugh at him as he laughs at us." I beg you: write to me again and tell me why all of this? There is no question of death for you; you would be crazy to commit suicide at the moment you are beginning to create. You don't even have the right to do it.
>
> At the same time as your letter, I received the proofs of review in which one of my sonnets appeared which I dedicated to you, because Gide claims it is one of my best. I send it to you; I am your friend; I don't want you to forget it.
>
> Pierre Louÿs
>
> Why aren't you in Paris today for the inauguration of the Banville monument? Give me also Oscar's address. Here's mine: "Soldier of the second company of the first battalion of the 78th. At the line in Abbéville (Somme)."[6]

Before Gray received this letter, a momentous intervention had occurred. Under the heading of "Follies of the Week," a former friend of Oscar, André Raffalovich, had attacked the prose style of Wilde and Gray. Furious that his name had once again been linked with Wilde's, Gray wrote a vitriolic reply.[7] Dorian was acquainted with Raffalovich's reputation as a frequenter of the Uranian literary demimonde, but had shunned him as a known antagonist of Oscar.[8] Anyway, the sheer magnitude of his wealth, his mansion in the West End, his elaborate dinner parties which lionized such celebrities as Ouida and George Meredith and Robert Browning, assured that they moved in mutually exclusive circles. Yet it was Arthur Symons, his fellow writer from the Temple, who invited them both to a literary gathering in early November. It was enough to have seen Gray and Oscar together in the last months at the Café Royal to know that something was dying between them. Symons decided, on pure instinct, that Gray and Raffalovich ought to know each other.

When Gray met Raffalovich at Symons's rooms in the Temple, Gray was considerably abashed, uncertain as to how he might be received. To his surprise, Raffalovich was gentle and affable, and asked him to dinner the following week.[9]

It was to inaugurate—what?—Gray thinks abruptly, sitting down at the table to complete his task. His back aches. The fire seems to be spluttering. Over dinner, Raffalovich had told him all about his early flirtation with Oscar; the teasing; the affectionate innuendoes; then the ensuing rudeness and the gibes. Oscar arriving with other guests for dinner at Raffalovich's house in South Audley Street; when the butler answered, raising his fingers and saying: "Places for five, please." Oscar saying that Raffalovich had come to London from Paris to found a salon and had merely opened a saloon, a remark he thought so well of that he wrote it into the egregious *Picture of Dorian Gray*. Wilde's monstrous egotism, self-absorption, love of influence. Then the infamous remark about his "nice improper talks" to Constance, after which Raffalovich vowed never to speak to Oscar again without witnesses. How over the months, distaste had turned to distrust, distrust to revulsion. Eventually, he had made public his rejection of "the whole set," explaining how he came to feel about Oscar that

> everything he did or said annoyed me. He could do nothing right in my eyes. When I say he could do nothing right in my eyes, must this apply to the past as to the present? to his way, for instance, of always selecting the youngest in any company and talking to him endlessly, turning his head (as I said) for the mere pleasure of doing so, even though they were never to meet again.[10]

Raffalovich had leaned over the table, looking into Gray's eyes. It is not so much what he does or doesn't do with his boys. I know about all that; once I might even have been part of it. But it is the *influence* on the society of young men that I object to.[11] They admire, they copy him; it is an infection; it is pernicious.

Gray had drawn back, like a snail into his shell. He had tried to remain impervious, as if his clothes were just an elegant carapace to hide the naked man; his face a painted mask, fixed and immobile. But something had touched him; was it André's peculiar face, pulled one way and another as if it had been stepped on as a child; or his bright eyes that caught every flicker of his own, that gleamed with a soft affection? He had heard of André's wealth, his love of glitter, his pursuit of the hard and elegant celebrities of the day; from this quarter he had not expected such gentleness, nor such sympathetic and intelligent attention.

At that moment Gray knew, as he recalls now, that something had grown instantly between them. Gray rises restlessly from the long table and walks towards the fire. He will stand near it until at least part of his body thaws from the January cold, even if his shirtfront is roasted while his aching back freezes. Looking again into the small creeping flames, he thinks: I knew at that instant desire had taken hold with Raffalovich. Dorian is beautiful; it is common for men and women to desire him. But he has done with desire. (Years later, when Gray is at Scots College, Rome, Raffalovich would write him on the anniversary of this meeting:

> Still after all Symons the artist brought you and me together 7 years and 3 months ago. There was plenty of mental manure on which our fraternity could grow, n'est-ce pas, petit frère. And it has so thrived that I do not often bring into conscious thoughts how through eternity nothing I could ever do could quite atone for all I made you undergo . . . It is curious that two human beings can get sure enough of each other not even to have to ask for forgiveness . . .[12])

They had talked until the butler had cleared the table and blew out the candles. Of London, Paris, the new writing; André is shockingly well read, in English as well as European literature; the new movements, decadence and *symbolisme;* Uranianism and its future. Gray was shocked, but not surprised, that Raffalovich ended that dinner with an ultimatum: "You cannot be Oscar's friend and mine."[13]

It is a matter of only two months before Gray decides to move from his rooms at the Temple. He is no longer at home in Bohemia. He is not at home, full stop. Perhaps he will never be at home. Work is simply a kind of competent slavery: the "galley where life has chained me."[14] The Temple is full of old associates, part of a world which is dying for him; has died on him: "Of late I have consorted with the dead."[15] Along with Teixeira de Mattos and Sherard, he has located new rooms. As Dowson writes Victor Plarr: "This morning Gray who is finally leaving the Temple—quantum mutatus ab isto— fat but friendly, I fear incurably given over to social things—& about to take up his abode in Park Lane! This is sad."[16] The Park Lane address is not, as was generally assumed, the residence of André Raffalovich, but a house leased to eleven residents, a few minutes' walk from Raffalovich's mansion at 72 South Audley Street.

Gray writes to Pierre Louÿs with the news of his removal.

> My dear Pierre
>
> I thank you with all my heart for your sympathy. I have written a long letter to Robert & I have asked him to send it to you, I am so far from being able to write much. It explains my troubles sufficiently and as there is not in the world a triple friendship more perfect than ours please do not mind. I am better today than since months and I promise to write to you as soon as I can get my breath again. It is so strange to me that you are a soldier—are you a dragon [dragoon?]. If so I want a full length pastel portrait of you at once.
>
> Ever
> j.g.[17]

A day later, a "chère dépêche" arrived from Louÿs himself. Gray writes back that from the moment he received it,

> I have been inundated with health and joy; I am almost mad with it . . . All that remains of my sickness is a slight preoccupation with myself. How I bless you for the honour

which you do me in dedicating that noble sonnet. When I tell you my very dear that in structure, intention, in simplicity, in grace, in all these qualities, your poem is really *English,* I intend the most unbridled praise. It is typical of the *mature* Webster . . . and still surpasses a Keats. You ought to be proud to have overcome the difficulties of which we talked in the gardens of the Temple; you complained of the length of the sentence which failed to express in French the most simple ideas . . . I have promised to come and see you down there wearing your breeches peg-top, your republican frockcoat, your cap fabricated from English letters. Pardon—health is wicked and vile. At least if I have the same clothes and they are dignified enough. I always wear the same rags in which I was at the moment when you showed me around and they have truly fallen apart. When it doesn't matter where I am, I interlace my hands behind my head, which is not at all polite, but it allows me to air my elbows which appear and spread, gray and purple, according to the land or the wind.—This letter is mad. Write to me during your sparse leisure time . . . You have certainly taken me out of a vile year. I give you both my hands.

> always your,
> John Gray.[18]

Alarmed by a report from Louÿs that he had fallen ill, and having no response to his first letter, Gray writes again:

My dear Pierre

What a dreadful thing. But cannot you show from your attack of bronchitis that yourself and "the service" are not made for one another? I hope you are better. If you are yet alive you must be. For bronchitis does not mark time for very long. Now I am distressed. I wrote you a long letter. So long in fact that I used up all my French and have now to go back to the language of my adopted country. Now either you did not receive that letter, or for some reason you wish I had never sent it to you. In the first case it is a shame, for I wrote in it my admiration of your beautiful La Prairie, words which I can never repeat, and it contained the clue to the famous "toit" of some new rooms we are taking or hope to take. It also threw out a feeler to see if you would be glad to see me at Abbeville any chance Saturday. But I will keep Paris in mind. If you got my letter and did not like it you ought to say so. It was written in a furious impulse of high spirits which came to me with health—as I have never known it—suddenly returned to me—a true miracle. This access of joy has driven away all my fancies and worries and though it is alas a cold fact that they think that of me I cannot believe that they do.

Ever,

j.g.

P.S. But do get well my poor Pierre.[19]

They did think that of him, Gray knew: that he was one of Oscar's boys, part of the corrupt circle with which Oscar surrounded himself. Few knew he had broken with Wilde; his reputation as "Dorian" yet damned him. They still think that of me, he mutters to the fire, then surreptitiously bends down to prod behind the grate with the poker, displacing several coals in a firestorm of sparks. He turns to walk half the long room back to his place, accompanied by the shuffling of feet and maps, with the occasional sharp crack as one is disciplined to lie flat.

Leaning over his set of maps again, Gray wonders at his sudden shift in fortune. He has left the Temple. The recurrent fever, the bronchitis, the hallucinations, have all deserted him, leaving him at first drained and flat; then he is suddenly overcome by a surge of joy and health such as he has not felt in years. His sudden collapse in late November now seems just a nightmare; "I am so very well," he writes Louÿs. "It is *impossible* for me to have convulsions again."[20] At the center of his turn of affairs is Raffalovich. André— kindly, discreet—has made him write out an account of his haunting over the last year.

André regards himself, in an age when titles are still elastic, as a kind of doctor—not so much a healer, as a diagnostician. His specialty is probably the mental and physical condition of those men he knows to be Uranians—because so little has been written on them and they seem to have special claims on medical attention, particularly that of the new field which is emerging as the study of the psyche: psychology. Raffalovich's contact with writings from both French and German authorities convinces him that there is a new impetus to name and research the phenomenon of same-sex love in England, where it thrives in such fertile—if hidden—ground. He will begin with his friendship with John Gray.

His new friend, as Raffalovich gathers from rumor, is in difficulties. His finances are chaotic; he is poor, but dresses well; nevertheless there is a large family dependent on his Civil Service pay. His health has disintegrated under various strains: the most obvious being that he is neither sleeping nor eating properly. He has reason to fear he is going mad. His father has just died. His beloved Master, his dear friend Oscar Wilde, has just taken up with another lover, Bosie Douglas. (Years later, confronted by a photograph of his younger self, Gray "makes confession of the old days—their reckless destruction of health by exotic habits—their low company; their idle hours at the Foreign Office—their long nights of vain pleasure." [Gray implies that this entails frequenting "the haunts of the world & the devil not in sin—a conversing with sin not so much sinning . . ."] "A good doctor, seeing death sure in two years if such life were continued, broke the spell & got the fair young wreck to eat meat at each meal & take sleep in nature's way. The beginning of redemption was made! The Doctor was preparatory master for the seminary & the priesthood."[21])

Following Raffalovich's prescription, Dorian had written down, as completely as possible, the account of his haunting by "the person in question." Dorian knew, by the time he had completed its composition, that there was only one friend who could help, and "he would never forgive my treachery in keeping my secret."[22] The secret was shared. Raffalovich forgave. He did more. He assured Gray of an income, settled on him each month. He backed his decision to move from the Temple, the scene of dissolution of his health and sanity. And above all, he strengthened Gray in his resolve to break with Oscar Wilde.

To the larger world, as to Oscar and his circle, the move to rooms near Raffalovich is taken as a sign of a formal break with Wilde. (Robert Sherard wrote years later of speculation that, in befriending Gray, Raffalovich had "avenged himself . . . on Oscar Wilde for one or two gibes about his personal appearance and his social success by breaking up a new friendship to which Wilde attached great value."[23]) But in common with all endings, the actual falling out with Oscar happens gradually, then suddenly. When they meet briefly in the Café Royal in late November, just before Wilde is to leave for winter quarters at a house in Barracomb Cliffs, Gray finds himself looking at Oscar's white face as if it had been already embalmed. Since his father's death, he had moved through a world of the dead—some, like Oscar, who did not even know they were dead. But it came to him that they had, along with his whole world, died to him. Dorian does not say much; he orders an absinthe; between one cigarette and another it is decided, almost offhandedly, that Wilde should be released from the contract he had signed with the publishers at the Bodley Head in June for the cost of the design, manufacture, and advertising for Gray's first book of poems, *Silverpoints*.[24] (In January, another contract will be drawn up, stipulating that the costs will be paid entirely by the publishers, with a royalty of 20 percent for Gray. Wilde, for "the help we have received in this matter," is to receive one free copy of the special and one of the ordinary editions.[25])

This morning at the Foreign Office Library, Gray arises from his seat and takes a turn about the room, ostensibly looking to see if anyone has a correspondent map to the one he is perusing, actually to restore some semblance of warmth. It is almost lunch time. Everything since his father's death has turned about; his firstborn book charts out the change of direction. When Gray had announced at the Vale the advent of his first book, Ricketts had volunteered to do the cover. But his plans are almost a state secret, Gray muses; and he has during the past year or so not been often enough at the Vale to keep in touch with Ricketts's doings.

Anyway, Ricketts is notoriously slow and, as Gray has learned, becomes more secretive the more overdue the work.

Within the book there will be many of the translations inspired by the blazing talk at the studio: the renditions of Verlaine are among his best, Gray reckons; "Un Crucifix," which he plans to dedicate to his fellow convert Dowson, has a quiet mastery the others lack. But Gray discovers that his publisher, John Lane, is hopelessly conservative; being nervous of the new label "decadent," while hoping at the same time to capitalize on it: scandal sells well, but only safe scandal. So Lane has expressly requested that this new and provocative poet remove one poem, "The Song of the Stars," from his roll of poems. Expressions such as those about "swollen women" or references to a "corpse lying naked and robbed," Lane insists, must be "suppressed from the volume on the ground of indecency."[26] For reasons of prudence, Gray himself has withdrawn the poem "Sound," which draws so obviously on a passage from *The Picture of Dorian Gray*.[27] People will only think he is trading on his "Dorian" nickname—when, in fact, Wilde had stolen it from him.[28] Predictably, the translations from the French are going to be trickier. Baudelaire's notorious "Femmes Damnées" is deemed admissible—but only on the condition the last verse is left out; no apotheosis of these unnatural women must be sanctioned, certainly not in print or in public. Frank Harris's censoring of the Rimbaud piece, "Charleville," is left intact; the Mallarmé poem to the "Mother creatrice," a Madonna of flowers, simply truncates itself by extending into territory where the available resources of the English language cannot reach.

Despite the volte-face with Wilde, despite John Lane and other censors, Gray is conscious that in this book he has at last found his voice. He looks towards the dying fire, then at his hands, held in front of him, scrupulously manicured. In *Silverpoints* Dorian Gray will become himself, beautifully bound, wonderfully printed: a work of art. He has worked out the details with Ricketts. The paper will be expensive: Van Gelder handmade paper; the type, italic: delicate to the point of being unreadable, floating in a sea of margin. The "build," or shape, of the book will be tall and slim, modeled, as Ricketts dictates, on "one of those rare Aldus italic volumes with its margins uncut."[29] It is to be bound in vellum or green cloth stamped in gold; design as yet unknown. It is to surprise; but it will be elegantly clothed. Inside, the poetry will be as extravagant as its binding, as precious as the restricted numbers of the edition—only 250 ordinary copies, with 25 in a deluxe edition. Every touch, from the epigraph of Verlaine to its last languishing phrase, will mark it as rich and rare, the precocious child of "decadence."

Returning to his mapwork, Gray ponders briefly on the mysteries of naming. Here, on the map of Ireland, the names are a jumble of arbitrary translations. Sometimes the surveyors simply rendered the Irish into what they considered to be English equivalents—with, to the English ear, occasionally bizarre results; sometimes they attempted to transliterate the Irish name into an anglicized equivalent; occasionally there was just a bald substitution with an English imperial denomination. Moreover, as his task makes painfully and abundantly clear, the new names are not always coordinated or systematized, so that two or sometimes three different versions of the same name appear on different maps. He throws up his hands. He is cold and hungry. Time for lunch.

On Fleet Street, the January drizzle is mixing everything into an atmospheric blur; the jumble of hansoms, horsecars, and wagons merge with the London smoke and fog into a study of black and gray, the sky commingling with the moving traffic in a ghostly effect, shifting suddenly out of the mist into sharp reality and then sinking back into it and disappearing into an agitated murk. Dorian ducks into a dimly lit pub—the Cheshire Cheese—for a beer and a quick, cheap dinner; he seats himself near a window to stare out past the line of steaming cab horses, blanketed against the cold, towards the street. Even in the January cold, there is always life on the streets. The whole world is there: aristocrats and beggars; cabmen and merchant princes. Some walking or greeting; some hawking or selling; others attending to horses or sweeping the crossings. Some simply loiter, sitting on doorsteps or propped against walls. They live on the streets. Gray too spends more time now walking aimlessly through London; he senses he is no longer at home, either with himself or with his "adopted country." He no longer has a place or a name. He is no longer Dorian, but neither is he John Gray; neither from Woolwich nor the Temple. He writes poetry, but his readers will not necessarily recognize it as English; already he is aware of the ambivalences attaching to the new name: decadence.

Gazing out onto the controlled anarchy of the street, Gray recites again softly: "Je suis l'Empire à la fin de la décadence." He did not need his godless cousin, straight back from Ceylon, nor even Oscar, still silently grieving for his great lost leader, Charles Stewart Parnell, to tell him about the decadence of empire. A week in the Foreign Office, examining maps and editing dispatches to all its corners, was enough to do that.

The French, being French, had codified that sense of an ending into an aesthetic movement, which they defined as *déca-dence*. Its expression in literary movements such as symbolism and impressionism is neither well known nor understood in England. His own modest efforts in educating the public to the work of the Goncourts had sunk like a stone. Those who read Huysmans's *A Rebours* thought it must be a joke. The word "decadence" in English had about as much precision, Gray reflects, as the scene outside the window—or of the English names for Irish places on the maps which he had been told to reconcile.

What "decadence" has come to mean to the English public, Gray ruefully concludes, is to be preposterously and poisonously— French. He was trying to live up to this reputation in his translations, which, he knew, would compose the bulk of his first collection. But the real test was to use their techniques within the traditions of English poetry. A performance on the edge of a precipice, as he is discovering. To extend the resources of English poetry on one's own, without maps, without guidelines, without even the support of fellow poets, is a performance on the edge of a precipice, a performance in which one occasionally falls over. There is no consensus in any case on the direction in which English poetry is going. The Rhymers are themselves grotesquely divided on the value of the new French poetics: Symons is all for importing it, theory and all, wholesale. John Davidson and others dismiss it as utter rot—and rotten.

Rotten is what it should be: a rotting poetry for a rotting empire, Arthur Symons announces definitively, to the whole room. His mustache, ever a register of strength of feeling, quivers in the wavering light of the Café Royal. Look, Gray. I'm working on a manifesto to proclaim the tenants of the new writing: I will call it "The Decadent Movement in Literature." The paper quivers in his hand. I've enlisted Verlaine and Mallarmé, the Goncourts and Huysmans, the Belgian Sensitivists—your translation of Couperus's *Ecstasy* did much, Gray, to advance his cause here—and Ibsen, of course. And, of course, Pater.

Pater? Gray pulls back in shock. He will not thank you, Symons. You know he still feels badly burnt about his association with the hedonistic philosophy of Dorian Gray. He will not thank you.

Ah, but Gray, consider the divine pathologies of his *Marius the Epicurean* or *Imaginary Portraits*. "Have they not that morbid subtlety of analysis, that morbid curiosity of form, that we have found in the works of the French Decadents?"[30] Is Pater not the disembodied voice of the very sensibility of our age? Does his style not mime in its tremulous cadences the collapse of all our certainties? the very temperament of our times, riddled with the consciousness of its own degeneration? Look at the way he writes English— as if it were a dead language, decomposing from its own weight, laying each phrase out as if it were in a shroud. Does not his own imaginary poet, Flavian, seek to imitate the decaying Latin of *The Golden Ass,* "full of the archaisms and curious felicities in which that generation delighted, quaint terms and images picked fresh from the early dramatists, the lifelike phrases of some lost poet preserved by an old grammarian, racy morsels of the vernacular, and studied prettinesses:—all alike, mere playthings for the genuine power and natural eloquence of the erudite artist."

It is our golden book, Gray murmurs. A sacred text. I myself have fallen under its spell. I wrote a little thing for Shannon full of such "studied prettinesses." Would you like to hear it?

Please, Symons quivers.

> Purple and white the crocus flowers,
>> And yellow, spread upon
>> The sober lawn; the hours
> Are not more idle in the sun.
>
> Perhaps one droops a prettier head,
>> And one would say: Sweet Queen,
>> Your lips are white and red,
> And round you lies the grass most green.
>
> And she, perhaps, for whom is fain
>> The other, will not heed;
>> Or, that he may complain,
> Babbles for dalliaunce, with a weed.
>
> And he dissimulates despair,
>> And anger, and surprise;
>> The while white daisies stare
> —And stir not—with their yellow eyes.[31]

Excruciating, Symons murmured. You are just asking for the kind of parody Owen Seamen is going about reciting: you know, the one called "Disenchantment"?

> My love has sickled into Loath,
>> And foul seems all that fair I fancied—
> The lily's sheen a leprous growth,
>> The very buttercups are rancid.[32]

What do you think you are doing? Symons inquired, as if asking for the rationale of a particularly bizarre music hall act.

Well, Shannon loves flowers. He was scattering marigold seeds in that wilderness they call a garden at the Vale and I followed him around reciting Tennyson's "Maud"—and then that wonderful song from "The Princess," "Now sleeps the crimson petal, now the white"—Ricketts observed that I did so "with the subdued relish of an epicure."[33] Then to tease me, he began to recite the passages about the talking flowers in *Alice's Adventures in Wonderland*. So dead as to be daring, Dorian, he said; it teeters between the sickly sweet and downright silly, don't you think, Chubbus? Since Shannon did not exactly spring to my defense, I told Ricketts: it is as I wrote of the Belgian Sensitivists—"in the end, the language they play tricks with thanks them."[34] What I seek in poetry is a stasis of the mind. If the words or phrases are dead from centuries of overuse, or deadened by previous handling, they are more useful for me in quieting the mind, in deploying them in patterns of sound in which they resonate subtly with allusions to other poets, other eras. Placed in patterns as if for entirely decorative effect, they arrest by means of a relation to each other; they bring the mind to a halt and they arrest the heart in a silent stasis of aesthetic pleasure, and in that state achieve something very much like that cardiac condition which the Italian physiologist Luigi Galvani, using a phrase almost as beautiful as Shelley's, called the enchantment of the heart.

Symons, silent and still, gazes at Gray as if he no longer recognizes him. Then abruptly, coughing, announces: that poem still sounds silly to me.

Well: I like clever poetry, just as I like charming people. Both depend on a kind of overt manipulation, it is true. Just as with the *symboliste* poets we both so intensely admire. "New-found freedom is apt to realize itself a little too vividly, and first experiments with a language loosed from the moorings of its tradition are like to be carried out with more impulse than balance. But the temerity of these forerunners has it immediate reward . . . in the inevitable youth and cleanness of their language; every word they write is with intention." When I compare my attempts to bring into English what they have done with French, I see that you may be right, that "all I have done has been a performance on the edge of a precipice, usually rewarded as such deserves, and more for reproof than applause even when I did not fall over."[35]

No, no, some of it is wonderful, Gray. The Verlaine poem "Un Crucifix" is masterful. And your version of the Baudelaire "La Voyage à Cythère" far surpasses my own feeble attempts to render the same poem. I admit in the one Mallarmé poem you undertake, you do not do justice to the Master. I myself am struggling with his "Hérodiade." But you are right to try, even if you must take large risks. If you do not, as you say, perform on the edge of a precipice, you are not taking enough chances; there are times when real art must fail and fail again.

A silence; one that burns. Then Symons suddenly becomes the public critic. Take heart, Gray, the voice from behind the mustache booms. It is worth the risks. You have done things that will mark the hour. What about that sonnet you wrote to Robert Burns? Ah yes, recite it now, Gray, and you will find your true voice.

Gray bows his head, then raises it, and recites towards his double in the mirror:

Geranium, houseleek, laid in oblong beds
On the trim grass. The daisies' leprous stain
[Seamens again, interjects Symons]
Is fresh. Each night the daisies burst again,
Though every day the gardener crops their heads.

A wistful child, in foul unwholesome shreds,
Recalls some legend of a daisy chain
· That makes a pretty necklace. She would fain
Make one, and wear it, if she had some threads.

Sun, leprous flowers, foul child. The asphalt burns.
The garrulous sparrows perch on metal Burns.
Sing! Sing! they say, and flutter with their wings.
He does not sing, he only wonders why
He is sitting there. The sparrows sing. And I
Yield to the straight allure of simple things.[36]

A moment's silence while the clatter and talk of the Café Royal settles about them. Were you there, Symons? asks Gray. I mean, there at the statue's unveiling by Lord Rosebery at the Victoria Embankment Gardens in 1884?[37] I believe it was my first literary event—the first time I saw Oscar Wilde—and my present master, Lord Rosebery. He is now foreign secretary, but they say he will be up for prime minister soon—despite the rumors that he is of that school. Gray trails off at the glazed look in Symons's eye. You see, it was the first time I understood what it meant—to be known as a poet. There was Rabbie Burns, the brawling bard of moor and tavern, frozen into bronze on a pink marble—a *pink* marble—plinth, taunted by the tame park sparrows. I looked about and thought: the child is foul; the daisies are unkillable; but at least they have a sordid vitality that mocks poor Rabbie: frozen now into the attitude of composition, a parody in apotheosis. The asphalt burns, but not metal Burns—cold, hard, aloof; worse, prettified— that is what they have made of this Scots ploughboy, who was of his people and lived among them. The English have tidied him up and made him charming: sitting there on a bronze tree stump beside a broken plowshare with a scroll of his writings beneath his feet. Oscar would have called it: the revenge of Caliban.

You are angry, Gray.

No. When I am angry, I am silent. I am irritated. I am raw with irritation. Do you not know what I mean? "At a certain time one is apt to want to live for grace. Soon the better ideal comes to live well and chance the grace. And is it not so with poetry? Have you come to the determination to write *well* at every risk? To put more fire into your work than anyone else could ever find out."[38]

Gray notes a skeptical glint in Symons's eye. I know what they think of me, Symons. That I am severely conventional, bland, impassive; a mere civil servant. Not enough fire to warm a tea kettle. Perhaps even that I am as cold and hard as metal Burns. But they do not know my life as even you do, Symons. They do not know that my whole method is to work by contradiction. "A Truth in art is that whose contradictory is also true," as Oscar says.[39] I am severely conventional only because I come from the working class. My new religion has taught me that the way to grace is through the necessary, the therapeutic sin; Symons looks up abruptly. Fire kindles from the spark of two stones. It is the same for writing. I will tell you how I do a poem; I made these poems "seven days alone before they went into proof, by getting 2 ideas (often incongruous) & clapping them to bake" in my brain—"repeating the process till the dish was single."[40]

A silence. Symons's pale eyes settle on Gray as if in appraisal. The mustache stills, then twitches. An original method. I begin to understand metal Burns. But do you not think, Gray, that one is less a victim of one's audience than of one's art? That Art is like Pygmalion's statue, which destroys him in coming alive? That the real danger for the artist is in becoming the creature of one's own creation? Just as you have scented danger—as Dorian—in becoming the creature of another's creation?

Something flashes between them. Gray disappears for a moment beneath the table, pulling out a portfolio that had been placed at his feet. He rights himself again, nearly tipping over his drink, then pulls a foolscap sheet from the portfolio. Read this, Symons. I have just proofed it.

I. I dreamed I was a barber; and there went
Beneath my hand, oh! manes extravagant.
Beneath my trembling fingers, many a mask
Of many a pleasant girl. It was my task
To gild their hair, carefully, strand by strand;
To paint their eyebrows with a timid hand;
To draw a bodkin, from a vase of kohl,
Through the closed lashes; pencils from a bowl
Of sepia to paint them underneath;
To blow upon their eyes with a soft breath.
They lay them back and watched the leaping bands.

II. The dream drew vague. I moulded with my hands
The mobile breasts, the valley; and the waist
I touched; and pigments reverently placed
Upon their thighs in sapient spots and stains,

Beryls and crysolites and diaphanes,
And gems whose hot harsh names are never said.
I was a masseur; and my fingers bled
With wonder as I touched their awful limbs.

III. Suddenly, in the marble trough, there seems
O, last of my pale mistresses, Sweetness!
A twylipped scarlet pansie. My caress
Tinges thy steelgray eyes to violet.
Adown thy body skips the pit-a-pat
Of treatment once heard in a hospital
For plagues that fascinate, but half appal.

IV. So, at the sound, the blood of me stood cold.
Thy chaste hair ripened into sullen gold.
The throat, the shoulders, swelled and were uncouth.
The breasts rose up and offered each a mouth.
And on the belly pallid blushes crept,
That maddened me, until I laughed and wept.[41]

Symons pauses. The mustache works itself briefly, then stills. The pale eyes rise to fix on Gray: your ancient mistress I suppose? Or the one you attribute to Alexander?

Gray flushes. His visits to brothels are no secret to Symons, who prefers the whore to the society woman; he claims the whore is more his intellectual equal.

It is brilliant, Gray. Brilliant. It is La Mélinite, dancing before a mirror in Le Jardin de Paris: she was "young and girlish, the more provocative because she played as a prude, with an assumed modesty . . . She had long black curls around her face; and had about her a depraved virginity. And she caused in me, even then, a curious sense of depravity that perhaps comes into the verses I wrote on her" dancing on that night of May, "in her feverish, her perverse, her enigmatical beauty."[42] Ah, but this woman, Gray. She is truly fatal. When the barber rouses her, she responds like the black widow spider: she devours him. She is madness; she is death; she is the black widow, death. The mustache twitches; then is still.

Yours, Gray, has the true chill of the Hérodiade of Mallarmé or Wilde's Salome; she freezes the blood.

Gray flinches. Symons is too near the mark, for one of the lines, in which the barber paints "in sapient spots and stains, / Beryls and crysolites and diaphanes"—a line he had honed to suggest her glittering, inner corruption—had been culled from one in the manuscript of Oscar's *Salome*, which Wilde had briefly shown him; while teasing him about the fate of another namesake, St. John the Baptist.[43] The resemblance—either of the line or of the name—would hardly be noted, he thought. But the publication of *Silverpoints* has now become inextricably mixed up with Wilde's unfortunate play, delayed from September to next February by the change of contract, by Ricketts's secretive procrastinations. Frustrated, Gray had written Ricketts:

> Please do not let there be any unnecessary delay with you in sending back the pulls [proofs] . . . Forgive me mentioning this to you but the friends for whom I am having the poems printed are dying off one by one and I also want to see the book complete in my lifetime—for I hate posthumous works.[44]

Now the debut has been further postponed for some weeks because, as Gray explains in a letter to Louÿs, "The editors have the idea of having me appear on the same day as Salome—an idea which warrants as little wisdom as it does satisfaction."[45] How little wisdom is to become clear from the reception of *Silverpoints*. A few weeks after his book's publication, Gray is seated in Raffalovich's dining room in his house on South Audley Street. They dine under the gaze of Madame Raffalovich, whose large portrait dominates the room. Her dark beauty is offset by her richly embroidered gown; her soulful gaze follows the progress of her younger son through the meal and seems to note each sentence, each silence. Gray has learned already, after an initial blunder, not to refer to her at all. He has heard from others of her prodigious learning—she is the reputed mistress of eight languages; her important intellectual contacts; her fashionable salon on the Avenue Hoche. Her elder son,

Arthur, acts as the financial editor of *Journal des Debats*. Her second child, Sophie, had been received into the Catholic Church upon her marriage—after an improbable and wildly romantic courtship—to William O'Brien, the Irish nationalist leader and member of Parliament, some three years earlier. Ever the name-dropper, André mentioned that Charles Stewart Parnell had made the wedding speech.[46] But for all pride in her other children, there was a painful constraint with her younger son, even as she fostered his literary talent. It is said that she had taken a dislike to André as an infant "because he was so ugly."

The association with *Salome* is most unfortunate, André concedes in his low guttural English. Wilde's play is already tainted. And the French is so ragged! I understand he had several French writers at work on it; Pierre Louÿs was the last and best, so he dedicated the play to him. No one will read it here; although I understand Mallarmé has praised it.[47] André briefly resumes the meal, then lays the fork down deliberately. You have arranged, of course, to have a copy of your *Silverpoints* sent to Mallarmé?

Well—indirectly. To Whistler, who will show Mallarmé. To all the dedicatees. To Ellen Terry; to Alice, Princess of Monaco; to Marcel Schwob, as you know, "the editor of *Paris* the only French daily." I have given Frank Harris copies to distribute for review. He promised an appreciation in the *Times,* but I have not seen it; nor one in his own *Fortnightly Review.* One to Swinburne. Also, of course, to Dowson and Shannon. And, need I add?—he glances surreptitiously up at the portrait—one to my mother.[48] Who will not understand, but will approve.

A nod from André.

Dowson of course wrote immediately. What did he say? All the right things. That he took "extraordinary and subtle pleasure" in "the wonderful little book. It is beyond my expectations even, in exquisiteness."[49]

Another nod from André; a bright glance. And the photograph?

Have I not yet honored you with a copy? Allow me to send it by the first post. It turned out well; I look as unearthly as any poet, and as elegantly bound as my book. You will like it: I appear quite unlike myself.

Ah, yes. It is important that you be as elegant as the book—for to most people, you will *en effet* become the book. André's eyebrows rise slowly, regarding the impact on Gray of this observation. The book, he announces, has the appearance of a masterpiece: it is only the superficial who will not judge its contents by such a binding. Raffalovich rises as he takes down the newly minted edition from the dumbwaiter. Ah, he murmurs, handling it; green leather stamped with gold. What is the design? Is it of gold flames lapping against the wind? Or feathers floating against the waves? It is exquisite; it is ambiguous; it is highly stylized. Is it of your own design?

No, no, Gray demurs. It is by Ricketts. A surprise. I did not even know of it until it was complete. We have not been in touch; apparently he wrote Lane suggesting this design, and complaining in his usual acid way that he sees me only "sometimes"—"about once every two years."[50] He invented this design; he says it is of "little ships on wavy lines," but I think it resembles more "lime seeds over a stream. The 'flame' is the leaf with a twig at the bottom and seeds round it—these last are falling into the stream—the wavy lines."[51] It is typeset to Ricketts's instructions as well: in a delicate, almost unreadable italic in a sea of margin. It made the proofreading hellish. But the end result is astonishing.

And is the cause of astonishment, André exclaims. I hear that "The Sphinx"—you know, Wilde's friend, Ada Leverson, is already raving to everyone about the new book by "the incomparable poet of the age," John Gray, and how she opened it to find "the tiniest rivulet of text meandering through the very largest meadow of margin." She is said to have "suggested to Oscar that he should go a step further than these minor poets" and "publish a book *all* margin; full of beautiful unwritten thoughts, and have this blank volume bound in some Nile-green skin powdered with gilt nen-uphars and smoothed with hard ivory, decorated with gold by Ricketts (if not Shannon) and printed on Japanese paper." Each volume is to "be a collector's piece, a number one of a limited 'first' (and last) edition: 'very rare.'"[52]

André's voice trails off, his eyebrows rising in amusement as Gray studies his plate, embarrassment becoming acute. Noting it, Raffalovich begins to tease him gently: Ah, behold the incomparable poet of the age. The smile vanishes suddenly with a turn of mood. Surely even from such a source, Gray, such a remark can only do you good. And, talking of society women, you did send a copy to the Princess of Monaco—along with your photograph, I hope, my dear Gray?

Ah yes. I have her reply here. She had written before that she appreciated my "strange, weird, fascinating verses." So I took care to order a vellum-bound edition of *Silverpoints* to be sent to the Palace in Monaco—along with a portrait of its father.[53] Would you like to read her letter? Gray fishes in his pocket, pulls out a small note in a large scrawl, and hands it over to Raffalovich:

> My dear poet,
>
> The photo has just come with the book and I can't say what pleasure both gave me—Since I first heard you recite, that evening Frank Harris gave us a dinner. I was most enthusiastic. They carried me very far away. Since then I saw you again, heard of more of that soft music & the charm was to me greater. Now I get that lovely work of art & am intensely grateful & happy.[54]

Of course, she knows me as "Dorian," Gray murmurs.

You must make your own name for yourself, André remarks, rather sharply. I do what I can for you.

Naturally, dear André, I am intensely grateful. The evening with Walter Pater was very helpful.

He is very sweet, André replies. I have heard from Symons about that reading; he has become quite a champion of yours. Symons wrote to remind me that after reciting one of your poems, "A certain expression passed over Pater's face and he asked Gray to say it over again. 'The rest is silence.'"[55]

And, André continues: did you notice that review in your old outlet, *The Artist and Journal of Home Culture*, which mentions that "Mr. Pater, Mr. Swinburne and Mr. Theodore Watts, have praised the 'Silverpoints' of Mr. John Gray . . . "[56] Oh, dear, all those misters. Is this Kains Jackson's way of saying he never heard of you before? André looks quizzical. Then abruptly changes direction. And the others? he asks. I mean of the published reviews?

Well, there's the poet's—you know, the "Log-Roller"—Richard LeGallienne. It probably has done the most damage; in trying to rescue *Silverpoints* from a vulgar misinterpretation of "decadence" he simply succeeds in fixing the epithet in the public's mind. He is entirely at cross-purposes with himself, saying that "the real core of decadence is to be found in its isolated interests. Its effects are gained by regarding life as of but one or two dimensions." Then he concludes (as parody?) that "in spite of his neo-Catholicism and his hot-house erotics, Mr. Gray cannot accomplish that gloating abstraction from the larger life of humanity which marks the decadent."[57] What neo-Catholicism? Is he talking about Verlaine? Erotics? Come, come. Gray realizes he is almost shouting and suddenly stops. Sorry, André. I suppose he merely means it is all too French. Or at least, too French for him.

Well there is always the *Pall Mall Gazette,* André smiles; no ambiguities there. It simply calls you "le plus décadent des decadents."[58] André laughs, a quick short laugh; then his smile disappears as suddenly as if it had been wiped off a slate. He reaches over the dumbwaiter again and takes down a page from a newspaper. Gray, he said: this is what worries me. You must listen carefully—and mark it. It is not signed and it is about Oscar. It reads—André stabs at the newsprint with his finger—so:

> If he [that's Wilde] had lived in the days of Socrates he would surely have been impeached on a charge not only of "making the worse cause appear the better"—for paradox as a method is never acceptable to the many—but also of "corrupting the youth"; he would have been condemned, and would have drunk the hemlock under protest, and one of the corrupt—perhaps Mr. John Gray—would have written another *Phaedo* in his memory. Indeed, the harm that Mr. Wilde has done within a certain radius is incalculable. For the love of beauty for its own sake, which has absorbed his whole system and

inspired everything he has written, is a very rare thing indeed. It is inborn and cannot ever be communicated. And thus the young men who have tried to reproduce not only the manner of "the Master" but his spirit also have, for the most part, failed absurdly.[59]

This is dangerous, Raffalovich announces. I have long since broken with the man. Gray looks steadily at the mobile face which has become a mask of cold distaste; the black eyes blaze at him, boring through his front of impassivity. Gray looks down again. It has been months since I have seen Oscar, he murmurs diffidently, toying with a dessert spoon. I believe he is only back from the house he had rented for the winter near Torquay. All his set knows that Bosie joined him for long periods there. I have left a note for him at the Albemarle.

Just remember . . . André rises, wiping his mouth briefly and placing his napkin beside his plate. You cannot be Wilde's friend and also mine.

In early March, a few weeks after the appearance of *Silverpoints,* Gray meets Oscar by appointment for the last time. He had refused an invitation to lunch at Wilde's hotel. Rumors were already circulating everywhere that Wilde had left his wife and his children—whom he visited only occasionally at Tite Street—and set up with Bosie in rooms at the Albemarle. These were rumors that strayed near the edge of what, in decent society, could be said. Then there were the other rumors: whispers, innuendoes of what could not be said. Miscellaneous sightings of uncouth boys going in and out of the rooms at the Albemarle; stories of consequent attempts at blackmail—these were not gentlemen; reports of Oscar and Bosie arriving arm-in-arm at the Savoy; accounts of terrible quarrels between them, at restaurants or even on the street.

Gray looks through the smoke-filled gloom, trying to avoid the face that follows him from the mirror. He has avoided the Café Royal recently, but it seemed the inevitable place to meet. Then, suddenly, Oscar is upon him, large, overwhelming, and radiant as of old. My dear boy, he huffs. It has been a long time.

For a moment, Gray finds himself beaming back at this sun who for so long has been the very pivot of his universe. My loved Master; my dear friend. Homage. Recollecting, he draws back into himself and gestures towards a chair. With great play of drawing off gloves and coat, then gesturing to a boy who relieves him of the burden, Wilde seats himself. He is heavier, slower, his speech more guarded and mannered. He produces a cigarette case, opens it, elaborately lights a cigarette, then offers it to Gray, who declines. Oscar waits until the silence is heavy.

You have seen the *Silverpoints?*

Ah, yes, dear boy. It is wonderful, exquisite, subtle. It breaks new ground, opens up new worlds: it will be the sign of a renaissance of our poetry and of you, Dorian—its acknowledged father.

It is the benchmark of our friendship, Gray murmurs. Which must now end.

Oscar feigns surprise, then hurt. *Friendship? End?* Dear boy, what nonsense is this? *What* friendship? I tried to act as your mentor; offered to pay the expenses of your exquisite first book. I made you, Dorian; you are my creature. Because of my gilded words you are now famous—or infamous, which is the same thing. I am not your friend: I am your lover; your inventor: your maker. You are the lover of my soul, as I have told you many times: "my real life, my higher life" is with you and Louÿs and such as you.[60] But know this, Dorian—a large forefinger is waved as Oscar looms towards him over the table—henceforward I do not have friends. I have only lovers.

In the silence, a wave of talk and clatter from the neighboring tables enters the agitation of his own mind; Gray feels something collapsing within himself, like the walls of a city long under siege. The magnificent city is open now to devastation; the walled garden open to the enemy.

It takes an immense effort to find his voice again. He knows he is only one among many of Oscar's friends who have tried to dissuade him from his folly. He sees now that it is useless. Like a watchman on a tower who sees the enemy advance in such numbers that to cry out would itself be futile, he simply turns away. Something breaks, silently and in secret. He gives up; he lets go; he thinks: nothing can now be saved.

Oscar leans back, takes a deep drag from his cigarette and watches the smoke jet out from his nostrils and then swirl into the encircling gloom. As it dissipates, he says, gently, Dorian: you have changed. You have become in some way ashamed. Perhaps you are afraid? But shame itself is beautiful. Bosie has put it wonderfully: "I am Shame / That walks with Love; I am most wise to turn / Cold lips and limbs to fire; therefore discern / And see my loveliness, and praise my name / . . . Of all sweet passions Shame is loveliest."[61] Shame, Dorian, is what others think of us. It is not guilt, which is what we think of ourselves. I am not ashamed that I love Bosie. I am guilty of nothing but love. I am determined to live my life openly; I will not become an abject slave to public opinion and public hypocrisy, which are simply other names for English stupidity. Henceforth, I am determined to live my life as a free man.

In the ensuing silence, Gray retrieves the lines he had practiced. He says them as slowly and coldly as possible, avoiding the face in the mirror:

Oscar: I cannot see you again. I do not wish to see you again. I do not wish to talk with you again. It is over.

A heavy silence, as Wilde registers the blow, turns pale—with anger or sorrow?—then blows out one slow exhalation of smoke. Very well, Dorian. You have judged me; but you will not change me. I will not change. And whether you know it or not, you will not change either. You will always be Dorian Gray.

Flinching, Gray rises; decides not to offer his hand; walks rapidly to the door and into the raw chaos of Regent Street. In his head are singing the bittersweet lines of farewell which he had printed in *Silverpoints*—dedicating it to Oscar Wilde:

> There was the summer. There
> > Warm hours of leaf-lipped song,
> > And dripping amber sweat.
> > O sweet to see
> The great trees condescend to cast a pearl
> Down to the myrtles; and the proud leaves curl
> > In ecstasy.

Fruit of a quest, despair.
Smart of a sullen wrong.
Where may they hide them yet?
    One hour, yet one,
To find the mossgod lurking in his nest,
To see the naiads' floating hair, caressed
    By fragrant sun-

Beams. Softly lulled the eves
The song-tired birds to sleep,
That other things might tell
    Their secrecies.
The beetle humming neath the fallen leaves.
Deep in what hollow do the stern gods keep
Their bitter silence? By what listening well
    Where holy trees,

Song-set, unfurl eternally the sheen
    Of restless green?[62]

Deep in what hollow do the stern gods keep / Their bitter silence? The naiads have fled the Seine and the Thames; the fauns have abandoned the Bois de Boulogne and St. James's Park. No one will return again after a day in the woods to recount their elaborate adventures or report how Salome wore her silver slippers or the fisherman lost his soul in a bargain with a merman. Looking now through the gray fog enveloping the black shifting shapes of horse and carriage, pedestrian and hawker, Gray wonders at how suddenly all the color of his world has drained away, leaving only the dreariness and turmoil of this street.

Returning to the Foreign Office, he writes Pierre Louÿs: "About the falling-out with Oscar. I say it to you only and it is absolute. It will suffice that I recount its origins when I see you in London."[63] Gray is careful now not to put anything on paper. Louÿs arrives in April. Mindful of the dedication of *Salome* and other favors, he is slow to break with the man who had introduced him to Sarah Bernhardt, among others. At Wilde's invitation, he attends the first performance of *A Woman of No Importance*. But Oscar's companions of that spring fill him with consternation. "London is charming," he writes his brother Georges; "but I am in a group of people who make me a little uncomfortable."[64] The decisive moment comes one morning. Dropping by the hotel room which Oscar shares with Bosie, Louÿs notes one large bed with two pillows. Worse: while he is there, stammering out his mission, Constance comes by, bringing Oscar's mail from Tite Street. Pierre watches while this slight, fragile woman tries gently to persuade her husband to return home with her, to their two young sons. Oscar, wandering towards the window, turns curtly, cutting across her words: Constance, it has been so long since I have been to Tite Street that I do not remember the number of the house. Constance turns her face as if she has been slapped, trying bravely to smile while tears trickle down her cheeks.

Louÿs takes in a sharp breath and leaves. Back in Paris, he recounts what he sees to several friends, including Henri de Régnier, who in turn tells it to Edmond de Goncourt, who in turn confides it to his diary:

> On hearing the name "Oscar Wilde," Henri de Régnier, who has come to see me, starts smiling. I ask why. "Ah, you don't know! Well, he's not hiding it himself. Yes, he has come out as a pederast . . . You don't know that following the success of his play in London, he left his wife and his three [sic] children and set himself up in a hotel, where he is living conjugally with a young English Lord."[65]

Wilde's situation has become the talk of the town, both in London and Paris. After long discussions with his brother Georges, Pierre Louÿs decides he cannot remain Oscar's friend unless he admits the error of his ways. Accordingly, when Oscar arrives in Paris briefly that May, Pierre decides to visit him in his hotel. Entering the room, Louÿs bows briefly, refusing his hand. Oscar, he says, I have come on only one mission. You should know your relationship with Lord Douglas and the abandonment of your family is known here and harshly judged. I have considered the matter and reached this conclusion: you must either leave Douglas or bid farewell to our friendship.

Oscar steps back; he had had little warning of such an ultimatum, although in London it is becoming something of a tired stage line. He looks at Pierre with great sadness. Louÿs, we are wonderful friends, friends of the soul, friends of the spirit. Your reproaches hurt me deeply. But I love Bosie. He has made me feel alive in a way I have not ever felt before. The danger is part of the pleasure; being with him is like feasting with panthers. I cannot give him up; I cannot even think of giving him up. There is no question of a choice. He is my fate, and all that may befall us in future is also fate. I am powerless to change it. So farewell then, Pierre. Wilde walks towards him with his hand outstretched. "I wanted to have a friend; in future I shall just have lovers."[66]

Pierre flees, writing that week to John Gray: "I would very much like to see you for a while, but I cannot come to London. You know I have fallen out completely with Oscar Wilde, and can never meet him again, anywhere."[67] (Nor was he ever to do so. There follows, in the letters from Louÿs to Gray, a black hole of more than two years: a black hole of silence and fear, filled with the charred remains of letters given to the fire.)

In London, John Gray attempts to repossess himself. For Dorian Gray is dead; ironically, just when his poetry is just becoming known. In the Foreign Office, conditions are becoming difficult. As the reviews of *Silverpoints* trickle in, its author begins to achieve something approaching notoriety—which serves only to irritate the other John Gray, posing as a colorless civil servant. For during the spring of 1893, this John Gray has become an object of curiosity. In one recorded incident, "an explorer" who ventured to the second floor of the Foreign Office "discovered a second division clerk employed in the Library, who was also a minor poet. Delighted with his find, he was wont to escort parties of friends to the spot, who peeped at the poet one by one."[68]

Gray's disgust with Dorian becomes disgust with his creature, *Silverpoints,* the book in which he is bound and circulated. (Father Gray will later refer to it as "the odious *Silverpoints.*") Of all his friends, Symons is the most attuned to the siege of remorse, writing: "I understand well enough your present feeling about it, but it is a book which will certainly be remembered as marking a certain hour of the day. Every line is packed; and in most books there is so amazingly little ore, when one looks into them."[69] But Gray has a plan. Now, thanks to Raffalovich's regular checks, he is financially secure, and so begins a lifelong campaign to buy up and thus "immobilize" as many copies as possible of the limited edition of *Silverpoints*.[70] He wishes to make it part, now, of his past. And he wishes the past to *become* the past—and so finds himself almost welcoming the review of his poems which states: "As a collection the book is a failure. Mr. Gray is often clever and occasionally an artist; and on the whole, one may say that he is a young man with a promising career behind him."[71]

Emotionally, the past is not so easily abandoned. Gray throws himself into the new life offered by Raffalovich, a life of introductions, dinners, private theatrical events—the opera! He has been looking forward to it since February and by the time he writes of his new life to Louÿs on 6 June, Gray sounds like the most jaded of critics: "The opera here is loathsome so far but Alvray is in London . . . Next Wednesday they are giving Lohengrin in Italian! With Albani!! Vignas!!! Giulia Ravogli !!!! Tannhauser with Albani & Vignas last Wednesday was so wretched that I left in the middle."[72]

The new life is comfortable; not extravagant, but Gray can eat and sleep again. There is the comfort that Raffalovich knows of his past and has even, through his own relationship with Wilde, been a part of it. He does not judge; indeed, Gray finds it a relief that André not only understands but is sympathetic to the life of the invert—or the *uraniste* as he calls them—and even talks of writing a semiprofessional essay on the subject.

At first, such is his impulsive temperament, there is a question of actually holding André off. Extravagant in the Russian fashion, André showers Gray with affection—and gifts. Gray knows himself to be the taker, not the giver of affection; he recoils still at any sign of physical tenderness. After Oscar, Gray finds he cannot trust himself. He meditates on a few sentences that Alice, Princess of Monaco, had uttered concerning her own widowhood and remarriage. And from those meditations, a short story writes itself: about a princess who, believing herself in love with one man, inadvertently finds herself returning the kiss of another. The second love makes dust of the first; but she finds she cannot reciprocate the feelings of the man to whom she had so impulsively responded. "That was eighteen years ago, and that is why she has never loved, never married, and why year by year she has grown more strange, more eccentric, more dull also, more suspicious of herself and of others, and why she has narrowed her life for fear of losing her freedom."[73] That is the way "The Yellow Princess" ends.

Sitting by the fire in André's West End mansion, Gray tries to explain what he can only register as a lack of feeling—a kind of sexual anesthesia. How once loving Wilde and being cruelly disillusioned now makes it impossible ever to love anyone else. But all he can find to say, as André comes across and sits on the arm of the chair, putting his fine hand on his arm, is a faint stammer: I can't; I can't. Gray turns his face to the fire; it is hot and flushed and he finds tears pricking his eyes. André has been so intelligent—so kind. He has assured him of a permanent income; a place to stay; a home; a friend. No, more than a friend. For as they talk, Gray is aware how eager little André is to enter into all his ambitions. I will make you a writer, he had cried, pacing the room. We will have readings: I will invite Pater, I will invite Swinburne; I will invite every reviewer that matters. We will write things together—little things that can be produced in private theaters to select audiences. I have enough money to finance anything you wish to publish.

It is true, is it not, my brother—André had fallen into this intimacy as a way of reassuring Gray that a Platonic relationship might, after all, be possible—it is true that we have both been bruised by the world. They think of me as ill favored—look at this face! Not even my mother can stand me! But my friends laugh and just say that I am so gloriously ugly that to call me plain would be offensive. I have an accent! Well, you can't be both Russian and French without speaking English with an accent. Of course I am foreign! But I am also a Jew—and rich. And *that* my dear Gray is *unforgivable!* Because I am rich they make jibes about me being a Jew; because I adore geniuses and invite them to dine with me, they call me a parvenu. I know what it is to be an outsider. You have learned what it is to be an outsider. Particularly in London—such a provincial city!—where to be ostracized from proper society is a fate worse than death. We are bruised by the world. The hand, now gripping Gray's sleeve, moves to André's face—to brush away a tear? But we are together, no, in this? "We hate the world, you and I, a slanderous servant, an evil master. We can conquer together. You are unconventional. I am unconventional. Separate, we are at the world's mercy; together we are perfect strength. We can laugh at the world's unkindness. We can shut the door and be happy with silence and music, and beauty and friendship."[74] I have written this all somewhere. I should have written it to you, my dear John Gray.

Suddenly, André is kneeling before him, at the edge of the hearth. The flames seem to illuminate his face; his eyes shine—is it with tears?—but the mobile features are set in a mask of grief. He clasps his hands before him, looking Gray intently in the face: "Oh, mon frère," André cries: "if I could pour myself out for you like water, I would."[75] Gray stares at him, stupified. Then very gently leans forward, kisses him on the forehead, and, standing himself, lifts him to his feet and puts an arm around his shoulder. Dear André: we will always be friends. I feel we will be friends for life. We have suffered too much not to have an understanding between us. But you must know that I can never be more to you than a friend—a friend who is a brother.

André covers his face with his hands and weeps, quietly and softly. Then, after a few minutes, recovering himself sufficiently to wipe eyes and nose with a large rose silk handkerchief, murmurs: Let it be so between us.

That July, Gray moves with André to his summer retreat in Weybridge, Surrey, commuting up and down daily from the Foreign Office until the August break. They are joined, as is the custom, by Miss Gribbell. Miss Gribbell's position is unimpeachable. Indeed, Miss Gribbell is herself unimpeachable.

Miss Florence Truscott Gribbell is of Scottish origin, a bank manager's daughter. She had entered Madame Raffalovich's Paris household as a governess to André, "whom she found to be a shy but very intelligent little boy, rather neglected by his mother who was too busy being a great hostess to give him much attention."[76] When André left Paris for London in 1882 he was not yet eighteen; his mother's trusted *dame de compagnie* accompanied him. André's first intention had been to enter Oxford: he stayed there long enough to be warned by Professor Keats "to avoid the acquaintance of Pater and Symonds. The latter I did not admire, and was not curious about, too inexperienced to be excited by so clinical a case."[77] Ostensibly Miss Gribbell was there to look after André because of his poor health; but—in such company—the health of his morals might also have been in question. When Raffalovich left Oxford for London, he began to entertain his "lions"—literary celebrities such as Browning and Swinburne, Burne-Jones and Whistler, Pater and Meredith.[78] For these social events, Miss Gribbell proved an adequate and even formidable hostess for her young charge.

Now in the glory of her middle age, Miss Gribbell supervises André's households in the West End and in Weybridge, Surrey. When André first pointed out John Gray at the opera, she surveyed him carefully with her opera glasses, announcing: no one can be that beautiful! But now that John Gray comes frequently to the house for dinner and tea, she finds she has taken a particular liking to the slightly distant young man; such a suitable friend for André! Literary and still respectable, with a steady job at the Foreign Office. And such wonderful manners!

The first summer that Gray joins this little household in Weybridge, a new routine is established. Gray takes the train up in the morning and down in the evening, like any other suburban commuter. The weekends are given over to punting and archery, to reading and tea under the great pine trees at the end of the garden near the river. André has bought another new contraption: a box Brownie camera, with which he takes photographs at every opportunity.

André's sister, Sophie O'Brien, borrows it one summer afternoon to take a picture of Gray practicing his archery: the bow pulled to its full arch, both arms at stretch; Gray perfectly poised in his flannel whites and straw boater, eyes narrowed against the strong sun. Behind him, André naps discreetly, head bowed so that his face is shaded from the early afternoon blaze by his straw boater, while Miss Gribbell, in a dress of white muslin, employs herself quietly with her embroidery.

That summer, Sophie finds herself a bit put out with John Gray. She admits he is beautiful, but distant; a passive object for André's intense affection. She knows André can be effusive and sentimental; maybe it is the pressure of this kind of emotional extravagance that makes Gray behave in a manner that seems to her spoiled and pettish. But she has come to regard him as selfish, overconcerned for his own comfort, inclining to be greedy—and not always polite. She considers that Gray is taking Raffalovich and his generosity entirely too much for granted.[79]

Perhaps too, there is a little jealousy at play. Raffalovich has begun to address Gray more informally, sometimes as "brother." He is Gray's senior by only two years, but Sophie notes that he is inclined to fuss about Gray's health and the minutiae of his daily life. Was the train too stuffy this evening? Is the dear boy spoiling for a cold? Does he need lighter/heavier/more suitable clothes? Sophie's patience is further frayed by Miss Gribbell's habit of referring to this grown man as "our child" and "the dear child" and, during any absence, writing long, chatty letters addressed to him.

Sophie notes too that Raffalovich's generosity now extends to include Gray's sisters. Abandoned in Woolwich with the death of their father, Hannah Gray has been struggling to raise the last of her eight children; the youngest, Beatrice, is still only six. The boys will find work; but the girls are more problematic. For young women of their generation, the only realistic career is marriage; until then, they will live at home or go into service. Certainly, Gray's own modest salary is not enough to ensure their security. Absorbed as he has become in Gray's concerns, Raffalovich takes it upon himself to assist in arranging for the future of the two younger sisters, Sarah and Beatrice. They are to be educated at a convent school near Regensburg, Germany, far from their "miserable island history"—and from Gray's mother, not necessarily considered a good influence. She has become a Catholic—one mark in her favor. But she is willful and quite offhand about the lot of her girls. In Germany, Sarah and "Trixl," as Beatrice comes to be called, will have an excellent education far removed from Woolwich. It is arranged that Sarah, now sixteen, will go first; then in two years, she is to be joined by Trixl. While they are abroad, they are to be visited at least once yearly by their oldest brother, who will anxiously note their progress.

But during this first of the holidays in Surrey, Trixl joins her adored John at Raffalovich's summer house. (This is the way, as an old woman, she remembered it:

> We must go back as far as 1893. On a hot August afternoon in a Surrey garden there lay in a hammock slung between tall pine trees a slim young man of twenty-seven, wearing white flannels. Very close beside him was to be seen his six-year-old sister and god-child. We looked up and watched the red squirrels enjoying their pine cones and throwing down their leavings on our heads. After a while we sat on the side of the hammock, while "Brother John" (as I then called him), having rubbed an amber cigarette-holder on a pink silk cushion, demonstrated its power of picking up small pieces of paper. This came, of course, as a revelation to me; but I attributed the miracle more to him than to the amber. Indeed, in my small mind, all things were possible to this god who dominated my entire childhood.

> Let me recall another scene. This time it was a Sunday afternoon, which we were spending in a punt on the River Wey. Although he was considered the best punter on that stretch of water, he landed the party on a sandbank. Soon a storm came up and rain fell in torrents. The general hilarity which ensued must have struck me as somewhat profane. How dare they laugh at Brother John being baffled by the elements! I gave full vent to my feelings, thereby rendering the god so weak with mirth that he was a very long time pushing us off the sandbank and getting us home in safety. As far as I recollect, his two favourite pastimes at that period were archery and punting. While staying at Weybridge he would rise very early, go on the river, return for breakfast and change into his London clothes before going up to the Foreign Office [he was not due there until eleven]. It used to be my privilege to be summoned to his room each morning to choose his handkerchief, and the socks and tie he was to wear. In the late

afternoon it was my delight to run along the sandy road to meet him coming from the station.[80]

Yet at the end of this golden summer, the storm clouds would gather: this golden glow would darken into two of the most tumultuous years of her brother's life.)

4 | TRIALS OF THE SPIRIT

(SEPTEMBER 1893–AUGUST 1898)

DURING THE BURNING AUGUST AFTERNOONS, Raffalovich confides in Gray his plans for their literary and social debut. They are to write playlets—brittle little pieces for private invited audiences. The first pair of these is given on 17 April 1894 as part of an "At Home" for which Raffalovich rents the West Theatre, Albert Hall. They are two one-act plays. The first, *Sour Grapes,* is described on the program as "A Masque, Written Entirely in Rhymed Couplets by John Gray." The second, *Black Sheep,* "a Pantomime Pastoral, with Spoken Prologue and Epilogue . . . Concluding with a Dance," was concocted by Raffalovich.[1]

Perhaps finding the whole exercise too precious, Gray decides to open the program with what one guest describes as the "Dynamiter's piece"; in the character of "Etienne Rozenwaltoff," Gray gives the stage to a foreign (Franco-Polish?) anarchist—who confesses to killing for "fun."[2] Gray intends to shock. Even if it does not shock, the poem is timely. It is the opening of what is to be the "black year" of anarchism in France. As he knows from his contacts in France, what had long been theory was now issuing in the propaganda of the deed. (From March 1892 onwards there had been no less than eleven major bomb explosions in Paris, the chosen method being tin cans filled with dynamite and nails.) On 4 April, nearly two weeks previously, the crowded, fashionable restaurant at the Hotel Foyot had been bombed—the device planted in a flowerpot on the windowsill. There were no fatalities. Less than a week after Gray's recital, his friend Félix Fénéon is arrested and charged with the bombing.[3]

Looking at the portrait of Raffalovich which hangs in the dining room of the South Audley Street house, Gray decides to choose this sort of man as the target for the hatred which detonates his dynamiter. Gray understands anarchists; they are among his friends. Was not Oscar, at bottom, simply an anarchist? And an Irish anarchist at that (Gray wonders for a moment whether that is not, in fact, a tautology.) Calling to mind again Raffalovich's portrait, Gray imagines his wild Pole ranting at the "fine young fellow" wearing a white carnation. It is nothing personal: his actions exhibit the cheerful neutrality of a force of nature. Nor does any other tone best convey the twisted logic of class warfare. Gray knows his man: he is the rank outsider, in exile at home. Breaking with Oscar, Gray discovers a new hardness, a new coldness within himself; it is to be a powerful weapon.

After the April recital—done as ferociously as his sotto voce will allow—after the studied frivolities of the "Masque" and the "Pastoral," the guests are merely polite. Upholstered by privilege, Gray murmurs to himself, comparing one lady novelist, Mrs. Lynn Lytton, to the overstuffed button-backed sofa on which she languishes after the play. The dramatic monologue did provide a nice contrast, she murmurs solicitously, touching his sleeve softly: "the masculine note . . . in the midst of the more fanciful & more tender pieces."[4]

But this was merely a trial run. Their real debut as playwrights comes two months later. On 7 June, they launch a full-length melodrama at the Prince of Wales's Theatre, Tottenham Court Road. It is entitled, tantalizingly, *The Blackmailers*.[5] It is the first (and, as it turns out, the last) public production of this or any other work by the two collaborators. The audience is polite; but the press implies that to call it a debacle would be a kindness. Under the tall pines near the bridge on the Wey, Gray and Raffalovich take tea and nurse their wounds. Raffalovich is scowling at the latest review, a prominent one from the *Theatre*.

1. John Gray, Senior; Gray's father

2. Beatrice ("Trixl") and Sarah Gray, Gray's sisters, c. 1896

3. Beresford Square, showing the gates to the Royal Arsenal, Woolwich (1913?)

4. Furnace and steam-hammer in the foundry of the Royal Arsenal (c. 1910)

5. Ricketts and Shannon.
Lithograph by William
Rothenstein, 1897

. John Gray, from a drawing by
Reginald Savage (c. 1890)

7. "Dorian" Gray (1893)

8. Pierre Louÿs

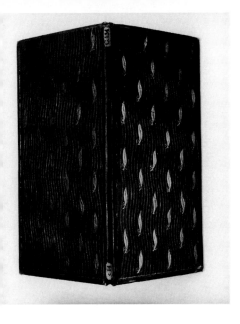

9. Silverpoints, 1893

GREEN

Leaves and branches, flowers and fruits are here;
And here my heart, which throbs alone for thee.
Ah! do not wound my heart with those two dear
White hands, but take the poor gift tenderly.

I come, all covered with the dews of night
The morning breeze has pearled upon my face.
Let my fatigue, at thy feet, in thy sight,
Dream through the moments of its sweet solace.

With thy late kisses ringing, let my head
Roll in blest indolence on thy young breast;
To lull the tempest thy caresses bred,
And soothe my senses with a little rest.

FLEURS. IMITATED FROM THE FRENCH
OF
STEPHANE MALLARMÉ

HE tawny iris—oh! the slim-necked swan;
And, sign of exiled souls, the bay divine;
Ruddy as seraph's heel its fleckless sheen,
Blushing the brightness of a trampled dawn.

The hyacinth; the myrtle's sweet alarm;
Like to a woman's flesh, the cruel rose,
Blossom'd Herodiade of the garden close,
Fed with ferocious dew of blooddrops warm.

Thou mad'st the lilies' pallor, nigh to swoon,
Which, rolling billows of deep sighs upon,
Through the blue incense of horizons wan,
Creeps dreamily towards the weeping moon.

Praise in the censers, praise upon the gong,
Madone! from the garden of our woes:
On eves celestial throb the echo long!
Ecstatic visions! radiance of haloes!

Mother creatrice! in thy strong, just womb,
Challices nodding the not distant strife;
Great honey'd blossoms, a balsamic tomb
For weary poets blanched with starless life.

11. André Raffalovich, from a painting
by A. Dampier May (1886)

12. André Raffalovich by Max Beerbohm

13. André Raffalovich in the garden of his summer house at Weybridge, Surrey

Previous page: Oscar Wilde and Lord Alfred Douglas ("Bosie")

14. John Gray, Sophie Raffalovich, André Raffalovich, Florence Gribbell, and Georges Raffalovich (?) c. 1896

15. The Cowgate, Edinburgh, during Gray's lifetime

16. Katherine Bradley and Edith Cooper ("Michael Field")

17. St. Peter's church, Edinburgh

18. Interior of St. Peter's church as it was in Gray's lifetime

19. John Gray on Skye (c. 1930)

20. Eric Gill in the engraving shop at Piggotts (c. 1940).
Photograph by Howard Coster

21. Eric Gill, Canon John Gray. Collotype of pencil drawing (1928)

22. Canon John Gray

They say the plot is repetitive, Gray. Listen to this: "Blackmail is levied right and left; there is nothing but that in the play."[6] Of course it is repetitive—Raffalovich bangs down the fragile Limoges teacup with unexpected force. Why do they think we named the play *The Blackmailers?*

Gray nods in the sun and looks down, towards the river. The question requires no answer; they have talked it to death already. Perhaps, he murmurs to Raffalovich, perhaps what is wrong is that we relied too much on the drama of actual events to carry us through. Since the uproar over the publication of *Salome* last February, with the provocative drawings by Beardsley, tongues have been on fire with rumors about Oscar—and Bosie—and his rent boys. It is now said openly in the clubs and the streets that Wilde will be blackmailed—that indeed he has already been blackmailed. That Bosie and he first came together when Douglas approached him over a letter threatening blackmail. That Oscar calls him openly such endearments as "my dear Hyacinth"—so in having our character Clyde called "dear Hyacinth" we have certainly tipped our audience as to the real subject of our play. Not that we are not already marked as associates of the man, Gray adds, somewhat acidly.

But the theater is no longer on the boards, dear Raffy; it is in the streets, at the clubs, the crushes, the first nights, the private views. How could we hope to capture it? As Oscar used to say, everything that has happened in real life is already ruined for art.

Raffalovich nods a little distractedly, then leans eagerly towards Gray. But Oscar is so damned foolish. Taking such huge risks. Everyone knows that the Criminal Law Amendment Act will not be invoked unless it is flouted repeatedly—and publicly. Why does Oscar goad his public this way? Why act the *agent provocateur?* Does he not know he cannot win in this? Wilde acts like an English lord—but he is regarded as foreign. He is Irish by origin. He claims to be French in spirit. He even threatened to become a French citizen after the Lord Chancellor refused a license to produce *Salome.* Anyway: he is emphatically *not* English. *I* have some experience of what that means. He also has no position in society. Wilde is not Lord Rosebery, who can protect himself by strategic silences, strategic absences. Oscar has no staff to hide behind; no institution whose interests are served in protecting him. Has he not learned, as I have had to do, to be discreet—careful? Does he have no idea of what danger he places others in? The danger for those who choose to live their lives quietly? For those, like us, who try to regulate the passions that we have inherited? Who are inverts, but of the superior kind, who practice a daily discipline of celibacy and restraint? So that we can concentrate our energies on the life of the spirit and the intellect and develop the kind of love for each other that we express as brothers?

Gray winces, thinking of how much he and Raffalovich had gone through already to reach this delicate compromise. How both of them, in writing the play, were aware that, with their history, the important thing was to suspend judgement—if possible, to escape from moral judgement altogether—about the world in which their fictive hero, Hal Danger, finds himself.

But it is unforgivable—Raffalovich's guttural accent thickens—I mean the fiasco of the production. I have replied to the *Theatre*. He reaches under the morning papers; here it is. This is what I have written: tell me what you think of it. The play as given, he intones, is only

> a mangled and mutilated version of the first four acts . . . It was only a consideration of honour which prevented us from withdrawing the play when we found to what a state it was being reduced from rehearsal to rehearsal. We saw scene after scene ruined by cuts, omissions, impoverishments and slip-shod. It is no wonder that we refused to own the play by answering the kindly call of a disconcerted audience.[7]

Gray cringes, recalling their hasty exit through the stage door to the scattered applause from the invited audience; recalling, too, the visits to South Audley Street the next afternoon, visits that had all the marks of an at-home after a bereavement. He almost anticipated the tart reply from the critic of the *Theatre* to their letter, "that if authors choose to delegate their authority to unreliable people, or to resign their power of control, they have only themselves to thank for any mangling done on the theatre premises."

It is the end of their public bid for fame as dramatists; perhaps the end of their public life in this era, full stop. But in this end is a beginning. Like most beginnings, it is unforeseen and its growth, secret and inevitable.

It begins with a journey. John Gray decides to go to Edinburgh in December 1893. (Why he is to go or for how long, the biographer never discovers.) That night, restless, he has a dream: he arrives in a square in a large town. A garden is in the midst of it, and it is enclosed by large, gaudy buildings lit up, though it is day. At one corner of the square there is a bookshop, over which is a poem written in gold letters. The poem has eight lines: four which rhyme correctly, and in continuation four others, not rhymed, which seem to dwindle away. In the dream this has a deep meaning, but he only retains the concluding words:

> . . . it was a wondrous thing
> To be so loved.

Turning around he sees that the square has an oriental aspect; then the dream becomes stupid; then unpleasant. Waking, Gray smiles with the click of recognition: of the bookshop he haunts on the corner of Leicester Square. That explains the oriental coloring, he thinks—it is the gaudy exterior of the Alhambra Theatre. But this is not gaudy London; this is gray Edinburgh. Nevertheless he is on the watch for a bookshop, a poem in gold. So much so that when it appears, book in shop window, open to a long poem beginning with four rhymed lines and proceeding with others unrhymed, he steps in and without hesitation buys it. The title, stamped on the cover, reads *The Excellent Way*. Its author is Jacopone da Todi. His own name rendered strange: Jacopone. Gray is beginning to believe in providence—or at least to trust in signs.

On the train back to London, he opens at random:

> O love, all love above,
> Why hast thou struck me so?
> All my heart, broke atwo,
> Consumed in flames of love,
> Burning and flaming cannot find solace;
> It cannot fly from torment, being bound;
> Like wax among live coal it melts apace;
> It languishes alive, no help being found;
> Seeking a grace to fly a little space,
> A glowing furnace is its narrow pound.
> In such a deadly swound,
> Alas, where am I brought?
> Living with death so fraught!
> O leaping flames of love![8]

The words flare and die; but the flame, being lit, would not be quenched. Gray attempts to describe to himself what the words do to him; in the end, he writes them into a story. On the surface, it is a simple tale. A smith's wife, a modest woman, decently poor, not given to reading books and certainly not to buying them, dreams his dream. Guided by some inner instinct, she finds the bookshop on Leicester Square, buys the book, smuggles it into the house. Reading this poem of Jacopone, she thinks: "the words had no special reference to her own condition at the time, probably none at all; yet such was the force of this unlooked-for revelation, she knew once and for all and at the first glance that these words were meant for her."[9]

The words take possession of the smith's wife, never named. In the midst of her stolid, strangely formal routine of housework, she finds herself directed by an "inner voice." From the time she reads the poem, ordinary experience is transfigured; a thirst for perfection dictates all her household duties, however menial; behind them surges the ecstasy of "tempestuous, chaotic prayer" until, at last, the poems take possession of her entire consciousness. The village women keep watch, whispering that she is raving; but as she dies, the smith alone recognizes her holiness. Gray calls the story simply: "Light."

During the Christmas of 1893, John Gray begins a notebook marked "Spiritual Poems."[10] It is to be a map of a search for a life of the spirit. It begins in bitter self-reproach, where he speaks as "Oliver" in a piece he titles "Rosary of the Cross":

> Holy Christ, upon thy cross of torture,
> Deign to see the sinner at thy feet,
> Ignorant, besotted,
> Even in despair effete.

And ends:

> Holy Christ, upon thy cross of pity,
> Deign to see the sinner at thy feet,
> Ignorant, besotted . . .
> Be thy work for me complete.[11]

Gray takes to visiting the British Museum on odd days off. He comes as a pirate—to ransack the hordes of religious poetry—from the Latin, Spanish, German, French. Origin or period is a matter of indifference to him, as long as they approximate in words what is surging inside him, a song of something so far beyond him that words will never be able to reach, except perhaps, in the sheer desperation of the search. When Gray finds a poem that speaks to him, he takes it in any way he can: translating, approximating, even composing limp imitations. The poems change under his hand: so the fierce and hard lines of Jacopone da Todi swoon and languish. Sometimes, it all seems like failure; but the poetry is no longer the point. Was it Symons who pointed him towards the poems of St. John of the Cross? They cut into him as nothing else does. He even begins to write of St. John, turning his extreme, skewed, even grotesque imagery back upon him to imagine "the Lover of the Dark Night's tryst"

> . . . folded in the hands of Christ.
> He lay upon their wounds, and wept the whole

Of longing that was in his holy soul.
Those molten hands were silent. And made speech:
"Weep not for us, sweet Pity, lest thou teach
"Us even greater sorrow than our own;
"The angels weep not, nor doth Heaven make moan.

. . . .

And John was locked within the riven Side.
The Wound said: "Sleep, beloved, and be calm;
"I, in thy flesh, made wounds upon thee balm.
"My torrent poured for thee; thou art my son;
"I ached for this dear hour, my darling one."[12]

Even as he writes, Gray knows this is not great poetry; it is not even good poetry. The poet in him tells Gray: it is not enough that it is deeply felt. But the poet is being remade: "All dead & living men" Gray writes,

> Bear witness how a charming pen
> Went into the fire of God & came forth new.[13]

He imagines himself, like St. John of the Cross, enclosed within the wounds of Christ's side like a babe in the womb. The darkness within which he moves, he tells himself, is not the darkness of extinction but the dark night of the soul, from which, through pain, he will be reborn.

("I have invincible love of S[t.] John of the Cross," he will confide to a friend almost fifteen years later, "because, I suppose, he made a hole in the covering which I had woven about myself to hide me from God."[14] And, a month earlier: "I love him very much with a firm persuasion that I should now be in hell but for him. But I do not more than ask his intercession once or twice a day & take an extra glass of wine on November 24 & make fervent resolutions not to become a Carme[lite]." The confidante reports in her journal that Gray was, in the pitch of his spiritual crisis, thinking of becoming a Carmelite, but when asked if he could live on boiled cabbage for the rest of his life, discovered he had no vocation.[15])

He isn't a poet, you see, Gray finds himself explaining to Symons as they wander back to his rooms in the Temple. The curious thing about St. John of the Cross is the way "his love of God produces a literary quality in his expressions."[16]

Ah, but you and Raffalovich admire the baroque, is that not so? Symons looks up quizzically. I know you both admire Crashaw.

Gray glances for a moment at the mustache, which twitches like a small weather vane in the winter wind. Well, Symons: take a poem like George Darley's "The Bee." It "stirs an old craving for the impossible in poetry—something to be got from words & images quite exterior to words & thought."[17] Like Huysmans's hero, Des Esseintes, I relish the morbid excesses of late Latin poetry. It was not until I saw Grünewald's great altarpiece that I understood why. To me Grünewald seems a "modern soul capable of willful revolt against the sugared trash of the devotional picture."[18] Gray turns his face briefly against the biting wind, then looks towards Symons again. You must understand, Symons, at some point the poetry no longer matters. "The odd thing [about the poems] is that the poetical interest is there by accident. S[t.] John seems to regard them as a kind of *aide mémoire*."[19] The poetry is only a spiritual instrument; it must be abandoned when one finds the real thing.

Symons ponders a moment, then gazes towards the Thames, hesitating only briefly in the bitter evening wind. You must meet someone: Garth Wilkinson. I am trying to get Yeats to meet with him. He notes the blank expression on Gray's face. You know: Yeats. The Irishman who is organizing the Rhymers.

Ah, yes, said Gray. I knew him from the early days at Horne's. But the last time we were in the same room together—at one of your at-homes—he seemed so abstracted that I never took the chance of speaking to him again. He kept gazing out the window. Gray glances up towards the windows of Fountain Court, now looming into view, the soft light of lamps suffusing in their glaze of early frost. It is darkening, and he can see his breath rising in a ghostly cloud before him. Who is this Wilkinson?

A student of Blake. A translator of Swedenborg. I thought Yeats might be interested in knowing him as he was working on his edition with Ellis of the Blake manuscripts. It should be out any day now. Wilkinson now thinks of himself as a poet; he follows Blake's methods of writing by inspired dictation.

Clutching Symons's letter of introduction in his hand, Gray finds himself pulling the bell of a modest house not far from Bedford Park. Blake seems to be the presiding deity in this neighborhood, he muses, thinking of Yeats at home down the road and Ellis not far distant. Of Blake he had heard from Ricketts and Shannon, who regard him as a kind of Pre-Pre-Raphaelite, a forerunner of the mystical brotherhood they revere. Yeats, said Symons with distinct glee, thinks Blake is Irish. I have had to cruelly disillusion him. Not for the first time, either.[20]

Gray hands the letter to the girl who answers the door and is kept waiting in the dark and shabby hallway as she makes her way to the study. There is a muted conversation; a dark male mutter answered by the light girlish voice; then silence. A tall shape fills the study door; a long shambling man with a face that would pass for God's: long whitish hair, long whitish beard; blazing blue eyes that look at Gray intently as if in question. Under the scrutiny, Gray hides behind his face, withdrawing into himself. The man does not offer his hand, only gestures Gray silently into the study, book strewn, untidy, a small fire crackling in the grate, some pictures of serious men watching him grimly from the walls.

He stutters out his mission. He wishes to write something. They sit and as Wilkinson begins to warm slowly to his topic, Gray takes notes. I write from Influx, he says, gravely. Influx is like Pentecost; it is a pentecostal event, if you wish. The spirit descends. The tongue burns with holy fire. Most people think it is either holy—or insane. "Writing from an Influx which is really out(-side) of your Self, or so far within your Self as to amount to the same thing, is either a religion or a madness. In allowing your faculties to be directed to ends you know not of, there is only One Being to whom you dare entrust them: only the Lord. Of consequence, before writing by Influx, your prayer must be to Him, for His Guidance, Influx, and Protection."[21] The speech flows, like his beard, from his mouth, and as he grows more fluent, he seems to grow more abstracted, gazing towards the solemn head of Swedenborg in the oleograph above the desk, glowing with an enthusiasm that seems to seep into the dingy room like a shaft of dusty sunshine, gently shifting the scale of the room into something larger and more grand; a theater, perhaps, of the spirit.

Returning to his rooms in Park Lane, Gray writes up the extraordinary afternoon for the new edition of *The Dial,* still limping into production at unpredictable dates. Ricketts finds it fascinating, although as a craftsman he is suspicious of anything that comes automatically, without effort or skill. But Gray begins to experiment. The techniques for automatic writing are similar to those he is learning from the *Spiritual Exercises* of Ignatius Loyola for making the mind receptive to spiritual influence. He begins, as directed, with prayer; then trusts to the consequences. These productions are duly printed—privately, by Raffalovich's subscription—and sent out for the next and subsequent two Christmases under the title *The Blue Calendar.* They are modest works; they reflect a new modesty of spirit. The poem for May 1895 reads:

> Good Saint Mary fumbled deep,
> With a saintly gesture.
> In this bag (said she) I keep
> All the Infant's vesture.
> Ah Lord! How great is my reward.
> *My soul doth magnify the Lord.*
>
> . . . .
>
> Here be little cambric shirts,
> Very small and slender.
> Here the band His body girts,
> Which is frail and tender.
> So carefully must He be dressed.
> *Henceforth all nations call me blest.*[22]

For the former recipients of *Silverpoints,* the poems are a shock. Automatic dictation does not improve their quality, Gray observes, always the hardest on his own performance. But it does work towards a new freshness and naiveté. Not all of his circle are taken aback. His old friend Dowson is to write in December 1895 praising the "rare, audacious, successful—admirable" effects of that year's *Blue Calendar,* particularly its "'Moyen-Age-fin-de-siècle'" flavor.[23]

It is a question of finding the right words, Gray explains slowly to Ricketts. The Vale has been left behind, probably to be destroyed, like all other vestiges of countryside within an expanding London. Shannon and Ricketts had moved to Beaufort Street, where Gray visits them once in a blue moon. Ricketts, along with a sedate man called Charles Hacon, have started a new imprint, the Ballantyne Press. Ah, Gray—the very man at the very moment. Ricketts approaches him eagerly, waving his thin hands before him as if conducting an invisible orchestra. We need editions. Of anything you deem worthy of print: fine print. I am designing the fonts, the woodcuts for initials, the bindings. This will be very fine work: continuing where Morris left off with the Kelmscott Press. But we need words—we need authors!

Gray still finds himself bemused by Ricketts's suddenness, his tyrannical energy. Yes, yes, Gray laughs a conciliatory laugh. I am already working on a volume of religious poetry. Are you interested? I intend to call it "Spiritual Poems: Chiefly Done Out of Several Languages."

Ricketts throws his hands to the sky. A prayer answered, he laughs. Manna from heaven. Alleluia. Although I am beginning to worry about your evident religious mania.

No, says Gray. It is just words. I can find you some more bread-and-butter stuff: Thomas Campion; Michael Drayton; Sir John Suckling. I spend a good deal of my time now in the British Museum.

Wonderful! pounces Ricketts.

He does not tell Prince Charles that he is also translating the poetry of Friedrich Nietzsche.

Such is his new sense of urgency that Gray sometimes wonders if it is about poetry at all. He reads Boehme; he finds a formula there that makes sense: imagination as a vehicle of divine revelation. Writing from Influx has loosened him up. He knows he will now try anything; he is a spiritual desperado, like a man who is drunk running through a hotel corridor and throwing open one door after another to find the right room.

Raffalovich has opened one of the doors: to spiritism. He knows it is not respectable; that is part of its charm. He loves intellectual slumming. He takes notes for his future memoirs: "Madame Blavatsky, purple-lilac . . . [in] her livid earth-gray skin . . . sat on the great sofa in the great drawing room in Richmond Terrace, Whitehall . . . She was attacking Frederick Myers, the Zelator of the Phantasms of the living, as I came in: no doubt the S[ociety for] P[sychical] R[esearch]'s adverse report, though not yet published, was known to her. She was afraid and indignant . . . and she cried out: 'Mr. Myers, if you had not made me so angry I would cause all the bells in this house to ring' (we all held our breaths—would she relent?), 'but I will not do so.'"

> Then there was dear Mrs. Wentwy, handsome and placid, [who] patiently related the surprising discomforts of her daily life: "the spirits plague me so some days that I retire to my bath, zinc is a non-conductor . . . Yes, I won't pay my rent any more, because the man who pretends to be my landlord is a changling. He is no longer Mr. Hussey, though he looks just like him. I told him he was not himself, and he bowed himself out. The neighbourhood of the Albert Memorial accounts for much. A tall, handsome man arrived one evening at the Mansions. [Much like you, Mr. Gray; perhaps indeed it *was* you? It looked distinctly like you.] I saw him get out of the cab. He left the next morning under the guise of two short plain men. That's what the spirits do now . . . I often come across people going to their own funeral. Mrs. Booth stood near me at hers. But in the bus last week we passed a hearse. I said to my *vis-à-vis*, quite a pleasant sickly-looking young man, I wondered he was not at his own funeral. He got out at once. [Then she looked very sharply at my companion: And don't you think you will be late for yours, too, Mr. Gray?]

Her world had never seemed to me so queer as one evening in the country [when she had made her way down to the summer retreat in Weybridge]. I was seeing her off after a long day in the garden and in the pine wood. [She had exhilarated our lively group by pointing out John Gray and saying: Why do I always see two of you? Who is the other who walks always beside you? When we arrived at the station she] gravely assured me when I complained that the last train did not always start from the same platform: "You see, they have to dodge Them."[24]

Gray laughs with the rest when Raffalovich returns with the story, but somewhere inside he does not laugh; he is afraid; no, he is desperate. All ways are one to him now; he accompanies Raffalovich in his ventures to mediums as he once accompanied Louÿs and others to brothels. Once again, it is Pater who indicates the path, urging his reader to break up habits, to live in the moment, not to exclude or discriminate, but to "grasp at any exquisite passion, or any contribution to knowledge that seems by a lifted horizon to set the spirit free for a moment": that is the goal. "To burn always with this hard, gemlike flame, to maintain this ecstasy, is success in life."[25] John Gray burns now with a rapacity of the spirit; like a pirate, he would seize at anything that promises treasure, that promises to give a sense of splendor to experience amidst its awful brevity, to gather all "into one desperate effort to see and touch" and thus, perhaps, to feel his way into the dark—towards the future.

The future is a wall of mist. With Raffalovich's mediums as guides, he seeks to pierce it. But it is hard to know how seriously one can take them—or oneself. Raffalovich suffers from the same ambivalence:

Close to my Surrey pine wood resided Mrs. Stephenson, the rotund medium . . . She during her trances (I never knew her decline to be entranced) held forth about *hhorgans*, 'ealth, past, present, future . . . She was so stout that sitting down she appeared to be standing up. In every class these spherical women with an accent are persuasive . . . [One evening I took Gray to the medium's cottage.] She saw something in his hand. She took for granted that he was an author, as she connected me with people who wrote. [Gray was disappointed; she was no good. So we decided that our dear Lady G. would be part of] our gay impudent hoax. In the front drawing room in South Audley Street she sat disguised as a Muscovite seeress, thrice veiled, muffled, long-coated, a thimble in her mouth (for the Russian accent), in her hand a Willie Benson paper-weight of metal. Madame Céleste we called her. She teased Meresia Nevill, tantalised charming Lady Clementina Maude, she over-teased the Pocahontas of Park Lane, a lady so truly ethnic that the tufted eglantines of her coiffure suggested feathers, and her fan a sheaf of presumably poisoned arrows. At supper Madame Céleste in her frock of violets and cream feared herself detected, so cold was the eye of Pocahontas, so exotic her silhouette.[26]

So much like theater, my dear Gray, Raffy said afterwards: persons like Edward Maitland professing to be St. John the Evangelist and Anna Kingsford "under his guidance as the reincarnation of St. Mary Magdalene. She also remembered herself as Ninon, Anne Boleyn, St. Joan of Arc."[27]

I do not think I need any more theater, dear Raffy, Gray murmurs. No more representing of one person as another. I wish to find what is real—the bedrock behind appearance. I wish to see beyond this blank wall that is my future.

Ah. I will take you to Cheiro, Raffalovich says decisively, in his guttural accent, looking at Gray hard, then blinking. I have great faith in Cheiro, even though his rivals accuse "him of clairvoyance and of using short cuts to knowledge instead of the slower road of scientific palmistry." But, Raffalovich confesses, I have found Cheiro "shrewd, entertaining. With his glass rod he pointed out islands and mystic crosses, and pleasantly 'curdled the blood and agonised the mind' of self-seekers . . . I have outlived my island." I begin to think; England is beginning to suffocate me. But perhaps "my mystic cross remains." Your poetry alone brings me to it, dear

Gray. You know what Cheiro said at the end? "'Why don't you go in for palmistry? . . . you would succeed.' I was flattered."[28]

At the Bond Street premises, Gray is escorted into a semi-darkened back room divided by a heavy velvet curtain. A voice said: I am Cheiro. Do not speak; I wish only to see your hands. If you place them one at a time through the slit in the curtain, I will read them for you. You must place your left hand in first, as that denotes hereditary tendencies; then the right hand, which denotes individual developments. I will read each hand only once and I will not elaborate on my readings. You must trust to them, for they are secure.

Gray hesitates, then places his left hand through the slit. He feels it taken firmly and spread, as if for an operation, a finger tracing the lines; he winces at the exquisite tingle that runs through him.

A gentleman's hand, the voice says, as if in incantation. But it began as a workman's. The scars are still there; they will always remain. Give me now your other hand.

Gray withdraws the workman's hand and pauses. His past he knows. But the future?

The hand is taken as before, and spread. As the finger traces the line through the palm, he feels a suggestion of the slightest tremor, but one which sends a chill through his spine. There is a heavy silence; the man behind the curtain shifts in his chair, then clears his throat—and intones:

In the middle of the lifeline, there is a split. One part of it fades out, as if you were not wholly alive, nor yet actually dead. It persists, it can be still traced to the end of a usual life span. Another line continues, but beneath it: a hidden life.

When? Gray falls into speech, despite the injunction. He hears his voice from a distance, as if he were talking in his sleep; it sounds hoarse and strange.

Soon; you are soon at midlife; so it will be soon. I do not know what it means.

Gray snatches his hand away and leaves hurriedly.

In the outer room, Raffalovich throws him a strange look. As they leave, Gray regards himself in the shop window across Bond Street; he is unearthly pale, the eyes hooded, the hair thinning. He will grow old, he suddenly thinks. And old, he will be haunted by his youth as Dorian Gray is haunted by the picture in the attic.

As they progress down Bond Street amidst the reflecting windows, Raffalovich quizzes Gray obliquely about the outcome; concedes the reading is puzzling, if not downright opaque. Disturbing, he murmurs in agreement. Then adds, more cheerfully: Come, my good Gray. Cheiro is bound to be paradoxical. You know what he is reputed to have told Oscar? The night of the opening of *A Woman of No Importance* he dined at Blanche Roosevelt's house. Before dinner, she arranged a reading for her guests by Cheiro—a curtain was rigged up in the drawing room and they went in one by one. Dear Blanche was *most* disconcerted when Oscar rushed back into the hallway; he was as pale as a ghost. She cornered him as he was putting on his coat. But you have not even eaten, my dear Oscar. What is wrong? He simply muttered his apologies and rushed out. Blanche only heard months afterwards: Cheiro had told Oscar that his left hand was the hand of a king, but his right that of a king who will send himself into exile. When Oscar asked, "At what date?" Cheiro answered apparently: "A few years from now, at about your fortieth year."[29] What age would Oscar be now, do you say?

Gray pauses and, looking up, says: I think he would have been thirty-eight at the time—that is, about a year ago. As I recall, *A Woman of No Importance* opened on the nineteenth of April of last year. Just after *Salome* was first published. And *Silverpoints,* he added ruefully. I recall the occasion because Oscar invited Pierre Louÿs to the first night; but, according to his brother, Georges, Louÿs had written to him that "Oscar Wilde has been charming on my behalf, I have lunched with him almost every day. But I should have been glad if he had provided different company."[30]

Douglas, says Raffalovich darkly.

Douglas, Gray confirms. Apparently Douglas and Oscar told Louÿs they were anxious about the possibility of blackmail; you know the story, Raffy—about the letter addressed to Douglas as "My dear Hyacinth" which fell into the hands of that vile creature Alfred Woods. So Oscar came up with this scheme that the letter be transformed into a work of art and Louÿs obligingly turned it into a passable poem in French to be published in the *Spirit Lamp* in

May. But you know, Raffy, that once Louÿs saw Wilde and his clique at close quarters, he became thoroughly disgusted. He wrote to me shortly afterwards, from Paris, that he had broken with Wilde and can never meet him again anywhere.[31] So, my dear Raffalovich, you must have been among the first to break with Oscar; but Louÿs and I are now only two among many. Many others are following suit; especially since *Salome* has appeared in English with those upsetting drawings by Beardsley. He is a genius, of course; but his illustrations have inflamed Mrs. Grundy. And you know for yourself, dear Raffalovich, how narrow-minded and vindictive the English public can be.

Wilde is simply preparing his own exile, that is all, replies Raffalovich firmly as they both turn into South Audley Street. The late spring evening is beginning to darken.

At the steps to his house, Raffalovich turns to Gray to offer him his hand. Will I see you again perhaps on Friday evening? I have arranged for Mrs. Stevenson to come up from Surrey to entertain my guests with her prestidigitations. Perhaps, John Gray, she will help you pierce the wall of mist which you say obscures your future.

That Friday the drawing room at South Audley Street is "the scene of a triumph of Mrs. Stephenson. She had been invited to London; she had no accessories, her cockney speech was worth all the thimbles, her corpulence outweighed Madame Céleste's muffled slimness (Madame Céleste was more at home in the hunting field than as a clairvoyante). Lady Inglefield, soon to be Baroness von Haucqwitz, was the first introduced to the squat Sybil. Through the narrow windowed passage connecting the two drawing rooms we heard not the words but the voice of Lady Inglefield, high, full of inflections. At the end of a quarter of an hour she joined us, triumphant, puzzled by our laughter.

'That woman knows all about me!' she exclaims.

'No wonder, we answered, we heard you tell her.'"[32]

Despite his earlier disappointment with Mrs. Stephenson in Surrey, Gray enters the back drawing room expectantly. He recalls the poem he is composing in his head, about a flying fish, who lives between earth and sky, driven by the "aspiration born of fear":

> not to be one of the sons of air;
> to be rid of the water is all his prayer;
>
> all his hope is a fear-whipped whim,
> all directions are one to him.[33]

Desperation drives him to this, he reflects; to consulting a fat lady about his future. He sits before her quietly, wondering whether she recognizes him from the earlier encounter. What intelligence lies behind the cornflower-blue eyes, which seem to pull shutters down before his steady gaze?

Be'ind you, young man, I see someone standing, she says. His 'ealth is not good. 'E's big, you see, and 'e's been something of a toff. 'E's lost his 'ead, 'e 'as. An' 'e's shambling like an old man; 'is 'ead 'anging—'e looks as if 'e's one of the living dead, 'e does. Do you know 'im?

Gray looks down. If he's big, he couldn't be his father. He shakes his head silently: no.

Then there's another. 'E's lying down. 'E has a face like a hatchet. 'E looks cruel, but 'e's only a boy, really. 'E's laughing, more like a giggle, really, but then there's an awful cough that jus' jerks him up like a puppet. 'E's a goner too. Know 'im?

Gray shakes his head again, decisively: no.

After a moment's silence, he leaves, nodding to Raffalovich as he enters the front drawing room. I haven't the slightest notion of whom she's talking about. Perhaps she thought I was someone else.

The year of 1894 is one of gathering anxiety. On 17 April *The Yellow Book* is published, to howls of outrage. The two women poets who write as "Michael Field," passing the window of the Bodley Head in Vigo Street—the home of their own publishers, and Gray's—cry out to their journal: "We have been almost blinded by the glare of hell."[34] *Silverpoints* had already done much to establish the Bodley Head as publishers of the most decadent of books. Now the yellow covers seem to lick at the windows like sulphurous flames. The very color chosen was that of the notoriously immoral French novel; but it might as well have been the color of brimstone, as far as the public was concerned. Aubrey Beardsley is the art editor and illustrator. His pictures—modern, provocative, impudent—reveal to the public for the first time an astonishing artist. "Women who saw Beardsley's portrait of Mrs. Patrick Campbell aspired to look like his conception of her with that slim long body and enigmatic head weighed down by the dense black of the hair as with oppressive dreams. They yearned for those overdecorated boudoirs in which he loved to place his voluminously draped figures whose heavy lids and sullen lips imparted to the face the suggestion of forbidden adventure. He played with powder boxes, rouge pots, phials and puffs with aggressive sensuality. And always there were the candlesticks, so constant . . . they might have served as a signature."[35] (Of the explosion that was the "Beardsley boom," Gray is to recall a few years later:

> In an instant he was famous. Music-hall writers adorned their verses with his name. Publishers anxious to make a fortune proffered their attentions. Women's dress conformed to his wish. Wagnerian concerts were thronged with his characters. As for himself, he did nothing but draw, unmoved, and was none other than Aubrey Beardsley.[36])

Suddenly everyone recognizes Beardsley, who has become a celebrity.

> Now whenever he went to the Café Royal there was no need for people to ask who he was. The loose-limbed, gaunt apparition in a black cutaway, silk hat and lemon-coloured gloves held in the long spidery hands, the youth with the startling hair and cold, agate-like eyes, moving feverishly among the tables as if every instant had to be lived, was as well known as the type he had invented. He might almost have stepped out of one of his drawings. Everyone was soon talking of the "marvelous boy" and society came forth to meet him . . .

First night audiences and concert crowds became familiar with the angular, fleshless face drinking in life from avid eyes. One cold night a friend was shocked to see him on the steps of the Opera House, wearing no overcoat.

"Aubrey, you will kill yourself!" he remonstrated.

"Oh, no . . . I am always burning."[37]

And so he is, Gray observes, always burning with the fever of ambition that knows it has little time to fulfill itself. For Beardsley is already walking among the graves. Was it Haldane Macfall who had seen him stumbling, panting for breath, among the gravestones of Hampstead Church after the unveiling of the bust of Keats? Did Beardsley on that occasion know himself to be fatally stricken, like Keats, fighting for time to fulfill his obvious genius?[38]

Gray notes the efforts of his fellow artists to account for the detonation of this talent, as startling as the bombs now shaking Paris:

Theories followed; in the end he was *explained*. For some he was a monster with a contrary vision: what was meant, for example, by his fauns dressed in lace? his hideous women firmly convinced of their charm, or beauties with a tranquil and unpitying air? According to others, he had to wait, to possess himself in patience. Beardsley would begin to learn the way of the world; before long, weary of shocking good people, his whimsical imagination would be exhausted, and he would draw like everyone else; he would show himself at last responsible.

Responsible! What did they want, his judges, his admirers? His seriousness was in fact precisely to mock, but in a kindly way, without malice. One would wait long for something else from him.[39]

Gray observes the frantic efforts of Beardsley's fellow editor, Henry Harland, and of Mathews and Lane, the publishers, to render *The Yellow Book* respectable. For its first issues, they commission such safe names as Richard Garnett, Edmund Gosse, and Henry

James; even the staid poet William Watson—who had, as Wilde noted, not enough fire in him to warm a tea kettle—is approached in an effort to provide the ballast of old decency.

But everyone reads *The Yellow Book* for the new names, the authors and artists who take risks: particularly the wicked caricatures, the delicious rodomontade of that rogue Max Beerbohm. His "Defence of Cosmetics" is agreeably naughty, particularly in an age when decent women do not "paint." So un-English, so provocative: so positively and subversively French! His aggressive teasing of the public bemuses Gray, as does the predictable overreaction of the *Westminster Gazette*—that great guardian of public morals—which demands "a short Act of Parliament to make this kind of thing illegal."[40]

"What kind of thing?" Raffalovich asks quizzically one day. Well you know, Raffy: almost everything. Particularly any tendencies not to take Public Morality seriously. You know how the Great English Public distrusts laughter. Listen to this—I've just come across it—by someone called, improbably, Mostyn Piggot, writing under the pseudonym "Testudo" in the London *World*:

> 'Twas rollog, and the minim potes
>> Did mime and mimble in the cafe;
> All footly were the Philerotes,
>> And Daycadongs outstrafe.

Raffalovich splutters. The old "Log-Roller" LeGallienne would like that—and as a "minim pote" yourself, Gray, you should revel in the "Daycadong" strife with the "Philerotes"—by which I suppose he means the Philistines.

But hear this, Gray smiles wryly:

> Beware the Yallerbock, my son!
>> The aims that rile, the art that racks,
> Beware the Aub-Aub Bird, and shun
>> The stumious Beerbomax.[41]

Ah, yes, says Raffy, the smile beaming and then suddenly disappearing, wiped off his face by a moment of anxiety. The "Aub-

Aub bird" is good, is it not? He seems more and more like some fantastic tropical bird—an ibis perhaps—that has flown into London for a brief visit and will soon depart, probably for the south of France. But Beerbohm—he is becoming almost as dangerous as Wilde, although his conduct of his life is far more innocent. The English public is getting tired of being teased; it is like an irritated child on the verge of a tantrum. *The Yellow Book* will be the victim of a public temper tantrum yet. At least Mathews and Lane had the sense to cut Oscar. But I am not sure in the end whether that action alone will save them—or their latest publication.

For his own part, Oscar is smarting at the cut. Scandal is now his métier and to be excluded from one so successful is hurtful indeed. But Beardsley is an instigator, with Harland, of this latest project, and the mutual distrust engendered by the illustrations for *Salome* still simmers. Beardsley also harbors a superstitious dread that any association with Wilde will bring bad luck. Moreover, John Lane has no more desire than Beardsley to include Oscar among the contributors. To publish his new poem, *The Sphinx,* in a small quarto with exquisite designs by Charles Ricketts is one matter. In any case, *The Sphinx* is about as dangerous as a stuffed pussycat. But to unleash Wilde onto a large and unsuspecting public would be quite another. Wilde's dealings with the Bodley Head's office boy, Shelley—the one Gray remarked on as having "the eyelashes of a poet"—who is now drifting like a hopeless human wreck as the result of the great man's "interest" in him, has made an indelible impression on Lane.

"Have you seen *The Yellow Book?*" Wilde asks Ada Leverson in a petulant little note. "It is horrid and not yellow at all." He is even more candid with Bosie. "*The Yellow Book* has appeared. It is dull and loathsome: A great failure—I am so glad."[42]

He nurses the grudge. So many of his disciples are there— Max Beerbohm and Arthur Symons and Richard LeGallienne—and artists who were his friends from the Vale days: William Rothenstein and Walter Sickert. Oscar carries his childish pique to Ricketts's new quarters on Beaufort Street, ostensibly to confer on the binding of *The Sphinx*. "My dear boy, do not say nice false things about *The Yellow Book*"—rebuking Ricketts with a mock-injured look, one that Ricketts knows is preparatory to some ridiculous yarn.

> I bought it at the station, but before I had cut all the pages, I threw it out of my carriage window. Suddenly the train stopped and the guard, opening the door, said, "Mr. Wilde, you have dropped *The Yellow Book*." What was to be done? In the hansom, with the subtlety of a poet, I cunningly hid it under the cushions and paid my fare . . . when came a loud knocking at the front door, and the cabby, appearing, said, "Mr. Wilde, you have forgotten *The Yellow Book* . . . "

And so on, Wilde putting on the most absurd expressions in a pantomime of injured pride. He rejoices in these little performances.[43]

But Wilde's revenge comes in a vicarious *succès de scandal*: an "undergraduate of strange beauty," the editor of an obscure little Oxford magazine called the *Chameleon*, asks Bosie for a contribution to its first issue.[44] Bosie complies, then asks for one from Oscar Wilde. Oscar supplies him with a set of aphorisms, which he entitles "Phrases and Philosophies for the Use of the Young."[45] They show a reckless disregard for the darkening mood of public solemnity. "Wickedness is a myth invented by good people to account for the curious attractiveness of others . . . Pleasure is the only thing one should live for . . . No crime is vulgar, but all vulgarity is crime. Vulgarity is the conduct of others . . . To love oneself is the beginning of a life-long romance." These prove merely sparks that detonate the explosive mixture within. The two poems by Bosie are among the most direct on the subject of inverted love. The sonnet "In Praise of Shame" boldly proclaims:

> I am Shame
> That walks with Love; I am most wise to turn
> Cold lips and limbs to fire; therefore discern
> And see my loveliness, and praise my name.[46]

"Two Loves" speaks more plainly still. It is a dream-vision, set in a flowering garden:

> And lo! Within the garden of my dream
> I saw two walking in a shining plain
> Of golden light. The one did joyous seem
> And fair, and blooming, and a sweet refrain
> Came from his lips; he sang of pretty maids
> And joyous love of comely girl and boy . . .
> But he that was his comrade walked aside;
> He was full sad and sweet, and his large eyes
> Were strange with wondrous brightness, staring wide
> With gazing; and he sighed with many sighs . . .
> A purple robe he wore, o'erwrought with gold
> With the device of a great snake, whose breath
> Was fiery flame; which when I did behold
> I fell a-weeping and I cried, "Sweet youth,
> Tell me why, sad and sighing, thou dost rove
> These pleasant realms? I pray thee speak me sooth
> What is thy name?" He said, "My name is Love."
> Then straight the first did turn himself to me
> And cried, "He lieth, for his name is Shame,
> But I am Love, and I was wont to be
> Alone in this fair garden, till he came
> Unasked by night; I am true Love, I fill
> The hearts of boy and girl with mutual flame."
> Then sighing said the other, "Have thy will,
> I am the Love that dare not speak its name."[47]

Raffalovich's voice trembles at the last line and he places the slim volume carefully on the table near the fire, as if it might break. There is a moment's silence, an instant in which Gray senses, rather than smells, a brief waft of apple blossom; then the smell of fear. Raffy moves in an agitated manner, first to the window, then back to the fire, where he leans upon the mantlepiece, looking slightly down at the seated Gray. It is true, he says, the guttural accent unaccountably thickening. There is no name. I have, in my recent writings, called it "inversion"—that is what most people think of this kind of love. As a kind of inverse of what is "normal"—whatever that is. Perhaps a bit like the negative of a photograph; everything reversed. Of course it is not so, but it is the best name we have. To call people like us "Uranians" is silly; who recalls that the Uranian Aphrodite is the goddess of pure and ennobling love? And anyway the pun is appalling. Almost as bad as naming such love after the act of sodomy. People like us should not be named after physical acts in any case; we are not just the summary of our acts. We are a certain type of person, who lives in a certain kind of way. I have been reading widely for my recent treatise on "inversion" and I think perhaps the German Krafft-Ebing comes nearest when he gives us the name "homosexual." But I prefer Edward Carpenter's "homogenic love"—as the love between those of the same sex—as the most neutral. We have no name, people like us, for our comradeship. Few will admit it as love. But Carpenter recognizes it as love, and a love dedicated to higher ends—to our own self-development—and to art.

Gray, still and silent, looks into the fire, his fine profile shadowed against the light which plays over the room. Ah, yes, Raffy. Carpenter is fine—he believes in the higher love. He recognizes it as the blaze which illuminates heroism, which lights up romance. But you forget its true source; in the fire of the spirit.

Raffalovich looks at Gray hard, then turns abruptly. No: I do not. But I object to the crudity of such pieces as "The Priest and the Acolyte." He picks up the *Chameleon* again, abruptly, rifling through its newly cut pages. Have you read this trash? Do you know who it is by?

Gray looks up at Raffalovich as if from a long distance. It is crudely written, that it is all. It cannot help itself. It is a *cri de coeur*. Silently, Gray reaches out for the slim book, takes it in his fine hands and opens randomly to a passage: Listen.

> When they reached the vestry and the boy stood before
> him reverently receiving the sacred vestments, he knew that
> henceforth the entire devotion of his religion, the whole ecstatic
> fervour of his prayers, would be connected with, nay, inspired

by, one object alone. With the same reverence and humility as he would have felt in touching the consecrated elements he laid his hands on the curl-crowned head, he touched the small pale face, and, raising it slightly, he bent forward and gently touched the smooth white brow with his lips.[48]

Pater does it so much better in *Marius the Epicurean,* Raffalovich mutters darkly. Does it have to be spelled out?

Gray shrugs briefly, places the book back on the table, then stares into the fire. After a minute's silence, he says, slowly and deliberately, as if weighing the measure of each of the words:

Raffy, you know how it has been with us. It is only when we gave up bodily love that we found the true love between us: the higher love that allows us to dedicate ourselves to Art. You know how it has been with us. It is only now that we repent bitterly our actions of the past that we begin to find our way to God.

Raffalovich moves to the side of the chair; he stands as if stilled by another hand, placing his own quietly, in consent, on Gray's shoulder. It trembles slightly. Yes. The voice is final, quiet. But it is the name of Oscar Wilde who sullies us and those such as we are.

Gray nods silently; in the silence there is pain—and fear.

Oscar for his part is horrified at seeing the printed *Chameleon.* He had no idea when Bosie came to him asking for a contribution that his comparatively innocuous "Phrases and Philosophies" would usher in such explosive material. He senses now, instinctively, that he is walking along a precipice. He does not regret—nor does he intend to modify—his flamboyant behavior with Bosie. But two months before something had happened which had changed the whole public tenor of their very public affair. In October, Bosie's older brother and the heir to the estate, Drumlanrig, had died with shocking suddenness. The newspapers reported a shooting accident, but among his friends and associates, suicide was generally suspected. Drumlanrig was private secretary to Lord Rosebery, who as foreign minister under Gladstone was tipped to become the new prime minister. In certain circles, Rosebery was also suspected to be a lover of boys; was Drumlanrig's suicide the result of the threat of blackmail? If their relationship were discovered, did Drumlanrig fear it would bring down Rosebery or even the government that supported him?[49]

Oscar's newfound caution, however, is not systematic enough to prevent him writing Ada Leverson:

> "The Priest and the Acolyte" is not by Dorian: though you were right in discerning by internal evidence that the author has a profile. He is an undergraduate of strange beauty.
>
> The story is, to my ears, too direct: there is no nuance: it profanes a little by revelation: God and other artists are always a little obscure. Still, it has interesting qualities, and is at moments poisonous: which is something.[50]

The poison is spreading. Three days into the new year of 1895, Wilde's latest comedy, *An Ideal Husband,* is produced at the Haymarket Theatre. Its immediate success is becoming almost routine, but the glitter is tarnished by the shadow of Bosie's father, the notorious Marquess of Queensberry. Having lost one son in what is rumored to be a homosexual love affair, he is determined not to lose another. The fear seems reasonable; but the "mad" Marquess of Queensberry is not a reasonable man. He stalks Wilde, insults him, threatens him, creates scenes. He is to become a locus for all Wilde's enemies—and for growing public disquiet that gathers about Oscar. Wilde's fellow Irishman, George Bernard Shaw, catches the public temper perfectly when he observes of the audience of *An Ideal Husband:* "They laugh angrily at his epigrams, like a child who is coaxed into being amused in the very act of setting up a yell of rage."

> All the literary dignity of the play [Shaw continues], all the imperturbable good sense and good manners with which Mr Wilde makes his wit pleasant to his comparatively stupid audience, cannot quite overcome the fact that Ireland is of all countries the most foreign to England, and that to the Irishman (and Mr Wilde is almost as acutely Irish an

Irishman as the Iron Duke of Wellington) there is nothing
in the world quite so exquisitely comic as an Englishman's
seriousness. It becomes tragic, perhaps, when the Englishman acts on it; but that occurs too seldom to be taken into
account, a fact which intensifies the humour of the situation,
the total result being the Englishman utterly unconscious of
his real self, Mr Wilde keenly observant of it and playing on
the self-unconsciousness with irresistible humour, and
finally, of course, the Englishman annoyed with himself for
being amused at his own expense, and for being unable to
convict Mr Wilde of what seems an obvious misunderstand-
ing of human nature. He is shocked, too, at the danger to the
foundations of society when seriousness is publicly laughed
at. And to complete the oddity of the situation, Mr Wilde,
touching what he himself reverences, is absolutely the most
sentimental dramatist of the day.[51]

The forces of danger converge in Wilde's most perfect
comedy. *The Importance of Being Earnest* opens on St. Valentine's
Day of 1895. It is snowing. Among the broughams, hansom cabs,
equipages of all kinds, the Marquess of Queensberry arrives,
carrying a grotesque bouquet of vegetables he intends to hurl at the
author when he is called upon to make a curtain speech. Warned
beforehand, certain men are placed strategically to prevent the
Marquess of Queensberry from entering; but he prowls about for
three hours, closely watched by Scotland Yard men. When the doors
are finally shut, the Marquess leaves, shaking his head in wrath and
muttering to himself.

On stage, as if it were a play within a play, *The Importance of
Being Earnest* ridicules every solemn institution of the Empire, from
the deference of servants to the masculinity of the paterfamilias.
Most crucially, it ridicules solemnity itself. The Marquess of
Queensberry—though universally regarded as mad—is still a mar-
quess, and a father of sons, one of whom has already died tragically.
The fuse is lit which is to detonate the explosion.

No one is quite prepared for the first blast. On 1 March, the
Marquess of Queensberry is arrested and charged at Great

Marlborough Street Police Court with criminal libel. The warrant of arrest was obtained by, of all people—Oscar Wilde. What the papers do not give in detail is filled in by Raffalovich's hairdresser on Bond Street—whom he shares, grudgingly, with Wilde. Queensberry had left a card for Wilde at the Albemarle Club, which Oscar read only ten days later, on 28 February: "For Oscar Wilde posing somdomite [sic]."[52] Trimming Raffalovich's drooping mustache, the hairdresser murmurs: Can't even spell, Mr. Raffalovich; can't even spell.

On 9 March, Queensberry is remanded at Bow Street for trial at Old Bailey. Alarmed, Gray engages one of Wilde's barristers, Mr. Charles Willie Mathews, to attend the trial with a watching brief on his behalf.[53] A "watching brief" is purely precautionary; no defense need be launched unless John Gray's name is mentioned during the actual proceedings of the trial. The same instinct which had prompted Gray to threaten *The Star* with a libel suit three years ago now comes to his aid. Gray has a premonition that *The Picture of Dorian Gray* will certainly be mentioned in the trial; as will the name of Edward Shelley, the office boy at the Bodley Head. He senses the danger, too, in the sensational story "The Priest and the Acolyte," commonly assumed to be by "Dorian." Gray's actions are clear, direct, decisive. (And, as it transpires, effective: in the event, neither John Gray's name nor his association with Wilde is ever mentioned, at this or any of the subsequent trials.)

It proves an eerie spring. During those weeks in March, the Café Royal empties out. Dinner parties and crushes and private views are either ablaze with rumors about Oscar Wilde or surround his name with an iron cage of silence. With grave deliberation, Raffalovich and Gray lie low, seeking lives of quiet obscurity. In their separate dwellings around the corner from each other, they read the headlines each morning with trepidation; it is too late to step aside from the slide towards what now seems inevitable. They agree on no written communications. On certain mornings when the reports are particularly disturbing, Raffalovich makes an early morning call to Park Lane before Gray sets out to the Foreign Office. The Foreign Office is solemn, silent. But hushed whispers speculate as to whether the trials will involve the name of the now prime minister, Lord Rosebery. An election is pending; what effect will such a connection have on the government? After the years of tremors and jolts, the earthquake is upon them.

On 3 April, the Queensberry trial opens. As Gray had foreseen, the philistine mind makes no distinction between literature and life: *The Picture of Dorian Gray* is presented as evidence, as is "The Priest and the Acolyte." Gray smiles at the newspaper reports of Wilde's condemnation of "The Priest" as "perfect twaddle"—and his brilliant justification of *Dorian Gray*. When asked by the defense, "Then a well-written book putting forth perverted moral views may be a good book?" Wilde replies: "No work of art ever puts forward views. Views belong to people who are not artists."[54]

Gray winces at the word "perverted." As he does at the letters to Bosie which are read out in court, in words Oscar once addressed to himself: "Your slim gilt soul walks between passion and poetry."[55]

Then the descent into sordid transactions, detailed by the newspapers: the evidence concerning Wood, Parker, Taylor. Wood he had seen in the Café Royal a few years back, pointed out to him by Frank Harris, who knew all sorts of assorted low-life. The itemization of lunches, teas, drinks of iced champagne, gifts of cigarette cases. The squalid commerce of sex rental, the misplaced glamour of the prostitute, and, beneath it all, the relentless logic of the Criminal Law Amendment Act of 1885, which made all such transactions between men, whether public or private, consensual or not, a criminal offense and punishable as such. In fact, Gray muses, since Oscar discovered boys within a year or two of its ratification, was this law not itself the instrument he chose for his own destruction, for an indulgence that he found exciting precisely because it was dangerous?[56]

At the end of the second day, the newspapers reported the fatal exchange. Carson, representing Queensberry, questioned Wilde about Douglas and the servant at his lodgings at Oxford: "Did you ever kiss him?"—"Oh dear no. He was a peculiarly plain boy . . . I pitied him for it."—"Was that the reason you did not kiss him?"[57]

The trap had been sprung. Wilde is ensnared by one final, fatal witticism. With that sentence he had sentenced himself. Wilde, as the prosecutor, withdrew from the proceedings the following day on the advice of counsel. Queensberry meanwhile instructed his solicitors to send the files to the Director of Public Prosecutions. Wilde was arrested that evening.

Wilde's precipitous descent stuns his friends, even those no longer friends. Those who recall the sparkling, idealistic Wilde find him now besmirched: revealed is the Oscar who pays over money to rent boys for sordid, hidden fumblings in hotels. How have the mighty fallen! Raffalovich recites the words of Milton's Lucifer, the son of the morning, to his next of power, fallen from heaven:

> If thou beest he—but O how fallen! how changed
> From him, who in the happy realms of light
> Clothed with transcendent brightness didst outshine
> Myriads, though bright . . .

His friends, shocked at the speed and violence of events and foreseeing the inevitable, urge Oscar to escape to France. But he stays: whether through misplaced heroism or Irish fatalism or fatal indecision. He is arrested, imprisoned in Holloway jail, then brought to trial. Once the second trial opens, on 26 April, Wilde's friends veer between hope and despair. The papers chronicle every exchange. In one, there flashes the fire of the old Oscar. He is asked again about the contributions to the *Chameleon;* in this case about the poem by Lord Douglas that ends, "I am the love that dare not speak its name." What is "the love that dare not speak its name?" The old Oscar, once loved friend and Master, rises again to his former heights, responding in the old resonant voice:

> The "Love that dare not speak its name" in this century is such a great affection of an elder for a younger man as there was between David and Jonathan, such as Plato made the very basis of his philosophy, and such as you find in the sonnets of Michaelangelo and Shakespeare. It is that deep, spiritual affection that is as pure as it is perfect. It dictates and pervades great works of art like those of Shakespeare and Michaelangelo, and those two letters of mine, such as they are. It is in this century misunderstood, so much misunderstood that it may be described as the "Love that dare not speak its name,"

and on account of it I am placed where I am now. It is beautiful, it is fine, it is the noblest form of affection. There is nothing unnatural about it. It is intellectual, and it repeatedly exists between an elder and a younger man, when the elder man has intellect, and the younger man has all the joy, hope and glamour of life before him. That it should be so the world does not understand. The world mocks at it and sometimes puts one in the pillory for it.[58]

Max Beerbohm is in the public gallery and, cynical as he had become about the influence of this Socrates on the youth of the day, he writes Reggie Turner:

Oscar has been quite superb. His speech about the Love that dare not tell his name was simply wonderful and carried the whole court right away, quite a tremendous burst of applause. Here was this man, who had been for a month in prison and loaded with insults and crushed and buffeted, perfectly self-possessed, dominating the Old Bailey with his fine presence and musical voice. He has never had so great a triumph, I am sure, as when the gallery burst into applause—I am sure it affected the jury.[59]

But for all their passion, the bright words are tarnished by the ensuing evidence: of hotel servants; former lovers like Shelley; of rent boys: Parker, Atkins, Wood. Stories of unholy intimacies, of sordid blackmail, of stains on linen—and reputations. Is it this conflict between idealistic love and sexual squalor that causes the jury's failure to reach a verdict?

A new trial is ordered. After much wrangling, Wilde is released on bail. His lover, Douglas, and his friends Robert Ross and Reggie Turner are all fugitives in France. While Wilde had been in prison, the entire contents of his family house in Tite Street had been put up for public auction. Some of his friends had gone there on the afternoon of 24 April to buy back for him what little they could afford. They describe a scene of pillage, with the house mobbed by idlers, dealers, thieves, who went through the rooms helping themselves to whatever they could lay their hands on before the sale began. Letters and manuscripts disappeared without trace. Books, etchings, prints went for almost nothing while the mob tramped about, looting and forcing open doors and drawers, until the police were called in to restore some semblance of order. In the midst of all this, Raffalovich bid recklessly for boxes of letters and autographed copies that might contain some damaging inscription by "Dorian" Gray. But he failed to locate the copy of Gray's translation of Paul Bourget's *A Saint and Others* which Dorian had inscribed in 1892: "To my loved master my dear friend Homage."[60] Nor did he locate the letter Gray described to him as a holograph of the *Silverpoints* poem "Mishka," signed, "Yours ever, Dorian."[61]

In this interval, Gray hears from Frank Harris about how he tried to dissuade Oscar from standing further trial. He reviews with relentless logic the evidence of the past two trials, pointing out how everything had gone from bad to worse; that nothing would withstand the damning evidence of chambermaids and blackmailers.

"Oh, Frank," Wilde interrupted pitifully. "You talk with passion and conviction, as if I were innocent."

"But you are innocent, aren't you?"

"No, Frank," said Wilde. "I thought you knew that."

To Harris's credit, this avowal makes no difference. Some nights later, he arranges for a brougham and a fast pair of horses to take Wilde to a steam yacht anchored at an obscure landing place up the Thames. He walks Wilde quickly to the brougham, urges him with all the strength of will at his command to climb in and flee—to a new life, outside of England.

The tears streaming down his cheeks, Wilde can only repeat: "It is impossible, Frank, impossible. It would be too wonderful—but it's impossible!" Harris begs, threatens, prophesies. Wilde will not be moved. "I am caught in a trap, Frank. I can only wait for the end."[62]

Gray understands also, as does Raffalovich, that events are moving towards an inevitable catastrophe. Shortly after the third and last trial opens on 20 May, in an extraordinary lapse of taste, if not common sense, Raffalovich decides to attend a session of the proceedings:

Was it malevolence or sheer curiosity [he wonders years later] that sent me walking with one of the Palmers from Grosvenor Square to the Law Courts? He had a ticket: we parted in the crowd: I wished to find my way to see this unheard-of spectacle of a twofold poetical justice, allured not only by the onslaught on Wilde, but by the flouting of Mrs. Grundy. *Les sociétés ont les criminels qu'elles méritent:* I have always bowed to that axiom of Lacassagne. A handsome youthful policeman stopped me: "It is no place for you, Sir; don't go in."—"Thank you; you are right," I murmured, and went away. This policeman fair, almost luminous, like the Archangel Raphael, deserves from me this tribute. I did not question his advice.[63]

Before the verdict of the final trial is given, however, Raffalovich discreetly takes himself off to Brussels, where he has arranged to be wired news of the sentence by his, and Wilde's, hairdresser. "I tore open in the lift the telegram . . . announcing the verdict," he recalls: "I must confess my approval . . . I could almost have said what Alphonse Daudet said to Sherard: 'I admire a country where justice is administered as it is here, as is shown by to-day's verdict and sentence.'"

John Gray hears the news while walking up Coventry Street near Leicester Square. A stranger approaches and imparts a few words into his ear. Devastated, Gray makes his way to a nearby French church, Notre Dame de France, and, in the quiet of the nave, collapses on his knees. His lips move, but the words are not his; it is as if the words speak through him, in the voice of the Blessed Jacopone:

> O Love, all love above,
> Why hast thou struck me so?
> All my heart, broke atwo,
> Consumed with flames of love,
> Burning and flaming cannot find solace;
> It cannot fly from torment, being bound;
> Like wax amid live coal it melts apace;
> It languishes alive, no help being found.[64]

The words, he knows, have no special reference to his own condition; and yet they strike him with the force of a blow. Under its force, his spirit splits, and from his broken soul, a stream issues, as of hot blood, as of fire. It flows in words, not his own, not belonging to him, but of voices that speak through him. Sometimes he recognizes fragments of the song of his nominal ancestors—the Blessed Jacopone and the now beloved John of the Cross. At other moments they are the voices of those other mystics he had been laboriously translating out of several languages. But in the end the speech is the language of the spirit, uttering itself through him in tempestuous, chaotic prayer. As he kneels, he watches the light, springing as if in four flames from the crucifix hung in the chancel. Long fluted golden tongues of somber sheen, like four flames joined in one, spread their glory around the head, radiating from the broken body, robust and frail, shuddering in the last convulsion of the dying breath.

The light gleams, and is gone. Darkness seems to gather in the dim emptiness of the holy void. He kneels, a darkness within the dark, and as the shadows from the painted windows lengthen and the orange, blue, and gold deepen into shadow, the words assail him, forcing their way into consciousness as a river in flood forces itself through narrow banks—then overflows. It floods him then as if in the sweetness of love; the words now of St. John of the Cross, finding in this flight to darkness the night of the soul's great tryst:

> Under the night's dark wing,
> In secret, seen of no one in my flight;
> Nor saw I anything:
> No lantern and no guide,
> Save that which in my heart was all my light;
>
> Lighting the path before me,
> More surely than the brightest noonday light,
> To where he waited for me,
> Whom all my love endeared;
> Where no one else, save only him appeared.

O darkness, which hast guided!
O darkness, yet more lovely than the dawn!
O night, which hast united
The lover with the loved;
And changed into the lover the beloved!

Against my flowery breast,
Kept whole for him alone to lean upon,
The long night did he rest,
The while I entertained him,
And gentle swaying of the cedars fanned him.

His floating hair was fanned
By breezes falling from the tower above.
He, with his gentle hand,
Smiting my neck, bereft me
Of knowledge, so that all my senses left me.

Fainting and all distraught;
My drooping head was resting on my love;
Senseless, resisting not,
I cast off all my cares,
Fallen among sweet lilies unawares.[65]

A sweet odor fills the air; is it of apple blossoms? So this, after all, is love. Not the love that passes the love of women, but the love that passes the love of man: the Love that passeth all understanding. Gray kneels, assailed by the voices that speak of the wounds of love; voices of the Spirit, voices which he has, by translating, at last made his own:

Not iron nor the fire can separate
Or sunder those whom love doth so unite;
Not suffering nor death can reach the state
To which my soul is ravished. From its height,
Beneath it, lo! It sees all things create;
It dominates the range of dimmest sight . . .

Such light, he thinks, looking up at the dazzle of the candles, newly lit. Such sweetness in the "light without pause or bound" which lights the world as if from one's very body, bearing the Light within it. Such sweetness—

> The fetid sweet from sin,
> With sweetness overspread,
> The old forgot and dead,
> In the new reign of love.[66]

Someone touches him, tentatively, on the shoulder; startled, he jumps, as with an electric shock. It's time I locked up, sir, a cracked voice mumbles from a wizened, toothless mouth. It's night time, sir. You've been here all day. She jangles the keys in front of his face, as if to counter his dumbfounded look. He thinks: hours have passed, as if in minutes. He then first realized his fatigue, if not exhaustion. For hours his poor heart had been wrung with the love of Christ.[67]

Gray does not return to work. He is long due some official leave; this is the time to take it. The glances, the whispers are nothing; it is the public frenzy which grips him now. The name of Oscar Wilde is everywhere. Jubilation and revenge go hand in hand: Gray notes the billboards outside the St. James's Theatre, where notices of *The Importance of Being Earnest* are defaced with head-lines announcing: Oscar Wilde Sentenced: Two Years' Hard Labor. He moves in darkness, no light guiding him now, only the counsel of desperation. Robert Sherard, back briefly from Paris, remembers a man, unnamed:

> There was one face which often rises up before me, a face full
> of the intentness of the fixed idea, the face of a man who was
> always hurrying from place to place with a spirit-lamp and
> matches in his pocket, with no other thought nor preoccupa-
> tion in life than to rout out letters and to burn and burn. He
> was the humorous Wemmick of a tragic situation, a man
> whom the horror of the time had scared into a monomania of
> destroying documents by fire.[68]

(Both sides of the correspondence between Pierre Louÿs and John Gray are missing from January 1894 through January 1896—and from 1897 through 1899.[69] Only one letter, signed "Yours ever, Dorian," still exists between Oscar Wilde and Dorian Gray. And only one letter, signed "Robert," from Sherard to Gray. How can one enumerate what no longer exists? One can only mark the eerie silences surrounding the friendships of Gray, Wilde, and Raffalovich during these crucial years; the silence secured by fire.)

After that day of 25 May when Wilde is sentenced, London is gripped by a *Walpurgisnacht*. The crowd flits in and out and around Wilde's former Chelsea home in Tite Street. Constance and the two boys have fled; first to Dublin, then to Switzerland, where she takes refuge under a false name. "A wave of terror swept over the Channel," Sherard recalls, "and the city of Calais witnessed a strange invasion. From the arcana of London a thousand guilty consciences, startled into action by the threat of imminent acquittals, came fleeing South. Every outgoing steamer numbered amongst its passengers such nightmare faces as in quiet times one cannot fancy to exist outside the regions of disordered dreams."[70] Raffalovich leaves Brussels for Berlin, where he is joined a short time later by John Gray and Miss Gribbell.

In Berlin, Raffalovich writes an essay that is to gain the dubious distinction of being the first sustained account of the trials of Oscar Wilde.[71] Commissioned by the editor, Lacassagne, for the *Archives de L'anthropologie Criminelle de Criminologie et de Psychologie Normale et Pathologique*, the very title of the journal dictates the context in which the account is to be placed. Such an account could be published only in French and in France. In considering the Wilde trials within the context of criminal behavior, Raffalovich is very clear as to what aspects of Wilde's behavior are most culpable. When he accuses Wilde of criminality, it is not the sexual acts with which he reproaches him, but the role Wilde has played, the influence he has acquired and so perversely employed, over the young and vain men he has warped, and his influence over their vices, which he has so much encouraged.[72]

Reading it, Gray is struck again by how well informed Raffalovich has been of every aspect of the trial; the account is accurate, if condensed. Raffalovich had not attended the trials himself, he knew; but his sources have been impeccable. But what arrests his reader is the unmistakable tone of injury—and revenge. It gives Gray occasion to remind himself that Raffalovich is a kindly man—and a committed "invert." How much of that vitriol, Gray wonders, has been distilled from his own suffering and self-recrimination during these months? Would Raffalovich feel so exposed if he were not now known as the companion of the man who was once Dorian Gray? Or had he not witnessed Gray's anguish at the news that his brother, William, had torn up his photograph after the Wilde trials as a protest against the life he had been living?[73] (Thirty years later, when Raffalovich tries to explain to a young friend disconcerted by his admission of "approval" of the verdict and sentencing of Oscar Wilde, he will write: "If you had lived through that time and seen at least one tortured victim as I did, and sinister shadows cast on whole tracts of human relationships, you would have understood my feeling . . ."[74])

As Gray knew, Raffalovich had been refining his theories on what he called "unisexuality" since 1894, when he had responded to a questionnaire set by Lacassagne on inversion. A series of articles followed, of which the Wilde piece was only one. But in the wake of the Wilde trials and the growing public consciousness of the "invert" as a distinct type of person—a man with a woman's spirit, usually an artist—Raffalovich decided to write with a larger treatise in mind: it is to be published in 1896, again under the direction of Dr. Lacassagne, under the title *Uranisme et Unisexualité: Etude sur Différentes Manifestations de L'Instinct Sexuel*. What Raffalovich asserts here—with all the confidence of a "scientific" opinion, when "scientific" was a term more elastic than it is now—has been tested against the very pulse of experience: against his love for his friend, John Gray.

Raffalovich addresses his treatise to the medical profession as well as to the intelligent reader; but he is painfully aware of the kind of baggage implied in the original series title: the *Archives de L'anthropologie Criminelle*. Drawing on classical and Christian sources, Raffalovich defines a type of sexual inversion that is blameless and noble: that of "superior" or "sublime" inverts who seek to sublimate their sexual desires through friendship, religion, art. Opposed to this kind of invert is the pervert or sodomite, who engages in sexual acts—such as anal and oral sex—and who sometimes entertains a vulgar infatuation with Wagner. Disconcertingly, Raffalovich here invokes exactly the homophobic diatribes he seeks to challenge: "We have arrived here at the borders of madness and crime," he asserts; "passive sodomy is akin to madness and active sodomy to crime."[75] Oscar Wilde personifies this kind of criminal madness; he is the very type of the "inferior" invert who acts as a "corrupter of youth." The "superior" invert, on the other hand, seeks, in the name of Platonic love, what Raffalovich terms "sexual decentralization."[76] (More than a century later, one commentator is to observe: "in an account of sexual development that reads startlingly like Freud *avant la lettre,* Raffalovich describes this libidinal decentralization as a rejection of adult genitality and a return to the sentimental friendships and polymorphous sensuality of childhood."[77]) What Raffalovich seeks is a return to "childish innocence," the kind of innocence he has reinvented with his friend John Gray. "With his chosen friend, conversations, tender caresses, long intimacies, all help to curb, suppress, annihilate this feverish insurrection of the flesh."[78] "The loves of uranians," Raffalovich notes ruefully, "are very frequently without sexual satisfaction."[79]

Gray recalls how they have struggled with the fevers of the flesh; he has had to ward off Raffalovich, he knows, but out of those deflections, which are inherently part of his own nature, they have come to the point where Raffalovich too has acknowledged the necessity of being chaste—and has even found it less difficult than he had anticipated. After all, Raffalovich admitted to him one day, "it is easy to be chaste if one has a friend who is chaste."[80]

Raffalovich is content with this arrangement, which liberates them both from the condemnation of society and the law, if not wholly from the suspicion of the public. For his own part, Gray finds it a relief. (A few years later, separated from Raffalovich, Gray is to write him about a professional dispute that Raffalovich has had with the psychologist Charles Féré: "I am curious to know if Féré agrees with me about the overwhelming, superabounding-and-all-that-is-superlative-importance of the first sexual act. All the passion of making the discovery that man is naturally chaste comes back to me."[81])

In the "sublime invert" Raffalovich invents a kind of sanctified homosexual, going so far as to speak of uranianism as a "vocation." It is Gray's translations that allow him to locate a prototype of such a lover, in the adoration, for instance, of the virginal invert for the "young God, naked and bleeding, disfigured and transfigured, wounded and wounding,"[82] which is the love of Christ's own body. Raffalovich writes:

> The soul of man, affianced to Christ, has throughout the centuries expressed its desire and its adoration in poetry and prose. Angelus Silesius, Friedrich von Spee, Saint John of the Cross, Saint Teresa, and so many other illustrious and gracious figures have languished in love on the shoulder of the Divine Lover. Hafiz has approached the "obscure night" of Saint John of the Cross. One might well read these poems and not recognize that it is the soul of man that cries out and clasps the feet, the hands, the merciful flanks, a lover of the sort that Krafft-Ebing describes in his *Psychopathia Sexualis* as suffering from sadism, masochism, and unisexuality.[83]

After dinner, by the fire, Raffalovich reads to Gray his latest installment on uranianism and unisexuality. Have you not been the one to teach me, dear brother, how the fire of sexual instinct can become refined into the effulgence of Divine Love? Look at your translations: at how the mystics express their love of God through erotic effusions. Of course, that eminent psychologist Charcot and his followers use this connection between the lives of the saints and the modern science of sexology to condemn priests as frustrated celibates. But I do not see it that way. Surely many priests are born inverts who have transformed their sexual urges into the very language of devotion, making of their inverted nature a vocation which mirrors the Love of God.

Look at St. John of the Cross, to whom you have introduced me. Do you know this passage?

There are people of a frail and delicate complexion, and of a nature tender and sensitive. From the time they really occupy themselves with spiritual things, their nature experiences a very great sweetness, and it is from this sweetness that these emotions come. When the spirit and the senses enjoy possession of each other, each part of the man is thereby excited to pleasure according to his particular characteristics, knowing: the spirit, or spiritual pleasure, which comes from God; and the senses, or sensible pleasure, which is born of the flesh.[84]

Surely if "one studied the mystics, the sectaries, the Church fathers, one would find for the superior invert a wisdom and an elevation and a practice altogether comparable to Plato in its self-sacrifice—and for the weak invert, a discipline."[85]

We were weak once, Gray smiles ruefully, watching André's bright eyes glance into the fire. We have at last found our discipline. Do you recall the poem I wrote for us? "The Two Sinners"? With you as Godfrey, signifying "earth"; myself as Oliver, signifying "air"?[86] Or our poem "Repentence"?[87] But now we burn as brightly as cold gems, in the fire of the spirit, and so

> O lord, remain, with us, remain;
> Ignite in us a flaming vane;
> Inflame the pulses of the brain
> Fulfill the world with sweet again.[88]

Raffalovich turns to him, bright from the fire, and recites back the divine poem of Jacopone da Todi:

> For thee, for love, I languish and I burn.
> I sigh for thy embraces soon and late.
> When thou are hence, I live and die; I yearn
> And groan and whine in very piteous state
> To find thee; and my heart, at thy return,
> Fainteth with fear lest aught should separate.[89]

Gray smiles now, without bitterness: "Consume my heart with love," he murmurs. And so it has been, dear brother; our hearts have been consumed with another love.

Having arrived at this consummation, where one writer is virtually thinking the same thoughts as the other, why then is it such a shock that Raffalovich suddenly—as it seems—one bright January day in 1896, decides to be received into the bosom of the True Church? (Canon Gray still recalled the jolt almost forty years later, writing shortly after Raffalovich's death:

> His was a conversion *coup de foudre*. His friend from boy-hood, Florence Truscott Gribbell, had, in the glory of her young fifties, been received into the Church. There was a "ghastly row", as the phrase of the day was; but the mettle-some youth soon compromised, watched Chère Amie to see that she did not injure her health through medieval pen-ances, saw to her Friday menu, and started every Sunday from South Audley Street at a quarter to eleven to walk round the park. She might report at lunch who had preached or whom she had seen at Mass. No reply. Then, all but suddenly, André was himself a Catholic. No one can disclose how this came about.

But, Gray added, with "thoroughness which knew no exceptions he was soon conversant with Catholic devotions, Catholic ways."[90]) Raffalovich was formally received on 3 February 1896.

Now working in a completely Catholic household and undoubtedly swayed by its influence, Raffalovich's Swiss butler, Joseph Tobler, converted to the Roman Church shortly thereafter.[91]

Nothing seems to have prepared Raffalovich's circle for this abrupt rejection of his native Judaism. After all, as many knew, his father had fled Odessa for Paris before Raffalovich was born in order to escape the czar's edict that all Jews convert or leave the country.[92] So his family must have been painfully surprised, even though Raffalovich's sister, Sophie, had formally converted to Catholicism before her marriage to the Irish member of Parliament, William O'Brien, some six years previously.

Of all his acquaintance, it was William Butler Yeats who told the most embroidered story. "According to Yeats, Gray and Raffalovich had gone cruising in the Mediterranean in a yacht which they had painted black and christened *Iniquity*. They put in at a small Italian port where some religious festival was in full swing; and there it was that their change of heart took place quite suddenly."[93] Of course, when Gray heard this story, he burst out laughing; most of his friends knew of his earlier conversion; such gorgeous nonsense could only be taken as amusing. But where Yeats's story is acute, Gray acknowledges, is in its instinct for the agonized self-recrimination that harrows him, even as he sees that he is not the only "tortured victim" in the wake of the Wilde debacle.

Another has already made his way to Raffalovich's door. In the spring of 1895, Aubrey Beardsley too had become a casualty of the public hysteria over the Wilde trials. When the press reported that Oscar Wilde was arrested with a novel in yellow paper covers under his arm, the game was up. A very frightened John Lane unceremoniously dismissed Beardsley from his post as art editor of *The Yellow Book,* removing all trace of his projected drawings for the next issue.[94] (Writing as an old man, Raffalovich remembered how he had been persuaded by Beardsley's sister, Mabel, to go to hear him lecture: "The slender youth did not attract me nor his lecture."

> Not many weeks later, when I returned to South Audley Street from an early call in Park Lane, . . . I found a strange visitor in the drawing room, near Gustave Moreau's Sappho. "Mr. Beardsley said he would wait," I was told. He had travelled through the night from Paris. He was in a fix. His sister had suggested his consulting me. Could I advise, help? I heard his difficulty. We conversed amicably. He returned to Paris, and when he came back our intimacy started . . .[95])

From that morning in April 1895, Beardsley's welfare, in all its aspects, becomes for Raffalovich a major concern.

Their intimacy begins in May, when Beardsley returns to London to resume his work. Raffalovich begins to court him. (In later life, Raffalovich recalls:

When I remember him I remember his youth: but at the time
I was thirty and he twenty-three . . . Of course I admired him;
he arrested me like wrought iron and like honeysuckle;
hardness, elegance, charm, variety. I delighted of course, in
his fame, in his notoriety. Wherever we went he was gazed at.
They sang about him at the Gaiety; Max caricatured him;
strangers credited him with unfathomed perversity; acquaintances all recognised his simple boyishness.[96])

Raffalovich is in his element. There are invitations to lunch,
to teas, to the theater and the opera, invitations to join Raffalovich
in Berlin; Beardsley refuses the last: "it will be impossible with all
the work I have to get through."[97] And gifts: chocolates, walking
sticks, a sonnet, flowers from Goodyear's, Bond Street's most
elegant florist. As well as books, of every sort and description,
from a "delicious" Crashaw to the latest Huysmans novel. When
Raffalovich produces his tract *L'Uranisme,* Beardsley sees it before
publication; and Raffalovich has taken the trouble to read aloud
at least part of "L'Affaire Oscar Wilde" to Beardsley from manuscript.[98] Beardsley shares Raffalovich's distaste for Wilde; the
aftermath of the *Salome* drawings has left a permanent rift between
the two artists.

Inwardly, Raffalovich rejoices in finding so perfect a kindred
spirit. Part of him even acknowledges that Beardsley at last allows
him to have his cake and to eat it to: to enjoy the pleasures of
notoriety while indulging his keen interest in the demimonde
without any slur on his consummate respectability. After all, is he
not now at last a genuine patron? To an artist of acclaimed genius?
Raffalovich relishes the delicacy of his position.

Raffalovich is also capable of conducting himself with consummate tact. Rather than offer money outright, he proposes token
commissions. He asks that a portrait be made; it is planned—"it
must be in pastel on brown paper—full length,"[99] but never
completed. Beardsley undertakes to illustrate a playlet published by
Gray and Raffalovich, *A Northern Aspect,* as well as a new translation
by Gray of Benjamin Constant's *Adolphe.* Neither materializes.
Beardsley did come up with a frontispiece for Raffalovich's latest

volume of poems, *The Thread and the Path,* with an illustration of the first line of the first poem—"Set in the heart as in a frame Love liveth"—he drew a magnificent winged Amor set in a heart which in turn is part of an elaborate candelabrum. Raffalovich liked it, but the publisher refused the picture, claiming that the figure was hermaphroditic. Beardsley tried to soften the blow by explaining to Raffalovich that it had been rejected because it was a "nude Amor." In fact, Beardsley had read Raffalovich's epicene poems correctly; but in the end the book was published without a frontispiece.

In the beginning, Beardsley is swept along by Raffalovich's effusive concern. ("We called each other Mentor and Télémaque," Raffalovich recalled, "more out of affectionate playfulness than because he could then brook interference or guidance.")[100] Beardsley occasionally gets himself into difficulty by forgetting the odd lunch invitation; so sensitive is Raffalovich to any slight that he refers to this as a "declaration of war," which baffles Beardsley. But for all the business of commissions and publications, all the overheated exchanges and endless gifts, particularly of books, theirs is not a literary friendship. ("My conversion in January, 1896, did not long precede his first haemorrhage of the lungs, 'and the cloud began to gather which meant death in the end,'" Raffalovich recalled.)[101] By the end of January, Beardsley has stopped addressing Raffalovich as "Mentor," just as some months before, Beardsley had abandoned the sobriquet "Télémaque." The scene has shifted— and darkened. From this time on, Raffalovich and Gray are caught up in the drama of a protracted death watch.

Gray initially plays a minor part. His relations with Beardsley are cooler, confined by their admiration for each other's art. (Writing of Beardsley immediately after his death, Gray observed that "one finds in the force of his inclinations an assurance of his genius.") For his part, Beardsley urges Gray to write: specifically, for a new magazine, *The Savoy,* which he hopes will replace the now emasculated *Yellow Book.* Arthur Symons is the driving force behind the new venture; Beardsley, as art editor, sets out to persuade Gray to contribute. Gray submits "The Forge," a vivid meditation on his early days as a metal-turner's apprentice at the Woolwich Arsenal; it is published in the 1896 issue.

In early July, after receiving *Spiritual Poems*, Beardsley writes Leonard Smithers, one of the editors: "Gray has just sent me a copy of a new book of verses. They are *really admirable* & might be reviewed (I should have thought) in our monthly. I wish Gray was asked more frequently to contribute for us, he is one of the few younger men worth printing."[102] Arthur Symons too admires Gray's work, praising his recent translations of Goethe and of Neitzsche's poems—the first such translation to appear in English.[103] (But some tension must have arisen between them, for Gray in later years is to refer to Symons as "by me in the past, so much disliked & then liked.")[104] For whatever reason, more of Gray's poems do not manage to appear in *The Savoy* before November, when Symons announces its imminent demise. The spirit which infused *The Yellow Book*—the very spirit which infused the movement called "decadence"—has died with the imprisonment of the "High Priest of Decadence," Oscar Wilde.

Another death is to follow. After the first flush of intimacy, Raffalovich and Beardsley grow more distant after the new year. Although he has frequent and dramatic collapses of health, Beardsley finds himself well enough to work—that is, well enough to live. His letters to Raffalovich become often perfunctory, sometimes merely polite. But after January 1897, a new note enters the relationship. Gifts of chocolate and books, at least one gift of money, make their way to Bournemouth, where Beardsley has retired for his health. "Your sweet friendliness," Beardsley writes, somewhat dutifully, "helps me over such alarming difficulties."[105] In February he writes—of Raffalovich's Swiss butler, who had converted to Catholicism a little more than a year after his master: "I am most envious of Joseph [Tobler], whose conduct of life puts no barriers in his way to the practical acceptance of what he believes in . . . Do not think, my dear André, that your kind words fall on such barren ground. However I fear I am not a very fruitful soil; I only melt to harden again."[106]

Gray and Raffalovich—they work now as very much a pair—spend a few days in Bournemouth this February of 1897. While there, Raffalovich arranges for a Father David Bearne to visit Beardsley. It is a brilliant choice. Bearne is not only a convert, but a writer of boy's books. Is it the suppressed child in each that ensures he and Beardsley hit it off immediately? Shortly after this visit, Mrs. Beardsley sought out kind Mr. Raffalovich to confess her distressing financial circumstances. Aubrey is visibly dying, but to pay the rent, Mrs. Beardsley must go out to work, leaving her son unattended. True to his generosity, Raffalovich immediately proposes a regular monthly payment, so that the mother can attend to her critically ill son. Beardsley writes immediately to thank him for such "wonderfully kind help . . . offered with so much intention and so much gentleness." In helping with "so much judgement," Beardsley observes gratefully, Raffalovich is helping him "doubly."[107]

When Leonard Smithers, who had been commissioning drawings from him, visits Beardsley in the last days of February, he finds stacked near the bed numerous lives of the saints; Beardsley confides to Smithers about the frequent visits from Father Bearne. No wonder, as he teases Smithers a few days later, his visitor is "haunted . . . with visions of designing Jesuits."[108] A few weeks later, in early March 1897, Beardsley admits for the first time that he is dying. His doctor had recommended against going to London; even Beardsley could read the signs. "I may not have many months now to live," he confesses to Smithers.[109]

As the winds of March grow shrill and Beardsley grows weaker, Raffalovich's solicitude begins to justify the name of "brother," with which he opens his "kind letters." Living with the daily specter of death, Beardsley's doubts begin to pale; finally, he casts them out. On 30 March 1897, Beardsley announces to Raffalovich: "Tomorrow, dear André, the kind name of brother you give me will have a deeper significance."[110] The following day, Father Bearne receives Beardsley into the Roman Catholic Church, an event which he names as "the most important step" in his life. Three days later, he writes Raffalovich that the Blessed Sacrament was brought to him in bed. "It was a moment of profound joy of gratitude & emotion. I gave myself up entirely, utterly to feelings of happiness, & even the knowledge of my own unworthiness only seemed to add fuel to the flame that warmed & illuminated my heart."

"Oh how earnestly I have prayed that that flame may never die out!"[111]

Beardsley is to die almost exactly a year later.

During the previous week, Gray and Raffalovich had been at Beardsley's bedside. In an "obituary memoir" for a French journal, Gray recalls: "Fifteen months ago, in Bournemouth, he was thought to be dying: his whole appearance condemned him. Nevertheless he kept repeating: If I went to Paris, I would recover." Shortly afterwards, Beardsley and his mother travel to Paris at Raffalovich's expense and then, with Raffalovich's own doctor in tow, continue on to Paris. "After arriving by some miracle at the Quai Voltaire," Gray recalls, "his expectations seemed to be realised. He made a recovery." At the end of April, Beardsley is joined in Paris by John Gray, Florence Gribbell, and Raffalovich, who are on their way to holiday in Touraine. Visiting him in his hotel, they discover "numbers of people frequented his sickroom and spread hope there. For a short time even he regained the strength to handle his industrious pen."[112] Beardsley welcomes his patrons warmly: "It's amusing to have them," he writes his sister Mabel. "Yesterday we had a charming lunch party at Lapérouse. Rachilde [Madame Alfred Valette, critic and novelist] and some longhaired monsters of the Quartier were with us. They all presented me with their books (which are quite unreadable)."[113] "It is like a dream that we lunched with Rachilde and her husband, and Mlle. Fanny and Alfred Jarry," wrote Raffalovich some thirty years later.[114] Raffalovich also attempts to arrange a meeting between Beardsley and Huysmans, believing them kindred spirits, but in this one plan he appears to have failed.

Meanwhile, in Paris, Beardsley is not the only object of his patronage. Raffalovich has of course told his mother about John Gray; they have stayed with her a few times, quietly, at the elegant apartments on the Avenue Hoche. But on this occasion, Madame Raffalovich organizes a large party in his honor, in which Gray is to be introduced formally to the family's "lions." Of the many important figures from the worlds of science and politics, there is one in whom Gray immediately recognizes a friend, Thadée Natanson, whose brother, Alexandre, had established the remarkable *Revue Blanche*. Gray knew that since its founding in 1891, this journal had attracted every important contemporary artist in

France: not only Verlaine, Mallarmé, and Laforgue, but also Cézanne, Gaugin, Toulouse-Lautrec, Bonnard, and Vuillard. Now Gray's old friend Fénéon, imprisoned and then released after his alleged part in the anarchist bombing of the Restaurant Foyot, has become the chief editor. He immediately takes it upon himself to persuade Gray to contribute—perhaps as London correspondent? He contributes a short story in passable French, "Daphné."[115] It is something of a triumph of Gray's new "clinical" style. (When he wrote it, he could not foresee that his next contribution would be an obituary of Aubrey Beardsley.)

In the end, Beardsley's understanding of theater comes to his aid: he is to become a performer of his own demise. He even draws a picture of it in "The Death of Pierrot"—and himself as a small, childlike creature engulfed within a huge bed. "Undoubtedly," Gray writes of it, "the dying Pierrot is Beardsley; and in the group of people who tiptoe near to the bed, finger on lips, he has quite simply turned to the advantage of his art the half gestures and the hidden compassion that a discerning invalid is aware of chancing upon around him. But it is the symbol itself which interests the artist, and not what is symbolised."[116]

In his drawings, as in his letters, Beardsley creates a theater for himself, and conversion is part of its drama. But so is the thinking against, the skepticism, the waspishness which have always given Beardsley's sweetness its sting. At times the effusions of his "Russian Prince" grate on his nerves. At times the pressure of the two, both Gray and Raffalovich, apostate and new converts, would bear too heavily on his delicate and subtle nature. Is he to be a vindication of their newfound faith? Is he to be their celebrated victory over the pagan excesses of decadence? Certainly there are times he senses—and resents—his role; he is quite capable of writing, "How good you are to me, dear André, a brother in fact out of a fairy tale," while confiding to his sister Mabel some months later: "If A. [André] is all right in January I need not get rid of them [Gray and Raffalovich] in any indecent haste."[117]

By the last day of November 1897, a week after this letter, Gray officially resigns from his position as librarian in the Foreign Office, bidding his colleagues—and the smoky fire—adieu. In the next month, he leaves for a week's retreat with the Jesuits at Manresa House, Roehampton, seeking in prayer a new direction for his life. He prays too for Beardsley, who grows increasingly weaker during the first months of the winter, disguising his terror with a stoical, if pathetic, gaiety. (Gray later wrote of Beardsley's "reputation for sweetness and resignation . . . during the martyrdom of his last eight days, those days of choking blood coughed up in torrents, and of painful attempts to cure."[118]) Nine days before his death, Beardsley scrawls in a note to Leonard Smithers:

> Jesus is our Lord & Judge.
>
> Dear Friend,
>   I implore you to destroy *all* copies of Lysistrata & bad drawings. Show this to Pollitt & conjure him to do same. By all that is holy—*all* obscene drawings.
>   Aubrey Beardsley
>   In my death agony.[119]

"Nothing could be done to save him," Mrs. Beardsley writes; "his marvelous patience and courage amid very great sufferings . . . touched all who were near him."[120] Beardsley dies, having received the last rites, on 16 March 1898 in Menton. He is only twenty-five.

For *La Revue Blanche*, Gray writes an obituary memoir prescient in naming Beardsley a "genius." As one would expect, Gray defines Beardsley's artistic gifts precisely. Implicitly, Gray responds to the taunts of "degenerate" which follow Beardsley everywhere: his love of the French, the foreign, the exotic.

> For he loved Paris in a direct and special way. All that he observed there with such clarity, he set down. He had an extraordinarily precise vision. And with this gift he wanted to be able to single out the most delicate lines as far as the eye could reach; which, in London, at least, is difficult.
>   One finds in the force of his inclinations an assurance of his genius. This was a man who never hesitated: for all his delicate appearance and awkward gestures, he had the stamp

of a great man. All that he was, all that he did, was good. He laid down his views. And, for him, the matter was settled, decided once for all.[121]

Gray's appreciation of the daemonic in Beardsley goes far beyond assertion that "All that he was, all that he did, was good." For Gray is alone in understanding that Beardsley was not merely a phenomenon in his own right, but that he would stamp his name on a whole era.

With Beardsley's death, that era comes to an end. With it too, dies at last, in the public world, "Dorian" Gray: dandy, poet—the most decadent of decadents. Pierre Louÿs and Fénéon unconsciously inscribe Dorian's own obituary when each write separately to Gray that his reputation has been made in Paris as the importer of the fashionable new word: "smart." Its triviality is a fitting epitaph to John Gray's decade as dandy.[122]

With Wilde imprisoned and Beardsley dead, Gray considers the demise of his reputation as the man who was Dorian Gray complete. (A confidante of Gray's later years recounts how Father Gray had told her of the hours after he received news of Beardsley's death—wandering around Piccadilly aimlessly, murmuring to himself: "I must change my life. I must change my life."[123])

It is summer again. Gray lies in the hammock beneath the pines in Weybridge, waving his cigarette airily in its amber holder, contemplating the swans on the river, recalling his twin poems, "Leda" and "The Swan." There Leda moves, as if in the summer's heat, through an atmosphere of oppressive heaviness, the claustrophobia of a world which operates, like the jewel she wears, by the law of "exact similitude":

> All palpitant and dazed,
> Across the lawn doth Leda haste,
> To where the dreaming water lies;
> Therein to cool her mirrored eyes.

She moves as if in a dream, caught in a world of Swedenborgian correspondences:

> The awful heavens burn
> Repeated in the hollows; yearn
> With ruddier purpose, to unfold
> The swelling destiny they hold.

> And, in a certain place,
> Suspended on the water's face,
> The doubled swans sit motionless.
> For ease against the summer's stress.

Here—in this visionary paradise, the very world of doubling and equivocal appearance—is the world Dorian Gray has made for himself: a world of mirror images and doubles; his face in the mirrors of the Café Royal; his name created for him by a master, in a book. Now in this world, the god appears, changed into a swan. There is no resistance; Leda is lured into the pool and, with "timid hand leans out/ And folds his downy breast about." And then,

> The swan and Leda break
> Triumphant the spreading lake,
> . . . .
> Till sudden lightnings split
> The burning sky, and empty it;
> And raucously as eagles cry
> An eagle screamed across the sky.[124]

As the burning sky darkens and heat lightning plays above the pines, Gray gathers himself up to go into the house. Moving away from the lake, from the world of London and that of art, he moves away from the world created in his own image to a world simply accepted, no longer distorted by what he now sees as an empty and perverse form of will. (Some years later, he will explain to Raffalovich the peace that has overtaken him as priest:

> Do you think there is an interesting psychological study to be
> made of the religious attitude of mind? . . . My own conversion
> in my mind nearly exactly coincides with the action of passing

from a world of dreams to a world of *things. Thus* my ideal was the *inexact* (au fond) *now* it is the exact. I deliberately wanted desired things not as they were *but as I wanted them.* Now I want them *as they are*[.] All this is very badly expressed.[125])

Inwardly, Gray submits to the voices burning within him. Published by Ricketts as *Spiritual Poems*, they puzzle his friends. On receiving the first *Blue Calendar* in December 1895, Dowson had written Gray a letter of praise. Yet even Dowson—himself a convert—confides to Arthur Symons some seven months later: "John Gray has sent me his new book 'Spiritual Poems.' I can not determine whether his mysticism is sincere or merely a pose— but I begin to think it is the former."[126] About this time, Gray's former acquaintance from the Vale, William Rothenstein, reports how he saw Dorian Gray wandering around Chelsea under the name of John Gray.[127] And from Pierre Louÿs comes the shocked response to Gray's announcement of his intention to enter the priesthood:

> Mon cher ami,
>
> What does this extraordinary vocation mean and how can you think that you have nothing more to say when you have just published the volumes I have received? I understand that you are going to settle in Rome; happiness is a hot-house plant which does not grow in our wretched countries. But why become a religious there, even if you no longer wish to write?[128]

Gray discovers in himself a fatal disillusion with words. His work as editor and translator of poems over the last few years "stirs an old craving for the impossible in poetry—something to be got from words & images quite exterior to words & thought."[129] In *Spiritual Poems* he had reached the limits of a language. In his own turning to the life of the spirit he had learned from Huysmans "a deliberate rejection of symbol."[130] Both his stories about conver- sion, "Niggard Truth" and "Light," describe the effect of an "attouchement divin": not as a spiritual crisis but as a germ growing with irresistible force, so assuming the direction, so absorbing the attention, of its subject, that suddenly he is aware only of the fact that he *believes*, with not a trace in memory of how he passed from the somnambulance of everyday life to the anxieties of an awakening faith.

In his library, Father Gray kept a copy of the *Pageant*, which had published "Niggard Truth." To the endpapers, two press cuttings had been secured. One describes John Gray's work as "interesting." The other describes it as "silly, unsuitable, senseless, incompetent, affected, precious, laboured, ineffective and ignorant."[131] Father Gray relished such contradictions. They also vindicated his rejection of his work as an artist, when, in the closing months of 1898, John Gray resolved the question of the role of his art by announcing he would never write again.[132] Shortly afterwards, he took his final leave from London to study for the priesthood at Scots College, Rome.

The man who was Dorian Gray had died. To rise again.

5 | LA VITA NUOVA

(OCTOBER 1896–APRIL 1907)

IN OCTOBER, THE SUN IN ROME IS STILL WARM. John Gray rests for a moment before the altar of a small medieval church, San Clemente. The mosaics shimmer in the mellow autumn light. His thoughts follow the path by which he has reached this resting place, traveling from London by a roundabout route; stopping first in Regensburg in Bavaria to visit his two younger sisters; then making his way to the Holy City by way of Verona and Bologna, where he made a visit to the tomb of Saint Dominic. He had discovered in himself an attraction for the Blackfriars, who have custody of this particular church. Perhaps it is after all one of the enthusiasms caught from Raffalovich, who in order to regularize his spiritual devotions has this autumn become a lay member of the Dominican Order, taking the name "Brother Sebastian." Or perhaps it is only part of the extraordinary sympathy which now exists between them. They call each other "brother" and "child." They act as both father and son to each other. Had his health allowed, André confessed that he himself would like to have become a priest.[1] As it is, it has been agreed between them that John Gray will become a priest for both of them.

In the dazzle of the late October sun, the mosaics of the apse seem to flicker and move, the gold gleaming within the peacocks' tails and glinting behind the deer lapping from the stream. "As the hart panteth after the water brooks, so panteth my soul after thee,

O God." It is the only regret of his conversion, Gray muses, that with it he lost the King James Version of the Bible; the Douay is no match for it. Now the old words fill him with a yearning—is it for home, or rest, or for God? He hopes now to find rest in giving his life to God.

What life I have left, he thinks suddenly, in a moment of pain. The past can never be changed; it lurks like a dark night escaped, a night ready to envelop him again, a night against which he must hold all the powers of light. Will he ever be able to escape his past? Already Raffalovich has reported to him by letter that rumors are circulating around London that, of all the seminaries, Gray had chosen to attend Scots College because he was attracted by its uniform, the most colorful in Rome: purple cassock, red cincture, and black *soprano,* or robe. The wide-brimmed beaver hat is enough to mark out one of their seminarians from all others in the city. Raffalovich had replied tartly to one such speculation that Gray was attending Scots College because of his Scots descent. But Gray knows already, with the dark wisdom of foresight, that it would be said he chose this college "out of abhorrence of 'Naughty Nineties' memories."[2]

For the nineties, although not yet officially over—and already advertised as "naughty"—are as dead as the dodo. The very phrase evokes poor Oscar. Gray gazes again at the apse mosaic, glittering with all the subdued rich splendor of the light of heaven itself, of a field of grass glazed with dew, full of the promise of morning. What divine mind knew that the Triumph of the Cross would bring with it the spring freshness of peacocks and deer and the wealth of acanthus leaves, curling against the gold? He knew, even as Dorian, that he nursed within himself a love of the visible world that would scandalize a Manichee.

That is it, he suddenly thinks. I am a heretic, but one who has become Christian. And will the heretic become subdued in the Christian, or the dandy within the priest? Surely, as certainly as this building, one will be raised on the foundations of the other, until they are absorbed, one layer into the other; distinct, but part of the same continuum. Like San Clemente itself. He had come to meet a Dominican, one of the Irish order who were supervising the excavation of the church begun by a Father Mulooly in 1857. Beneath the exquisite twelfth-century basilica there had been uncovered a fourth-century church; below that again, ancient Roman buildings, which, although now flooded, appear to include a temple of Mithras: an all-male fertility cult which flourished during the age of Imperial Rome and a bitter rival to Christianity. Gray had read sufficiently in *The Golden Bough* not to be shocked at the precursors to Christianity in such cults as those of Mithras. He knows intuitively, also, that his own past as a member of another pagan cult could never be eradicated nor even sought to be eradicated, but must be kept painfully alive as a memento of those years in which he had denied God.

He thinks of the informal tour given by Father Lawless, a name mentioned to him by one of the Dominicans in England as a contact here. With diffident courtesy Father Lawless has asked a few quiet questions about Gray's origins, his bushy eyebrows raised slightly at the mention of London and the Brompton Oratory. And did you know Oscar Wilde? the good father had asked in his Irish accent; he was one of us you know—I mean Irish, of course, not Catholic. Gray confined himself to an enigmatic smile and a formal shake of the head which could have meant either I did not or I do not mean to answer. Poor man, said Father Lawless, and his poor mother, dead just two years ago, and his poor wife, dead just this spring. The wife's family were once known to my own relations in Dublin; but we never speak of them now in Ireland. Only in Rome, you know—where such things are forgiven.

Or too distant to matter, Gray muses. He had forgotten how small a place Dublin is, where everyone knows everyone else's business; when she married into the country, Raffalovich's sister Sophie had discovered that salient fact all over again. Gray is discovering too how easily it is assumed that, as a student at Scots College, he can be appropriated immediately as a fellow Celt, as well as a brother in religion.

That afternoon of 28 October 1898, John Gray makes his way to Scots College in the Via Quattro Fontane. From the first day he finds he is set apart, being, at thirty-two, almost twelve years older than the others in his class. (Some months later the disparity of age will permit Gray to undertake the shortened course of studies for those with "late vocations": a course of three-and-a-half years rather than the usual six. By temperament, Gray is always to remain to a certain degree aloof. One of the thirty students who later became a friend, Dominic Hart, recalled of Gray that "apart from special occasions such as concerts, at which he used to sing songs, he did not have a lot to do with the rest of us . . . There was always a certain remoteness about him, although he was, as we knew, very kind."[3]) He is not a rank outsider, however. He becomes close to Willie Mellon (afterwards to become Bishop of Galloway), whom he is to describe as "a solid mass of goodness," and to a younger student also named "John Gray," who goes by his middle name, Alan, to avoid confusion. (Will he ever escape these doubles? Gray wonders.) Since both Grays were good with their hands, after dinner it became a habit for them to hive "off to a lumber-room [where they] did carpentry, plumbing, etc." thus saving the rector, Monsignor Robert Fraser, many a lira.

As a new rector, Monsignor Fraser is concerned to turn the college around after years of neglect by the previous incumbent, the Very Reverend James Campbell. Monsignor Fraser clearly appreciates Gray's practical skills and good humor. Indeed, Gray himself is beginning to sound happy—although he keeps his letters to Raffalovich uniformly neutral, conscious always of the censor who would read both outgoing and incoming mail. One observer, Sophie O'Brien, clearly thought the new regime a trial to both Gray's temper and his health; indeed, André's letters this year are burdened with such concerns; Rome itself is a risk and the Scots College food is nothing short of penitential. What could be done by André was done. He sends food parcels regularly (were they censored, one wonders?): packages of game, caviar, asparagus, and so forth arrive almost weekly. Also, perhaps because of his age and status, Gray is permitted certain privileges denied the others: he is allowed to go out "in black," for instance, rather than wearing the conspicuous college uniform, which also means that he can go out unaccompanied, normally against the rules.[4] André has invoked his connections, arranged introductions: Gray attends the occasional dinners at the British Embassy, over which Lord Currie, the husband of

Raffalovich's friend, Lady Currie, presides. Gray is invited to dine with several prominent churchmen known to Raffalovich. He is already acquainted with many of the resident Dominicans; fellow students tease him when they see a black robe approaching, saying, "Look out Gray here's a friend."[5] Most importantly, André writes frequent letters full of the acceptable London gossip, news of friends and family, warm greetings to "the dear child" from Miss Gribbell, and endless advice about keeping well and content under difficult circumstances.

Despite all this, the Tridentine system, by which all Roman Catholic seminaries are at this time conducted, is very demanding. Its discipline is geared to instilling in the student the habit of absolute obedience, unquestioning attention to regime. To one student of nine years previously, Frederick William Rolfe, alias Baron Corvo, it proved insufferable. Expelled after a year on vague charges of unsuitability, he took his revenge in a partly autobiographical novel, *Hadrian the Seventh*. There Rolfe/Corvo, now the first English Pope, revisits "St. Andrews College." He recalls the ugly refectory and gaudy chapel, the library "where he had found impossible dust-begrimed books," and the large helpings of coarse food. His fellow students were "immature cubs mostly" or, more curtly, "savages," whose choice recreation was murdering stray cats: an act which encapsulated "the altogether pestilent pretentious bestial insanity of the place" which was his "homeless home."[6]

Gray hears about Rolfe, has read some of the stories, and knows, whatever the trials of Scots College, that he is no Baron Corvo, whom he regards as something between a legend and a joke.[7] After all, how much of Corvo's bitterness could be put down to the fact that he was expelled virtually at the insistence of his fellow students?[8] For all his fastidiousness, Gray finds himself at home. Coming out of a retreat on All Saints' Day, he writes Raffalovich of an extraordinary happiness which he takes as "indicative that I am in the right place & going the right road":

> From the moment of coming in here (5 minutes before the retreat began) I have been the object of special grace beyond any doubt or possibility of doubt. I have been as happy as ever

before, and the more the retreat unfolded the more I took to it: and the same thing applies to the life in general. I have grown quite used to this new order of things though I am still fully conscious of the *bien être;* but in the first hours & days I was quite beside myself to explain my ease & peace & satisfaction . . . Everyone seems very happy though I think I must be the happiest. My health is perfect; sleep appetite and everything quite up to the mark . . . I like the food . . . I take to my clothes perfectly. They are very comfortable. Of course you see it is simply the everyday garb of the 16th Century.[9]

The rigid scheduling of his daily activities suited Gray as well. A week later, he summarized it all for Raffalovich:

We rise at 5:30. Morning Prayers and meditation at 6. Mass at half past six. Breakfast at 7:15. Start to schools 7:45. For me Moral [Theology] at 8 Natural Theology at 9 till 10. Go back & read till 11:45. Then Litanies at 12 dinner 1:30 study 2:15 (at present) start for schools 1 hour of Metaphysics. Thence to the Pincio. 5:15 Ave and visit to the B. Sacrament. 5:30 study 7:45 Rosary. Litany of Loreto. 8 supper. After supper no one may go to his room without permission 9:15 night prayers. Every Thursday is a playday i.e. no schools but study, morning trip to Pincio for an hour & what one . . . likes in the afternoon. There are extra playdays too. On Thursdays we turn housemaid and "do" our room. We make our bed & shave between Mass & breakfast. Clean our boots between breakfast & schools. We talk at breakfast but not at other meals. On Saturday we sing plain chant and those who are ignorant have drill about how to behave in choir . . . I continue getting on well & even face the thought of being asked questions in class without going mad at once. Best love to Miss Gribbell from whom I long to hear.
Yours ever afftely,
Jacopone[10]

These are the letters of a happy child. The ease and satisfaction with which Gray submits himself to this regime does not extend, however, to his academic work, which elicits a new humility. Soon Gray confesses to Raffalovich that "It is a fact that I have never had a moment of self-complacency about my present work—and I lived largely on complacency once."[11] The studies are a jolt to his self-esteem; the rapid lectures in Latin reduce him almost to despair. But the quasimonastic rule of the college appeals to Gray: it releases him from self-preoccupation, from personality, even from conscious thought. What it seeks to instill is a systematic distrust of oneself, one's mind, one's instinctive life. After two years at Scots College, Gray confesses to Raffalovich that "now I am in such a confirmed & salutary state of mistrusting all my own thoughts & listening to what others have to say that I have practically no thoughts at all as I dare say you have found out. You always ask how I am & I say: never better."[12]

Yet under the still, white purity of this new life there lurk crevasses: the pits of remorse. Occasionally Gray falls into them, as when he writes Raffalovich in February of his first year:

> On the 14th is the anniversary of my baptism. It will be, as far as I can make it so, a day of oblation and resolute resignation to the will of God. I suppose the longer I live the more tragic each anniversary of this day will become. I went through instruction as blindly and indifferently as ever anyone did and immediately I began a course of sin compared with which my previous life was innocence. The sequence of miracles which has brought me where I now am is beyond my comprehension. To contemplate it means to realise as much dread as security.[13]

To which Raffalovich replies,

> Mon frère, mon frère, be happy and well. Your past can be explained in this sense: that you were baptized because you were God's and had to come back from [sic] him. Think how many saints have been brought back from sins against the known truth: St. Andrew Cossini, B. Bernard of Scammacra, etc., etc., against a truth known and practised.[14]

The shadow of the Master is always present. Not like a decomposing picture in the attic, but as a picture of himself young and beautiful and desired. It is like a grief, but for someone still living. About five weeks later, Gray responds to the news of the death of Wilde's brother: "Poor Willie Wilde: & poor t'other one too, he was foolishly attached to Willie when he was ill in any way."[15] As much as he wishes it behind him, the past is not always past, but has a way of ambushing him, as on that day the Scots College students are walking to Santa Maria in Aracoeli. Their intention is to pray before the miraculous Christ Child whose wooden image is said to have the powers of resurrecting the dead. Moving up the slope of marble steps, some instinct makes John Gray suddenly look up: and there, staring down at him are, unmistakably, Wilde's friend of friends, Robbie Ross, together with a slim, curly-headed boy, arrested in their descent: "both parties looked at me as a *bête curieuse*," Gray dryly reports to Raffalovich, well aware of the spectacle he made in purple robe, red belt, and large plate-shaped beaver hat.[16] He had not counted on the wooden babe's powers to be so potent.

Scarcely more than a year later, Gray is again walking, in company, in the Vatican Gardens. Although only April and not quite two weeks after Easter, it is burning hot. He had chosen the gardens at random, as being convenient and, he hoped, deserted, being officially open only to the Pope and his attendants, seminarians in Rome, and, for reasons he could never discover, only two special groups of pilgrims, the Bohemians and the Portuguese. In fact, the gardens seem deserted, and in that "desolate park, with its faded Louis XIV gardens, its sombre avenues, its sad woodland," he wanders silently with his companion, who honors his sudden speechless melancholy.[17] A peacock screams, and, looking up, Gray finds in his path "a large form planted as if to waylay him." Beside this figure, a slim gilt youth, who looks up instinctively to the man beside him. Following his gaze, Gray finds himself staring into the large, haggard face of Oscar Wilde, silent, expressionless—waiting. But for what? ("There was complete silence," Gray confided to a friend years later: "but mockery dangled it.")[18]

Shaken, Gray returns hastily to his room and to the silence of the Thursday play day, in which he is sure not to be interrupted.

Taking up pen and paper, he writes out words which have been haunting him; they shape themselves as a poem:

"The Lord Looks at Peter"
My lips were like my steps a song,
and all my thought of Follow me;
but when the march was over long
I turned away from thee.

When not alone thine eyes, my God,
but all thy sacred body wept,
and every tear was ruby blood,
I shut my eyes and slept.

A night alarm; a weaponed crowd;
one blow, and with the rest I ran;
I warmed my hands, and said aloud:
I never knew the man.[19]

In his past he had betrayed Christ; but in breaking with Oscar, he had betrayed his past. Yet he feels with every instinct that his only hope is within the True Church, within the arms of God. And so it is not harshness but love that urges Gray to bring others into her fold. Of Oscar: he had always regarded him as a secret Catholic; and perhaps his presence in Rome now confirms it. News of Oscar's death six months later comes as no shock; for in the moment they had met he looked as if he had died already. (No letter from Gray registers Oscar's death nor rumors of his deathbed conversion to Catholicism, although in later years Father Gray will be known on rare occasions to refer to "poor Oscar.") A month before their last encounter, Gray heard of "poor Dowson's death." "I used to like him very much & his poetry more if possible,"[20] Gray writes in requiescat. Of the death of Lionel Johnson—rumored to have fallen off a barstool—Gray is more detached, observing that it was a "funny case, it would be more so if one did not know that the man was as eccentric as he was."[21] His detachment however does not conceal his own consciousness of a near escape. He is a survivor who has learned that his own demands on himself for spiritual perfection can make him bitter over the waywardness of others and, finally, coldly indifferent if they persist.

A case in point is his friend from early days, Marmaduke Langdale. Gray can never forget that it was Marmaduke who, by bringing him into his family household in Brittany, had brought him to God. And yet Marmy, always the black sheep, had gone from bad to worse. Never gainfully employed for any length of time, after the turn of the century he had taken up "any kind of hack work which would enable him to earn a few shillings." At this point he began drinking seriously, and, after a flirtation with taking holy orders, Langdale compounded the "despair of his very respectable family" by marrying the divorced wife of an Anglican clergyman.[22]

During that crucial period when Langdale is considering joining the Congregation of the Oratory of St. Philip of Neri—a congregation of diocesan priests living in community, known informally as the "Filipinos"—Gray encourages him to come to Rome. By the end of 1899, however, Langdale changes his mind, prompting Gray to write Raffalovich in exasperation, "and so you despair of Marmion. Why doesn't Fr. James tell him that if he doesn't work he'll go to hell. The silly ass has to be a Filipino. I should like to see him *in the novitiate*. The daily screw would bring the sense to the surface."[23] (Three years later, Father Gray will write to his favorite among Langdale's sisters, Fanny, about Marmy's "lamentable disregard for his health." Although Marmy has "suffered terribly," Gray will counsel, "I advise you very strongly however to put a check on your impulse to make sacrifices on his account. A good deal of money has passed through Marmie's hands and so little remains to show for it . . . Though you may think this a cruel point of view I hope never the less you will consent to be guided by it."[24] If this was harsh advice, Gray accurately foresaw the inevitable outcome. Writing to Fanny some twelve years later, Father Gray will chide Fanny:

> Really if I were you I should not vex myself about Marmy. Pray
> for him and be ready in the last extremity to make sacrifices.
> He has a lot of good qualities mixed up with other things: but

the truth is through all his craziness enthusiasm and suffering there is in him a profoundly selfish man. I like him both for the past & the present too & do not care a hang what he thinks about me . . . He does not contrive pleasure for others. Don't think about the marriage. You can't influence him—or her.[25]

When Marmaduke dies in 1924, Father Gray will write to console Fanny, saying: "Relations and friends have secured in Marmy what they would wish for themselves, a happy death. Such is the reward of prayer."[26])

Marmy is the past. He is "Dorian" unregenerate; "Dorian" unmade. At Scots College, Gray remakes himself as a priest: the gifts of those years are hardness, detachment, commitment. Gray's vocation feeds on penance: an unsparing grief for his past life; a lively consciousness of the sensuous, complacent, even spoiled man who still lives within him. ("I know what some folk think of me," Father Gray will one day confess to a fellow priest, "but I just have to do it in self-defence. If I were to relax for a single moment, only God knows what might happen to me.")[27] He did not need to meet Robbie Ross or Oscar Wilde to know what might have happened. Having found what he regards as the only effectual mode of salvation, within the faith of the Catholic Church, Gray's mission is now to save others, insofar as they can be saved, from the wreckage of the past.

In the case of his own family, the mission is urgent. Gray and his mother had always been close; only his own rediscovery of faith in 1893 could have led to her own conversion that year, together with the three youngest children—Alexander, or "Alectryo," Norval, and Beatrice Hannah, or "Trixl." Beatrice and Sarah are still at convent school in Regensberg, Germany. It becomes Gray's habit to stop regularly on his trips to and from Scots College to visit "my creatures" or "my children," as he refers to them. (In old age, Beatrice recalls these visits as "unmitigated bliss." The handsome "Hansl"—as she named Gray—has become something of a pet of the nuns and on his visits is given more or less the complete run of the school. "He was known to assist at open-air needlework classes," she recalls," and show off his skill at hemming with a child's thimble on his little finger. Once he even penetrated to the Junior's dormitory and gave the occupants affectionate goodnights.")[28]

After each visit, the reports flow in to Raffalovich; they are firm, even harsh, concealing hidden anxiety about the future. This autumn of 1898, taking up residence in Scots College, Gray writes that "My sister Trixl's character shows no modification . . . Last April she was known to say: 'My brother has gone three days. I am beginning to be a little cheerful again.'"[29] Does she mean, Gray wonders, that Beatrice felt his departure so acutely that it has taken three days to recover? Or, more likely, that "Hansl's" presence could be just a little bit oppressive? He knows he is critical; judging himself so harshly, it is hard to be lenient on the youngest one, particularly since she seems so intractable. Two years later to the month, Gray reports to Raffalovich that Trixl, despite being "greatly improved in temper" and "a little more grown up . . . remains however a decidedly low-comedy woman, and still takes no trouble to conceal or disguise her thoughts."[30]

(In retrospect, Beatrice did indeed turn out to be his "creature," becoming, after the turn of the century, Sister Mary Raphael of the Benedictine Order. She lived out her life in Princethorpe Priory, Warwickshire, writing a few years before she died: "I feel out beyond all human appreciation or otherwise of my brother. He fulfils a certain role in my life, which is too spiritual to be put on paper—and which outweighs all other aspects in value and importance.")[31]

Gray encountered difficulties with his mother. On more than one occasion he finds himself meeting her spirited opposition to what she may have resented as interference with her own plans for her younger daughters. In terms of will, they are almost evenly matched; their last confrontation occurs in the autumn of 1902, almost a year after he has become Father Gray. Sarah has set her mind on becoming the second wife of one Rear Admiral Arthur Roger Tinklar, for whom Gray has a high regard. Gray's mother, however, objects strongly to the union, probably on the grounds of a large difference of age, for Tinklar's two daughters are about the same age as the intended bride. Stepping in as mediator, Gray attempts to reconcile mother and daughter. "Everything started as badly as it could," he reports to Raffalovich,

> and towards evening my pent up feeling gave expression in such a violent form as I have never seen before. I thought it best to get Sarah out of her sight as soon as I could . . . Poor Trixl begged me not to leave her with my mother but I persuaded her to stay though I could have wished to bring her with me. I left my mother in a calmer frame of mind this morning—Sarah says more pleasant than she has been since Christmas—and she & Sarah made peace at my instance . . . [32]

With every such encounter, Gray feels again the urgency of saving the children from their mother, from the influence of their past. Accordingly, Gray becomes very angry when his mother seems to resist the instruments of grace. A month after this scene with Sarah, Gray is again writing Raffalovich, that

> talking of my mother, she has been trying all she knows to make me unhappy, but hitherto without success. This day however, I hear that she is going to make a confession, the first since January; it is an amelioration for which I am devoutly thankful, for I said mass two days ago with a view to bettering the situation . . . [33]

Gray's mother dies suddenly the next March, from what Gray melodramatically describes as "the red death" of Poe's tale. Gray writes to tell Sarah—now safely married and on a visit to Regensberg—while at the same time confiding to Raffalovich that "she must have had an unpleasant moment, poor girl; for all the miserable island history must have come back to her memory."[34] That miserable history is always present, always a marker of what must be escaped, put firmly behind.

In this sense, his life's work has already been decreed before John Gray becomes Father Gray on 21 December 1901. Although he has not completed his full course of studies, Gray is ordained by Cardinal Respighi in the basilica of St. John Lateran, the cathedral church of Rome.[35] A few months later, while still in Rome, Gray suffers what he describes to Fanny Langdale as a "thorough breakdown of health."[36] The doctors discover him to be suffering from a heart condition, although his letters to Raffalovich speak only of gout, neuralgia, and various minor ailments. He is advised to finish his theological studies at the University of Fribourg in Switzerland on the grounds that the climate would be better for his health. He goes; he recovers. By September the doctors deem Gray strong enough to take up a position as curate at St. Patrick's in the Cowgate, Edinburgh.

Gray knew that rumor would say that he was sent to the Edinburgh slums as penance for his decadent life in London. Or that he had been prevented from taking up a more reputable position in England by the Pope, or the Marquess of Bute, or some other prominent Catholic, because of his association with Oscar Wilde. But he had chosen this course for himself, sounding out the idea to Raffalovich after his first few months in college, writing: "What do you think of my putting myself under the aegis of a Scots bishop when the time comes—with the view after ordination of working a year or two in a manufacturing town entirely among the hopelessly poor?" He had mentioned Dunkeld, Edinburgh, and Glasgow as good settings for such a venture. It is not that he was impervious to his previous reputation. After a few years of such work, he noted, "I could then withdraw without any shadow of impropriety[,] betake myself to London or join a congregation— say of the Filipini establishing themselves in Scotland." He asked Raffalovich to take the question into serious consideration: "You know we have often said it is *your* vocation we are struggling to set on foot. We are waiting to know what God will do with his lamentable subject and you are just as likely to hear as soon as I— or do you leave me to find out for myself?"[37]

Father Gray is dispatched as curate to a parish of the most desperately poor in Edinburgh. Those who attend St. Patrick's, Cowgate, are the families of the Irish brought over to Scotland as cheap labor. From the time of the Famine onwards they have been crowding into the tenements and lodging houses; with them lodge tuberculosis, alcoholism, violence, early death. "There are ten thousand of us Catholics here in a very small compass," Father Gray writes his niece in the first year; "and not a few of us drink; but on the other hand our faith is unbounded and we have moments of sorrow for our misdoings which a saint might envy."[38]

The conditions are harsh; and yet, doing his rounds, Father Gray expresses an eagerness and joy he has not known for years. In fact, his enthusiasm, born of a gratifying conviction that at last he has found his life's work, chimes oddly with reports of the desperate condition of his parishioners. Shortly after assuming his duties, he writes Raffalovich: "It is a very consoling life, what with the bad and the good. It is also full of surprises; every hour brings the news of a tragedy: as one goes out there are all sorts of people with all sorts of tales, in all degrees of drink, want and impudence."[39] All that autumn the letters to Raffalovich, now visiting his family in Paris and traveling around the Continent with Florence Gribbell, remain jublilant. Father Gray's efforts to save souls never seem more fruitful. "It is beautiful work," Gray writes. "I don't want to exchange it for no matter what. It is all so simple: there are the open arms of God, and one has just to push people into them."[40] He no longer regards sickness, desperation, or even death as merely evil, but as the very occasion for the soul to find God. "It no longer needs an effort of my will for me to thank God," he confesses to Raffalovich, "when I hear a man is dead."[41] Two days later, he sends Raffalovich an example of a routine pastoral visit:

I went the other night into a house of a couple belonging to us when there was a bit of a row going on. The wife "had drink in her" as the phrase is here, and was by way of putting her husband out of his misery, to the screaming of five children ranging from a girl of eighteen down to nothing. My arrival quieted the storm and I bound them over as well as I could, while the combatants and the children tried to put the few things the room contained into their proper places. As I turned to go, almost immediately, I saw a small boy sitting in the middle of the floor, pen in hand, calmly going on writing on a small piece of paper, dipping his pen judiciously into a bottle of penny ink which was standing on the floor. I saw the woman the next morning, and learnt what I was very keen to know, what had been the instrument with which she was attacking her husband. It was the door of the oven . . . She gave a very convincing account of the natural and acquired wickedness of her husband. Balzac could hardly have done it better. So we came to the euphemistic conclusion that there were many faults on both sides. Life is like a dome of many-coloured glass—with most of the panes smashed.[42]

This is bedrock; it proves a relief. Visiting the sick, Father Gray observes that "the utter common sense of the hospital charms, and after the years of *voulu* nonsense, looks like the very way to God."[43] Looking back, he recalls that once "I deliberately wanted desired things not as they were *but as I wanted them*. Now I want them as *they are*."[44] Being saved meant being saved from himself, from the willful pleasures of his life as "Dorian."

Gray now understands that such acceptance is a sign he is saved. Within himself he has discovered resources of humor and joy and sheer relief. He lives now beyond himself, not in the role dictated by a scandalous book by a scandalous author, but in a role dedicated to the life of the spirit. If he is another's creature, he is now God's. His faith gives him security; his position gives him a role that is respected, useful, but also one removed from the world. As Father Gray he may remain detached, apart, literally untouchable. Now he is one of another aristocracy, that of the True Church. As its servant, no one will question why a scrupulously dressed, well-spoken, even fastidious man walks in the rough neighborhood of the Cowgate. He belongs by right; he feels no reason to minimize the great distance between himself and his parishioners, nor confess to the same origins in poverty and despair. Once to Raffalovich he describes the constraints between a priest and his people as "the great wall of China"[45]; the fate of the late emperor of China has given him an image for the burden of his own vocation:[46]

Too sore upon a human frame: too great
This heavy priesthood, royalty, immense
Fatigue, the office of the exalted Bonze:

Lonely, endeavourless, terrific state,
From inattentive eyes too closely screened.
In sombre courts of adamant and bronze,
Time polished and from age to age patined,
And quaking service all his recompense.

His sparrow, in the broad air, where he plays,
Delighted, in much light, with many a shrill
Contention, summoned, drops, a parachute:
By gardens and by devious covered ways
Sweeps silent, to the sacred hall addressed,
A satin flesh mailed marmelukes salute,
Wheels steadily to the Presence, preens his breast,
Waits gaily, back and forth, the sovereign will.[47]

As the sparrows mocked the statue of metal Burns, so in the sparrow's flight, delighted, free, Gray finds the definition of his double state: joyous confidence within; an aloof detachment without. The impassivity of the Buddhist monk recalls the Father Gray of later years, with a face said to resemble a mask; a priest described as cold, inscrutable, silent. Yet for those who know him, his aloofness is offset by the inner delight of his faith, which grants him a fine careless access to the Presence, waiting gaily, back and forth, so unconscious of its commonness, its triviality.

For those who grew to know Father Gray, both aspects are part of the real man. A friend of his later years, Father Edwin Essex, thought that Gray's distrust of himself came from an idea of the priesthood so exalted that he kept himself on the tightest of reins.[48] But Gray also fights for a bitter self-control out of a lively fear of his past. He knows what some folk think of him; he knows his reputation for coldness, for habitual restraint. He just has to do it; if he were to relax, "God knows what might happen to me."[49] And yet there are many stories of Father Gray's kindness, particularly to women parishioners. It is not kindness he intends to offer. He comes to give spiritual aid, by means of the sacraments. But he would also scrub floors, mend fuses, give hardheaded practical advice. Above all, his parishioners sense that here was a man who had been through it all and could sympathize. "'You have not lived if you do not know that there is a pit in life,' was one of his sayings, which he left as it stood."[50] Keeping an eye on the pit makes Father Gray particularly sensitive to the rites of penance. ("Everyone said he was very proud," one old parishioner said to the biographer, "but he was awfully kind in the confessional.")[51]

Other reminiscences reveal other extremes. There is the intolerably precious priest who organizes a Toy Exhibition at Outlook Tower, Castlehill, in Edinburgh for 1907; the humble, kindly man who comes to know "everyone" on summer holidays in Iceland and who, back in Edinburgh, entertains the captain and crew of Icelandic fishing boats putting into Leith harbor.[52] For Father Gray there is no contradiction. An interest in artifacts grew from his first days at the Woolwich Arsenal. He knows from firsthand experience that art can come from the folk. Thus the exquisite poet can turn his mind, without embarrassment, to an article entitled "Some Scottish String Figures," illustrated by designs held in his own fine hands.[53] Nor is he a Luddite; he is ready to greet machines, too, as works of art. But he does not value only the most modern. In common with many of the avant-garde, Gray is fascinated with the primitive, (which had already exercised his imagination in several early short stories). Now Father Gray takes the opportunity to organize a trip for some of the parish boys to see an exhibition of early weapons, confessing to Raffalovich, "I scored a beautiful morning in the museum yarning with the subdirector, a bow and arrow man, the most purely selfish two hours I have spent in Edinburgh."[54]

Yet for all this interest in the practical and the primitive, for all his grounding in the working class and acquired sympathy for the Irish, Father Gray is never a man of the people. When meeting with the men of the parish, he confesses, "from my desire to see the thing do the men good I become a little nervous, with a small temptation to diffidence. The 'men of the parish' are so vague, silent, mysterious, and yet they are very concrete all the same . . ."[55] The note of respect is there; he came to be respected in turn. Not because Father Gray shares their taciturn and mysterious nature, but because he comes with work to do and he does it. In these years at the Cowgate, Father Gray sets up—with resources donated by Miss Gribbell and Raffalovich—a hostel for illegitimate children. He also conducts surveys: of housing conditions and rents; of working conditions in local factories. All this on top of a heavy workload of normal parish duties: serving Masses, confessing, confirming, catechizing, marrying, baptizing, ministering to the sick and the dying, burying the dead.

His years here are nothing if not exhausting. It was said of Father Gray that he soon began to be known in the parish as a priest who would go to places which, even in daylight, the police would patrol only in pairs, and that he would go no matter how late the hour or dirty the night.[56] It does not surprise, then, that Gray discovers he has little time for himself, writing Raffalovich,

> To be a curate here is to feel like the Salisbury crags, a fixture; we do not get away . . . The summer holiday is an abandonment of the people one has to look after, and the impression on return is . . . of beginning the whole thing over again, while in fact of course it is not so. I am hoping I am making for the time when I shall have my work well in hand, and at the same time be able to live a life for myself, and find scope for the hypothetical intellect I possess; work and a sort of half-piety, cemented together with bits of wasted time, make up the whole for the present, but experience will amend this.[57]

At first, much of his "spare" time goes into writing sermons, which achieve a kind of fame in themselves. "My sermon went off all right," he writes Raffalovich. "Here of course we only hear what is wrong with our work; it seems the monotony of my voice drives to drink. In vain I tell them that the subject of Purgatory requires a monotonous voice . . . "[58] When Raffalovich plans a visit, Gray warns him: "Don't build expectations on hearing me preach. I prepare my sermons conscientiously, and I am not shy; the bizarrerie of my mind too sometimes keeps the congregation awake, but the rest is very uncertain."[59] (In later years, Father Edwin Essex describes Gray's sermons, writing that they

> were always in character with the man. "No matter where or how be begins," a listener remarked appreciatively, "the

Canon always brings us in to the terminus." And that described his technique fairly enough. He could never be obvious, either in theme or phrasing, and from his opening statements it was impossible to deduce what was to be the trend of the sermon. Then very deliberately, in that quietly incisive voice, the Canon would proceed, using always the right word in the right place [second nature to him], until suddenly, often by wayside tracks of thought, the listener found he had been led to the essential point of the discourse.[60])

The sermons arise naturally from Father Gray's own reflections. In one, talking of the terrible grandeur of the Mass, Father Gray emphasizes how no church, not even St. Peter's in Rome, no rite, however grand, could be worthy of an event so stupendous. Father Gray's own great dignity at Mass is notable; he is beheld as a lesson in reverence, gravitas, self-possession. On rare occasions, however, his own preoccupations take over; it is then that his fears of relaxing an iron self-control become justified. In one instance, virtually in midsermon, Father Gray suddenly goes off into a tirade about women who dance naked on stage and send men's soul's to hell. (Had Salome come back to haunt him as St. John?) A slight wave of astonishment ripples through the congregation, so out of key is this diversion from their reserved pastor's usual tone.[61]

But the past will reassert itself, if only in a return to writing. Father Gray begins, initially, by composing some harmless verses on the Life of the Blessed Virgin Mary. They (probably) arose out of a course of evening instruction for the boys of the parish in the autumn of 1902.[62] That very year, Father Gray also agrees to translate a book by a former professor of his at Fribourg, a Dominican by the name of Father Vincent Rose. Translating gives Gray at last "a means of forcing me into the rule of two hours work for the intellect in the day," as he tells Raffalovich.[63] While working on it, he comments astutely on the gathering crisis within the Roman Church which goes by the name "Modernism," reflecting, with his unregenerate Protestant instincts, that "it is consoling to think that the operation of submitting the scriptures to the historical method is passing so peaceably; it had to come, and there had to be a certain number of 'morts et blessés.'" And, he adds: "Don't forget that this uproar may have for one good result to remind some of the good plodders [fathers] that there is such a thing as scripture. I am often called a protestant by those who should know better— but I go on smiling."[64] Yet in doctrinal terms the Scots College had rendered Father Gray acceptably orthodox. (Was it for this reason—or just sheer mischief—that many years later he described his *Spiritual Poems* as "a lot of heretical rubbish"?)[65]

Both of these pious works are published in 1903, a year that ends with reverberations from the past. A fire guts the publishers Leightons and Methuen; Father Gray reports that the remaining copies of his *Spiritual Poems* have been "burnt out. It was he [Leighton] too who cased [put in hardback?] *Silverpoints*," Gray continues, "and a pity he didn't burn that too."[66] In January 1904, Gray announces that *Ad Matrem,* revised scenes from his dramatized life of the Blessed Virgin, will be out soon; would Raffalovich buttonhole Arthur Symons for a review? Symons replies, saying he would like to turn any review into a retrospective of Gray's work. To which Father Gray responds: "Arthur Symons might see his way to a serious article, if he were to take the present 'corpus' of my work. There is nothing in it but shame at any given point, but it has always had an aim, and that sometimes redeems even failure . . . "[67]

During this year, the past continues to boil up around Gray, like steam from a simmering volcano. By the autumn of 1904, Father Gray finds himself responsible for editing for publication the *Last Letters of Aubrey Beardsley*. Most of these were letters from Beardsley to Raffalovich, along with a few to Gray, written from the time Aubrey appeared in André's parlor in 1896 until his death in Mentone in 1898. Gray's first act is to expunge all proper names of those living and, at the insistence of the publishers, Longmans, Green and Company, most of the details of the "horrors of consumption."[68]

What inspires such an enterprise? Surely Father Gray wishes to escape his association with Aubrey, of all people: next to Wilde the blackest of the beasts labeled as decadent. In fact, it is exactly this reputation that Raffalovich and Gray wish to counter: the notion that Aubrey was, in the words of Roger Fry, "the Fra Angelico of Satanism." Others are set to fatten themselves on his notoriety.

Raffalovich reports in alarm that Madame Strindberg, the estranged wife of the playwright, had begun to collect Beardsley's letters and pictures—particularly the "distressing" ones, those erotic drawings Beardsley on his deathbed had ordered to be burnt. Sensing a killing, Beardsley's publisher, the disreputable Leonard Smithers, had kept and then sold them. Now Madame Strindberg—"Swindleberg," Raffalovich calls her—is proposing their publication; she is pressing Beardsley's sister, Mabel, for the German rights. Conscious that their mother has been in dire poverty since her son's death, Mabel confesses to being tempted by the offer. To make matters worse, Raffalovich observes, "Madame S. said she could not fit belief in God or the religious sense into Aubrey: his conversion to Catholicism, yes, but not a religious sense before he found he could not live."[69]

In the six years which have passed since Beardsley's death, an era has ended. The nineties are dead; Wilde is dead; "Dorian" has died. The past now looks like a different country. From his present perspective, Father Gray welcomes an opportunity to redraw the map, to represent Beardsley's history in a different light. Rather than challenge Madame Strindberg's assertion about Beardsley's "religious sense," Gray vindicates it. From his own experience as priest, Father Gray describes how serious illness

> seems to do what nothing else could. What appears to the observer is the gradual humiliation of the physical economy being accompanied by the proportionate emancipation of the spiritual. It is a spectacle so moving, the reduction of a coarse brute to a frank-eyed youth, the renascence of a gentle-souled factory-girl, supposed to have been long ago drowned in drink and gone for ever, from the wreck of a wild virago, that in the presence of it the words tuberculosis, cancer, and even the euphemistic G.P., cease to curdle the blood.

Among the rough people of the Cowgate, Father Gray muses, he has at last found the paradigm for Beardsley's conversion:

> Aubrey Beardsley might, had he lived, have risen, whether through his art or otherwise, spiritually, to a height from

which he could command the horizon he was created to scan. As it was, the long anguish, the increasing bodily helplessness, the extreme necessity in which some one else raises one's hand, turns one's head, showed the slowly dying man things he had not seen before. He came face to face with the old riddle of life and death; the accustomed supports and resources of his were being removed; his soul, thus denuded, discovered needs unstable desires had hitherto obscured; he submitted, like Watteau his master, to the Catholic Church.[70]

It is with this paradigm in mind that Father Gray angrily opposes Longmans' efforts to "clean up" the letters, writing: "We are strongly of the opinion that whatever there is of horror is vital to the interest of the letters, inasmuch as it serves to exhibit the moral victory of the sufferer & the power of divine Grace in him."[71]

But shortly afterwards, he confesses to having come to "a better frame of mind about the ghastliness of some of the health details;"[72] rather than a moral tale, the book in his mind has now become a "literary curiosity." Certainly, he reflects, "it is unique in this, that never before have letters written with so remote an idea of subsequent publication been given to the public except in the interests of science, and only then I think as criminological documents . . . "[73] There is also the possibility of a *frisson nouveau,* which Father Gray contemplates with a certain glee: "I anticipate a horrible explosion in the press," he writes Raffalovich shortly before publication, "which we expect, having loaded the gun and applied the match."[74]

Father Gray waits; but there is no "explosion." Rather what happened was a slow and subtle sea change in the public's sense of Aubrey Beardsley. (How the perspective shifted might be indicated by a letter Henry James sent to Raffalovich some years later, thanking him for the volume of

Beardsley's letters by which I have been greatly touched. I knew him a little, and he was himself to my vision touching, and extremely individual; but I hated his productions and thought them extraordinarily base—and couldn't find [perhaps didn't try enough to find!] the formula that reconciled this baseness, aesthetically, with his being so perfect a case of the artistic spirit. But now the personal spirit in him, the beauty of nature, is disclosed to me by your letter as wonderful and, in the conditions and circumstances, deeply pathetic and interesting. The amenity, the intelligence, the patience and grace and play of mind and of temper—how charming and individual an exhibition! . . And very right have you been to publish the letters, for which Father Gray's claim is indeed supported.[75])

Instead of explosion, there is collapse. In late November of 1904, within weeks of the publication of the Beardsley letters, Father Gray falls dramatically ill. It appears to be a complete breakdown of health. Indeed, it had been anticipated more than a year and a half earlier by Father Gray's superior, the parish priest of St. Patrick's, Monsignor William Grady, who had taken it upon himself to voice his concerns to Raffalovich. Hearing of them, Gray had responded, "I do not in the least resent being the object of solicitude, and I have not really the maniacal devotion to my work that is supposed, but I have an abject fear of instability subjective or objective."[76] Now in his sickbed, Father Gray reflects that he has been under strain. Shortly before Monsignor Grady's intervention, his own mother had died unexpectedly. Raffalovich had been abroad with Miss Gribbell; Sarah had been in Regensberg visiting Trixl; there had been no one close to soften the blow. They had been horribly close; the frictions therefore at times almost unbearable; but he was her first child and of all the family she had been his ally. Also, Gray reflects grimly, his rule of two hours' intellectual work a day has, over the last two years, pushed him to his limits. It is true, his *Fourteen Scenes in the Life of the Blessed Virgin Mary* has been published; Father Rose's *Studies on the Gospels* is in press; the Beardsley letters are about to see the light of day. But he is now forced to confess that the "strenuous life of the Cowgate" has been taxing his reserves, observing to his sister Sarah that his work requires "a lot of physical stamina . . . and as the life consists entirely in the work one does, the situation is serious."[77] But he has come to the realization that it is not what the work requires of him, but what he has required of himself, that has now nearly killed him.

The doctor diagnoses pneumonia. Father Gray finds himself confined to bed. But it is January and in the raw Scottish climate there is no hope for improvement. Advised by the doctor to decamp for London, Gray stays for several days with Raffalovich before they leave together for Rome, where André remains intermittently at his side for the next six weeks. His condition is critical; recovery is slow; it is becoming clear that Father Gray can never go back to the Cowgate.

On 16 February 1905 two visitors make their way to his bedside in Rome: the Most Reverend James A. Smith, Archbishop of St. Andrews and Edinburgh, and Gray's former rector at the Scots College, Monsignor Fraser. Two days previously, Gray had observed the anniversary of his conversion as if it had been the anniversary of a death. Would he never escape the surge of grief that overcame him once again, recollecting his perverse plunge into a life of sin? Now ill and far from home, he knew it was a time for taking stock. Slowly, painfully, he and Raffalovich had worked out a plan for a new life. The exhausting work in the Cowgate must be abandoned. But Edinburgh is congenial; the work of the Church growing despite the violent sectarianism. As the Archbishop observes, it is not only the poor who need a priest; there is at present no focus for the growing number of prosperous Catholics in the Edinburgh diocese.

During the long days of convalescence, he and Raffalovich piece out a possible future. It involves building a new church, largely with their own resources. One day, musing on its shape and form, Gray's eye is suddenly caught by the small, primitive church below his window, so typical of Rome: a square, Romanesque campanile; low terra-cotta roofs around a courtyard; an unpretentious priest's house tacked on the third side; an entrance gate: self-enclosed, rosy, modest, and of a fabric and design complete within itself. He has looked at it every day for about a month but now he sees it with new eyes. He draws Raffalovich over: There, he says. There is our church.[78] And so seizing the occasion of the archbishop's visit, Father Gray and Raffalovich together raise the first formal suggestion that they should build a new Catholic church for Edinburgh, over which Father Gray would preside.[79]

Such a plan is not merely expedient. It had has a long gestation between them, from what they have come to see as a shared religious vocation. Once Raffalovich had written to Gray: "What matters most to me is our relation towards God, that you and I should do his will here, and be with Him for an eternity. That is the prize, the aim of all and everything, and our history, yours and mine, does point to such a scheme, to such condescension of God's part."[80] For almost a decade now, their relation to God had bound them together. They had sealed it when, in October 1898, Raffalovich had joined the Third Order of Saint Dominic, and Gray had followed his example a year later.[81] By doing so, they were each bound to observe within their daily lives a modified version of the order's rule. As Raffalovich observed in one letter, their both joining the order formalized their relationship as "brothers." At the time, Gray was studying for the priesthood; Raffalovich had also considered such a course, but had been prevented by his health, having been warned as a young man about a weakness of the heart.[82] It was in this sense that Gray became a priest for both of them.

But now God's scheme demands more. Resigning his post at the Cowgate, Father Gray returns to Edinburgh in May 1905. At once, he opens negotiations for a site in the fashionable district of Morningside. Raffalovich intends to finance both the purchase of the site and the building costs. But Father Gray will allow him to bear only a portion of the cost, feeling that parishioners would not consider the church their own unless they too contribute.[83] Also on Raffalovich's behalf, Gray purchases a substantial house within walking distance of the new church on Falcon Avenue. As it turns out, 9 Whitehouse Terrace will be where he is to live—along with Raffalovich and Miss Gribbell—until the completion of the church and its adjoining priest's house in 1907. For Raffalovich has decided to move to Edinburgh, claiming that the climate better suits his health. In any case, Gray's serious illness now makes it inconceivable that the two should any longer live apart.

The foundation stone is laid in April 1906; the church dedicated almost exactly a year later. Father Gray chooses the architect himself: Robert Lorimer, later known for his work on the Scottish War Memorial. Gray's sure sense of excellence in workmanship and design never fail him; in choosing Lorimer, he again reveals a taste as innate as perfect pitch. He does so despite the rabid sectarianism of Edwardian Edinburgh. "There is . . . for a moment a violent set against Lorimer," Gray reports to Raffalovich, "but the chief complaint is that Lorimer is 'anglican,' which is vague. I do not see how his anglicanism is to affect me."[84] Gray simply decides to ignore the pressure of these factions. What he knows is that he will be able to work with Lorimer to impose his own interpretation on the design.

In designing the church, Gray and Raffalovich translate into the native idiom their vision in Rome. Above all, they seek its humility, its intimacy. (Those today who pass through its gates into the inner courtyard move into an altered ambiance. The street outside is gray and windswept, verging on a kind of desolate respectability. Inside, the courtyard is quiet and warm, the ochre-colored brick and red-tiled roofs infusing even the dim Scottish light with warmth. Yet when one enters the actual church, the mellow light of the courtyard vanishes. Here the light is stark. It bounces off the bare white loggia, leading the eye up the lofty piers to the coffered roof of Oregon pine. Coming from the intimate scale of the courtyard, one feels instantly diminished, almost crushed, by the height of the arches, the dark weight of the ceiling. As if Gray knew that the art of architecture studies not structure in itself, but the effect of structure on the human spirit. This was the shift of scale from Gray's Roman years: a new humility; an exacerbated guilt.

Gray named the church: St. Peter's. Father Dominic Hart always held that he did so "from Roman years." There are mementos placed strategically; the bronze replica of an ancient statue of St. Peter, for instance, and the copy in the Lady Chapel of the Madonna of Santa Maria Maggiore. But that is not what Father Hart meant; he considered the church was so designated "because both St. Peter and John Gray—in his unregenerate days—had denied their Lord. This was for him a matter of infinite regret."[85] There is a terrible severity here, not of mere style, but of first principle. It infuses every choice, every action relating to the church. As when Raffalovich's sister, Sophie, once asked if she could say goodbye to Canon Gray, then in the confessional, her brother rebuked her sharply: "We never speak in the church but of the things of God."[86]

Yet that bleak austerity, so much a piece of the architecture, is at odds with the detail of the interior. A gorgeously carved baroque confessional, now relegated to a side chapel, speaks of the elaboration of sin. There are dim paintings in the manner of the Pre-Raphaelites by John Duncan and Frank Brangwyn against the bare whitewash of the walls. The floor of the chancel is cipollino marble inlaid with little brass fishes in honor of the Fisherman; the wrought-iron rail itself signifies his net. Carved and gilded wood is used for the picture frames, the candlesticks, the chancel cross—a crucifix in the ancient form of an anchor, a symbol of Christian hope. All were commissioned personally by Father Gray, drawing on his contacts with the Vale and other artisans. Father Gray, too, laid the chancel with the first Persian carpets to be seen in Edinburgh. His alone is that exquisite, if precarious, balance between the severe and the self-conscious, the simple and the florid. Nothing so accurately reflects his sharp rejection of the world together with, as a fellow priest would describes it, a love of the sensuous so intense it would scandalize a Manichee.[87]

Despite recent changes, St. Peter's on Falcon Avenue still reflects Gray's singular taste. But it is within the priest's house that that taste achieved its most complete expression. A friend of Gray and Raffalovich, Peter Anson, recalled its effect upon first entering in 1919:

> Hanging on its walls were a few framed lithographs by Shannon and Ricketts. A heavy velvet-like fitted carpet added to the comfort. It was not until the following morning when the curtains were drawn back that I noticed the windows were very small leaded casements, filled with semi-opaque glass, through which the pale winter sunshine of Edinburgh hardly penetrated. The whole house was in a dim, mysterious, and elusive twilight. It was a world of half-tones: in fact it only

needed an invisible gramophone playing Debussy or bits from
Maeterlinck to make it quite perfect.[88]

On the ground floor, Anson continued, was a small dining
room. Nearby, a large, book-lined study held a few comfortable
green leather armchairs and a businesslike desk. The books attested
to Father Gray's wide range of interests: works in Icelandic, much
poetry and mystical theology, costly illustrated volumes on sculpture, painting, architecture. Father Gray's austerely furnished bedroom was perhaps even more characteristic: the sheets on the
narrow bed were made of black linen.[89])

Installed as parish priest of St. Peter's in April of 1907, Father
Gray is to serve there until his death in 1934. Curiously isolated
from everything around it, his new world is one created in his own
image, perfectly expressive of his own principled taste. Now that
Raffalovich has moved to Edinburgh, a new social world is invented
through his celebrated salons. Over the space of thirty years,
Raffalovich's Sunday dinners establish a fame of their own: for their
stylized, rather dated manners; their carefully chosen company of
academics, literati, young artistes, visiting celebrities. Moving
between the duties at St. Peter's and these weekly gatherings, Gray
now circulates within a wholly artificial if exquisite milieu, a whole
world of ceremony and symbol which "Dorian" Gray had sought
and lost. Father Gray puts it another way when he observes to
Raffalovich of the plans for St. Peter's: "I am sure the result will also
be exceedingly beautiful; things really for once being remoulded
nearer to the heart's desire."[90]

6 | FATHER SILVERPOINTS

(JANUARY 1906–SEPTEMBER 1914)

MANY HISTORIES ARE PLAYED OUT within the elegant setting of St. Peter's, Falcon Avenue. But they take place for the most part backstage, hidden from the world.

Few ever learn about Raffalovich's problems with his family—or his finances. The Russian estate he had inherited in part from his father, a tract of land larger than three villages, was sold and the money invested in German and Russian funds; but after World War I, these were worthless.[1] Nor do many learn of Raffalovich's discreet patronage of such artists as Eric Gill; nor his even more discreet acts of charity, many of them channelled through the Church. Hidden too are Father Gray's own efforts to help his family and friends—as well as the anxieties and grief at their difficulties or deaths. Outwardly, Father Gray has turned into a model of the respectable parish priest. He has succumbed to that archetypal Scottish passion, golf, even to the extent that he confesses to a close friend that the links at St. Andrews "competes with Jerusalem as a place I would choose to end my days."[2] In 1909, he founds the parish school of St. Peter's. He is elected a fellow of the Royal Anthropological Institute (a position he holds from 1903 to 1915); he is to be one of the founders of the Edinburgh Zoological Park. And before the Great War shuts down all travel to the Continent, Father Gray manages one extended trip during the summer of 1909 through Denmark to Sweden, this "wicked programme of movements" an indulgence in a personal pleasure trip.[3]

At some point he also acquires a silver Skye terrier, appropriately named Tobias, after his biblical precedent in the Book of Tobit.

With such credentials Father Gray has acquired a reputation for respectability bordering on immobility. Surely none of his parishioners would guess that their cool, aloof parish priest was about to embark on one final, passionate intimacy. It is all owing to his old friends from the Vale, Shannon and Ricketts. Through it all—the frenzy of the last years as "Dorian," the retrenchment of the mid-nineties, then the trials of Oscar Wilde—the Artists had stayed in touch. Gray's visits were intermittent, but persistent. He followed their moves from the Vale to Beaufort Street in 1894; then in 1898 to Spring Terrace, near the river in suburban Richmond; finally, in 1902, back to purpose-built studios in Lansdowne House in Holland Park, London. The Artists did not flee the country after the Wilde trials; no one knew for sure what the status of their relationship entailed, so there was no room for censure. Their friends retail the story of how the married but openly homosexual writer John Addington Symonds, who helped Havelock Ellis write his book *Sexual Inversion*, flouted all the laws of hospitality by following Ricketts around the house shouting, "But you are, aren't you?" Ricketts walked to the front door and opened it, declaring imperiously: "Out!"[4]

Yet Ricketts suffered; he felt the condemnation of Wilde was an attack on all artists. "To me, the shock and stupour were slow to pass away... something happened from which I have never quite recovered, a mistrust of the British conscience, a mistrust of modern civilization ... I have never forgiven the emminent [sic] men of the time, Meredith, Morris, Hardy, who were silent."[5] He poured out his grief over the news of Oscar's death into his diary (his accustomed misspelling even more disastrous than usual):

> I feel too upset to write about it, and the end of that Comedy that was realy Tragedy. There are days when one vomits ones nationality, when one regrets that one is an Englishman. . . I know that I have not realy felt the fact of his death.[6]

Later he tore out the entries from 6 to 19 December, but at the end of the year he noted that the death "at first heardly felt . . .

affects one at stray moments, when one is off one's guard, at Sundown or at Sunrise, moments with me of introspection, hesitation, or regret." Only several years after Wilde's death did he come to realize that

> Oscar was always better than he thought he was, and no one in his lifetime was able to see it, including my clairvoyant self. It is astonishing that I viewed him as the most genial, kindly, and civilized of men, but it never entered my head that his personality was the most remarkable one that I should ever meet, that in intellect & humanity he is the largest type I have come across.

After the trial, the Artists seem never to have mentioned Oscar. But their lives had changed. Ricketts and Shannon devoted themselves to a new enterprise, the founding of the Vale Press. In 1896 they opened a shop in Warwick Street, putting their old friend Holmes in charge. The Artists aimed to produce books as beautiful as those from William Morris's Kelmscott Press, founded in 1891. Every aspect of the book was to be newly created: from well-designed type, considered placing of lines, perfect positioning of the page on the paper, beautiful ornaments and pictures, so that the books themselves might be total works of art. For this Ricketts offered his own definition in the bibliography of the Vale Press publications: "A work of art is a whole in which each portion is exquisite in itself, yet co-ordinate."[7]

The designs for the fonts and the woodcut initials were distinctive, but the border decorations were simply breathtaking; Ricketts's inventive, intricate patterns employed a myriad of different motifs, whether vine leaves and grapes, wild byrony, hops, or knot-work derived from Celtic manuscripts. As in the design for *Silverpoints*, Ricketts aimed to equal books of the Italian Renaissance, which he described as "full of light."[8] John Gray was solicited for poems. He at first offered many of the pieces he had been working on since 1893, which appeared as an early edition of the Vale Press under the title *Spiritual Poems* in 1896. For the next two years, Gray fed Ricketts selected editions. They were not done on any special principles, except that of taste and common sense. During long hours at the British Museum Library, Gray gathered collections of the poems of Michael Drayton and Sir John Suckling (both produced in 1896); of Henry Constable (1897); of Sir Philip Sidney (1898). Copies of the new books followed Gray to Rome and back with him to Edinburgh, from whence, in 1902, Gray made the occasional foray down to London, to visit with Raffalovich—and the Vale.

Undaunted by the calamity of a fire which destroyed all the wood blocks for the Vale Press in 1899, in the intervening years the Artists have become recognized connoisseurs, reasonably prosperous, and collectors of formidable acuity. Twice, dropping in for a visit, Father Gray missed them at home; the second time he was greeted by a note, similar to that left for others, apologizing for not being at home: "The maid has instructions to give you tea," it read. "You will find the new Egyptian things and the new Intaglios in the drawers of the new case. The fine Greek vase is in the lower shelf of the old case (window corner). The new Mycenean vase . . . is also in the old case, unless it is basking on one of the tables."[9] What that man knows! Gray thought, wandering around the room, sipping his tea, then indulging in a cigarette. His sense of Ricketts crystallized around one sentence: it is knowledge that he has and how he has it. Glancing about at the fine eighteenth-century English furniture, the Persian rugs, the Japanese prints, he recalled Oscar's words about how fine things of different periods belong together. Certainly the dining room of Lansdowne House was the most perfect place he had ever seen. His thoughts might well have echoed those of another acquaintance, who remarked:

> Ricketts had that unique quality of taste which enabled him to distinguish an object of merit whatever its period or use. You would not think that old master drawings would be at home with a Chinese bird-cage; you would not think that red and green marble-topped tables could live in amity; you would fancy that Empire chairs might swear at Morris chintzes, French knives could not harmonise with Georgian silver, and a modern blue glass bowl could never stand at the foot of a Grecian statuette; the whole could certainly not be lit hard

with clear bulbs handing from sixpenny porcelain shades. Yet, strangely, all combined to give a sense of luxury and elegance that was incomparable. Each object, being in itself perfect, added its lustre to the whole, so that the room, which was, winter and summer, filled with flowers, glowed with a radiant and compelling beauty.[10]

So it is, Gray reflects, looking out the window of the express once again coming down from Edinburgh to London, so it is with the Artists' friends. He recalls Ricketts saying of his collecting that "perfect good luck" was an integral part of all genius, for "the work is of the spirit, and knows no place."[11] It is the same with his associates: Ricketts gathers around him those whom he values in spirit, from whatever place. Gray reflects on those he has already met there: the artist William Rothenstein, the poet W. B. Yeats. And on the occasion of this visit to London, the Artist has insisted—true tyrant that he is—that Father Gray meet two others of their intimates: the poets "Michael Field."

As the countryside rushes by, Father Gray muses on their reputation; like the lone tree punctuating the misty morning, the name of "Michael Field" had punctuated the blurring years, now seeming to fall away behind him. Years ago, "Michael Field" had written an appreciation in thanks for a copy of *Silverpoints*. André, who knew everybody, had explained that "Michael Field" was really the pen name of an aunt and niece, both poets. The aunt, Katherine Bradley, was the elder by sixteen years; she went by the name of "Michael." She had virtually raised her niece, Edith Cooper, nicknamed "Henry," the child of her invalid sister. They had studied together at University College, Bristol; joined the debating society and the antivivisection group; then became, together, writers. To date, they had written about twenty plays—the Vale Press had produced the more recent ones—and an early book of poems. André was sure that they were *inverti*, most probably chaste. (His instincts, for once, failed him; but with women, who can tell?) André repeated to Gray their remark that as collaborators they worked so closely together that they could not tell, in the end, who had written what; he confessed to the same ambition in their own work. But Gray had also heard of "Michael Field" from others. Lionel Johnson had once confessed to being their devoted admirer. Rothenstein had said often how he prized their friendship. (Years later, in his memoirs, he would write of them: "Proud and aloof, they tended their minds as precious vessels prepared to receive all they held lovely, both in the physical and the spiritual world. They were the feminine affinities to Ricketts and Shannon with whose work they had fallen in love."[12])

In January 1894, "by express entreaty" from the Michaels, Will Rothenstein had brought them to the Vale.[13] On his occasional visits to the Artists, Gray had heard of their calls, infrequent, but increasing. He did not realize until years later, reading Edith's diary, the impact of those early meetings. In the entry for May 22, Edith immediately marks Ricketts as "a decadent Christ," while Shannon is "like one of the comely angels of Della Francesca." She remarks on Ricketts's "expressive eyes"—that he "is one of those delightful people who seem complex but are simple at the end of a good talk. He is an ardent lover of Shannon—his elder by a year—loving him as My Love loves me—following him about with rippling banter & eyes that deprecate the Beloved's willfulness," his "nervous hilarity" countered in Shannon's "self-inculpating laugh." Then comes to rest on the observation of how exactly parallel their relationships are: "These 2 men live & work together & find rest & joy in each other's love just as we do."[14] They take their leave "with a sense we have walked into friendship as deep as moving grass."[15] Gray knows too from the Artists how the Michael Fields had expressed the hope that, although devoted to Oscar Wilde, the Sacred Ones "don't imitate their idol in more than conversation."[16] Gray finds himself smiling at his dim reflection in the window, a slightly rueful smile. How had it taken until this late date to meet these two extraordinary women? After *Silverpoints,* his visits to the Artists had become intermittent and, for some periods, were even suspended. The grip of the Wilde sensation; his life with André; then Beardsley; then the decision to leave London for Rome; finally, the Cowgate. The years had slipped by as seamlessly as the landscape now slips by behind the rain-rattled window of the first-class carriage.

Now, as Ricketts had decreed, Gray ascends from the depths of the Underground to Holland Park to meet these soulmates, whom the Fields denominate their "male-doubles."[17] It is January 1906. As ever, Father Gray is in his clerical clothes. He is seldom recognized now as "Dorian" even in Chelsea; he looks older: the fine profile has blurred, the hair is thinning. He passes his hand over his hair and, before ringing at the large door of Lansdowne House, lights a cigarette nervously. Ricketts throws open the door. My dear Gray, how good of you to come. Michael is above. As Ricketts ushers him up the stairs, Gray thinks again with amusement of the description of Ricketts as "Christ in a fit"—his mission shines from him, through the doorway into the drawing room. As they enter, there advances upon them a "small, ruddy, gay and buoyant" woman in middle age holding out her hand, her eyes bright.[18] She speaks quickly: So John Gray, at last this is you, the inventor of the exquisite *Silverpoints*. You have become quite a mystery to us. Now I see why. She pauses, gazing into his face, as if she could see someone behind him, someone she expected to see rather than this very plain clerical gentleman before her. She releases his hand, steps back, and proclaims: I see a face behind the face; could it be Dorian? But a Dorian so subdued that he is refined out of existence, invisible, like a shadow without the sunlight to fix it . . .

Her strong voice dwindles off, but the stare for an instant remains, before she recalls it might be rude, and turns away.

Ricketts decrees tea. Then brazens out a conversation, baiting Shannon, laughing immoderately, teasing "Michael," whose goat is very gettable. She returns his banter with flair, her quick, bright manner adequate to his imperious wit, his outrageous exaggerations. Gray places himself obliquely to the wordplay, sometimes intervening with a grave word or phrase, but most often wandering restlessly about the room, picking up a small Greek thing here, an Egyptian fragment there. When the visit draws to a close, he senses they are already friends. Something silent has passed between Michael and Father Gray; is it the half-wounded reference to "poor Oscar," or their sense of a shared past in the pagan rites of the nineties, or simply that unspoken fellowship of the Vale, the high mission of the Artists, that ties them together now? Gray takes his leave to catch the night train back to Edinburgh. After seeing him out, Ricketts confronts

Michael: Well . . . what do you make of our John Gray? "Rosy, inscrutable and kindly," Michael flashes back.[19]

That evening Michael returns to her home in Richmond, where the Poets had been lured to live by the Artists—who then, in an irony of fate, moved back to London leaving them there, in their cottage at Paragon, near the river. Michael returns to find their beloved companion, a Chow dog whom they christened Whym, to be in grave distress, dying. For the Poets, Whym had become a focus of their love for each other; their feeling for him is more than that for a child or another person; it is, as Michael observes perceptively, more "a desire to get into another kingdom."[20] Ironically, it is that love that is to lead them, tragically, literally into another kingdom. How this comes about is told by Michael to Father Gray, months, maybe even a year, after their first meeting, when they are exchanging confidences of how the spirit turns at last to God:

> Dear Father Gray—
>
> that is best—the search—light—in response—I will do all I can to aid—And now I am sending to you a little picture. It is a picture of our Bacchic altar—taken before we left our old home of Durdans, Reigate, in think 1899. I said—we must have our Bacchic cub [Whym Chow] at the foot of the altar—& he obediently fell asleep there . . .—that day I met you at the Palace Jeu [the Artists' studio in Lansdowne House], Tuesday 1906— I went home to learn my Chow was already in frenzy—(stricken of some awful brain disease). I nursed the little creature day & night—ready at once to part with him . . . Vets, said I ought to give him a chance—till on the Sunday—for the bright eyes were growing blind & the little feet wandering in circles—that no gentle caress wd stop—I resolved to kill him . . . It was in sacrifice—& indeed much for the sake of Love itself—& then— through blunderings as pitiful as painful as Goscommon's [Edith's then confessor, Father Goscommon]—I was nearly 5 hours seeking to quench that too sturdy life . . . And no prayer was listened to—And I heard the cries of my little Whym— when after chloroform—he was being driven by the vet—for the final puncture—I *hoped* unconscious—

Then I came home, & took down the candles from the altar of the Trinity—& was left—oh—*a very brief while*—without God. Before Whymie was brought home to be buried at the foot of the altar of Dionysos in the garden—we were able to pray—& to ask God to accept that sacrifice—And presently—a month or two—after—at Rottingdean—I was quietly told of Heaven; that we three Henry, & Whymmie, & Michael were accepted—to reflect as in a dark pond—the Blessed Trinity—

It is our Mystery—*it is our secret*. In return for our blasphemy—Whymmie returned to us to be our guardian angel . . . & little living Flame of Love. He is a little Fellow, as Henry is my Fellow.

There! I have told you of my intercessor, as simply & bravely as you confide in me; & I shall never forget them[?]—the story of yours.

—I knew nothing of Sacrifice—till I offered one. It has been accepted. To my dear Henry the price was worse—for she loved him most—and from this I have learnt all I know of the Sacrifice in the bosom of the Trinity, and the search light you must cast—in on my *blasphemy*—and God rewarding *that*—so!

—There is nothing in my life worth talking about to God! I suppose it would be wrong to say—Would there were! I have had so sweet & noble parents—my nature lies all at unity with itself—vainly, as it seems to me[?] by happy instinct from the Seven Deadly Sins. There is deeply, heretic blood in me—and I pray—by penance—by all that . . . help—that I may be cleansed to receive the mysteries.

Pray for me—Michael[21]

They buried Whym Chow under the altar of Dionysus in the garden, the Poets reciting that great song of Jacopone da Todi, learned from John Gray:

O love, all love above,
Why hast thou struck me so?

All my heart, broke atwo,
Consumed in flames of love,
Burning and flaming cannot find solace;
It cannot fly from torment, being bound;
Like wax among live coal it melts apace;
It languishes alive, no help being found;
Seeking a grace to fly a little space,
A glowing furnace is its narrow pound.
In such a deadly swound,
Alas, where am I brought?
Living with death so fraught!
O leaping flames of love![22]

They retire to the exquisite house to begin the poems that are to be published under the unabashed title *Whym Chow: Flame of Love*.[23] The Artists are impatient with their grief; but Father Gray takes it on its own terms. And, leaning on that tenderness, the Poets travel to Edinburgh to visit Father Gray. Encountering him for the first time, Edith records in her journal: "The round little priest comes in quietly—as happy as a rose on a bow . . . greets Michael eagerly, bows to our hostess, . . . &, as with a pause of revelation & praise, he sees me beyond her & his eyes rest over me. A strange moment: the apprehension of the mystic & the approval of the man of the world in unison in that gaze." Later, she refines her perception, noting in the appearance of Father Gray "the wild beast in the mystic," all more or less kept under control.[24]

When they return to Richmond, Gray finds himself haunted by the vision of a tall, pale woman, gliding over to meet him in a shimmer of gray silk, like a ghost. Then a long, elegant hand extends, a touch, momentary, almost as if of air; as Edith plays the wan and wistful spirit to Michael's energetic bustle. "I grow in the dark," she said of herself.[25] Her shyness extends to letters. Throughout that winter, it is Michael to whom Father Gray writes: Michael demanding books and inquiring on points of dogma; Father Gray answering always by return. By December 1906 they are going to Mass regularly, reading a Latin missal (early nineteenth-century Venetian) and recording in their journal their amazement that the year of their "worst loss" is also the time of their greatest "marvel."[26]

By the time they travel up to Edinburgh together for the dedication of St. Peter's on 11 April 1907, Edith has decided to enter the Catholic Church. The news comes as a shock to Michael, who exclaims: "But this is terrible! I too shall have to become a Catholic!"[27] Michael, now determined not to be separated from her Fellow in matters of the spirit, demands that Father Gray receive her into the Church then and there. Firmly, Father Gray explains he is unable to oblige her, but arranges for her baptism to take place on 8 May, the feast of St. Michael, to be followed the next January by her confirmation.

Reconciled to Edith's decision—by sharing it—Michael now devotes her energies to helping Edith resolve her dilemma over "my secret sins."[28] Her first confession is to take place immediately, as preparation for her baptism into the new faith the week of their return. But Edith decides there is no way she can confess these to the bungling Father Goscommon since he clearly has no idea of her concerns; she wonders to her journal as to how she can speak to the good father "of the anguish of the 3rd, 4th & 5th Verses of *Femmes Damnées?*" (He would not have caught the reference anyway: this particular poem of that name was banned from French editions until 1949.[29]) Would she have to spell it out? "I know he thinks I have to confess forbidden relations to men," she writes in exasperation, "with whom the relations of my lifetime have been abstract & blameless."

Edith panics, sending Michael off to tell Father Goscommon to cancel the baptism scheduled for 19 April, while confiding to her journal: "There is nothing this young seminarist might not misconceive . . . even our Sacred Relation to each other!" But if confused, the good father is kind and his kindness calms her down. When Edith makes a "vow of chastity," he does not probe; Henry is duly baptized in Richmond on 19 April 1907. Michael seizes the occasion to make her own first confession, and as Henry records in the journal with no little defiance, she "comes straight down the Church to me, bearing a kiss ready on her lips . . . while the Priest prays she presses the kiss home with a brave sound . . . The Priest heard."[30]

Edith's acceptance of her new faith is in character, deep and serene. But for Michael, turning to the Catholic Church is only the beginning of her acceptance of it. She has, she confesses to Father Gray, "deeply heretic blood." Michael knows herself to be an instinctive rebel against all forms of coercion, however subtle. Older and more forceful, she dominates her tall, pale "Fellow," her Beloved Henry. For Father Gray nothing else, not even their poetry, captures their personalities as do their letters: Michael's scrawl across the page, high pitched, fervent, even reckless in its pursuit of the absolute. Henry's more careful hand, reticent, the keen mind shaping each sentence. Henry suffers from the bunglings of Father Goscommon, but Michael (probably advised by Father Gray) has taken as her confessor an Irish Dominican, Father Vincent McNabb, who assures her that "the Church welcomes poets" and intuitively accepts their companionship. (He writes after their death of their unique "fellowship in life and love."[31])

There are others for whom the welcome of the newly baptized Michael is qualified; she dreads telling the atheist Ricketts, and does so only after the final step of being received into the Church is taken; then writing:

> Being a serpent & so wise I trust this news will not startle you; for you must have seen how 'the ruddy Mass Book' has been with us all the winter . . . I invoke your Catholic mother of the many lovely names to plead with you to be glad.[32]

Shocked, Ricketts sends gallant congratulations; then bequeaths them "his mother's coral rosary, portable candlesticks, a crucifix and a small Spanish reliquary with fragments of the True Cross." He will resent her conversion, he writes, only if he finds his chair in Paragon usurped by the "*chers pères*."[33] On a later visit, when Henry absent-mindedly calls him "Father," he finds it hilarious. Knowing that one of the "dear Fathers" is in fact John Gray has made it all easier to accept.

With their conversion, a wall of sorts arises between the Fields and the Artists. But with Father Gray there are no restraints. Here is a man who has been through it all: translated verses from the "Femmes Damnées," entered the circle of the damned himself, but now shriven in chaste fellowship with André Raffalovich.[34] More than that, Father Gray also shares their past. Once the Michael Fields had been part of the new "aesthetic" movement, friends of Robert Browning, George Meredith, and Oscar Wilde. Now, after the turn of the century, Michael's letters, impulsive and often scrambled, are full of nostalgia for "those eighties, & their damnable aestheticism—there have been moments when I have . . . cursed it, & its lovely void." Although she admits once that "I did seek to flee," the older Michael has gained enough perspective to value "the work of those eighties & early Nineties—the good & vital work of Oscar—rising up from the folly—the good & the harm of Pater— your work—ours!"[35]

Because Michael shares this history with Father Gray, both artistically and spiritually, she is able to perceive that quality in him that others miss, exclaiming to her diary: "It is almost appalling to find how strong the capricious dominion of the senses still is in this devoted servant of God! Oh! how our past is our tragedy."[36] Michael is shocked by the intensity of Gray's delight in the visible world; perhaps, too, by his sensual pleasure in food and drink or his keen response to flowers, which drives him to become a keen botanist. Like Henry, she also notes that the "wild beast in the mystic" is kept under iron control by the discipline of his vocation, now incarnate in the actual church of St. Peter's. "Yesterday," she wrote him after its dedication, "how I rejoiced in our blessed church, & gave thanks it had been given to you to build it—surely in reparation—for all we were in deed or con- cept—in those years 85-95."

In honor of the past they share, Michael rebaptizes Gray "Father Silverpoints." In one sense, they feel at home with him also because, as Henry writes playfully, "the Priest is Man on Woman's terms."[37] But Michael also knows that, like herself, his past life as an artist was a bid for freedom—one now cruelly suppressed, she finds, in "Sancta" or "Holy Mother Church." Although she declares herself free "by happy instinct from the Seven Deadly Sins," the artist in her draws on "deeply heretic blood." Even before she submitted to the Church, she feared it as an institution that would compromise her hard-won autonomy, both as an artist and a woman. For aid against her own rebellious nature, she turns more and more to Father Gray:

> My dear Father—
>
> Of Lent—yes—I know you wd. not fail me. But I wrote to you when the great crisis of my life had come—when I had to give up my entire liberty, & abandoning every fastidiousness of choiceness & mood be . . . everyday with the Bread from Heaven.
>
> I wrote to you, as my Father in God, to you, as perceiving how dimly I walk on the orders of things—
>
> I know you did not understand I made appeal for help.

There is the difficulty of submitting herself, proud and aloof as she is. There is also the complexity of understanding the role of her past: "My terror is to *deny him in my past years,*" she wrote. "I have received Him in Communion—He has sought me from a Child—and again & again I have forsaken Him & broken away in the great wave of 'Modernism' that swept over us in the eighties— Sometimes deliberately I have turned my lamp upside down."

The great "Modernist" crisis of 1907 enacted her private spiritual dilemmas in public. Briefly, "Modernism" was advocated by those who believed that the Catholic Church should adapt "what was considered sound in modern thought even at the expense of radically changing the Church's essence."[38] Under the liberal policies of Pope Leo XIII, the "new thought" gathered momentum; but when Pope Pius X succeeded him in 1903, firm action against the "Modernists" was undertaken. A series of papal decrees placed the work of many scholars, such as that of George Tyrrell, a member of the Society of Jesus in England, on the Index of prohibited reading. At this time, Tyrrell had become a friend of Raffalovich, who followed all these developments closely, often reporting them at length to Father Gray in Edinburgh. By 1906, Tyrrell had been dismissed from his order; by 1907, he was excommunicated; when he dies two years later, "Modernism" in England is considered to have died with him. In some rough sense, George Tyrrell becomes to liberal Catholics what Oscar Wilde was to the pre-modernist artists of the 1890s.

Caught up between the forces of revolution and reaction, Michael tries desperately to reconcile the assertion that "the Church *is the home of freedom*" with its action in expelling George Tyrrell from the Society of Jesus as the result of two letters he wrote to the *Times* criticizing the encyclical *Pascendi:*

> My dear Father,
>
> The Times of this morn. brings to me *very great trouble.* I deplore also extremely the letters (or rather the temper of the letters) of Father Tyrrell.
>
> I maintain my right to criticise the encyclical letter. It has no claim to infallibility; & it is manifestly full of human temper, cleverness . . .
>
> The enclosed extracts this morning are far more serious. I am told that the Church *is the home of freedom.* And if today I purchased the reply of men on their defence, & considered what they need to say—I incur (officially) mortal sin—& may be excluded from the Sacraments of the Church.
>
> But English Michael will read his Times attentively every morning. (Not all the Pope's horses nor all the Pope's men will keep him from the Times!!! & large extracts will surely be given from the defence. English Catholics fought for freedom against the Armada, & surely they will have to do this again.)
>
> . . . If anyone has suffered from Modernism—I more. As you know, Father, I have cut it away from my life in so far as it could infect me.
>
> Henry suffers worse than I—she suffers as a man when tight cords are drawn across his brain. We have very narrow priests here . . .
>
> Personally I take refuge in the Mass against schism—I seek every day to love his Church with Christ, as the Church he died for . . .
>
> Yet I feel that any day the most terrible of deprivations might be mine. Do give me help. I wish you had told me of this

letter. *How does it affect you?* And how about the Church being the home of freedom? All this when every day we are growing profounder in our love to "Sancta" [Mother Church]—our whole lives filled with happiness because of her.

Such amazement in my heart!

Michael[39]

The happiness and the torment grow in Michael and Henry together. Just after Michael's baptism, she wrote Henry this short poem:

BELOVED, NOW I LOVE GOD FIRST
THERE IS FOR THEE SUCH SUMMER BURST
WHERE IT WAS STIRRING SPRING BEFORE,
LO, FOR THY FEET A BLOSSOM FLOOR!

PATIENCE A LITTLE WHILE TO WAIT
TILL I POSSESS MY NEW ESTATE,
THEN TO ASSUME THY GLORIOUS PART
IN MY ENRICHED AND FEASTING HEART.[40]

While their poems endure, as does their love each for the other, thriving now in a new dispensation, the correspondence between Michael and Father Gray is often strained, occasionally broken. (Did the fire claim those letters which, returned to Father Gray at their deaths, he deemed too exposed? In any case, no reply exists to Michael's plea as to whether the Church is *"the home of freedom."* Perhaps he did not answer at all.) Father Gray could be evasive. Partly it is his instinctive sense of the radical privacy of Michael's experience: "I know—or think I know—well how it is, that any word I write reads irrelevant, intrusive as a stone in one's shoe," he responds after one exchange, shortly before Michael appears for the dedication of St. Peter's.[41] Rather than tackle hard points of dogma, Father Gray advises on the practical difficulties of the spiritual life. Or speaks plainly of his own, in particular of his affair with St. John of the Cross. Growing easier with Michael, he is apt to tell her about his own reading of the moment—literary rather than "spiritual"—or about his attempts to write again: "I am expiating: when I should have chosen things I cared for nothing but words: now things grind my face and I pine for words."[42] Sending the Michael Fields his poem "The Emperor and the Bird," he comments, "It shows well how the remnants of my talent are limited—by the queer."[43] He speaks to Michael as poet to poet, remarking on effects he would like to achieve and those he admires. Only in rare moments does he speak intimately of his own spiritual experience, as in that letter (now lost or burnt) which relates his own moment of revelation in a Breton church.[44]

For Michael's part, her letters (or, to be more accurate, those which Father Gray thought proper to preserve) speak almost entirely of spiritual difficulties which become, under pressure of events, spiritual emergencies. For Michael's is instinctively a protestant soul; obedience comes hard to her and perhaps she knew her course was not to be an easy one in any case. Facing perhaps a familiar enemy, Father Gray throws his energy into strengthening Michael in her struggle with herself. "Michael had the look, the laugh, and many of the thoughts of a child," Father Gray once remarked.[45] Certainly Michael flung herself unto the strength of Father Gray with all a child's trust and impetuousness. His occasional obscurity or apparent harshness frightened them. Once Michael wrote: "Henry & I go on wondering about your last letter— we don't understand it: it seems like a vexed, angry arrival, & indeed we don't know where we have offended." Here Father Gray's habit of writing in aphorisms works against him. Again and again Michael's letters repeat the accusation: "You put me in a very hot temper last night—I could not understand your letter." On yet another occasion, she observes to her diary: "Monday and Tuesday filled with distracting letters from Father Gray. Not one of the simple sentences gives a simple meaning, the meaning is scattered as the leaves of the pythoness."

Despite such apparent obscurities, Father Gray proves a rock of consolation during the next few years. For some time Henry has been frail. Her beloved younger sister, Amy, contracts pneumonia in January 1909; making the grueling trip by boat and train to Dublin, the Michael Fields arrive in time only to see her across the threshold; they return with her body to the cottage in Richmond, to bury her near them. But Henry never recovers her uncertain health; she collapses just over a year later; the doctor is not optimistic in his prognosis. Father Gray writes,

> My dear Michael
> The terrifying news. It is only a threat: the blow must not fall. I thank God that Henry will loyally use all the means of safety: and use good will—perfect will—to the same end. I am consoled by what you write of the long sleep. Michael has now a fine pact—to double the sollicitude [sic] which is already complete ... I shall make the solemn momento [sic]— immediately before communion—until all fear is past.[46]

Michael replies:

> I read again & again the opening sentences of your letter. And also—"I shall make the solemn memento immediately before communion—until all fear is past."—
> Oh thank you.
> this will steady me.
> —Reprove & strengthen me: teach me how to behave to Henry.
> MICHAEL

Weeks later Michael writes in her journal: "I offered Divine Sacrifice for Henry's restored eyesight and Henry's restored wits."[47] But Henry's precarious state declines into mortal illness: in late January she is diagnosed with terminal cancer. She has just turned forty-nine. Henry herself writes Father Gray of how, on that "Monday when the specialist was silent & I knew the worst," she was gripped by the "agony of a doom that reft Michael & me apart, who lived a bone-of-bone, a flesh-of-flesh life."[48] Refusing "a hideous operation of alleviation," Henry also decides against using morphine, lest it cloud her mind. Within her newly found faith, the pain also makes sense to her: as penance for her "great, flagrant sinning"; as a way she can now share in Christ's suffering; as a way of making spiritual progress; as a help to Amy in making her way from Purgatory to Heaven. But often the pain is at the limits of the endurable. "When the pain is very bad," Henry writes at Easter of 1911, "Michael takes me in her arms, & the vital warmth of her being is of such power the pain goes to sleep."[49] When even Michael's warm embrace is no longer a help, Henry grips the crucifix as if it were a lightning rod, praying for the agony to pass through her.

For Michael, having to watch this is almost as hard. "The days are inconceivably terrible," she writes to Father Gray. Henry's decline is ruthless. At one point, Henry develops dropsy; her legs have to be punctured to drain them; her swollen throat produces "a sound like that of a dove that fights against choking corn." Michael writes it into a poem to God:

> SHE IS SINGING TO THEE, DOMINE!
>> DOST HEAR HER NOW?
> SHE IS SINGING TO THEE FROM A BURNING THROAT,
> AND MELANCHOLY AS THE OWL'S LOVE-NOTE;
> SHE IS SINGING TO THEE FROM THE UTMOST BOUGH
>> OF THE TREE OF GOLGOTHA, WHERE IT IS BARE,
> AND THE FRUIT TORN FROM IT THAT FRUITED THERE;
> SHE IS SINGING—CANST THOU STOP THE STRAIN,
>> THE HOMAGE OF SUCH PAIN?
> DOMINE, STOOP DOWN TO HER AGAIN![50]

In the grip of this mortal illness, they face into another year. Following the example of Gray and Raffalovich, they have become members of the lay order of Dominicans. And so, at midnight of the new year, they greet 1912 in their Dominican scapulars (cloaks) and sing a "marriage-song." A short time later, they make a further Solemn Profession as a sort of joint marriage to Jesus with "the *two* gold rings & the lovely spousals [making us] Brides of the Heavenly Bridegroom together."[51] If Henry's illness binds them as never before, it also renews many of their friendships. Ricketts visits frequently, bearing gifts: a rare plant; rose-leaf conserves; some very fine chocolate.[52] But his love for them both stumbles at the frontiers of the spirit.

And so it is to Father Gray alone that Michael turns for help, or confesses her terror. "Michael lies bleeding, & in the dust," she writes: "Help me more, Father, I have none save you to help." Who can be equal to such entreaty? There are the difficulties of distance; the pressure of work; the shortage of time. Father Gray does not reply promptly—perhaps he does not know how to respond. When at last he does write, his letters are, Michael rages,

> inexplicable . . . O poet of Silver-points, if you are back in that world of spleen, & pique—Michael, alas!—is only too able to follow you—to take revenges, & plan the most exquisite tortures but we have not so learned Christ!—When the great darkness of the spring fell on me—Henry's pain, & my injured health—I turned to you for help: and you cut all communication wires.
>
> Unravel please, Inexplicable No. 2. Much as I desire to see you Father. It is not as a rosy riddle I would see you.
> Michael

In the end, Father Gray writes: clearly and strongly. He visits. He prays with and for Henry and Michael. Their suffering—and their redemption—mark forever the watershed between their shared past and shared present.

"I think constantly of you and Henry in your joy & suffering," he writes (in the last letter to survive from his side of the correspondence):

> Great is the Beloved who has chosen us. I feel much confusion under the sense of His goodness: and that I think produces the most quickening movements in my life. I ran about the world seeking the objects of my desires: and the longer they were unfulfilled increasing my demands. And when it was clearly of no use for me to continue kicking up the dust of the desert & there seemed nothing left but to hide myself & my failure without delay the heavens opened and the world revealed is so wonderful that it hardly surprised to meet Michael in the white robe of the redeemed. We never met in the desert.[53]

Months later, a part of one of Gray's letters is copied into the private journal: "Michael, I join with great joy in thanking God for your birth. I have watched the day coming near. I hear with much gratitude about the sufferer and whatever consolations or mitigations are found: I wonder with deep sympathy, how you Michael, can keep the balance between attachment and detachment." In Michael's hand the entry continues: "He speaks of a November visit and the opportunity to him most precious of sight with Michael and a word with her. Now *he* realizes her tragedy with fellow feeling and the intelligence of the heart."[54]

In response, Michael thanks him for the "strong words, so helpful to Henry & to me," resolving, "I will make a tremendous effort to overcome my hysteria. It grips me: it is cruel, edges of pain all about my body." She veers from terror to resolution and back again, pleading, "Teach Michael more of 'her part.'" At the last, the help that Father Gray gives is a tribute to the sure strength he has now found as a priest. "Father dear, what a bond you love me," Henry writes a few months before her death. "It reminds me of the way, so intimate & powerful in [which] Whym Chow & I used to share our appreciation & love of Michael's self. Such a bond!"[55]

That very month Michael, feeling broken, consults a doctor; the verdict is breast cancer. She is offered an operation that might save her life, or at least prolong it. She refuses. She wishes to share in the suffering of the Beloved, to go step by step the way Henry has gone. Or is it that Michael, perhaps, once again, does not wish to be left behind?

Only Father Gray and her confessor, Father Vincent McNabb, know of her condition. Absorbed in her own dying, Henry thinks that Michael has some heart trouble and that the doctor's concern is exaggerated. Over the next few months, every detail of their lives takes on an preternatural significance, as if it were happening before them in an enlarged form. In the midst of terrible pain, Henry has some easier intervals; during these, she takes note of what agony is teaching her: "It is a great solitude. And I have been able to think of things with a quietness I would not have lost . . . Pain is so real it may even be a key to the fresh motions of childhood. It makes all things new."[56] Speaking of being with

Michael, "It is infinitely soft between us," Henry writes. "Warm buds open."[57]

On 25 November, Henry stops writing; she saves all her energy now for prayer. Ricketts visits, bringing clay angels and a camel laden with pearls for the Christmas crib. She and Michael had planned the deathbed, but when Henry dies on 13 December, she does so whispering, "Not yet, not yet." The funeral brings on Michael's first hemorrhage; "Two days after thou wert gone, bleeding came," Michael tells Henry in their journal. It is no longer possible to keep the truth from herself or others. Now ill and alone, Michael turns once again to Father Gray in her own great need. At first she rebels at the Church's version of Henry's present life after death: of her being first in Heaven and then in Purgatory:

> Father Gray comes. We have a solemn talk. I open up my grief at the Church's action—first speaking of my Love as among the Angels; then after a few weeks, in Purgatory. I tell him how this has checked me and use the simile of Henry landing in Australia and enjoying the kangaroos, and Henry still tossed on unknown seas. "Michael," he says, "you must accept this paradox." He always thinks of a dead friend as with God. The awful thing is for it to become possible to God, to have His desire and to be able to admit man into His presence. Father Gray makes me feel how awful God's task is. Yes: what I feel about Henry's being gone is aridity: it happens, He commands me to be sure, whatever suffering is before me, sufficient grace will be with me to meet that suffering.[58]

In the last months, Michael consents to move from Richmond to a cottage on the grounds of the Dominican priory at Hawkesyard in Staffordshire—to be near her friend and confessor, Father Vincent McNabb. Her last (surviving) letter to Father Gray reveals a new control; but also a new fear of her "heretic blood":

> Beloved & most faithful Father
>   I have been in mortal struggle. Forgive.

The wonder & joy of being summoned here to die among the Dominicans—the joy that Father Vincent wants me near him to be with him at the last, I have longed to write you of: you see, please God, I have left Paragon behind for ever.

—I am suddenly asked to die in a stuffy drawing room with a grand piano, & lusters & every form of vulgar & horrible detail.

—I am a little afraid of my brain giving way & of turning blasphemer . . .

—*Pray.*

And come & help me *as soon as you can.*

. . . I am humbly your child.

michael

When World War I broke out on 5 August, Jenny the cook bursts into the drawing room to announce, "Good news; fifty thousand Germans killed!" Appalled at such bloodthirstiness, Michael also finds herself strangely excited. Death seems different now; she is calmer, happier; the nurse reports that Michael smiles all night in her sleep. On 18 September, the chaotic handwriting in the journal finally stumbles to a halt; but Michael continues to go to Mass at seven in the morning, wheeled to the priory in a Bath chair. On 26 September, she rises early, writes Ricketts; when the nurse comes to dress her for Mass, she falls into her arms and dies.[59]

Ricketts is the chief beneficiary under her will. Nine years later, shocked to hear that the Fields lay separate, in unmarked graves, Ricketts creates for them a tomb of black-and-white marble, asking Father Gray for a simple inscription. Thinking of the aunt and niece, bound by an earthly love but also married into a spiritual one, he sends back to Ricketts one line, which is duly engraved: "United in blood, united in Christ."[60]

Between the death of the old Queen in 1901 and the outbreak of the Great War, the histories of Father Gray's family are grouped around the drama of the Michael Fields like so many resonant subplots.

Of his old friend Arthur Symons, Father Gray first heard from Michael that he had been discovered in Bologna "mad and chained" (as she tells her journal).[61] Having made his own inquiries into the situation, Father Gray writes her an account, cautioning

> It is as black a case as can be—so horrible: don't speak much about it, or you will learn details. I should think at first glance that the chain is a gloss that has slipped into the text. There are plenty of horrors with or without. 2n. There is a little hope. The particular disease hitherto hopeless, has been treated in my madhouse by a physician a genius without much success . . . The whole treatment is largely experimental; but I thought good to try what was possible for the poor soul by me in the past, so much disliked & then liked.[62]

Symons had been (incorrectly) diagnosed as having general paralysis of the insane (whatever that might mean in modern terms). Father Gray recommends Dr. William Ford Robertson, pathologist to the Scottish asylums, who specializes in a serum treatment for this condition. But on his own doctor's advice, Symons is taken to a private home run by a Dr. Griggin at Crowborough. Here Father Gray visits him, arriving with a book of Dürer woodcuts. "To assure the people, [to] be magnificent and leisurely," Gray writes Michael, "characterizes the disease." He records the opening exchange:

> What is your name sonny?
> Edward the Seventh.
> Ah, I am a priest.
> Yes, I shall soon be that myself.[63]

From his visits, Father Gray is able to assure Michael that Symons is receiving good care; that his wife, Rhoda, is more than adequate to the task before her. In fact, Symons does "recover"— in the sense that he is able to lead a normal life; sadly, his prose becomes normal as well.

Sometimes the partings are hard; as with Mabel Beardsley, Aubrey's sister, loved by many artists. Shortly after her baptism into the Catholic faith, Father Gray wrote Michael, "It is true that Mabel Beardsley (AB's sister) and I are fond of one another."[64] When she too is diagnosed with cancer, Mabel becomes another to see across death's threshold. Whenever Father Gray and André can manage it, they spend long hours in the nursing home, playing cards, which they both detest, amusing her as only Mabel can be amused, with gossip, books, small gifts.[65] "Being Aubrey's sister little that is hidden to most young girls was unknown to Mabel," Will Rothenstein recalls, "& there was nothing that cd not be discussed."[66] Their mutual acquaintance from the Beardsley/Wilde circles; sexual inversion; the stage—Mabel had been an actress—or the new Russian ballet; nothing is immune from comment, query, critique. Ricketts comes frequently; he makes her a series of dolls, fantastically dressed. When William Butler Yeats visits in January of 1913, he finds them with their faces turned to the wall— "Because to-day is some religious festival / They had a priest say Mass . . ." Stirred by her courage, her gaiety in the face of death, he writes a poem sequence, "Upon a Dying Lady":

I.

Her Courtesy

With the old kindness, the old distinguished grace,
She lies, her lovely piteous head amid dull red hair
Propped upon pillows, rouge on the pallor of her face.
She would not have us sad because she is lying there,
And when she meets our gaze her eyes are laughter-lit,
Her speech a wicked tale that we may vie with her,
Matching our broken-hearted wit against her wit,
Thinking of saints and of Petronius Arbiter.[67]

"We have naught for death but toys," Yeats remarks. Yet, between the cards, the toys, the gossip, and the gifts, Mabel lives indomitably on until 1916.

Other blows fall. In 1911, Gray's younger brother Norval dies. The difficult Alexander, whose future Father Gray and Raffalovich had often discussed, at last settles down to a career as a military clerk in Africa (what country is never specified), marrying an African woman. In 1919, "Alectryo" dies, leaving two young sons, whom Father Gray takes in for a short period and then places for their schooling with the Dominicans at Hawkesyard.

With the old intimate world so visibly dying about him, Father Gray does not seem to feel the war. Yet it seems that Raffalovich's letters are full of the deaths of young men. Raffalovich has also lost a good deal of his income, invested in German and Russian funds.[68] He makes curious economies, although a guest recalls that *gateaux* were flown in from Sindar's or Rutenburg's in Paris right up to the early 1930s.[69] Yet Raffalovich decides to support two artists of merit: the young Cecil Wright, whose father is a friend, and the controversial Eric Gill, calligrapher and stone carver, who lives in a commune in Ditchling, combining there a rare religious fervor with a less public creed of free love.[70] The war is a test of everyone's nerves. Raffalovich and Miss Gribbell take the air-raid warnings over Edinburgh with studied calm. But Father Gray complains after one air raid that "the people in the street made so much noise that you did not get the full effect."[71]

After the first decades of the new century, Father Gray and André Raffalovich come to be regarded as something near to anachronisms. "I know you like *period* individuals and I am distinctly *period*," Raffalovich confides to a young friend in 1931.[72] But even before the 1920s, the pair must seem like cultural survivors from a forgotten age. For those who know about the nineties, they are a subject of curiosity. One who seeks them out is Ronald Firbank, a minor novelist and convert to Catholicism. He makes a formal call on Father Gray in September 1914. In doing so, he reflects, he has at last completed his living mementos of "the saint and martyr of homosexuality," Oscar Wilde. (His visit is later put to good use when he places both Father Gray and André Raffalovich in two of his novels, *Vainglory* and *Inclinations*.[73]) How Father Gray takes to being "collected" is not known. One who knew him well, Father Edwin Essex, recalls how the Canon, as Father Gray is to become, "could talk, when the rare mood was on him, with the familiarity of intimate, personal knowledge of Wilde ('Ah, poor Oscar,' it ever was), Beardsley, Johnson, Dowson, and the rest of them." At these times, he "would describe, but only when the humour took him,

> how Dowson scribbled verses on the tablecloth in a Soho restaurant, wooing his Cynara as she served the spaghetti; and what wailing and lamentation went up one day when Dowson was told she had eloped with a chef. And the Canon would indulge in a grim, mirthless chuckle, and recall: '*I have been faithful to thee, Cynara, in my fashion.*' Yes, John Gray was the man to have filled in the human background, spectacular, often sombre, of the gay nineties, and preserved in detail the lively touches that are apt to fade with the years. There was once a fine hubbub outside the restaurant door. 'Whatever's that?' someone asked. 'Only Lionel (Johnson) crying for his perambulator,' came the answer—from Gray himself, I was led to suspect, for L. J. in spite of his mighty dome of a head, happened to be a diminutive and somewhat peppery man.

But, adds Father Essex, "it was seldom indeed that the Canon would open up on the personalities of the past. Most of them ended their days as Catholics, but they belonged to an age that was dead, to an age that had nothing in common with the Canon's way of life . . ." Even though, as a Dominican lay brother, John Gray had been put "under obedience" by the Prior Provincial to write of his nineties acquaintance, Father Essex considers "it was asking too much of a man who had buried his past. Even the precious books that had survived the forgotten era were not allowed to show their faces on his shelves. Like so many naughty children they stood there—with their faces to the wall."[74]

But, far from destroying his past, Father Gray comes to embody it. One observer remarks of Father Gray's admirers—and, by implication, of Father Gray himself—that there was something as repulsive as attractive about all of them—a kind of hermetism that daunted, a ponderous *sic est & fiat* so alien to the late thirties and early forties—coupled with a ghostly delicacy/subtlety surviving from the Yellow Book—an epigrammatic skill in snubbing by implication— that to people of my generation as you might call it was incomprehensibly baffling, crushing and—you will hardly credit it—flirtatious.[75]

Such is the atmosphere of the priest's house. There, in monastic silence, a visitor would move through an unearthly gloom to confront Father Gray, who with the years has grown more formal, more ceremonious, more withdrawn. The house has grown to embody his elusive personality, at once seductive and forbidding. In the library on the mantlepiece stands a statuette shrouded from head to foot. Father Gray had once asked Eric Gill to carve him a small statue of a man weeping for his sins. But when it arrived, it was found to be too "fleshly" to expose to the general gaze. (How does one, after all, explain to visitors Gill's obvious belief that the phallus is an emblem of God's own virility or the potency of holiness?[76]) Certainly the unwary visitor learns to check his curiosity. Should he, in a moment of inattention, pick out from the shelves any book whose spine is turned towards the wall, it would, without comment, be gently lifted from his hand and returned to its proper place.[77]

And yet the ambience, oppressive to some, is imbued with the most hardheaded order. In Father Gray's house, a priestly colleague notes,

> everything went by rule. (Any failure put him out.) He had a special bath-towel which was like a dressing-grown, so that he could hop out of the bath and dry himself as he moved to his bedroom. For Mass he wore breeches under his cassock, so as not to spoil the crease of his trousers: of which he had seven pairs, one for each day of the week. After Mass and breakfast he dealt with as much of his correspondence as he could. (Once a month the arrears were tackled, and finished off.) His

letters were like telegrams. Yet they were *written*. After that, his first task was to take holy communion to the sick of the parish.[78]

Those who visit as guests write how "the orderliness, regularity and punctuality of his life and household, his tranquil, tidy soul and all about him reminded one of the monastery, and Father John Gray the humblest, most studious and devoted monk in it."[79]

At St. Peter's, a visiting Dominican each Sunday is the rule. The visitor would arrive on Saturday, dine that night with Father Gray in the presbytery, say the early Mass on Sunday, preach at the sung High Mass which Father Gray himself would celebrate, and preach again in the evening. After the High Mass, the visitor invariably would be taken the short distance down the road for the Sunday luncheon. This, together with the Tuesday dinner parties, have become Raffalovich's Edinburgh version of his former London salon. There, beneath the magnificent portrait of his mother, Raffalovich's table would at one time or another include every person of distinction within his orbit. Noted academics, artists, and writers were invited as a matter of course; occasionally there would be "a highly cultured Copt, a characteristically smiling Japanese, a Chinaman showing his interested audience the correct way of making tea."[80]

As the guest lists are ample evidence, Raffalovich no longer had any need to pursue his "lions." Once snubbed himself, he would reach out to the stranger, to the young, to the obscure. "People were welcomed for their own sakes, for some gift of heart or mind which he alone may have been fine enough to discover," Margaret Sackville recalls. She is a long-standing friend who would herself preside, in the later years, over these gatherings. She valued in particular that "curious delicacy" which dictates Raffalovich's taste in flowers, as in friends; his genius for choice and arrangement; his sheer social artistry. "And all these guests, so ingeniously contrasted, were held together, enveloped, made one, by their host's watchful, interested, all-pervading personality," Sackville observes.

He was conscious of each individually, just as a conductor is conscious of each separate member of his orchestra. His admirable talk would flash, skim, dart, with the swiftness of a dragonfly, over the whole: turning from books to vivid personalities, with none of the awful creaking of cart-wheels which so often a British lunch-tables announces a change of topic! The conversational shuttlecock was never allowed to fall; or if it did touch earth for a moment it was soon in the air once more. Not even the clumsiest player could spoil the game.[81]

Few who attend these occasions will ever forget their host. Diminutive but sitting ramrod straight, with impeccable white collar and clipped mustache, Raffalovich would follow the conversation with his quick black eyes, turning it one way or another with an adroit remark, or smiling at some sally with his beautiful smile, which would suddenly vanish as if it had been wiped off a chalkboard.

Presiding over these gatherings with practiced confidence, Florence Gribbell plays her essential part in the Whitehouse Terrace household. As Sackville observes, Raffalovich and Father Gray "considered her comfort and contentment in every detail: even seriously advising her on the choice of a new gown, and supervising her reading. Such solicitude was not officious but charmingly touching." As hostess of the Sunday parties, Florence Gribbell was, in Sackville's mind, "so *digne* (I can find no equivalent English for the expressive French word), so adequate in her behaviour."

As for Father Gray, Sackville sees him as a presence to be reckoned with at these Sunday congregations:

> If André Raffalovich's conversation was quicksilver, the Canon's provided the solid foundation on which these airy improvisations might rest. A little remote, even, some might think, a little stern, anyhow austere, it is not without significance that his favourite travels were made in Iceland. He never talked at random, his judgment, always weighty and considered, was, without arrogance, final.[82]

To these proceedings, Father Gray came to be considered a center of gravity. Despite a somewhat abstracted air, when appealed to in the course of a conversation he "was always ready with the type of comment that seemed to make any further discussion of the matter superfluous. He was a consummate master of the *mot juste*."[83]

The gravity extends to the purpose of these occasions. They are not mere social pleasures; they are, as Father Gray once explained to another priest, part of a mission. "Society," he said, "is something God has built into human nature. It is the medium by which . . . Christianity circulates."[84] On these occasions, Raffalovich's and Father Gray's sense of society as vocation weighs every detail; it accounts for the care with which food and drink are chosen and prepared; the guests selected; the conversation dictated and closely supervised. By such attentions does exquisite taste transmute itself into a finely tuned moral sense. The same conscious discipline extends to their own friendship. Recalling how André would welcome Father Gray at the door, a guest remarked: "Rooted, I felt, in an earlier generation, the high Edwardian handshake and slight formality of manner were of a different date. Always greeted by his host as an honoured guest (in spite of daily meetings), this special—some would think superfluous—courtesy belonged to the shape, the significance of Whitehouse Terrace hospitality."[85] Others perceive its shape and significance as distinctly *fin de siècle;* these assemblies, another guest explains, taken all round, were "rather like acting in one of Oscar Wilde's plays produced by Cecil Beaton in slightly off-period costume."[86]

"*Such* parties!" the young novelist Hugh Walpole writes Henry James. Walpole goes up regularly to Edinburgh, where his father is the Anglican bishop. He has been invited to High Mass at St. Peter's and dinner at Whitehouse Terrace. But rather than ritualized beauty, Walpole finds offense. In his own life, religion and homosexuality have been kept rigorously distinct. In the friendship of Father Gray and André Raffalovich, homosexuality had been sublimed into an ardent spirituality. Is it this sense of a continuum between these two lives that leads Walpole to feel that their spiritual life was, in some sense, still immoral? Something indeed happens that Sunday. Rather than spell out the complexities of his reaction to the service at St. Peter's, Walpole writes angrily to James about "immorality on stone floors." James's considerable sexual curiosity is piqued. He presses for details. Nor did Walpole's more extended account satisfy: "I could have done with more detail," he writes back, "as when you say '*Such* parties!' I want so to hear exactly what parties they are. When you refer to their 'immorality on stone floors,' and with prayerbooks in their hands, so long as the exigencies of the situation permit of the manual retention of the sacred volumes, I do so want the picture developed and the proceedings authenticated."[87]

Whatever Walpole thinks he witnessed, this is uncharacteristically heavy-handed for Henry James. For who but he could better understand the bittersweet discipline of their relations? "Never for a moment did they appear to relax into the free and easy communication of old friends," one of their circle writes:

> Whenever they met, as they did almost daily, it was as though they had been parted for months. There was the same handshake, the same question and answer as to health and activities. The sight of them greeting each other, with what looked like a detached, impersonal interest, was a thing to marvel at. Their approach was so schooled, there was such an element of sweet restraint about it, that one found it hard to realise they had been intimate friends for so many years.[88]

Another friend confesses bafflement over an intimacy so profound, its only sign is the ripple on the surface of ceremonial, somewhat overelaborated formalities. "Of the friendship of John Gray and André Raffalovich it is difficult to write," confides Peter Anson, who comes to know them both from December 1919 onwards, "because it was so aloof and detached":

> So far as the outside world was concerned it hardly existed. Their relationship—even after forty years—continued to be formal. Most Sunday evenings after a cold supper the front door bell would ring, and a few moments later the parlourmaid would open the drawing room door to announce "Canon Gray."

Had a complete stranger been present, his impression would have been that these two men were hardly more than acquaintances. André would jump up, bow slightly as he grasped the visitor's right hand, and say—almost in a tone of surprise: "Dear Canon, how kind of you to call!", or something to that effect. Then for an hour or so the conversation was as witty and epigrammatic as it had been at luncheon—possibly a little more intimate, but not much so. Then at 10 o'clock the parlour-maid appeared with a silver tray bearing whiskey, a siphon of soda-water, and cut-glass carafes of water and lemonade. "Dear Canon, will you be so kind as to serve the drinks?" And so, with further exchange of polite remarks, the typical Sunday came to an end, with more handshaking and bows.[89]

And yet, another friend asserts, for all this stiff ceremoniousness, "one was immediately aware of the affectionate reverence each lavished on the other."[90]

The same discipline extends to other relationships. "Did anybody ever understand John Gray?" Anson once wondered. "When conversing with him one had the feeling that he was wearing a mask. At moments the mask was raised very slightly; but I can honestly say that never once in fifteen years that I continued to meet him was the mask removed. He remained inscrutable, enigmatic, shrouded in mystery, and it was largely because of this polished reserve that he was so fascinating."[91] For some, Father Gray's manner is alien to the new generation of the 1920s, like that of the nineties poet satirized by Ezra Pound in his character M. Verog, "out of step with the decade / Detached from his contemporaries, / Neglected by the young." Yet that manner merely deflects attention from a keenly modern sensibility which is, after seventeen years of silence, at last to find distinctive speech.

7 | THE PICTURE IN THE ATTIC

(JUNE 1914–JANUARY 1930)

SINCE HE HAD SENT HIS CHINESE POEM to the Michael Fields for Christmas 1908, Father Gray apparently had written nothing except a few hymns. With the exception of translation or editing work and pious verses such as those published as *Ad Matrem,* he had kept his vow of silence since he had entered Scots College. Gray was not the only poet to find this a barren period. Of this first decade of the new century T. S. Eliot wrote: "I do not think it is too sweeping to say that there was no poet, in either country [England or America], who could have been of use to a beginner in 1908 . . . The question was still: where do we go from Swinburne? and the answer appeared to be, nowhere." The nearest he himself had come to "any living tradition," Eliot observes, had been in his reading as an undergraduate of the English poets of the nineties—who, he reminds us, culturally "were dead."[1]

In one sense Father Gray welcomes that designation. He has rejected his own nineties poetry, as having "nothing in it but shame at any given point," even though "it has always had an aim, and that sometimes redeems even failure."[2] (Thomas Sturge Moore, who had known John Gray from the early days of the Vale, cautioned another poet who wished to collect Gray's poetry in the thirties and forties: "I have always had the idea that John Gray's conversion proved by no means a salvation[.] He once wrote to me that he had nothing left but 'the ruins of a talent.' The church seems to be determined [to] suppress even the ghost of that talent."[3] For the Church, this was the expected and necessary sacrifice, one in which Father Gray not only colluded but gave wholehearted consent. At his funeral, Father Bernard Delany spoke of Father Gray as one who might have achieved acclaim as a poet. But "the Poet gave way to the Priest. He made songs and sang as a poet: but it is the songs and the poems he did *not* sing that give him his real, his royal, priestly greatness . . . How many songs must die that the supreme song of self-dedication may live?"[4])

Thus by the 1920s, Father Gray finds himself in the uncomfortable position of ex-poet. As if to drive the irony home, his work is now discovered by a new generation of writers. In 1905, he gives permission to John Masefield to use two poems in the anthology *A Sailor's Garland.* Two others from *Spiritual Poems* are republished in *The Oxford Book of Mystical Verse.* A. J. A. Symons, nineties scholar and biographer of "Baron Corvo," privately printed one poem suppressed from the *Silverpoints* manuscript, then went on to reprint six other of its poems in *An Anthology of Nineties Verse,* while speaking in the introduction of Gray's "Gallic elegance."[5] Of this selection, Ricketts wrote to Father Gray: "I thought you & Michael Field came out very well in the Verse of the Nineties. I found Dowson & Francis Thompson below their reputation."[6] Of course, Father Gray reflects, it is extremely irritating to regain a reputation as a period poet just as one is attempting to work out a contemporary style. For that is to be the great task of his late middle age.

Not that Father Gray is completely cut off. His correspondence during the first decades of the century includes such names as the distinguished French poet Francis Jammes, John Masefield, Laurence Housman, Lady Gregory, Edward Martyn, E. P. Ker, Percy Lubbock, Roger Fry, Herbert Read, and Sir Herbert Grierson, the editor of Donne.[7] Between them, Father Gray and Raffalovich have an eye for talent, particularly among the young. They befriend Graham Greene while he is an undergraduate at Oxford; after his conversion to Catholicism in 1926, young Greene becomes one of the people with whom they keep in touch. Of this period, Greene himself recalls that "it was the habit of Father Gray and Raffalovich to come to lunch" at Chipping Camden "when they used to make their yearly pilgrimage to Malmesbury . . . It was always an amusing occasion."[8] Describing Raffalovich as a "sweet, cultured and most ugly Jew," he reciprocates their hospitality by placing Raffalovich in his first popular novel, *Stamboul Train,* as Eckman, the convert Jew who keeps a copy of the Bible chained to the base of his toilet.[9]

Raffalovich has always been easy to caricature. Not only a foreigner, but a wealthy foreigner and a Catholic in a closed society, he is easy prey. But he is valued among his friends, and to Father Gray he is literally a godsend. His reading, his intelligent enthusiasms, his wide variety of social contacts, his hospitality, all render him invaluable as a focus of a lively social circle. His salon alone would give Father Gray the necessary environment for creative work. "You are a guardian angel to me," Father Gray once wrote him, "for without all these stimuli from without I should shrivel up intellectually at least if not also spiritually."[10]

Father Gray has also his own resources. In the later part of the twenties, he has come to know several poets of the "Georgian school," which had its heyday during 1911–12. Edmund Blunden and Gordon Bottomley both become enthusiastic admirers of Gray's mature poetry. There are also his books; between his and Raffalovich's joint libraries there are editions of T. S. Eliot, Robert Graves, Aldous Huxley, D. H. Lawrence, Ezra Pound, Edith Sitwell, and W. B. Yeats.[11]

Father Gray has also once again become involved with a community of artists—those who live and work with Eric Gill in Ditchling. Like that of Shannon and Ricketts, Gill's artwork is varied: from stone carving to wood engraving and typography. Like the Vale, the Gill commune becomes a center for fine bookmaking with the new partnership of Gill and Hilary Peplar. Unlike the Vale, the Ditchling community lives a self-consciously religious life— which does not stop Eric Gill from indulging secretly in unorthodox sexual practices.[12]

It is at one of Raffalovich's famous Sunday luncheons, in June 1914, that Eric Gill meets Father Vincent McNabb. At the time, Father McNabb was still seeing the dying Michael over the threshold at the Dominican house at Hawkesyard, where he was to become prior provincial. The Michaels had written effusive congratulations to Eric Gill on his conversion in February 1913, speaking to him as "Artist to artist, though stranger to stranger . . ."[13] In Father Vincent they have a common bond, for he is already well on the way to becoming one of the most charismatic of Dominicans.

Eric Gill finds himself attracted to this large, forceful Irish priest; he likes the idea of monastic orders anyway and is easily persuaded to become, like both Raffalovich and Father Gray as well as Michael Field, a member of the Third, or lay, Order of the Dominicans. This involves Gill in visits to Hawkesyard Priory; in a commitment to an orderly life of prayer; in reading and studying the works of Thomas Aquinas, whose theology he finds (as did James Joyce) complementary to the dedicated artistic life. Father Vincent McNabb, for his part, sees in Eric Gill and Ditchling the possibility of a radical regeneration of Catholic life in England, making the Gill commune a "kind of blueprint for the founding of other Ditchlings, self-sufficient Catholic communities all over England." The place dominates Father Vincent's thinking. "You ask 'Is Ditchling practicable?'" he writes. "In the Irish fashion I answer by a further question 'Is anything else practicable?'"[14] For both Eric Gill and Father McNabb, their meeting is in every sense seminal, leading to a founding of a community explicitly Catholic but also, in the kind of Catholicism it espouses, a site for subversion.

For Ditchling is now committed to a utopian ideal articulated most forcibly in Hilaire Belloc's *The Servile State*. Written just before the World War I, this is a vigorous polemic, as sharply anticapitalist as it is caustically antisocialist. Essentially, it argues that "the key to the right life" is *ownership:* but the ownership being that of small agricultural holdings away from state control and a return to private property in the ownership of tools, workshops, land. The theories have much in common with the Chartists of the 1840s; the difference lies in their Catholicism. These are Catholic visions for a new Catholic England and Ditchling, in Father Vincent McNabb's version of it, embodies many of the values of his Irish Catholic boyhood: the cult of the Madonna; the cohesiveness of family; the dignity and holiness of lowly occupation; the holdings of the small farmer, devoted to the land; and, finally, in Gill's studio, the image of the carpenter's shop—all informed by explications from the teachings of St. Thomas. Father Vincent loves his visits to Ditchling, for he sees there the incarnation of his ideal of the worker-artist-monk embodied in Eric Gill, as well as his vigorous and very masculine respect for paternity evident in his many children. Gill is also a talented spiritual parent. A succession of young men come to work with him at Ditchling, among them Desmond Chute, Hilary Peplar, David Jones. Many, if not all, also become Third Order Dominicans.[15]

Raffalovich praises Gill for his *"roominess* of mind," through which he can move around without knocking against mental furniture. (He compares his own mind to a curio stop in which one can pick up some bargains if one can stand the things one does not want.)[16] In acknowledgement of this spaciousness, Father Gray commissions Gill to engrave a bookplate: a knotted snake—to signify the danger inherent in certain of Raffalovich's books, particularly those dealing with the subject of inversion—the serpent being an image both of dangerous sin and of the healing arts.

During these postwar years, Father Gray visits Ditchling frequently, sometimes calling to check on the progress of his young nephew Norval, whom, after the death of their father, "Alectryo," he has placed during school holidays in the Gills' care. It is at Ditchling that Gill and Peplar establish St. Dominic's Press, summed up by one connoisseur as "The most private and at the same time the most commercial (and certainly the most individual) of the English private presses of the present century."[17] Partly this is because of the methods used: a deliberately primitive use of ink made from lampblack, linseed oil, and other traditional ingredients, applied to the type with homemade dabblers in the William Caxton manner, leading in the typeface to a pleasantly irregular effect. The press was ready to tackle anything, from missals to jampot labels. In 1922, Father Gray gives them a manuscript of a book of poems.

He calls it *Vivis:* you live—salutation to the poet who still speaks from within. Handprinted in an edition of seventy-five copies, it is, as Father Gray informs A. J. A. Symons, "strictly for a small part of my own circle."[18] Most of his friends from the nineties are now dead; would they recognize, in any case, the new voice of this resurrected poet—no longer languid, flaccid, deliquescent, but taut, laconic, reveling in the stark ironies of lessons learned, as in

Optimist
Too simply I took
the world as stated;
where nothing is straight,
and little crooked.[19]

It is an exacting form; it requires an exact account. Precisely
that is rendered in his estimate of his vocation:

Prelate
The rest of you enjoy the earth;
and drink the light, and taste the feast;
while I lie quietly deceased;
ordained to be so from my birth.[20]

His is the voice from under the ground, the voice from the
grave that he allowed to sing at times in *Silverpoints* or in his letters
to Louÿs, where it claimed its own rich territory. Now it is a mode
appointed, ordained in the orders of the priesthood, and consecrated to a life lived as if he were dead to the earth. But, no, he lives;
and now again, he quickens through his writing.

What leads to this quickening? Surely the new contact with
Eric Gill and the ferment of Ditchling. Perhaps a new ease with his
priesthood. A new dispensation for "Dorian," now safely far
removed from the decade that gave him his name. The Dominicans
have amplified his contacts with many of the lively intellectual
debates of the times. Their journal, *Blackfriars,* offers him a place
where his voice may be heard.

Practically, his voice found itself through his feet. His most
extended effort, *The Long Road* (published in 1926), is really a series
of short poems. They constitute, in part, a kind of diary of Gray's
walking tours: an accumulation of episodes, imaginary and actual,
over a number of years. Gray always loved long tramps; as a boy he
had learned London by foot. By the 1920s walking tours had
become an indispensable part of Father Gray's life. When he first
came to Edinburgh, he walked for the sake of his health; now he
walks for its own sweet sake. Pleasure does not always describe the

motive. A friend recalls how, "one biting December, he set off alone to one of the highest districts in Scotland; and how his telegram reached us by the fireside at Whitehouse Terrace: 'Conditions delightful: Snow.'" Sometimes, another recalls, Father Gray would "leave his presbytery in the late evening and tramp through the night, reaching his destination at breakfast time."[21]

Many excursions took him to the rolling hills of Banffshire and Aberdeenshire, which, as Father Gray once explained, "were so much more 'satisfying' than the loftier and steeper mountains of the Central and West Highlands because their subtle God-designed curves resembled those of the human body."[22] It is not the violent or spectacular but the tranquil that moved him, another friend explains. On the other hand on at least one occasion (probably in 1914) Father Gray tramped around Iceland, where he came to "know everyone" and to attempt to learn Icelandic.[23] On another excursion, he set out with Father Dominic Hart on a walking tour of France.[24] Usually Father Gray sticks nearer to home, however. Every summer he spends two to three weeks in the Cotswolds and the West Country—his "holiday ground," as he names it. These become quite a set piece. The routine is for Raffalovich to stay in Bath, at the Pulteney Hotel, while Father Gray makes his headquarters at the Old Bell Inn, Malmesbury. Sometimes Father Gray invites a companion to join him: Norman Wright is a particular favorite; a young man of promise whose brother's artistic career was subsidized by Raffalovich. They set out for a hike prolonged over several weeks, staying at carefully chosen inns. Then, on a given day, Raffalovich and Florence Gribbell collect Father Gray in their chauffeur-driven car to return to Edinburgh, sometimes after a detour of a few days in London.[25]

In an essay on "Winter Walking," Father Gray stipulates the necessary equipment: sound hobnailed boots, a Bartholomew's half-inch map—and a "good conscience." For Father Gray, walking is never walking; here he advances the case that "the essence of walking is spiritual . . . that it is a recovery of balance or of harmony . . . The walker does many things, and something more; walking is life."[26] By just such metaphor does Father Gray extend the significance of *The Long Road*. He makes it explicit in notes he sends his sister Beatrice:

1. The poem symbolizes life.
2. It charges the generality of men with two preoccupations: meals and death.
3. The monotony of life is varied with one excursion of the excursionist's own invention . . .
4. The paragraph "Along Wenlock Edge" is a march, not in space but in time, from 1 April to 31 December. The poem contains familiar, strange reflections on the nature of the road, an artificial river flowing both ways at once . . .[27]

That "artificial river" is the flow of consciousness, shifting restlessly back and forth between present and past, inner and outer landscape. It is the "road which ran with us" of the epigraph; the rush of loose, long catalogues, such as those on the names of inns; the jumps in narrative sustained by its strong, swinging rhythm. It is clear that Father Gray worked on these lines as he walked, keeping them in mind until he would write them down at night. The verses have all the preoccupations of the traveler, with specific names and spaces, designated flora and fauna, the reporting of weather and meals. At times the poem has the undigested quality of actual experience. But for all its slavery to circumstance, the journey justifies its vision—which ends, appropriately, in a graveyard:

> The slow pollen showers.
> Blue geranium to my knee
> and scabiouses; chicory
> with wondrous eyes is watching me.
> O sweet God, the flowers.
>
> This green; sultriness;
> This swelling ecstasy of earth
> is rising to unruly worth;
> the clay were yet for length and girth
> a clean sober dress.
>
> To ends known, unknown,
> perhaps where summits of desire

are touched by uncreated fire
and joy is as a just man's hire
the road passes on.[28]

Father Gray has found a voice: sober, precise, mellow, alive to the visible world. It is a craftsman's voice, patient with the flaws of the material, the difficulties they present in shaping them into form. Perhaps the most apt praise comes from a friend of later life, the poet Gordon Bottomley. Although puzzled by a few allusions— "I haven't made the leap yet, although your leaps are part of the delight"—he finds pleasure in the poem's "wayward beauties, its steady sharp vision, and its immediacy."[29]

The walking expeditions bear other fruit. Urged by the editors of the Dominican's new journal, *Blackfriars*, Father Gray begins to write occasional poems—and essays. Essays that live up to the name: trial excursions in print that track his actual excursions, on foot and in spirit, across the countryside. "An Island Cloud-Factory" (1926) meditates on the light effects on Skye. That particular expedition is forever marked as that on which Father Gray saved the life of his companion, Father Luke Walker, sitting down firmly between him and a cliff face to stop his near-fatal slide.[30] Another, "The Parting Guest" (1929), ruminates on the social intricacies of leave-taking. No names are mentioned, but the piece ends with the actual farewell of Eric Gill and his family to their four-year home in Capel-y-ffin, where they had continued their communal experiment among the Black Mountains of Wales.[31]

Other essays take bigger risks. "Brokenborough" (1926) uses a small Wiltshire hamlet to raise large questions: what does the eye find most satisfying in the arrangement of a village? What happens when, assailed by vision, the mind's eye "attains a quality not obviously justified by the object"? How does one balance rapture with experience? What Father Gray returns to is an almost Buddhist acceptance that "we take things for what they are"—such patient attention alone justifies epiphany. As an essay, "Brokenborough" provides the prototype for all that ensue; it begins and ends in lived experience; what arises always betrays an unusual turn of mind; its style is patient, easy, never slipshod. The essay "Cyder" (1927) opens: "Cider is vile stuff." Father Gray's perversity is systematic, revisionist: as in the composition "God-made and Machine-made" (1924), which deplores not the machine—which is reckoned a benefit—but the passing of those small artistic touches that distinguish the handmade from the factory-made artifact. Similarly, "Man's Visible Works" (1925) attacks the notion that human intervention violates the aesthetics of nature: "Permanent traces of man may be reasonable additions to subtler lines and surer colour: his dykes, his planting, houses, quarries, mills."

Two trial pieces are simply indulgent: the whimsical play with public notices in "Trespassers Will Be Prosecuted" (1928) and a Joycean "Dialogue" (1928), which commences, "Have a norange." Proceeding by way of the *New English Dictionary*'s definitions and choice exemplars—from Dr. Johnson's taste for orange peel in hot port to Robespierre's documented passion for oranges and on to Tennyson's suppressed poem—the dialogue closes with instructions on how to approach an orange: "Cut it through the equator, then across the poles: then image you are a meritorious negro." (The "meritorious negro" is to reappear in another context.) In these essays, nothing escapes Father Gray's sharp eye: the design of a cracker; the horrors of the "mountain sandwich"; the lines of buildings, contours of hills; the exact genus and species of wildflowers; those "exquisite vehicles," the new motor cars, "yomphing" down the road at ten miles an hour.

As in the prose, so in the poetry; there is a new cleanness, precision, patience of observation. *Poems* (1931; the final book) speaks in the modern idiom. But not without the resonances of the nineties; the opening "Ode" being something of a tour de force in onomatopoetic technique. In observing Walter Pater's dictum that "all art constantly aspires towards the condition of music," is Father Gray now so archaic that he is actually contemporary? Surely Proust—a passion of Raffalovich's—and James Joyce were simply catching up with the "incomparable" poet of *Silverpoints*. But even where Father Gray banishes the elaborations of the nineties, a mandarin disgust for the modern world remains; nowhere more so than in the poem "Odiham":

Put his head
and anxious face
out of a car.
Seemed to have said:
Yell's the name
Of this place;
seven, three, four.

Man addressed
tried to evince
interest,
as often before
and often since.
Said the name
of where they were
was Odiham.
Delighted, sir.

Fat, pale chap
seemed dissatisfied;
snatched a map
from those inside.
Engine tried
as much as it could
to drown the voices
with throbbing noises.
Man understood
him to say:
We know the way
to the south of France;
but Brodenham
is not in Hants;
we almost came
this way instead.

He said: I said
Odiham.

Odium: hatred.
Odi: I hate.
ham: ham.
A ridiculous name
in that point of view.

He said: Are you
then a Jew?

He said: No.

He said: Oh;
I thought I'd like to know;
but I can't wait.[32]

Here, he knew, was an exact sounding of himself—the dry wit, innuendo, distaste. Father Gray recalls the moment the fat tourist leaned from the car, shouting at him: obviously spotting someone who seemed to be a sort of deranged tramp, the shirt unbuttoned, hair thinning, with the face, as someone unkindly had said of him, of a village greengrocer. The exquisite features had coarsened, just as the mind has become finer, more discerning. The tourist cannot see a mind; only the recoil of the mandarin from the yobbo, which is the recoil of an older, finer civilization from the savage stupor of the contemporary.

At other times, the poet simply accepts. Standing in the haggard of Eric Gill's new commune at Pigotts, Father Gray contemplates the chaos of chickens and children before he goes to his room to write into the quiet of the night:

We are just barbarians.
Our camp is vast.
The present camp and the past
show little variance.

For today we do
whatever we did

in times bysped
and the years ago.
All over the ground
is bewildering;
scarcely a thing
where it should be found.

Children and hens,
wherever they group,
all mixed up;
not without offence.

A true to the life
Picture of us
ourselves, incongruous;
neither at peace nor strife.[33]

"We are just barbarians." The phrase sings through his mind during those months of 1931. Looking out from the candlelit room—the Gills never held much with modern convenience—Father Gray contemplates the now darkening yard. "We are just barbarians." He himself sprang from the most simple origins, its horrid history packed away until he came to the Cowgate. There followed the even more sordid history with Oscar: a picture in the attic, dusty, never visited except to excoriate himself, to remind himself of what he might have become. He was an outsider transformed into an insider: "Dorian" Gray—for a brief moment a celebrated poet of "decadence." A dandy. Then he lapsed; recanted the creed of dandyism for that of Catholicism, within he joined a new aristocracy of the spirit. Like a native American Indian brought to the court of King James, he is now like an aristocrat in exile, aware that the ancient civilization he represents never would—nor probably ever could—gain recognition from his contemporaries.

That night Father Gray dreams a strange dream. Waking, he writes down the first sentence of the plot which has conscripted him: "Mungo Park walked on in the belief, absurd as he knew it to be, that he had died."[34] It happens on his own "holiday ground," along the Oxford Road. Mungo Park—a fifty-nine-year-old secular priest and professor of moral theology—hears a long musical note, once, then repeated; then feels in his legs innumerable points of pain. "He tottered and fell. He had been well peppered. His last controlled thought was that the metaphor was good."[35] When Park comes around, he finds himself in the presence of a slight, powerful black man who takes him to a gamekeeper's hut.

Bit by bit, Park is able to piece together his situation. He appears to be the captive of a society ruled by black Catholic priests—the Wapami—committed to a utopian, pastoral existence in a region physically resembling the one Park was walking through. After many trials, his captors finally acknowledge Park as a priest, accept him into their own priestly society, enfranchise and ennoble him, although these acts bring him neither true recognition nor actual freedom. Then, abruptly, he awakens on the Oxford Road, eastward from Burford, having suffered some kind of collapse. He is later reassured by the doctor:

> You were asleep, said he; it was not a faint. It was a short, deep
> sleep; and what you experienced was a waking state.
>   A short sleep, said Park.
> But sleep is sleep, long or short.
>   And a long dream.
> Somewhat more elaborate than is usual.[36]

Father Gray recalls this dream. It first came to him during his collapse of health in 1904; he had been treated with heroin. Was it the heroin, he wonders, or the reading of H. G. Wells's *A Modern Utopia* that dictated this waking vision? He recalls writing Raffalovich about how violently he disagreed with Wells's premise, "the giant fallacy that the perfection of science is the solution of the human problem."[37] As a priest, he considers that to talk about "the human problem" at all is an offense—as if humanity were simply an equation to be solved. The saving grace of Catholicism is its deep, irradicable belief in original sin; evil is insoluble, ever present, even in the heart of utopia. Then he had fallen into reverie, recalling his vision: a community of black Catholic priests sufficiently wise to abandon as much technology as it employs. It is a particular satisfaction that they have banned the internal-combustion machine; they remain a people of the horse. Nor has the rising tide of democracy or the red tide of revolution obliterated their clear ordering of society. Wapami live within a theocracy. It is an empire kept in order by military force, but by those kinds of tyrants of which Father Gray has always approved. Yet he sees that, for all its civilities, Wapami society is impersonal, oppressive, and profoundly unreasonable. Its governance rests on suspicion. From his first appearance, Park becomes the subject of a formal commission of enquiry. The dream had ended with its official report; in it, Park recognizes only a strange counterfeit of himself. And in Park, as if in an opposing mirror, Father Gray recognizes an imposture of himself.

What could it all mean? By writing out the dream, he hopes to make its confusions clear—or at least to give a clear picture of its confusions. He begins with the walking: simple, practical. He had written in "Winter Walking" that the ramble is always "an ambit in imaginary space, where sensation is fruitful and its fruit imperishable."[38] Just so. Park's walk is into "imaginary space": which—as Park's name implies—is within the compass of his own mind and also becomes the name of his own estate. Park walks into a region of pure space, the kind of harmonious landscape which, Father Gray had once written, consoles man "for the horror of living in time."[39] But now Park confronts the horror of living out of time. Park's efforts to establish his age, for instance, are greeted with ridicule, and his insistence on chronological time, a major source of frustration. At least the space is tantalizingly familiar. The country named Ia is ringed by the unchanging hills, the flora and fauna that Father Gray meticulously chronicles in his essays for *Blackfriars*. Yet it is the natural phenomena alone that are unchanged; it is still England, but an England transformed.

Above ground, within its fields and hills, live the pastoral Wapami. A sophisticated/primitive community governed by black priests, they observe meticulously all the rituals of the Catholic Church and order their lives according to its seasons. Below ground live a race of rodentlike white men who inhabit the sunless tunnels of their former empire. They remind Father Gray of the first tunnels of the Underground, which so disrupted the London of his youth; but Park is told that they have been constructed by a people who present an "intolerable paradox: mechanical construction & genius we cannot overpraise, with moral degeneration the most complete."[40] Father Gray knows, but does not wish to know, that this is the region of hell: the London of "Dorian" Gray, now literally an underworld, explicitly condemned as "decadent": a *fin de siècle* become a *fin de globe*.

A citizen of both worlds, Park belongs to neither. A priest, he is denied the rights of his office. A native of the underworld, he lives in the upper air. Writing down his dream, Father Gray is aware he is delineating a psychic map of his own life. The past has been driven underground—it belongs there, having been in the demimonde of artist's studios, cafés, public houses, and music halls; the underworld of respectable London society. Now, in the public upper air, Park, like Father Gray, lives as a priest, speaking the sacred language of the Latin Mass, saying his office, observing the rites of the Order of Saint Dominic. But in the dream, there is constant, grinding misery: he is a priest, but without his *celebrat*—the letter permitting him to say Mass in a church other than his own—he is not recognized as such. He does not belong to either world; no one—including himself—knows who he is. Writing out the dream, Father Gray sees that the map of his mind is a map of dislocations, of false leads and dead ends; a maze from which there is no exit. No one really understands *Park*: not Park himself, not the reader, not its own cartographer. It is not tragic; nothing is clear enough for that. If anything, *Park* is about the misery of blank disorientation, of a white man lost in black country—lost to his time, lost to himself.

Suffering becomes Park's usual state. Among priests, but forbidden to act as a priest, Park finds Wapami society such torture he fears going mad. He is distracted only by his friend, Dlar; the comforts of the liturgy; his daily bath; the odd good meal. He understands that, although residing in the upper air, he is, as a white man, a true creature of the underworld.

Even before he knows of it as fact, Park intuits its existence in a dream on the first night of captivity—a dream within a dream, disorienting him still further. "He was in Westminster Cathedral and it was also a railway station of intolerable vastness & silence . . . Park went down the line in his vestments looking for the sacristy and a third-class smoking compartment. He had lost his server and his railway porter."[41] Later he is taken to a church that ministers to both worlds. Arrestingly sumptuous, it is a "two-stage rotunda with a flattened dome."[42] Looking down as Park in the dream, Father Gray recalls the sickening vertigo of the same view from St. Peter's in his Roman days. From the hung gallery at the spring of a cupola, Park gazes down into the sanctuary, from the upper to the lower world where the Mass is taking place. As the celebrant looks up, Park is sure he is a white man, one of the colonized race. "God is no respecter of persons," his companion explains.[43] Park feels dizzy. It is not the height, but the sense again of how far he had fallen, how far he again could fall, to the depths of his former life. When Park asks his guide the dedication of this church uniting lower and upper world, he is told: "The Martyrs of Uganda."

He answers only "Benedictus Deus."[44] But from the bottom of his mind Father Gray fetches up the history: the horrific deaths of the twenty-two pages of King Mwanga of Buganda; most of them in their twenties, but a few still younger, who, converted to Catholicism, had been horribly put to death because they refused the sexual advances of the young debauched king. He had read how they were martyred, between 15 November 1885 and 27 January 1887—he was then between the ages of nineteen and twenty-one—just before he met Oscar Wilde. At least one of them, Charles Lwanga, was his exact contemporary, born in the same year. He recalled their beatification in 1920.[45] Hearing them named, Park invokes the Blessed God; Father Gray shudders in the eternal martyrdom of his own guilt. Oscar's shameless courtship; his conscription as "Dorian"; the sin for which there is no atoning; he is not worthy to be a priest. The church that has saved him also condemns him; it unites both his worlds while dividing him against himself.

His distance from that past is confirmed by Park's visit to the underworld of the degenerate white man. He rediscovers the old ease and delight in its pleasures: the Reading Room of the British Library has become an enormous bookstore; the exotic books have their peculiar and intense gratification, as does the meeting with the great underworld scholar, Oli. But all is clouded by loathing, fear, an intense sense of being alien. For Park has, without knowing it, become acclimatized to the upper air. Those who live there are defined by two words: "black" and "dead." The dead he understands. He has left what he thinks of as life behind, in the underworld. Entering the dream, he realizes immediately that he has drifted outside the reckonings of chronology: "I shall never be back in time, he groaned. I shall never be back in time. Every thought has two meanings . . . 'Ever' is a property of time, & I shall never be back in time."[46] After the shock, there is a discovery, made in a dream: "That is a strange thing, he thought; to dream a fact I did not know awake. I am black."[47]

Shortly afterwards, Park is provided with a companion/guide—Dlar—who confesses to a strange immunity:

> No one, said he, is allowed to speak ill of me; the law protects me. I see, he said, that I puzzle you. I am one of the dead. It is a fiction; I am reckoned to be dead.

> Drak [the native mispronunciation of "Park"] had it on his tongue to make a whimsical remark, but refrained. Dlar spoke in great earnest:

> I have been condemned to death and reprieved.

> Drak leaned forward.

> I am in consequence regarded in many ways as though I had suffered the penalty I deserved. I am deprived of most of my civil and ecclesiastical rights; and also of many conveniences. I may not hunt, or have men-servants, or publish books. I cannot be a witness or a judge, or bring an action, or exercise a profession. But, on the other hand, no one may touch me either physically or morally: no one may sue me or send me samples or prospectuses, or ask of me alms or other favours; or, as I said, speak ill of me.

There must be some strange psychological consequences.[48]

Dlar, it transpires, is deemed "dead" as punishment for a crime in a previous life, one which he lived under another name. (Father Gray winces.) He is now directed "to try to behave in all ways" as though he were dead—"only awaiting the judgement."[49] (Is this his own purgatory? Father Gray wonders.)

As his history portends, Dlar is Park's alter ego. He is dead; condemned for a crime in a previous life. He is black. Park does not wish to be white, and greets almost with relief Dlar's sudden judgement: "Drak, your skin is white, more's the pity; but you are black inside."[50] It is Father Gray's own conviction about himself—one he has confessed only to his sister Beatrice. She writes: He was "deeply interested in the black man (he was a keen anthropologist) and used to say, although he was a white man he was black inside, and foretold in a general way that the black man would rule."[51] He had learned something of Africa from his brother "Alectryo," who had married an African woman. He had taken responsibility for his nephew Norval, who suffered in England as a boy of "mixed blood." But his curiosity had been piqued before, according to Beatrice. She writes that Gray was "very interested in a Zulu (called Mtembu) boy who came with a missionary priest and nun to A[ndré] R[affalovich]'s in Egerton Gardens—who seized some valuable arrows off the wall in order to try and shoot us. (Somewhere around 1902.) He liked pulling my long fair hair so I pulled his and discovered that his tight curls were long hairs rolled up like springs."[52] Of this visit Raffalovich recalls that "Mtembu wore a sailor suit; he shuddered when offered a pear; he had been that day to the British Museum, and with his pocket statuette of St. Joseph and his gestures he conveyed to us the conviction that he had seen the Elgin Marbles. The following day, in the garden, he shot arrows in the air; and when Father Gray undertook to photograph him, he whispered, tugging at his sailor suit, 'I can take them off.'"[53]

Father Gray recalls the moment vividly. Had he not ten years before he acknowledged the superiority of the black? He did so by penning "The Advantages of Civilization": a wicked satire on white Victorian prudery, so decisively exposed by one Zaccheus Bishop, the celebrated Fijian doctor, who leads a group of theological students on a tour of the British Museum. Stationing them in front of the Apollo Citharaedus, he draws their attention to its fine physique: "the students dared not yield to the temptation to look in one another's face."[54] Then, slowly, deliberately, with calculated relish, Bishop expatiates on the gastronomic qualities of the implied human flesh, and thus, in a kind of psychic jujitsu, returns the expectations of the white barbarians back on themselves.

Father Gray smiles. He is black inside: like the black priests of Ia, a barbarian more sophisticated than those who patronize them. He has always known he was black: is it not inscribed in his name? Would not a white man who is actually black inside appear to his public as "Gray"?

As he writes out the story of Park, Father Gray becomes more aware of how his dream has translated history to fantasy. He had always read his *Times* avidly. On 2 November 1930 the coronation takes place of Ras Tafari as Emperor Haile Selassie of Ethopia, Conquering Lion of Judah, King of Kings, direct descendant of King Solomon and the Queen of Sheba, now ruler of the ancient Christian kingdom of Abyssinia. For months before the coronation, the newpapers and cinema newsreels had been full of the preparations. Now the *Times*'s own "Special Correspondent"—a recent convert to Catholicism by the name of Evelyn Waugh—reports such engaging details as the withdrawal of Ras Kassa, Ras Tafari's closest rival to the throne, because "he prefers . . . to devote his time to the management of his own estates and the performance of his religious duties." Yes: this is the world of those sovereign priests of Ia, who have adapted the princely title of "Ras" to their own ends: A Ra [André Raffalovich?], Koti Ra, Edni Ra, Toni Ra.[55]

Even Waugh's reporting of how the tribal chiefs, on their first visit to Addis Ababa, showed "their consternation at the sight of motor-cars" or his account of how the native policemen had to beat back the people of the town with whips and canes enters into the brilliantly detailed work of the fantasy. Yes, there are transpositions. The Coptic rite of the Ethopian church has been replaced with the Latin rite of the European. St. Thomas—that great Dominican—is still the center of its theological gravity.

But above all, the country of Ia is John Gray's own I-land: the psychic terrain he inhabits. Again, it is inscribed in his name. The dream has chosen an ancient African kingdom which, from the later Middle Ages, had been the location of legends about Prester John, "the Nestorian priest-king who would liberate the Holy Land from the Muslims . . . The land of Prester John was black by race, Christian by religion and theocratic by government."[56] John Gray lived by denomination: his name had always had huge significance for him. Prester John has simply been the forerunner of this new kingdom now mapped out by another *presbyter Iohannes* or Priest John.

It is also, Father Gray ruminates, territory within which people notoriously disappear. Waugh himself visited Harar in the hope "of finding something new about Rimbaud," that spiritual poet-son of Verlaine who had disappeared into the dark of Abyssinia, to make there a death-bed repentance.[57] Is this the meaning of Dlar's status as a "dead man"? Now Park is, without notice, ordered to join him. Almost halfway through the tale, Park is granted new rights and privileges and a farm (also called "Park"). From now on, like Dlar, he is "for ever exempt from burdens fiscal, parliamentary and administrative. No one may cite him, sue him, ask favours of him or speak ill of him"[58]: a formula that echoes the one Dlar applies to the fictive dead. From this point on, both Dlar and Drak are referred to as "the dead men." What can this mean? For Father Gray, the meaning is obvious: they have entered into a priesthood, the black vesture being the mark of death to the world. Has he not declared this in his quatrain from *Vivis*, "Prelate"?

> The rest of you enjoy the earth;
> > and drink the light, and taste the feast;
> > while I lie quietly deceased;
> ordained to be so from my birth.[59]

Reborn as a priest, was he not also "ordained" to die? A tidy conceit. Was becoming a member of the Third Order of the Dominicans also not a sign of that death—its black habit having given its name to the journal in which *Park* is to be published? And had he not written to the Michael Fields: "'Si jamais je meurs' I should like to wear the habit and purple stole & have bare feet to look pitiable exposed to gaze upon the floor of S: Peter's."[60] The suffering here is not merely self-indulgent: it is death as one suffers it in life, with whatever self-command one can muster; with whatever wit, no matter how desperate. Gray greets death as a Catholic: as a necessary death, as the fruit of original sin. But also the death that brings resurrection—and life. Park is duly wakened from the dead.

And so, Father Gray asks himself, what is the nature of the death he has suffered? He has returned from Pigotts, only to be greeted a short time later by news of Eric Gill. One day at the end of September 1930, he had been found wandering about the farmyard. He could not remember who he was or where he was. After five days in bed at home, he was taken to hospital in London.[61] Hearing the news, Father Gray suddenly realizes how much of his fantasy has been shaped by Gill's communes: the vision of an artistic community—who are also Dominicans—among the pastoral English landscape, dedicated to the production, as in Ia, of beautiful books, and an eschewing of modern ways; as do the priests in Ia, Gill wears a version of the toga.

Is it Gill's breakdown that gives the dream a new turn? When Father Gray returns to write it up, it is not blackness or death, but the sense that he is himself lost that consumes him now. How could he have missed it? After all, the hero, Park, is named for Mungo Park: a Scottish explorer of the late eighteenth century who set out to find the source of the Niger. His first account, *Travels into the Interior of Africa* (1799), had suggested the alien enumerative systems which so vex Drak. There is no account of the second attempt—for Mungo Park simply never returned. The alien terrain into which Father Gray journeys is no Africa; it is into the darkness of himself, to follow, like Stanley tracing Dr. Livingstone, the tracks of a living man, presumed to have disappeared.

For, from the very beginning, Park has been subjected to some form of inquiry. "Do not let the fact distress you," he is told by a priestly official, "but it is as well for you to know that you are the cause of hideous excitement throughout the world. It is through no fault of yours; but the trouble is very great."[62] Some time afterwards, Park learns that a commission has been set up; he is to be questioned, informally tried. There is a general sense of alarm and confusion: what are the charges, what is the object of the inquiry? He is subjected to a medical examination. The particulars describe the actual John Gray down to his four missing teeth.[63]

The natives, however, remain unsatisfied. They refuse to accept Park's chronological age, as they are on "eonic" time. (And how often has this dogged John Gray in his early life, from the comic error on his birth certificate to the predictable miscalculation of his age, as Lionel Johnson had remarked, looking fifteen when he fact he was almost thirty.[64]) Aside from Park's own confusion as to whether he is alive or dead, black or white, is the added perplexity of names. Although Park is recognized as being a priest, he is accused of being a missionary.[65] Later, when asked to explain his name, Park answers that "Mungo was the name of a saint." He does not add that Mungo is a saint of special significance to the Scots, but he does explain that the name Park, "as it happens means in my language an enclosed property."[66] To add to the confusion, during the course of the story he is variously addressed as Park, Drak, and once as Dom Monaco Parek.[67] Only Father Gray can testify to the importance of being "John"—or "Dorian" or "Jacopone" or, finally, "Canon Gray." From the time he was a child he identified with those who shared his names: from Peter Gray (scalped by Indians) to "Dorian" (a kind of suicide à deux), from Wilde's John the Baptist to Saint John of the Cross and now Prester John, denomination realizes itself as a kind of fate.

The commission's enquiry issues, predictably, in a long report. Read to Park shortly before he awakens, he acknowledges, in externals, its accuracy:

> P. the subject is a normal human being . . . His body is complete, except that he has lost four teeth, unfortunately not replaced; slightly bald, good sight and hearing; intelligence fair; most of his reactions good.
>
> He is presumed to be well educated according to some unknown system . . . His knowledge of religion is wide and orthodox. Whatever other learning he possesses cannot, with-

out injustice to the subject, be judged . . . but he may be safely described as a cultured man, for he responds to tests which only a cultured man could satisfy.

He recognizes at once the good qualities of buildings & other works of art, even showing at times some little refinement. He can draw; but only indifferently well.

He is courageous, modest, perhaps diffident; he is bad tempered; he is truthful, with some power of dissimulation; but here allowance is due to his peculiar position. He has a sense of humour; and, among men he trusts (and his nature is affectionate), he is often vivacious.

He is not known to have any vices.[68]

It is a fair account, Father Gray muses. His aesthetic sense was always attuned to the spatial—perhaps even more than to the verbal. He has a fine eye. Courageous and modest: yes. Also an irritable devil. The blunt edge of his truthfulness is sometimes tempered by evasion. As for his sense of humor—well, poor Oscar was the first to acknowledge that, and in print, in his letter to the *Daily Telegraph*. Poor Oscar knew too how vulnerable he could be to affection; since then he had been more careful with his friendships, confining them to those he trusted: André, the Michael Fields, the Artists, a few poets and fellow priests. Most thought him cold and standoffish.

But there the perspicuity of the report ends. For it goes on, in its official way, to give a grotesquely speculative account of his past:

Hypotheses are almost as many as the persons who have advanced them.

That which is favoured by the best intelligence is (with permission) somewhat as follows:

The subject was born about 300 years ago, in some remote community, probably mountainous, for mountains have a peculiar and exhilarating effect on the subject, unknown to the infidels . . .

He may have been a theocrat; for it is the firm opinion of all who have interviewed him that he is, as he believes himself to be, a priest; and the possession of a chronometer by a man found almost in rags is significant.

The supposition is that through some great misadventure, whether vicious & excessive indulgence (favoured), bereavement, crime, disgrace, fear of torture, or rash psychic experiment (extremely favoured), he came under the domination of a remote ancestral survival in his consciousness; so thoroughly that he acts, speaks, thinks, and remembers in the person of that ancestor.

The hypothesis offers the best suggestion of how he reached Ia & why he came hither. He would have been impelled to return to the place of his origin as indicated by his hallucination . . .

The rapid survey, under the peculiar conditions, and the objective view of his own character, stiffened Park's spirit, quieted his nerves, & strengthened his dignity. But the voice of the prince awoke him from deep abstraction.

It's good, eh?

Yes, sir; it is good.

Filled with error, I suppose.

Yes, sir; so far as I am competent to judge.[69]

That is where the inquiry ends: as it does in life. Father Gray knows that in Edinburgh the question of his origins, his early life elsewhere, as well as most of his history up to the time of his arrival at Scots College are a mystery. To most who meet him, they are as hidden as the pagan temple or the early basilica under San Clemente—and as unforeseen. Or they are a subject of mystification. Sometimes Father Gray makes veiled references to a "near escape" in the distant past. At others, he exerts no effort to disguise the traces of his Cockney accent. Even his relationship with Raffalovich, he is aware, occasionally is the cause of speculation. How did such a strange—and yet strangely united—pair come to be friends? The hypotheses of their public are not more bizarre or more misguided than those who report on Park.

He knows what they think of him. The tragedy is, it has become what he thinks of himself. If he is a victim of a confusion of identity, it is a confusion he has engineered himself. Is not the dreamer the victim of his dream and the fantast of his own fantasy? Had he not simply, finally, become his own invention of himself, as the mask of the exquisite dandy had hardened into the pose of the ecclesiastical mandarin: a mask with a manner once described as "positively oriental in its false doors and booby-traps."[70]

Recovered, Eric Gill reads *Park,* commenting: "it is a thoroughly weird business, typical of its author. I think there are very good things in it, and things that only a Catholic could have guessed at."[71] Father Gray has approached him to print the book at his new art press set up at Pigotts with René Hague; Gill consents willingly. One of the early productions from Pigotts, *Park* is set in the Joanna Italic which had been especially designed for the press by Gill. He and Father Gray also agree to dispense with all quotation marks, preferring dashes instead: one of Gill's typically calculated measures for making the text more elegant. These, among other typographical oddities, set it apart as well as allowing *Park* to be read with a novel kind of speed—and intimacy.

Presented with the finished book, the poet Edmund Blunden writes Father Gray by return. It is in reply to this letter that Father Gray gives perhaps the clearest account of the fantasy. "Your astuteness has penetrated the whole matter," he writes; "the man stumbling in his dream upon a chance of vengeance & the free expression of repressed ambitions, yet dogged all the time by the obstacles of his waking life."[72] Vengeance is everywhere, corrosive: in the surreal vision of "Dorian's" London life, relegated to a purgatorial existence underground. Some relics of the lost decade might even have recognized themselves among the repellent inhabitants of that nether world, such as Oli. Later, it is said that *Park* also satirized local clerics in Edinburgh, particularly the ones whose personal habits irritated Father Gray.[73] Is not the reader constantly fidgeted by the feeling that some kind of esoteric joke is being played on him?[74] That all those names—A Ra, Svillig, Kottatil, Oli—are simply in code? The "most entrancing of anagrams" cited by Park is explained by Gray to Blunden—but can only be regarded as a calculated mystification.[75] In the end, its explication only confirms the suspicion that the book is a kind of esoteric puzzle made to tantalize—and exasperate—its reader.

To balance this is what Father Gray greets as "the free expression of repressed ambition." As Park, he moves within an England redeemed, at once returned and renewed in its pre-Reformation wholeness, both modern and medieval. It is a society of priests; Park is from the first acknowledged as a priest, one of those anointed, set apart. And the world is ordered according to priestly ritual; there is order and courtesy and an avowed love of beautiful artifacts, especially of books; a language—Latin—universally spoken; even an extraordinary diet. Although entering this world as a captive, Park has a meteoric rise in status, ending up as a landed aristocrat. Even though the commission cannot actually establish when he was born or who he actually is, Park is recognized as inherently noble.

But the accomplishment of desire, like vengeance, is "dogged all the time by the obstacles of waking life." These are two: the persistent inquiry into his identity; his subjection to a society which, ultimately, is unintelligible and arbitrary. These two are related. Because "they" do not know who he is, Park cannot know himself—or the alien world into which he is hurled. Park himself constantly wonders what "they" think of him. In the end, Park is forced to accept a relation to himself defined by his relation to "them." Surely this itself defines how he is "dead"—by viewing himself as others view him, Park has become as opaque, as inaccessible to himself as a pure object. "They" have defined his identity, taken possession of him as if he were defunct. It is for Park to come to terms with it, to seek, as he does at the last, for peace and ask for the prayers due the dead.

Before this death, there is another. Forty years ago, "Dorian" had written Pierre Louÿs: "It is Folly and Calumny who keep me company."[76] Likewise, Park finds himself the cause of "hideous excitement" in Ia—and is said to be notorious in the underworld. Is it not, in the end, folly and calumny which triumph, in the version of the official report on Park's identity? A "tormented prisoner" of this regime, Park has been deprived of his priestly right to celebrate Mass by his status as "dead"—is he being punished, like Dlar, for a past transgression? Father Gray, shaving, looks briefly at himself in the mirror. There is the face of the coarsened "Dorian" Gray, the picture in the attic, the sin that goes always with him. With his bizarre guides and companions, "Dorian" had written, he had entered into "the rich ground that hangs between Life and Death" which he is about to inherit. "I am going to enjoy my new estate presently," he had written Louÿs.[77] That estate is *Park,* which its narrator now inhabits as Park, coming finally into the true heritage of his imagination.

Now being "dead," has Canon Gray not at last become the picture in the attic: perfected as object, his own most perfect artifact? Those who know him well in his later years, such as Peter Anson, would not only say so, but would value him as such, writing of the canon's presence that

> He remained inscrutable, enigmatic, shrouded in mystery, and it was largely because of this polished reserve that he was so fascinating. His face often reminded me of Leonardo da Vinci's famous painting of the Mona Lisa, and it would not be irrelevant to adapt Walter Pater's description of it to John Gray: "His is the head upon which 'all of the ends of the world are come', and the eyelids are a little weary . . . He is older than the rocks among which he sits; like the vampire, he has been dead many times, and learned the secrets of the grave; and has been a diver in deep seas, and keeps their fallen day about him; and trafficked for strange webs with Eastern merchants . . . and all this has been to him but as the sound of lyres and flutes, and lives only in the delicacy with which it has moulded with changing lineaments, and tinged the eyelids and the hands . . . To burn always with this hard, gemlike flame, to maintain this ecstasy, is success in life."[78]

Having been, like the vampire, "dead many times," is not so much an acknowledgement of Father Gray's own death, spiritual or psychic, but a sign of the enduring vitality of the spirit. For Father Gray has not lost his life; he has found it with a fullness which the officially living cannot comprehend.

EPILOGUE

(FEBRUARY 1930–JUNE 1934)

ON 4 FEBRUARY 1930, Father Gray was made a canon of the Diocese of St. Andrews and Edinburgh. He had long enjoyed the confidence of the archbishop, Joseph McDonald. But the canonry was also a mark of the esteem in which Father Gray was held by his fellow clergy. Several other offices also came his way: Father Gray acted for several years as national president for Scotland of the Apostolic Union of Secular Priests. From its institution, he was the Catholic representative on the Scots Committee for Religious Broadcasting. Increasingly Father Gray was consulted by his archbishop, as well as by diocesan officials, on difficult and delicate matters of church business.[1]

A new decade brought new duties. Yet, in the age of the motor car, Raffalovich was still driven to St. Peter's in a landau or barouche; until, in later years, he compromised by taking the short journey by taxi. Every January Father Gray himself offered public prayers for the soul of Verlaine. Few of his congregation could have known how this great convert-poet has shaped the grave, aloof priest who ministered to them. As the years wore on, significant additions were made to the prayers for the dead. In 1929 Charles Ricketts effectively lost his beloved Charles Shannon; hanging a picture in their new home at Townsend House, Shannon fell, suffering irreversible brain damage. Ricketts himself died suddenly one October night in 1929, unattended. "Are we not dreadfully bereaved?" Father Gray wrote the poet Gordon Bottomley. "Death has seldom confused my mind more; for I feel a generation older than the impression my mourned friend made upon me."[2]

But it was the death of Florence Gribbell on 21 February 1930 that made the first momentous breach within his small circle of intimates. Just two and a half weeks after Father Gray had been elevated to the office of canon, she died—as she had lived, with dignity and presence of mind. To the last she was attended with great tenderness by Father Gray and Raffalovich. She had been nothing less than a second mother to André; at the age of eighty-seven she was the last surviving link with his own family. But for both men she had been also much more; she was the organizing spirit of the house at Whitehouse Terrace; its center; its gracious hostess. Her place in Father Gray's affections was bound up with his love for Raffalovich; they were nothing less than his family. "Our sorrow is very great," Raffalovich wrote their mutual friend Norman Wright, "and I don't feel as if the pain would ever cease in this life."[3]

A few months later, in June 1930, as if to ensure a final appearance in this drama, Max Beerbohm travelled to Edinburgh to receive an honorary degree and accepted Raffalovich's hospitality for five days.[4] Life continued much as it had, with Lady Margaret Sackville taking Florence Gribbell's place at the head of the table for Raffalovich's dinners. But at least one friend considered that Canon Gray no longer had his heart in such festivities:

> I was inclined to wonder now and then, especially towards the end of his life, if he still enjoyed meeting the guests at Whitehouse Terrace, interesting enough as they always were, hand-picked personalities in their own spheres. All of them the Canon could meet on equal terms; and André was his friend. But, as I glanced at him at table or in the drawing-room, I had a growing suspicion that their ways were no longer his ways, their thoughts and outlook no more his. I felt somehow that he had had enough, and I was right. In his closing years he was content to stay at home and eat his lunch with the curate. The time had come when he found it necessary to retreat into himself.[5]

Perhaps this same instinct that his life was coming to a close prompted Father Gray to accept an invitation to a reunion of his class in Scots College, Rome, in October 1933. He came as a guest of the rector, Monsignor Clapperton. Over the years, Father Gray had maintained a lively interest in the college and its affairs; indeed, it was he who had been chiefly, if not entirely, responsible for the production of the history of the college which appeared in 1930. During the five-day visit, Canon Gray was taken by the rector and students to spend a day at the college's villa in the Roman countryside. After lunch they all sang some verses of the song that John Gray had written for the college more than thirty years before. The author was called for. With some hesitation, Canon Gray stood up and modestly disclaimed any credit, explaining that when he was a student, the rector at the time, Monsignor Fraser, had said to him one day: "You write poetry, don't you? Well, write a song for the College." And "this [said Father Gray] is the result."[6]

Canon Gray "staggered" back to Edinburgh after the trip, "so dazzled in October that I cannot remember to whom I have written my impressions," he confessed. "I went out deliberately taking as my rallying point Bernini, so far as the external Rome of my rapid visit was to render impressions; and came back justified."[7] In another letter, to his old friend Fanny Langdale, he alluded to the "great excitement" of his Roman visit.[8] He was writing to accept an invitation to the ordination of a nephew, Eugene Langdale, whose career Father Gray had followed in his prayers. The date of the occasion was to be 29 June. But by that date, both André Raffalovich and Canon Gray were both dead.

The morning of 14 February 1934 was Ash Wednesday. It also marked the forty-fourth anniversary of John Gray's conversion to Catholicism. Early that morning André Raffalovich was found dead in his room by the maid calling in with the early tea he took before the accustomed taxi ride to Mass at St. Peter's. Raffalovich had died in his sleep, peacefully; there had been no warning. The previous evening he had appeared in his usual good health and spirits, having attended a lecture by Eric Gill, then staying with Canon Gray.[9] But another friend, Charles Cammell, remembers thinking how frail Raffalovich had looked when he had come to visit a few days earlier.

Canon Gray was summoned. He took charge, giving Raffalovich conditional absolution and extreme unction. Then he returned to St. Peter's to say Mass; on that morning, signing each brow with an ashen cross and repeating, "Memento homo, quia pulvis es et in pulverem reverteris."

Canon Gray never recovered from his friend's death. Father Dominic Hart remarked that the canon "seemed stunned by the loss, and for a while lost something of his mental balance. For instance, on the day after Raffalovich's death, Canon Gray was making preparations for the funeral, and, as was his custom on big occasions, he telephoned to Raffalovich to seek his approval for the arrangements."[10] The funeral itself took place in Mount Vernon Cemetery, outside Edinburgh. It was a bitterly cold day. Canon Gray officiated, standing in the cutting wind bareheaded and without a coat. Such indifference to his own well-being became characteristic of these final months.

In June a short appreciation of André Raffalovich by Canon Gray appeared in *Blackfriars*. It spoke, not without reticence, of Raffalovich's conversion to Catholicism; and of his personal qualities; in particular, his "natural kindness" and intelligence:

> He read (although, indeed, exactly what he chose), meditated, discoursed and liked to be understood; and, without any human respect, he withdrew when he was not understood. Hence the vast and varied character of his acquaintance; his elastic memory; his facility with languages; the disquieting alertness of his mind. He liked hyperbole and family jokes; but he was never heard to employ an unnecessary expletive.[11]

On an afternoon in the beginning of June, the very month this tribute appeared, Canon Gray was discovered in his study, sitting half-slumped over his desk, his head between his hands. He had developed a fatherly affection for his young visitor, Margaret George, the daughter of his solicitor. She asked him what was the matter with him; he replied he was not feeling well.[12] The next morning, the canon was removed to St. Raphael's nursing home, where he was diagnosed as suffering from congestion of the lungs and pleurisy. On 10 June he seemed to have passed through the crisis and was sleeping better; but an abscess was found in his left lung. The doctors decided to operate. The operation was successful; but the canon's heart, never strong, gave out under the strain. He died on the afternoon of 14 June. Margaret George found him dying and fled to the chapel for courage. She reports he died "almost alone," but other accounts disagree. "He was quite conscious," his sister Sarah Tinklar later wrote, "& tried to join with the priests round his bed in saying the prayers for the dying. His last words were an act of contrition, & his last act to bow his head at the holy name of Jesus."[13]

The office for the dead was said at St. Peter's on the evening of 18 June. It was crowded then and again for the Pontifical Requiem the following morning. The Archbishop of St. Andrews and Edinburgh celebrated the Requiem, and the Archbishop of Glasgow was present, as was the cathedral chapter of the diocese. There were as well, wrote Sarah, "Dominicans, Benedictines, Franciscans, Passionists & Jesuits, & of course all his sorrowful friends & parishioners." Sarah and her stepdaughter, Coralie Tinklar, were the only members of Gray's family present. His sister Beatrice, now Sister Mary Raphael, was prevented from coming by the rules governing her enclosed order. Afterwards, Sarah wrote to Fanny Langdale, "I feel very sad & lonely without him, for he was more than a brother to me."

In the panegyric at the funeral Mass, a friend of the canon's, the Dominican Father Bernard Delany, spoke of John Gray's "gift of vision and his power of giving rare expression to what he saw—all the instincts of his nature and the bent of his mind might have placed him, had he cared to use this gift, in the first rank of the literary history of the English tongue." But Father Delany praised John Gray's sacrifice in choosing "a higher and nobler immortality": the priesthood. "To me," Father Delany continued, "he always seemed the ideal priest":

> A priest gives his heart to God and there were some people who were disconcerted by John Gray's ascetic reserve. He did not easily admit the outside world within the inner sanctuary

of his soul. Yet those who knew him well knew a kindly, human priest with a depth of wisdom and sympathy, with the ready wit of a quick, lively mind, and the sense of humour that goes with humility. His was a keen mind, alert and always interested. He made no claim to scholarship yet his reading and learning were deep and wide—always directed by the apostolic zeal of the true priest.

"He was a priest and a *great* priest," Father Delany concluded.[14] And it is a conclusion to which many who knew him as Father Gray would greet with a fervent "Amen." Even those who dissent from this view would acknowledge genuine respect for a man who worked towards perfecting his life by great effort—and great sacrifice.

It is important to consider the nature of that sacrifice—and the cost to John Gray; a cost that can be estimated only in part. John Gray ensured that this would be so. There were the cryptic disclosures about the past life, veiled references to a fall—and a redemption. Something found, but something lost. By the terms of his will, all his and Raffalovich's personal papers and books were bequeathed to the Dominican Chaplaincy in George Square, Edinburgh. This legacy of letters and manuscripts showed clear signs of having been sifted through. The correspondence from Pierre Louÿs had been preserved—with the notable exception of those letters for the years 1894 and 1895, the years surrounding the Wilde trials. That kind of provocative behavior—of suggestion and denial—is all of a piece with Father Gray's habit of intriguing company with an anecdote about Lionel Johnson or Ernest Dowson—and then firmly changing the course of conversation.[15] Clues were dropped, but pursuit discouraged: it seems akin to opening, in a wall of adamantine denial, small peepholes to the past.

In other ways, Father Gray and his heirs did all they could to forestall enquiry into the life of John Gray. From the midnineties onwards, John Gray began to buy up copies of *Silverpoints* in order to "immobilize" or destroy them.[16] He kept many of his earlier books, but in his library with their spines turned to the wall—"like so many naughty children," as one priestly colleague remarked. Shortly after Canon Gray's death, William Butler Yeats was refused permission by Gray's executors to reprint poems in *The Oxford Book of Modern Verse:* acting, apparently, on what they interpreted as Father Gray's wishes.[17] And when Peter Anson, a friend of many years standing, proposed a memoir, he came up against what he described as the "strong & determined opposition of the Canon's two sisters, who feel that their brother would 'wish to be forgotten.'"[18]

The legacy thus confesses a certain ambiguous intention. On the one hand, Father Gray invites speculation; on the other hand, he has rendered definitive conclusions impossible. It is wholly in character with his tantalizing reserve. For if he did not wish to prompt curiosity, why preserve the letters and manuscripts at all? Why not simply build an immense bonfire and have done with it? It is obvious that Canon Gray could not bring himself to do so. This is neither oversight nor carelessness. Indeed it might be truer to say that Gray's decision to preserve at least part of this correspondence might be an act, on one level, of priestly humility. In its pages he could find again the portrait of "Dorian" Gray so closely locked in the attic of his past. It constituted exactly that witness to his "course of sin" which kept him, as a priest, on the right path. It gave him the touchstone to himself, at once lost and found: the working-class boy who became the prodigal poet, then the penitent priest. To understand John Gray one must know where he lived, and where he lived was pervaded by a lively sense of what, without the grace of God, he would have become.

The poet of *Silverpoints* imagined himself once as dead, speaking in a dialogue of lovers from the grave.[19] After his father died and he had broken off with Wilde, Gray proclaimed to Louÿs that he had now inherited the "rich ground which hangs between Life and Death." Now officially dead, he has come at last into his true estate, as a subject as fascinating and complex as the portrait for which he was once named. Whatever qualifications one may place on that death—and it offers itself both as a genuine death and as an entry into another state of being, both richer and more circumscribed than that actually available—it remains the mode by which John Gray lived, and still lives, within this actual world. It should not surprise, therefore, that among the accounts of Canon Gray are several that report him after death, still "sitting in his old confessional, and getting up afterwards to go into the clergy house" of St. Peter's, Morningside.[20]

May his soul rest, at last, in peace.

NOTES

CHAPTER 1

1. Edith Cooper, c. 8 January 1894. "Works and Days," journal of Katherine Bradley and Edith Cooper [Michael Field] [BM Add. Ms. 46782], British Library Manuscript Collections, London.
2. "a decadent Christ," from Ibid.
3. William Rothenstein, *Men and Memories: The Recollections of William Rothenstein,* vol. I (London: Faber and Faber, 1931), pp. 174-76. Rothenstein uses the word "disciple" of Gray, "then a fastidious young poet and something of a dandy."
4. Cooper, Ibid.
5. Frank Liebich, "Oscar Wilde," a typescript reminiscence, Wilde L716M3081 [191-?], Williams Andrews Clark Memorial Library, UCLA.
6. "cultivated and interesting" from Rupert Hart-Davis, ed., *The Letters of Oscar Wilde,* rev. ed. (London: Rupert Hart-Davis, 1963), p. 249, n. 2. The date of their first meeting is unknown, but the copy of the first *Dial* in the British Library is stamped 21 August 1889.
7. Cooper and Bradley, writing on the second edition of *The Dial,* Saturday 19 March 1892, "Works and Days" [BM Add. Ms. 46780].
8. John Gray, "The Great Worm," *The Dial* (1889): 14-18; reprinted in *The Selected Prose of John Gray,* ed. Jerusha Hull McCormack, no. 7, 1880–1920 British Author Series (Greensboro, N.C.: ELT Press, 1992), pp. 11-17.
9. John Gray, "Les Goncourts," *The Dial* (1889): 10; reprinted in McCormack, ed., *Selected Prose of John Gray,* pp. 4, 5.
10. Ibid., p. 12; *Selected Prose,* ed. McCormack, p. 8.
11. "horrid family troubles" from Gray to Francis Vielé-Griffin, no date, Beinecke Rare Book Room and Manuscript Library, Yale Library, New Haven, Conn.
12. "very simple" from Father John Baptist-Reeves, in taped reminiscences (19 March 1968), recounts that Father Gray had "distinct undertones" of a Cockney accent in his otherwise carefully modulated speech.
13. Father Edwin Essex, "The Canon in Residence," in *Two Friends: John Gray and André Raffalovich,* ed. Brocard Sewell (Aylesford, Kent: Saint Albert's Press, 1963), p. 154.
14. Wilde to Charles Ricketts [Autumn? 1890], Hart-Davis, ed., *Letters of Oscar Wilde,* p. 250.
15. Mentioned in a letter from Félix Fénéon to Gray, 18 December 1890 (?), John Gray Collection, John Rylands University Library of Manchester, England. I take some liberties with the dating here, projecting the project backwards by more than a year.
16. "all perfect things should be unique" from *Oscar Wilde: A Collection of Critical Essays,* ed. Richard Ellmann (Englewood Cliffs, N.J.: Prentice-Hall, Inc., 1969) p. 307.
17. G. Paul Delaney, *Charles Ricketts: A Biography* (Oxford: Clarendon Press, 1990), p. 45.
18. Cooper and Bradley, January 1894, "Works and Days" [BM Add. Ms. 46782].

19. Oscar Wilde, "Pen, Pencil, and Poison," in *Complete Works of Oscar Wilde* (New York: HarperCollins, 1994), p. 1096.

20. "miserable island history" from John Gray to André Raffalovich, 8 March 1903, referring to his family history on the death of his mother. Gray papers, National Library of Scotland, Edinburgh.

21. General Register Office, London. The eight other children were: Ada (Mrs. Pullen): b. 1868, d. 1945; Frederick William: b. 1870, d. 1961; William Thomas: b. 1872 (?), d. 1920; Emily (Mrs. Burbridge): b. 1875, d. 1950; Sarah (Mrs. Tinklar): b. 1877, d. 1950; Norval: b. 1880 (?), d. 1911; Alexander: b. 1882 (?), d. 1919; Beatrice Hannah (Sister Mary Raphael O.S.B.): b. 1887, d. 1963. For further histories of these members of the Gray family, see Brocard Sewell, "John Gray and André Sebastian Raffalovich: A Biographical Outline," in Sewell, ed. *Two Friends*, p.7.

22. Gray's birth certificate gives the date as 10 March 1866, but Gray corrects it in this letter to Katherine Bradley and Edith Cooper [Michael Field], 20 January 1908. Henry W. and Albert A. Berg Collection, New York Public Library, New York.

23. Gray to Pierre Louÿs, 3 December 1892. Quoted in Peter Vernon, "John Gray's Letters to Pierre Louÿs," *Revue de Littérature Comparée* 53 (1979): 98.

24. Brocard Sewell, *Footnote to the Nineties: A Memoir of John Gray and André Raffalovich* (London: Cecil and Amelia Woolf, 1968), p. 3. Sewell's account of Gray's ancestry is based on notes sent to him by Gray's sister, Beatrice Hannah.

25. Sewell, "Gray and Raffalovich," in Sewell, ed., *Two Friends*, pp. 7-8.

26. Heather Coltman to Jerusha McCormack, 26 April 1984, McCormack papers. Heather Coltman is the grand-daughter of the third son in Gray's family, William Thomas.

27. Gray to Raffalovich, 8 May 1904, Gray papers, National Library of Scotland, Edinburgh.

28. Gray to Sarah Tinklar, 31 January 1922, Brocard Sewell papers. Gray's name always had a large significance for himself, as evidenced by the many nicknames he adopted ("Dorian" being only one of a succession).

29. Marriage Certificate of John Gray to Hannah Williamson, 13 June 1864. General Register Office, London.

30. Gray's poem, "The Wheel," left in manuscript form at his death, was published in *The Poems of John Gray,* The 1880-1920 British Author Series 1, ed. Ian Fletcher (Greensboro, N.C.: ELT Press, 1988), pp. 72-73.

31. Brocard Sewell, *In the Dorian Mode: A Life of John Gray, 1866-1934* (Padstow, Cornwall: Tabb House, 1983), p. 1.

32. John Gray and André Raffalovich, "The Blackmailers," Gray papers, National Library of Scotland, Edinburgh. (Only the last act survives, in typescript.)

33. Gray papers, National Library of Scotland, Edinburgh.

34. Delaney, *Charles Ricketts*, p. 43.

35. Details of Gray's schooling here and below are taken from Sewell, *Footnote,* pp. 2-3. Gray's brother Frederick recalls his reputation for cleverness and the fact of other boys dropping in for help with their homework in Sewell, "Gray and Raffalovich," in *Two Friends*, p. 8. For discussion of Gray's Methodism, see Jerusha Hull McCormack, *John Gray: Poet, Dandy, and Priest* (Hanover, N.H.: University Press of New England, 1991), p. 263, n. 21.

36. Holograph of *Spiritual Poems*, Gray manuscripts, National Library of Scotland, Edinburgh. Braces { } indicate passages cancelled in the original which have been, for the most part, reconstructed. The poem has been printed, without the reconstructed passages, in Fletcher, ed., *Poems of John Gray,* p. 149.

37. Delaney, *Charles Ricketts*, p. 21

38. Ibid., p. 55.

39. Ibid., p. 49.

40. Ibid., p. 55.
41. Ibid., p. 56.
42. "inspired rot" from Ibid., p. 45
43. Ibid.
44. Ibid., pp. 18-19.
45. Hart-Davis, ed., *Letters of Oscar Wilde*, p. 488.
46. Delaney, *Charles Ricketts*, p. 57-58.
47. John Gray, "The Forge," *The Savoy* 2 (April 1896): 85-86; reprinted in Fletcher, ed., *Poems of John Gray*, pp. 69-70.
48. Holograph of *Spiritual Poems*, reprinted in Fletcher, ed., *Poems of John Gray*, p. 149. Following quotation from this source.
49. "The eternal dying of a summer's day." Sewell, *Footnote*, p. 4, gives the poem in incomplete form. A guess at the missing word, "centuries," is made by Margaret Mary McAlpine, "John Gray: A Critical and Biographical Study," (M.A. thesis, University of Manchester, England, 1967), p. 157. Reprinted in Fletcher, ed., *Poems of John Gray*, p. 42.
50. Details of John Gray's Post Office career given by F. Coates to McCormack, 17 June and 20 June 1970, McCormack papers.
51. According to records, Edmonds joined in January 1880, became a Lower Division Clerk in the Savings Bank on 17 August 1880, and moved to the Confidential Enquiry Branch 16 January 1882, where Gray presumably first met him. Appointed Surveyors Clerk in August 1885, he died in 1894. (Coates to McCormack, 17 June 1970, McCormack papers.) The "Parent" letter to Gray, 28 October 1891, headnote from the Post Office, is apparently from him. (Gray papers, National Library of Scotland, Edinburgh.) The letter reads in part:

> My dear Boy,
> I got the books all right—Many thanks. *Pour une nuit d'amour* is curious— very. I do not know if *Thérèse Raquin* was written first—but certainly Zola stands alone in making horrors ordinary. I took that corpse down—Moi.

52. Peter Vernon, "Introduction," in "The Letters of John Gray" (Ph.D. thesis, University of London, 1976), p. 16.
53. London University Records. At this time, London University was only a degree-granting institution. Since 1858, all examinations (except those for a medical degree) were thrown open to all candidates irrespective of their place of education, thus allowing students such as Gray to apply.
54. Following information taken from notes sent to Brocard Sewell by James Langdale, Fanny's nephew, Sewell papers. These are given in condensed form by Sewell in "Marmaduke Langdale," *Footnote*, Appendix I, p.101. See also Edgar Jepson, vol. 1, *Memories of a Victorian* (London: Victor Gollancz, 1933), pp. 219, 222, 254.
55. Gray to Fanny Langdale, 25 December 1969, James Langdale papers.
56. This and the following description of Fanny are taken from a letter by James Langdale to Sewell, 23 January 1968, Sewell papers.
57. Father Edwin Essex, "The Canon in Residence," in Sewell, ed., *Two Friends*, p. 158.
58. Ricketts and Shannon were great connoisseurs and their art collection was, given their means, exceptional. As most of it was achieved only after 1896, when they began to prosper, I use the device in this chapter of naming the actual artifacts eventually collected as a copy or photograph, to indicate the range of the artists' collection. In fact, during this period, they covered their walls with inexpensive Japanese prints, such as Hiroshoge, and tacked photos and other reproductions of their favorite pieces to brown paper pinned on the wall to provide a background. For details of actual items, see Joseph Darracott, *All for Art: The*

Shannon and Ricketts Collection, Catalogue for an Exhibition at the Fitzwilliam Museum, Cambridge (Cambridge: Cambridge University Press, 1979).

59. "an intelligent but vague young man" from Delaney, *Charles Ricketts,* p. 31.
60. "muddled brain" from Ibid., p. 32.
61. Ibid., p. 32. Thomas Sturge Moore was the brother of the philosopher, G. E. Moore, and himself the first translator of Rimbaud into English (John Gray was the second).
62. Notes made by Desmond Flower in his diary after an extended conversation with Father John Gray on 19 April 1932, papers of Jad Adams.
63. Cf. illustration by Reginald Savage of John Gray in a chair identifiable as similar to those in the Vale.
64. Sewell, "Gray and Raffalovich," in Sewell, ed. *Two Friends,* pp. 15-16.
65. Gray to Raffalovich, 10 February 1899, National Library of Scotland, Edinburgh.
66. Paul Verlaine, from an autobiographical article titled "Pauvre Lelian" (an anagram for his own name), originally published in *Les Poétes Maudits* (1884); in *Ouevres et Prose Complétes,* edited by Jacques Borel (Paris: Gallimard, 1972), p. 525.
67. "Ô mon Dieu, vous m'avez blessé d'amour . . . ," from *Sagesse* (1880), in *Verlaine: Selected Poems,* trans. by Joanna Richardson (Harmondsworth, Middlesex, England: Penguin Books, 1974), p. 135.
68. Hart-Davis, ed., *Letters of Oscar Wilde,* pp. 254-55.
69. Lionel Johnson, "The Cultured Faun," *Anti-Jacobin* (14 March 1891), pp. 156-57.
70. "Critic as Artist," in *Complete Works of Oscar Wilde,* pp. 1121-22.
71. R. B. Kershner, ed., *A Portrait of the Artist as a Young Man* (Boston: Bedford Books of St. Martin's Press, 1993), p. 97.
72. "Oscar Wilde: The Poet of *Salome,*" from a newspaper article that first appeared in March 1909, reprinted in *Oscar Wilde: A Collection of Critical Essays,* ed. Richard Ellmann (Englewood Cliffs, N.J.: Prentice-Hall, Inc., 1969), p. 60.
73. Delaney, *Charles Ricketts,* p. 54.
74. Notes made by Desmond Flower in his diary after an interview with Father Gray, 19 April 1932, papers of Jad Adams.
75. "as every artist must" from Jad Adams, *Madder Music, Stronger Wine: The Life of Ernest Dowson, Poet and Decadent* (London: I.B. Tauris, 2000), p. 53.
76. Ibid., p. 52.
77. Desmond Flower and Henry Maas, eds., *The Letters of Ernest Dowson* (London: Cassell and Co., 1967), p. 198.
78. Ibid., p. 172.
79. Darracott, *All for Art,* p. 67.
80. Cooper and Bradley [Michael Field], 22 May 1894, "Works and Days" [BM Add. Ms. 46782].
81. Gray to Raffalovich, 5 March 1900, National Library of Scotland, Edinburgh.
82. John Gray to Pierre Louÿs, 6 January 1894, in Vernon, "Gray's Letters to Louÿs," p. 104.
83. The text for "Passing the Love of Women" is from Jacqueline Wesley, "Bibliographical Notes and Queries," *Book Collector* 39, no. 1 (Spring 1990): 115-17. Wesley quotes the poem from its holograph copy, which came into her hands by private sale. I have verified the handwriting as that of John Gray. The version of the poem given by Ian Fletcher in *Poems of John Gray,* pp. 43-44, is not from the holograph but from a typescript made from the holograph by John Gawsworth. The title of the poem is taken from 2 Samuel 1:26, from David's lament for Jonathan, and was at the time regarded, according to one commentator on the period, as "well-nigh a fiat for paederasty." See Timothy D'Arch Smith, *Love in Earnest: Some Notes on the Lives and Writings of English 'Uranian' Poets from 1889 to 1930* (London: Routledge and Kegan Paul, 1970), p. 187.
84. Quoted in John Gawsworth, "Two Poets 'J.G.,'" in Sewell, ed., *Two Friends,* p. 70.

85. Ensuing biographical information about Raffalovich and his family is from Sewell, "Gray and Raffalovich," in Sewell, ed., *Two Friends*, pp. 10-13, and Sewell, *Footnote*, pp. 18-30.

86. André Raffalovich [Alexander Michaelson], "Giles and Miles and Isabeau," *Blackfriars* 9 (January 1928): 25.

87. Linda Dowling, *Hellenism & Homosexuality in Victorian Oxford* (Ithaca, N.Y.: Cornell University Press, 1994), p. 117.

88. Hart-Davis, ed., *Letters of Oscar Wilde*, p. 471.

89. Dowling, *Hellenism & Homosexuality*, p. 118.

90. Raffalovich [Michaelson], "Oscar Wilde," *Blackfriars* 8, no. 92 (November 1927): 694-702. Raffalovich's account of his relationship with Wilde is from this source.

91. "The Portrait of Mr. W. H.," *Complete Works of Oscar Wilde*, p. 344.

92. Ibid, p. 342-43.

93. Ibid, p. 343.

94. Ibid.

95. Ibid., p. 332.

96. Ibid., p. 327.

97. Ibid., p. 325.

98. Dowling, *Hellenism & Homosexuality*, p. 130.

99. D'Arch Smith, *Love in Earnest*, pp. 30, 44, n. 107.

100. Ibid., p. 33.

101. "Sonnet: Translated from Paul Verlaine," *The Artist and Journal of Home Culture* 11 (1 August 1890): 241.

102. Notes of Desmond Flower from a conversation with Father Gray, 19 April 1932, Jad Adams papers.

103. *Men and Memories: Recollections of William Rothenstein*, Vol. I, 1872–1900 (London: Faber and Faber, 1931), p. 174. The descriptions of the Vale ambience are indebted to Rothenstein's account of them in the early nineties.

104. Dowling, "The Socratic Eros," in *Hellenism & Homosexuality*, pp.67-103; in particular, p. 102.

105. Rothenstein, *Men and Memories*, p. 173

106. Gray to Katherine Bradley [Michael Field], 24 July 1907, Berg Collection, New York Public Library.

107. Notes by Desmond Flower of a conversation with Father Gray, 19 April 1932, Jad Adams papers.

108. Gray to Félix Fénéon, 18 July 1890, Paulhan Archives, Paris. I have chosen to give the correspondence in translation, so as not to reproduce Gray's painful and often incorrect French.

109. Halperin, Joan Ungersma, *Félix Fénéon: Aesthete & Anarchist in Fin-de-Siécle Paris* (New Haven, Conn.: Yale University Press, 1988), p. 8. Information about Fénéon's career and his friendship with Gray are taken from this source.

110. Gray to Fénéon, 20 July 1890, Paulhan Archives, Paris.

111. Gray to Fénéon, no date, Paulhan Archives, Paris.

112. Letters from Gray to Fénéon, Gray papers, National Library of Scotland, Edinburgh and the John Rylands University Library of Manchester, England.

113. John Gray, "Obituary: Dubois-Pillet," *Academy* 957 (6 September 1890): 205.

114. Gray to Fénéon, 20 November 1890, Paulhan Archives, Paris.

115. Fénéon to Gray, 18 December 1890(?), John Gray Collection, John Rylands University Library of Manchester, England. The lithograph of Gray by Ricketts is not traceable.

116. Only seven translations of Rimbaud into English were made before 1910: the first was by T. Sturge Moore (his translation of "Les Chercheuses de Poux" appeared in the 1892 *The Dial*). G. Ross Roy lists Gray's translation of "Charleville" in *Silverpoints* (1893) as the first; it is actually the second. Cf. G. Ross Roy, "A

Bibliography of French Symbolism in English-language Publications to 1910: Mallarmé—Rimbaud—Verlaine," *Revue de Littérature Comparée* 34 (Octobre–Decembre 1960): 645-59.

Gray reported to Fénéon that his attempts to translate the "Illuminations" strongly resembled the poetry of Blake—with a bit of Walt Whitman. Gray to Fénéon, 14 April 1891, Poulhan Archives, Paris.

117. John Gray, "Complaint," *Silverpoints* (London: Elkin Mathews and John Lane, 1893), p. ix, reprinted in Fletcher, ed., *Poems of John Gray,* p. 23.

118. Fénéon to Gray, 18 December 1890(?), John Gray Collection, The John Rylands University Library of Manchester, England.

119. Denys Sutton, "Neglected Virtuoso: Charles Ricketts and his Achievements," *Apollo* 83 (February 1966): 142.

120. "A charming young man, very young"; John Rewald, ed., *Camille Pissarro: Lettres à Son Fils Lucien* (Paris: Editions Albin Michel, 1950), p. 190.

121. William Sutton Meadmore, *Lucien Pissarro: Un Coeur Simple* (London: Constable, 1962), p. 60.

122. Gray to Gordon Bottomley, 3 February 1933, papers of Roger Lancelyn Green.

123. Ibid.

124. Rothenstein, vol. 1, *Men and Memories,* pp. 174-76.

CHAPTER 2

1. Oscar Wilde refers to Gray as "the poet" in his letter to Frank Harris, Rupert Hart-Davis, ed., *The Letters of Oscar Wilde,* rev. ed. (London: Rupert Hart-Davis, Ltd., 1963), p. 320.

2. The first version of "The Picture of Dorian Gray" appeared in *Lippincott's Magazine* as a novella in June 1890 and in book version (revised to tone down the homoerotic overtones) in April 1891. To differentiate between the two, I use quotation marks for the magazine version and italicize the title of the book.

3. On Wilde's use of the "Dorian" nickname, see Frank Harris, *Oscar Wilde* (East Lansing: Michigan State University Press, 1959), p. 73. Arthur Symons recounts how he was introduced by Wilde to "the future Dorian Gray" in what must have been late 1890, after the publication of the magazine novella but before its publication in book form; Karl Beckson, ed., *The Memoirs of Arthur Symons: Life and Art in the 1890s* (University Park: The Pennsylvania State University Press. 1977), p. 136. Lionel Johnson refers to Gray as "Dorian" on their first meeting; Raymond Roseliep, "Some Letters of Lionel Johnson" (Ph.D. dissertation, University of Notre Dame, 1954), p. 109; and Ernest Dowson routinely refers to Gray as "Dorian" in letters of this period; cf. Desmond Flower and Henry Maas, eds. *The Letters of Ernest Dowson* (London: Cassell & Co., 1967), pp. 182-83 and pp. 207-08. Finally, Gray signs off a letter to "My dear Oscar" with "Yours ever, Dorian." Gray to Wilde, postmarked 9 January 1891, Donald Hyde Collection, New York.

4. "The Picture of Dorian Gray," in *Complete Works of Oscar Wilde* (New York: HarperCollins, 1994), p. 96.

5. Ibid., p. 28.

6. Ibid., pp. 28-29.

7. For one account of this scandal, see Timothy D'Arch Smith, *Love in Earnest: Some Notes on the Lives and Writings of the English "Uranian" Poets from 1889 to 1930* (London: Routledge and Kegan Paul, 1970), pp. 24-25.

8. John Gray, "Les Goncourts," *The Dial* 1 (1889), p. 12; reprinted in *The Selected Prose of John Gray,* ed. Jerusha Hull McCormack, no. 7, 1880–1920 British Authors Series (Greensboro, N.C.: ELT Press, 1992), p. 9

9. Cf. "Pen, Pencil and Poison," in *Complete Works of Oscar Wilde,* pp. 1102-1107.

10. Flower and Maas, eds., *Letters of Ernest Dowson,* p. 169.

11. With characteristic laziness, Wilde seem to have lifted the instruments' names from a passage in a museum handbook; cf. Isobel Murray, ed., *The Picture of Dorian Gray* (London: Oxford University Press, 1974), pp. 134-35; p. 245, fn.

"Sound" first appears in the *Silverpoints* holograph, Princeton University Library [MSS Bd: O'Connell], Princeton, N.J. Published more than thirty years later as *Sound: A Poem* (London: Curwen Press, 1926) and reprinted in Ian Fletcher, ed., *The Poems of John Gray,* The 1880–1920 British Author Series I (Greensboro, N.C.: ELT Press, 1988), p. 46.

When a fellow priest remarked on an unusual adjective used by Oscar Wilde, Father Gray replied: "'When we met in the terrible cenacles of poets, we used to recite our poems one to another. I remember having composed a sonnet on spring and reciting it duly, and, Father, . . . I remember that Oscar Wilde was one of the company. Would you like to hear it?' Abashed beyond measure, I murmured, 'Please'. And then without a falter he recited the sonnet which included the epithet 'shrill.' 'So, you see,' he concluded, 'Oscar Wilde may have been the plagiarist.'" The Reverend Dominic Hart, "Memories of John Gray," Trudgian papers. Published in Brocard Sewell, ed., "Some Memories of John Gray," *The Innes Review* 2 (1975): 81.

12. "The Picture of Dorian Gray," in *Complete Works of Oscar Wilde,* p. 31.

13. Ibid., p. 29.

14. Ibid., p. 31.

15. Ibid., p. 32.

16. Ibid., p. 29.

17. Gray was described as Wilde's "disciple" by George Bernard Shaw in Stanley Weintraub, ed., *Shaw: An Autobiography, 1856–1898* (New York: George Braziller, 1969), p. 250 and by Max Beerbohm in "Appendix A: Oscar Wilde," in *Max Beerbohm: Letters to Reggie Turner* (London: Rupert Hart-Davis, 1964), p. 290.

18. John Gray, *Silverpoints* (London: Elkin Mathews & John Lane, 1893), pp. 13-14. Reprinted in Fletcher, ed., *Poems of John Gray,* pp. 25-26.

19. A reading which owes much to Linda Dowling, "Nature and Decadence: John Gray's *Silverpoints,*" *Victorian Poetry* 15, no. 2 (Summer 1977): 166.

20. Flowers and Maas, eds., *Letters of Ernest Dowson,* p. 177.

21. Roseliep, "Some Letters of Lionel Johnson," p. 109.

22. Flowers and Maas, eds., *Letters of Ernest Dowson,* pp. 182-83.

23. Notes by Desmond Flower of a meeting with Father Gray, 19 April 1932, Jad Adams papers.

24. William Butler Yeats, "The Rhymers' Club" (23 April 1892), in *Letters to the New Island* (Cambridge, Mass.: Harvard University Press, 1934), p. 143.

25. Gray to Mrs. Maclagan, 9 February 1916, O'Connell Collection [box 3], Princeton University Library, Princeton, N.J.

26. Jepson, *Memories of a Victorian* vol. 1 (London: Victor Gollanz, 1933), p. 225.

27. Notes by Desmond Flower on a conversation with Father Gray, 19 April 1932, Jad Adams papers.

28. Ibid.

29. Ibid.

30. Ernest Dowson, "Non sum Qualis Eram Bonae Sub Regno Cynarae Vanitas," *The Poems of Ernest Dowson,* ed. Mark Longaker (Philadelphia, University of Pennsylvania Press, 1962), p. 58.

31. Father Edwin Essex, "The Canon in Residence," in *Two Friends: John Gray and André Raffalovich,* ed. Brocard Sewell (Aylesford, Kent: Saint Albert's Press, 1963), p. 154.

32. Dowson, "Ad Domnulam Suam," in *Poems of Ernest Dowson,* ed. Longaker, p. 47.

33. Flower and Maas, eds., *Letters of Ernest Dowson,* pp. 207-208.

34. Ibid., p. 228. William Clarke Hall (1866–1932), barrister and later a distinguished metropolitan magistrate, was knighted in 1932.

35. Gray to Katherine Bradley [Michael Field], 11 November 1908, Henry W. and Albert A. Berg Collection, New York Public Library.

36. Essex, "The Canon in Residence," in Sewell, ed., *Two Friends*, p. 154.

37. Mark Longaker, *Ernest Dowson* (Philadelphia: University of Pennsylvania Press, 1945), pp. 247-48.

38. Notes by Flower of a meeting with Father Gray, 19 April 1932, Jad Adams papers.

39. William Butler Yeats, "The Rhymers' Club," in *Letters to the New Island*, p. 146.

40. Charles-Pierre Baudelaire, "The Painter of Modern Life: The Dandy," in *Baudelaire: Selected Writings on Art and Artists*, trans. P. E. Charvet (Hammondsworth, Middlesex, Eng.: Penguin, 1972), p. 420.

41. "The Picture of Dorian Gray: The Preface," in *Complete Works of Oscar Wilde*, p. 16.

42. From a reconstruction of this dinner, given by the 1890s scholar (and biographer of "Baron Corvo") A. J. A. Symons in "The Diner-Out," *Horizen* 4, no. 22 (1941): 253. My account follows this one closely.

43. Frank Harris, *Oscar Wilde: His Life and Confessions* (New York: Garden City Publishing, 1930), p. 86.

44. Harris to Gray, no date, Beinecke Rare Book and Manuscript Library, Yale University, New Haven, Conn. Gray's version of "Charleville," revised in line with Harris's suggestions, was published in *Silverpoints*, pp. 30-31 and reprinted in Fletcher, ed., *Poems of John Gray*, p. 36.

45. The two poems Harris refers to in this paraphrase of his letter to Gray are "Les Demoiselles de Sauve" and "Poem," both of which eventually are to be published in *Silverpoints*.

46. Harris to Gray. See above, note 44.

47. Richard Ellmann, *Oscar Wilde* (New York: Knopf, 1988), p. 322.

48. Ibid., p. 308.

49. "Les Demoiselles de Sauve," *The Dial* (1892): 23. Reprinted in *Silverpoints* (1893), p. 5, and in Fletcher, ed., *Poems of John Gray*, p. 21.

50. Alice, Princess of Monaco, to Gray, 15 January 1893, National Library of Scotland, Edinburgh.

51. Alice, Princess of Monaco, to Gray, no date, National Library of Scotland, Edinburgh. This letter specifically mentions Gray's recitation at dinner.

52. *Black and White*, I, no. 4 (28 February 1891):125. Reprinted in Fletcher, ed., *Poems of John Gray*, pp. 42-43.

53. National Library of Scotland, Edinburgh; quoted by Margaret Mary McAlpine, "John Gray: A Critical and Biographical Study" (M.A. thesis: University of Manchester), p. 90.

54. Gray to Félix Fénéon, 14 April 1891, Paulhan Archives, Paris. Although the only solid historical evidence of this period (April 1891-92) places Gray in Tours and not in Paris, circumstantial evidence—such as the sudden widening of his Parisian literary contracts—argues for a visit by Gray to Paris during this period—either before or after Wilde's.

55. Pierre Honoré Jean Baptiste Champion, *Marcel Schwob et son temps* (Paris: B. Gasset, 1927), p. 98. The date of the letter is not certain; Campion gives it as 1892, without specifying the month, but the context suggests January. For an account of Wilde's Parisian visit, see Ellmann, *Oscar Wilde*), pp. 346 ff.

56. Henry D. Davray, "Mallarmé as I Knew Him," *Horizen* 7, no. 41 (May 1943): 350.

57. Gray to Félix Fénéon, 2 January 1891, Paulhan Archives, Paris.

58. Sherard to Gray, no date, National Library of Scotland, Edinburgh. There is no further account of the incident or its eventual outcome.

59. Holbrook Jackson, *The Eighteen Nineties: A Review of Art and Ideas at the Close of the Nineteenth Century* (London: Jonathan Cape, 1931), pp. 207-208. For an

account of the cultural climate in which the Independent Theatre was born, see Allardyce Nicoll, "The Theatre," in *A History of English Drama 1660–1900* vol. 5 (Cambridge: Cambridge University Press, 1959), pp. 1-49. Details about the first two seasons of the Independent Theatre are taken from N. H. G. Schoonderwoerd, *J. T. Grein, Ambassador of the Theatre 1862–1935: A Study in Anglo-Continental Theatrical Relations* (Assen, Netherlands: Van Gorcum and Co., 1963), pp. 60-130; and from Anna Irene Miller, *The Independent Theatre in Europe, 1887 to the Present* (New York: Ray Long and Richard R. Smith, 1931), pp. 169-71.

60. John Gray, "Note," in *In the Garden of Citrons: Idyll in One Act by Emilio Montanaro*, trans. J. T. Grein (London: Henry and Co., 1892), p. 7. *The Star* review (6 February 1892) is quoted in Patricio Gannon, "John Gray: Prince of Dreams," in Sewell, ed., *Two Friends*, p. 108.

61. *Theatre: A Monthly Review of the Drama, Music and Fine Arts* 19 (January–June 1892): 146. Mrs. Alice Augusta Grein [Michael Orme], *J. T. Grein: The Story of a Pioneer, 1862–1935* (London: John Murray, 1936), p. 63.

62. "The Person in Question," in McCormack, ed., *The Selected Prose of John Gray*, p. 20.

63. See correspondence between Francis Vielé-Griffin and Gray, National Library of Scotland, Edinburgh and cited in Jerusha Hull McCormack, *John Gray: Poet, Dandy & Priest* (Hanover, N.H.: University Press of New England, 1991), pp. 30-31.

64. Joan Ungersma Halperin, *Félix Fénéon: Aesthete & Anarchist in Fin-de-Siécle Paris* (New Haven, Conn.: Yale University Press), p. 4.

65. Hart-Davis, ed., *Letters of Oscar Wilde*, p. 311.

66. Quoted in Gannon, "John Gray," in Sewell, ed., *Two Friends*, p. 108.

67. Flower and Maas, eds., *Letters of Ernest Dowson*, p. 225.

68. Ibid.

69. John Gray, "The Modern Actor," *The Albemarle: A Monthly Review* 2, no. 1 (July 1892): 20; reprinted in McCormack, ed., *Selected Prose of John Gray*, p. 30. Following quotations from this source.

70. The Reverend Dominic Hart, "Memories of John Gray," Trudgian paper. Published (in slightly altered form) by Brocard Sewell, ed., "Some Memories of John Gray," *The Innes Review* 2 (1975), p. 87.

71. *Players* (9 February 1892), p. 184, quoted in Gannon, "John Gray," in Sewell, ed., *Two Friends*, p. 112.

72. Flower and Maas, eds., *Letters of Ernest Dowson*, p. 223.

73. Quoted in Gannon, "John Gray," in Sewell, ed., *Two Friends*, pp. 111-12.

74. *The Artist and Journal of Home Culture* (2 January 1893), p. 8.

75. From the papers of Helen Trudgian, who attributes it to a letter Gray wrote to *Players* magazine, responding to its review of his lecture (9 February 1892), p. 184.

76. "Prologue: In the Stalls," in *Aesthetes and Decadents of the 1890s*, ed. Karl Beckson (Chicago: Academy Chicago, 1981), p. 154.

77. Beckson, ed., *Memoirs of Arthur Symons*, p. 109.

78. Cyril Pearl, *The Girl with the Swansdown Seat* (London: Frederick Muller, 1955), pp. 208-209.

79. "The Drama of To-Day," *Daily Telegraph* (12 February 1892), quoted in Christopher Millard [Stuart Mason], *A Bibliography of Oscar Wilde* (London: Bertram Rota, 1967), p. 53.

80. "The Soul of Man under Socialism," *Complete Works of Oscar Wilde*, pp. 1188-89.

81. *The Star* (15 February 1892), quoted in Gannon, "John Gray," in Sewell, ed., *Two Friends*, p. 109.

82. Wilde's collaboration in the action against *The Star* is underlined by new evidence in the form of a letter from Ernest Poole of *The Star* newspaper to Oscar Wilde, dated 16 February 1892, which reads:

Dear Sir,

I enclose for your perusal a letter which I have lately forwarded to Mr. Gray's solicitor that you may see my anxiety to repair the wrong.

Yours faithfully,
Ernest Poole
Oscar Wilde, Esquire

The text of the letter is given by Jacqueline Wesley, "Biographical Notes and Queries," *Book Collector* 39, no. 1 (Spring 1990): 117.

83. Hart-Davis, ed., *Letters of Oscar Wilde*, pp. 311-12.
84. Ellmann, *Oscar Wilde*, p. 366.
85. Ibid., p. 367.
86. Sherard to Gray, no date, National Library of Scotland, Edinburgh.
87. Review in *The Spectator* (26 November 1892), pp. 767-68. Attributed to Gray by Helen Trudgian, in whose papers a copy of it was preserved.
88. "Mainly About People," *The Star*, quoted in Gannon, "John Gray," in Sewell, ed., *Two Friends*, p. 114.
89. *The Daily News* (London), quoted in Gannon, "John Gray," in Sewell, ed., *Two Friends*, p. 114. In fact, Gray was experimenting with half-rhymes and visual rhymes (e.g., "feast" and "best"), a technique he was to develop further in *Silverpoints*; see typescript in the Lord Chamberlain's collection, British Library, London (Add. As. 53494). Published as *The Kiss*, with preface and notes by Ian Fletcher, by the Tragara Press, Edinburgh, 1983.
90. *Players* (12 April 1892), quoted in Brocard Sewell, *In the Dorian Mode. A Life of John Gray, 1866–1934* (Padstow, Cornwall: Tabb House, 1983), pp. 24-25.
91. *Players*, no date, transcribed copy from the Trudgian papers.
92. Hart-Davis, ed., *Letters of Oscar Wilde*, p. 352.
93. Becksong, ed., *Memoirs of Arthur Symons*, p. 136.
94. Sherard records his objections in *Bernard Shaw, Frank Harris and Oscar Wilde* (London: Greystone Press, 1937), pp. 154-55.
95. Oscar Wilde, "The English Renaissance of Art," *Essays and Lectures* (London: Metheun, 1909), p. 130.
96. "The Portrait of Mr. W. H.," *Complete Works of Oscar Wilde*, p. 343.
97. Hart-Davis, ed., *Letters of Oscar Wilde*, pp. 263-64.
98. "Decay of Lying," *Complete Works of Oscar Wilde*, p. 1083.
99. "Lord Arthur Savile's Crime," in Ibid., p. 165.
100. "The Portrait of M. W. H.," in Ibid., p. 302.
101. "The Critic as Artist," in Ibid., p. 1148.
102. "Phrases and Philosophies for the Use of the Young," in Ibid., p. 1244.
103. Roger Lhombreaud, "Une Amitié Anglaise de Pierre Louÿs: Onze Lettres Inédites à John Gray," *Revue de Littérature Comparée* 27 (Juillet–Septembre 1953): 344. The following paragraph is indebted to this article, pp. 344-45.
104. Peter Vernon, "John Gray's Letters to Pierre Louÿs," *Revue de Littérature Comparée* 53 (Janvier–Mars 1979): 88-107. My translation is indebted to that of Michael Spiller in *A Friendship of the Nineties: Letters between John Gray and Pierre Louÿs*, ed. Alan Campbell (Edinburgh: Tragara Press, 1984), pp. 11-12.
105. 29 September [1892?], Vernon, "Gray's Letters to Louÿs," pp. 93-94.
106. Dowson's middle name was "Christopher" and he signed at least one letter to Gray, "Kit Dowson"; when Gray inscribed a copy of *Silverpoints* to him, it was "To Kit Marlowe the master singer." Flower and Maas, eds., *Letters of Ernest Dowson*, pp. 271-72.
107. André Gide, *Si le grain ne meurt . . .* (Paris: Gallimard, 1955), p. 332.
108. Lhombreaud, "Un Amité Anglaise," (15 June 1892), p. 345.
109. Vernon, "Gray's Letters to Louÿs," (15 June 1892), pp. 89-90.

110. "Translator's Note," in *Ecstasy: A Study in Happiness* (London: Henry and Co., 1892), p. v.
111. "On a Picture," *Silverpoints*, p. 21 and reprinted in Fletcher, ed., *Poems of John Gray*, pp. 30-31.
112. William Butler Yeats, "Art and Ideas," [1913], in *Essays and Introductions* (London: Macmillan, 1961), pp. 353-54.
113. Vernon, "Gray's Letters to Louÿs," pp. 90-91.
114. Hart-Davis, ed., *Letters of Oscar Wilde*, p. 315-16.
115. Ellmann, *Oscar Wilde*, p. 372.
116. Vernon, "Gray's Letters to Louÿs," p. 91.
117. Cyril Pearl, *The Girl with the Swansdown Seat*, pp. 208-09. Its license was revoked in 1894. For the Corinthian Club, see Douglas Ainslie, *Adventures Social and Literary* (London: T. Fisher Unwin, 1922), p. 142.
118. Lhombreaud, "Une Amitié Anglaise," p. 346.
119. Ibid., p. 347.
120. Vernon, "Gray's Letters to Louÿs," p. 92.
121. Ibid.
122. Lhombreaud, "Une Amitié Anglaise," pp. 347-48. The transcription of the date is almost certainly wrong; it should probably be 15 July.
123. Copy from Wilde's library in the Houghton Library, Cambridge, Mass.
124. A sentiment Wilde will repeat in his famous letter from prison addressed to Lord Alfred Douglas, January–March 1897, p. 426.
125. Vernon, "Gray's Letters to Louÿs," p. 93.
126. Ibid., pp. 93-94.
127. Vernon, "Gray's Letters to Louÿs," (2 October 1892), p. 94, n. 28. Following quotations from this source.
128. Lhombreaud, "Un Amitié Anglaise," p. 348.
129. Vernon, "Gray's Letters to Louÿs," pp. 95-96.
130. Ibid., pp. 96-97.
131. Hesketh Pearson, *Oscar Wilde: His Life and Wit* (New York: Harper, 1946), p. 186.
132. "The Person in Question," in McCormack, ed., *The Selected Prose of John Gray*, pp. 19-28. Subsequent quotation and paraphrase from this source.
    The typescript of this short story was left among Gray's papers on his death. For dating, see McCormack, *John Gray*, p. 275, n. 127.
133. A "switchback" was a primitive roller coaster, popular at Victorian exhibitions and fairs at the turn of the century.
134. Hart-Davis, ed., *Letters of Wilde*, p. 426. This letter was only published for the first time in its entirety in Rupert Hart-Davis's edition of the *Letters of Oscar Wilde*. Initially appearing under the title *De Profundis* in 1905, this particular passage was not public during Gray's lifetime.
135. Arthur Symons, "The Café Royal," in *The Café Royal and Other Essays* (Westminster, England: Beaumont Press, 1923), p. 4.

CHAPTER 3

1. PRO Minute by A. H. Oakes, Assistant Librarian, Foreign Office (Library Correspondence, 366/ 392, 28 May 1896). Quoted in Peter J. Vernon, "The Letters of John Gray" (Ph.D. dissertation, University of London, 1976), p. 17, n. 9. Office hours were from eleven to five o'clock, with an obligation to remain until work was completed; no departure from these hours, in theory, was possible without the express permission of the chief clerk.
2. Desmond Flower and Henry Maas, eds., *The Letters of Ernest Dowson* (London: Cassell and Co., 1967), p. 295.

3. Paul Verlaine, "Languer," in *Selected Poems*, ed. Joanna Richardson (Harmondsworth, Middlesex: Penguin, 1974), p. 180.

4. The *Foreign Office Lists* give the salary scale for a Second Division Clerk as being from £70 to £350 (in 1897); presumably Gray originally took up employment at the G.P.O. at about the £100 mark and then received annual £25 increments, bringing his income to the £200 figure for 1892. On the price of rooms, see Vernon, "Letters of John Gray," p. 104, n. 2.

5. The remark on starving was made by Gray to Katherine Bradley [Michael Field] and recorded in the journal she kept with Edith Cooper, "Works and Days," 1907 pt.2 [BM Add. Ms. 46797 f.2], British Library Manuscript Collections, London. The anxiety over bailiffs is from Peter Vernon, "John Gray's Letters to Pierre Louÿs," *Revue de Littérature Comparée* 53 (Janvier–Mars 1979): 91.

6. Roger Lhombreaud, "Une Amitié Anglaise de Pierre Louÿs: Onze Lettres Inédites à John Gray," *Revue de Littérature Comparée* 27 (Juillet–Septembre 1953): 350.

7. Note by Helen Trudgian, Trudgian papers, cited by Brocard Sewell, *In the Dorian Mode: A Life of John Gray, 1899–1934* (Padstow, Cornwall: Tabb House, 1983), pp. 30-31; 200, n. 33.

8. Timothy D'Arch Smith, *Love in Earnest: Some Notes on the Lives and Writings of the English "Uranian" Poets from 1889 to 1930* (London: Routledge and Kegan Paul, 1970), pp. 29-34. That Raffalovich was indeed a familiar of the London homosexual underworld is based on his detailed knowledge of its practices, which he displays in his treatise, *Uranisme et Unisexualité: Étude sur Différentes Manifestations de l'Instinct Sexuel, Bibliothèque de Criminologie*, vol. 15 (Lyon: A. Storck, 1896).

9. Sewell, *In the Dorian Mode*, p. 200, n. 34. Trudgian's informant was André Raffalovich's sister, Sophie O'Brien.

10. André Raffalovich [Alexander Michaelson], "Oscar Wilde," *Blackfriars* 8 (November 1927): 700-701.

11. "L'Affaire Oscar Wilde," *Archives de l'Anthropologie Criminelle de Criminologie et de Psychologie Normale et Pathologique* (Paris) 10 (1895): 445. Reprinted under separate cover as *L'Affaire Oscar Wilde* (Lyon: A. Storck, 1895).

12. Raffalovich to Gray, undated [c. 14 February 1900], National Library of Scotland, Edinburgh.

13. Raffalovich [Michaelson], "Oscar Wilde," p. 701.

14. Vernon, "Gray's Letters to Louÿs," p. 89.

15. Ibid., 24 November 1892, pp. 96-97.

16. Flower and Maas, eds., *Letters of Ernest Dowson*, p. 295, and n. 4. "Park Lane," *The Post Office London Directory for 1895*. In December 1896, Gray moved from Park Lane to 92 Mount Street W., almost equally proximal to Raffalovich's residence at 72 South Audley Street.

17. Vernon, "Gray's Letters to Louÿs," 27 November 1892, p. 97.

18. Ibid.

19. Ibid., 3 December 1892, p. 99.

20. Ibid., 24 December 1892, p. 99.

21. Entry by Edith Cooper in "Works and Days" 1908 [BM Add. Ms. 46798, f. 202], British Library Manuscript Collections, London.

22. "The Person in Question," in *The Selected Prose of John Gray*, ed. Jerusha Hull McCormack, no. 7, 1880–1920 British Author Series (Greensboro, N.C.: University of North Carolina: ELT Press, 1992), p. 28.

23. Robert Sheraud, *Bernard Shaw, Frank Harris and Oscar Wilde* (New York: Greystone Press, 1937), pp. 90-91.

24. John Lane to Oscar Wilde, 17 June 1892, Princeton University Library [MSS Misc. WIA-WIL], Princeton, New Jersey.

25. Bodley Head files; printed in James G. Nelson, *The Early Nineties: A View from the Bodley Head* (Cambridge, Mass.: Harvard University Press, 1971), p. 95. The

second contract was highly disadvantageous for Lane; it is probable that Raffalovich was behind the scenes, guaranteeing him against loss. See Richard Ellmann, *Oscar Wilde* (New York: Knopf, 1988), p. 392.

26. Notes on the *Silverpoints* holograph and Gray to Lane: "By all means omit the 'Song of the Stars' from the Silverpoints." 18 June 1892, HenryW. and Albert A. Berg Collection, New York Public Library.

27. Isobel Murray, ed., *The Picture of Dorian Gray,* (London: Oxford University Press, 1974), pp. 134-35 and note, p. 245.

28. See the Reverend Dominic Hart, "Memories of John Gray," Trudgian papers; published in edited form by Brocard Sewell, "Some Memories of John Gray," *The Innes Review* 2 (1975): 81, for Gray's evident opinion that it was Oscar Wilde who stole from him, rather than the other way around.

29. Charles Ricketts, *A Defence of the Revival of Printing* (London: Hacon and Ricketts, 1899), p. 18.

30. Arthur Symons, "The Decadent Movement in Literature," in *Aesthetes and Decadents of the 1890s,* ed. Karl Beckson (Chicago: Academy Chicago, 1891), pp. 149-50. Following quotation is from this source.

31. *Silverpoints* (London: Elkin Mathews and John Lane, 1893), p. xix. Reprinted in Ian Fletcher, ed. *The Poems of John Gray,* The 1880–1920 British Author Series, no. 1 (Greensboro, N.C.: E.L.T. Press, 1988), pp. 29-30.

32. Owen Seamen, "Disenchantment," in *Punch* (14 July 1894), quoted in R. K. R. Thornton, *The Decadent Dilemma* (London: Edward Arnold, 1983), p. 43.

33. Derived from a fictive portrait of Gray as "Father Rosary" in Siegfried Sassoon's *Sherston's Progress* (London: Faber and Faber, 1936), p. 66, as identified by James Darragh in a letter to Brocard Sewell, 5 July 1976, Sewell papers.

34. "Translator's Note," in Louis Couperus, *Ecstasy: A Study in Happiness,* translated by A. Teixeira de Mattos and John Gray (London: Henry and Co., 1892), p. xi. Following quotation from this source.

35. Gray to Edith Cooper, 14 November 1909, Berg Collection, New York Public Library.

36. "Poem," *Silverpoints,* p. xx. Reprinted in Fletcher, ed., *Poems of John Gray,* p. 30.

37. Lord Edward Gleichen, "Robert Burns," *London's Open-Air Statuary* (London: Longmans, Green, 1928), p. 107. Gleichen notes that the statue was "unveiled by Lord Rosebery 26 July 1884."

38. Quoted by Olive Custance in a letter to an unidentified correspondent ("Lulu") in Brocard Sewell, *Footnote to the Nineties: A Memoir of John Gray and André Raffalovich* (London: Cecil and Amelia Woolf, 1968), p. 16

39. "The Truth of Masks," in *Complete Works of Oscar Wilde* (New York: HarperCollins, 1994), p. 1173.

40. Cooper and Bradley, 1907, "Works and Days," [BM Add. Ms. 46796 f. 216], British Library Manuscript Collections, London.

41. *Silverpoints,* p. xii. Reprinted in Fletcher, ed., *Poems of John Gray,* pp. 24-25.

42. Arthur Symons, quoted in Beckson, ed., *Aesthetes and Decadents,* p. 155, n. 1. See also Symons's poem, "La Melinte: Moulin-Rouge," pp. 155-56.

43. *Salome* was originally written in French by Wilde and translated, among others, by Alfred Douglas and Pierre Louÿs into an English version which was published by Mathews and Lane as *Salome: A Tragedy in One Act* in 1892 with illustrations by Aubrey Beardsley.

44. Gray to Ricketts, Berg Collection, New York Public Library.

45. Vernon, "Gray's Letters to Louÿs," 18 February 1893, p. 101, n. 57. *Silverpoints* was actually published in the week of 4 March 1893; *Salome* on 22 February 1893.

46. Brocard Sewell, "John Gray and André Sebastian Raffalovich: A Biographical Outline," in *Two Friends: John Gray and André Raffalovich: Essays Biographical and Critical,* ed. Sewell (Aylesdord, Kent: St. Albert's Press, 1963), p. 12.

47. Ellmann, *Oscar Wilde,* p. 375.

48. Gray to Lane, 4 January 1893 [Mss. Misc. GOR-GRA] Princeton University Library.

49. Flower and Maas, eds., *Letters of Ernest Dowson,* p. 271.

50. In a letter to John Lane, c. December 1892, Ricketts remarks on "Gray (whom I sometimes see, about once every two years) . . . " Houghton Library, Cambridge, Mass.

51. Notes made by Desmond Flower on a conversation with Father Gray, 19 April 1932, Jad Adams papers.

52. Violet Wyndham, "Reminiscences, by Ada Leverson: 1. The Importance of Being Oscar," in *The Sphinx and Her Circle: A Biographical Sketch of Ada Leverson, 1862–1933* (London: André Deutsche, 1963), p. 105.

53. Gray uses this expression in a letter to Louÿs, [14 February 1893]. Vernon, "Gray's Letters to Louÿs," p. 100.

54. Alice, Princess of Monaco, to Gray, no date, National Library of Scotland, Edinburgh.

55. Arthur Symons to Raffalovich, National Library of Scotland, Edinburgh; quoted in Margaret Mary McAlpine, "John Gray: A Critical and Biographical Study" (M.A. thesis, University of Manchester, 1967), p. 90.

56. Unsigned review, "Art Literature," *The Artist and Journal of Home Culture* 14, no. 161 (1 April 1893): 119.

57. "John Gray," *Retrospective Reviews: A Literary Log* (London: John Lane, 1896), pp. 229-31.

58. *Pall Mall Gazette* 56 (4 May 1893): 3.

59. The essay appeared in the *Anglo-American Times,* 25 March 1893, about a month after *Silverpoints*'s publication. Reprinted as "Appendix A: Oscar Wilde by [Max Beerbohm masquerading as] An American," *Max Beerbohm: Letters to Reggie Turner,* ed. Rupert Hart-Davis (London: Hart-Davis, 1964), p. 290.

60. Rupert Hart-Davis, ed., *The Letters of Oscar Wilde* (London: Rupert Hart-Davis, Ltd., 1963), p. 426.

61. Lord Alfred Douglas, "In Praise of Shame," *The Chameleon* (December 1894), quoted in Brian Reade, *Sexual Heretics: Male Homosexuality in English Literature from 1850 to 1900* (New York: Coward-McCann, Inc., 1970), p. 362.

62. "Summer Past," *Silverpoints,* p. xv, reprinted in Fletcher, ed., *Poems of John Gray,* pp. 26-27.

63. Vernon, "Gray's Letters to Louÿs," 16 March 1893, p. 102.

64. H. P. Clive, "Pierre Louÿs and Oscar Wilde: A Chronicle of Their Friendship," *Revue de Littérature Comparée* 43 (1969): 368. The subsequent account relies on Clive's work.

65. Jonathan Fryer, *André and Oscar: Gide, Wilde and the Gay Art of Living* (London: Allison and Busby, 1999), pp. 57-58.

66. Ibid., p. 58.

67. Lhombreaud, "Une Amitié Anglaise," p. 352 .

68. Sir John Tilley and Stephen Gaselee, *The Foreign Office* (London: G. P. Putnam's Sons, 1933), p. 144.

69. Symons to Gray, no date, National Library of Scotland, Edinburgh.

70. Father Edwin Essex, "The Canon in Residence," in Sewell, ed. *Two Friends,* p. 155. Also mentioned by Bradley and Cooper [Michael Field] in "Works and Days," 10 September 1909 [BM Add. Ms 46799, f. 138], British Library Manuscript Collections, London.

71. T. W. G. W., "La Garde Joyeuse IX," *The Artist and Journal of Home Culture* 14, no. 167 (4 November 1893): 329.

72. Vernon, "Gray's Letters to Louÿs," 6 June 1893, p. 103.

73. "The Yellow Princess," left in typescript among Gray's papers after his death, is published in McCormack, ed., *The Selected Prose of John Gray,* p. 67

74. Raffalovich, *Roses of Shadow,* privately printed and not for general distribution (no printer's name, no date), p. 13.
75. Raffalovich to Gray, undated [c. 1900], National Library of Scotland, Edinburgh.
76. Sewell, "Gray and Raffalovich," in Sewell, ed., *Two Friends,* p. 13, n. 6.
77. André Raffalovich [Alexander Michaelson], "Giles and Miles and Isabeau," *Blackfriars* 9 (January 1928), p. 25.
78. For an account of Raffalovich's London salon, see Philip Healy, "Raffalovich and His Circle: Part One. London in the 1880s and '90s," *Book World* 25, vol. 3, no. 1 (February 1984): 5-9.
79. Sewell, *In the Dorian Mode,* p. 60.
80. Beatrice Gray [Mary Raphael Gray], "A Sister's Reminiscences," in Sewell, ed., *Two Friends,* pp. 100-101.

CHAPTER 4

1. [Invitation] Gray to William Rothenstein, 29 March 1894, Rothenstein Collection, Houghton Library, Cambridge, Mass.
2. Gray papers, National Library of Scotland, Edinburgh. Published in Ian Fletcher, ed., *The Poems of John Gray,* The 1880–1920 British Author Series I (Greensboro, N.C.: ELT Press, 1988), pp. 61-65.
3. Joan Ungersma Halperin, *Félix Fénéon: Aesthete and Anarchist in Fin-de-Siècle Paris* (New Haven, Conn.: Yale University Press, 1988), p. 373.
4. [Mrs.] E. Lynn Linton to Gray, 18 April [1894], Gray papers, National Library of Scotland, Edinburgh.
5. Allardyce Nicoll, "Late Nineteenth-Century Drama, 1850–1900," in *A History of English Drama, 1660–1900* (Cambridge: Cambridge University Press, 1959), pp. 5, 390, 533. The final act survives in manuscript; National Library of Scotland, Edinburgh.
6. *Theatre: A Monthly Review of the Drama, Music, and the Fine Arts* 24 (8 June 1894), quoted in Brocard Sewell, "John Gray and André Sebastian Raffalovich: A Biographical Outline," in *Two Friends: John Gray and André Raffalovich: Essays Biographical and Critical,* ed. Brocard Sewell (Aylesford, Kent.: St. Albert's Press, 1963), pp. 20-21.
7. *Theatre* 24 (1 July 1894): 37-38. Following quotation from this source.
8. John Gray, *Spiritual Poems, Chiefly Done out of Several Languages* (London: Hacon and Ricketts, 1896), p. xi-xx; reprinted in Fletcher, ed., *Poems of John Gray,* p. 95-100.
9. John Gray, "Light," *Pageant* 2 (1897) I: 128-29. Reprinted in *The Selected Prose of John Gray,* no. 7, 1880–1920 British Author Series, ed. Jerusha Hull McCormack (Greensboro, N.C.: University of North Carolina: ELT Press, 1992), pp. 99-124.
10. "Spiritual Poems," holograph, National Library of Scotland, Edinburgh.
11. "Spiritual Poems," holograph, reprinted in Fletcher, ed., *Poems of John Gray,* pp. 147-148.
12. *Spiritual Poems,* pp. xxiii-xxiv, reprinted in Fletcher, ed., *Poems of John Gray,* p. 102.
13. "Spiritual Poems" holograph, National Library of Scotland, Edinburgh.
14. Gray to Katherine Bradley [Michael Field], 24 November 1908, Henry W. and Albert A. Berg Collection, New York Public Library.
15. Gray to Katherine Bradley [Michael Field], 24 October 1908, Berg Collection, New York Public Library. The journal entry on Gray as Carmelite is in "Works

and Days," Journal of Katherine Bradley and Edith Cooper [Michael Field], [BM Add. Ms. 46798], British Library Manuscript Collections, London.

16. Gray to Katherine Bradley [Michael Field], 24 October 1908, Berg Collection, New York Public Library.

17. Gray to Katherine Bradley [Michael Field], 3 August 1908, Berg Collection, New York Public Library.

18. Gray to André Raffalovich, 21 November 1904, National Library of Scotland, Edinburgh.

19. Gray to Katherine Bradley [Michael Field], 29 January 1909, Berg Collection, New York Public Library.

20. R. F. Foster, W. B. Yeats: A Life, Vol. I: The Apprentice Mage, 1865–1914 (Oxford: Oxford University Press, 1997), pp. 89-99.

21. Evidence of this encounter is contained in a letter from Wilkinson to Gray, 11 January 1893, National Library of Scotland, Edinburgh. The citation is from "Garth Wilkinson," The Dial 3 (1893), p. 23.

22. "May 1895," The Blue Calendar 1895: A Book of Carols (privately printed and not for general distribution, 24 December 1894), reprinted in Fletcher, ed., Poems of John Gray, pp. 159-60.

23. Desmond Flower and Henry Maas, eds., Letters of Ernest Dowson, (London: Cassell and Co., 1967), p. 337.

24. André Raffalovich [Alexander Michaelson], "Isis Unveiled," Blackfriars 9 (September 1928): 532-35.

25. Walter Pater, "Conclusion," The Renaissance: Studies in Art and Poetry (London: Macmillan, 1924), p. 250.

26. Raffalovich [Michaelson], "Isis Unveiled,", pp. 539-30.

27. Ibid., p. 537.

28. Raffolovich [Michaelson], "Parallets," Blackfriars 10 (January 1929): 784.

29. Richard Ellmann, Oscar Wilde (New York: Knopf, 1988), p. 382.

30. Ibid., p. 393.

31. No date, but probably late June 1893. Roger Lhombread, "Une Amitié Anglaise de Pierre Louÿs; Onze Lettres Inédites à John Gray," Revue de Littérature Comparée 27 (1953): 352.

32. Raffalovich [Michaelson], "Isis Unveiled," p. 540.

33. The Dial 4 (1896): 1, reprinted in Fletcher, ed., Poems of John Gray, pp. 255-60.

34. Katherine Bradley [Michael Field], 1894 "Works and Days," (BM Add. Ms. 46782) British Library Manuscript Collection, London.

35. Frances Winwar, Oscar Wilde and the Yellow 'Nineties (Garden City, N.Y.: Blue Ribbon Books, 1940), pp. 241-42.

36. John Gray, "Aubrey Beardsley," La Revue Blanche 16 (1898): 69. This article was published originally in French. Reprinted, in English translation, in Jerusha Hull McCormack, ed., The Selected Prose of John Gray, pp. 125-28.

37. Winwar, Oscar Wilde, p. 242.

38. Ibid.

39. John Gray, "Aubrey Beardsley," in McCormack, ed., Selected Prose of John Gray, pp. 126-27.

40. Winwar, Oscar Wilde, p. 243.

41. "The Second Coming of Arthur," in "Appendix," Aesthetes and Decadents of the 1890s, ed. Karl Beckson (Chicago: Academy Chicago, 1981), pp. 316-17.

42. Winwar, Oscar Wilde, p. 240.

43. Ibid., p. 243

44. The phrase is Wilde's. The Letters of Oscar Wilde, ed. Rupert Hart-Davis (London: Rupert Hart-Davis, Ltd., 1963), p. 379.

45. Complete Works of Oscar Wilde (Glasgow: HarperCollins, 1994), pp. 1244-45.

46. Lord Alfred Douglas, "In Praise of Shame," in Brian Reade, ed., *Sexual Heretics: Male Homosexuality in English Literature from 1850–1900* (New York: Coward-McCann, 1970), p. 362.
47. Lord Alfred Douglas, "Two Loves," in Ibid., pp. 360-62.
48. John Francis Bloxam, "The Priest and the Acolyte," in Ibid., p. 350.
49. Concerning Lord Rosebery's involvement, see Michael S. Foldy, *The Trials of Oscar Wilde: Deviance, Morality, and Late-Victorian Society* (New Haven, Conn.: Yale University Press, 1997), pp. 21-30.
50. *Letters of Oscar Wilde,* p. 379.
51. George Bernard Shaw, *Saturday Review* (12 January 1895) 89: 44-5, reprinted in Karl Beckson, ed., *Oscar Wilde: The Critical Heritage* (London: Routledge & Kegan Paul), pp. 176-77.
52. For wording on the card, see Ellmann, *Oscar Wilde,* p. 438.
53. Brocard Sewell, *Footnote to the Nineties: A Memoir of John Gray and André Raffalovich* (London: Cecil and Amelia Woolf, 1968), p. 35. Sewell names one "Frank (Francis) Mathew" as the barrister in question, on the basis of a private conversation with Father John-Baptist Reeves. However, no such person appears among the listing of solicitors or barristers of the time; therefore I can only make the educated guess that Charles Willie Mathews, already engaged for Wilde, must be the person in question. A "watching brief" is a brief instructing counsel to "watch" a case.
54. H. Montgomery Hyde, ed., *The Trials of Oscar Wilde* (London: Hodge and Company, Ltd., 1960) p. 124.
55. Ibid., p. 133
56. Wilde was "well aware of the dangers of being homosexual" (Ellman, *Oscar Wilde,* p. 275) and said: "It was like feasting with panthers. The danger was half the excitement." (*Letters of Oscar Wilde,* ed. Hart-Davis, p. 492).
57. H. Montgomery Hyde, ed., *Trials of Oscar Wilde,* p. 150.
58. Ibid., p. 256.
59. Rupert Hart-Davis, ed., *Max Beerbohm: Letters to Reggie Turner* (London: Rupert Hart-Davis, 1964), p. 102.
60. One of the books from Wilde's library now in the Houghton Library, Cambridge, Mass.
61. Now in the Donald Hyde Collection, New York.
62. Winwar, *Oscar Wilde,* p. 309.
63. André Raffalovich [Alexander Michaelson], "Oscar Wilde," *Blackfriars* 8 (November 1927): 701. Following quotation from this source.
64. John Gray, *Spiritual Poems,* p. xi, reprinted in Fletcher, ed., *Poems of John Gray,* p. 95.
65. Ibid., p. lxvii-lxviii, reprinted in Fletcher, ed., *Poems of John Gray,* pp. 123-24.
66. Ibid., p. xiii, xv, reprinted in Fletcher, ed., *Poems of John Gray,* pp. 96, 97.
67. Sewell, "Gray and Raffalovich," in Sewell, ed., *Two Friends,* p. 27 and Sewell, *Footnote,* p. 43. Sewell had the story from the late William Muir, one of Father Gray's Edinburgh converts, to whom Gray apparently spoke freely about his religious life. A similar incident occurs to Park in the novella of that name.
68. Robert Sherard, *Oscar Wilde: Story of an Unhappy Friendship,* (London: Greening & Co., 1905), p. 164.
69. Lhombread, "Une Amitié Anglaise," pp. 353-59.
70. Sherard, *Unhappy Friendship,* pp. 127-28.
71. "L'Affaire Oscar Wilde," *Archives de L'Anthropologie Criminelle et les Sciences Pénales* 10 (1895): 445-77. Some time later, it was issued under separate cover by A. Storck, Lyons.
72. Ibid., p. 445.

73. Information from Heather Coltman, granddaughter of William and Gray's grandniece, in conversation with McCormack, July 1989. She also spoke of "rifts" with other members of his family.

74. Raffalovich to Charles Ballantyne, 13 November 1927, National Library of Scotland, Edinburgh.

75. Raffalovich, *Uranisme et Unisexualité: Etude sur Différentes Manifestations de L'Instinct Sexuel*, Bibliothèque de Criminologie, vol. 15 (Lyons: Storck, 1896), p. 138. For assessment of the significance of this work, see Ellis Hanson, *Decadence and Catholicism* (Cambridge, Mass.: Harvard University Press, 1997), pp. 320-25.

76. Raffalovich, *Uranisme et Unisexualité*, p. 126.

77. Hanson, *Decadence and Catholicism*, p. 321, to which this account is indebted.

78. Raffalovich, *Uranisme et Unisexualité* p. 132.

79. Ibid., p. 130.

80. Ibid., p. 175.

81. Gray to Raffalovich, 5 March 1900, National Library of Scotland, Edinburgh.

82. Raffalovich, *Uranisme et Unisexualité*, p. 30.

83. Ibid., pp. 31-32.

84. Ibid., p. 32. Following quotation from this source.

85. Ibid.

86. *Spiritual Poems*, pp. lvii-lxvi, reprinted in Fletcher, ed., *Poems of John Gray*, pp. 118-22.

87. Ibid., pp. lxv-lxvi, reprinted in Fletcher, ed., *Poems of John Gray*, pp. 122-23.

88. "Jesus Angelic Gem," "Spiritual Poems" holograph, National Library of Scotland, Edinburgh, reprinted in Fletcher, ed., *Poems of John Gray*, p. 57.

89. *Spiritual Poems*, p. xvi, reprinted in Fletcher, ed., *Poems of John Gray*, pp. 97-98.

90. John Gray, "André Raffalovich," *Blackfriars* 15 (June 1934): 405.

91. Sewell, "Gray and Rafflovich," in Sewell, ed., *Two Friends*, pp. 12, 26.

92. Ibid., p. 10.

93. Ibid., p. 26 and Miriam J. Benkowitz, *Aubrey Beardsley: An Account of His Life* (Hamish Hamilton, 1981), p. 173 and p. 215, note 41.

94. Benkowitz, p. 122.

95. André Raffalovich [Alexander Michaelson], "Aubrey Beardsley," *Blackfriars* 9 (October 1928): 609-10.

96. Ibid., p. 610.

97. John Gray, ed., *Last Letters of Aubrey Beardsley* (London: Longmans, Green, 1904), p. 4.

98. Ibid., p. 12.

99. Ibid., p. 3.

100. Raffalovich [Michaelson], "Aubrey Beardsley," p. 610.

101. Ibid., p. 611.

102. Henry Maas, J.L. Duncan, and W.G. Good, eds., *The Letters of Aubrey Beardsley* (Rutherford, N.J.: Fairleigh Dickinson University Press, 1970), p. 142.

103. See Jerusha Hull McCormack, *John Gray: Poet, Dandy and Priest* (Hanover, N.H.: University Press of New England, 1991), pp. 163-64.

104. Gray to Katherine Bradley [Michael Field], 24 October 1908, Berg Collection, New York Public Library.

105. Maas, Duncan, and Good, eds., *Letters of Beardsley*, p. 244.

106. Ibid., pp. 249-50.

107. Ibid., pp. 255, 259, 260-61.

108. Ibid., p. 264.

109. Ibid., p. 269.

110. Ibid., p. 287.

111. Ibid., p. 291.

112. John Gray, "Aubrey Beardsley," *La Revue Blanche* 16 (1898): 68. Reprinted in McCormack, ed., *Selected Prose of John Gray*, p. 126.

113. Maas, Duncan, and Good, eds., *Letters of Beardsley*, p. 308.

114. Raffalovich [Michaelson], "Aubrey Beardsley," p. 613.

115. Gray, "Daphné," *La Revue Blanche* 12 (1897): pp. 758-62.

116. Gray, "Aubrey Beardsley," in McCormack, ed., *Selected Prose of John Gray*, pp. 127-28.

117. Maas, Duncan, and Good, eds, *Letters of Beardsley*, pp. 343, 379.

118. Gray, "Aubrey Beardsley," in McCormack, ed., *Selected Prose of John Gray*, p. 128.

119. Maas, Duncan, Good, eds., *Letters of Aubrey Beardsley*, p. 439

120. Stanley Weintraub, *Beardsley: A Biography* (New York: George Braziller, 1967), p. 243.

121. Gray, "Aubrey Beardsley," in McCormack, ed., *Selected Prose of John Gray*, p. 126.

122. Louÿs to Gray, 11 July 1899, Lhombreaud, "Une Amitié Anglaise," p. 356. Fénéon to Gray, 3 October 1898, John Gray Collection, John Rylands University Library of Manchester, England.

123. Mrs. Charles Cammell, in conversation with Jerusha Hull McCormack, May, 1970.

124. *The Dial* 5 (1897): 13-15. Reprinted as "Leda and the Swan" in Fletcher, ed., *Poems of John Gray*, pp. 82-85.

125. Gray to Raffalovich, 18 March 1903, National Library of Scotland, Edinburgh.

126. Flower and Maas, eds., *Letters of Ernest Dowson*, pp. 337, 372.

127. Letter from William Rothenstein, G. F. Simms Catalogue No. 25, item 245, quoted in Patricio Gannon, "John Gray: The Prince of Dreams," in Sewell, ed., *Two Friends*, p. 110.

128. Lhombreaud, "Une Amitié Anglaise," p. 355.

129. Gray to Katherine Bradley [Michael Field], 3 August 1908, Berg Collection, New York Public Library.

130. The phrase is Gray's, "The Redemption of Durtal," *The Dial* 4 (1896): 7. The following passage is a paraphrase of the paragraph on p. 9.

131. No. 209, *Catalogue 1: Anthony d'Offay, Books and Autograph Letters Mainly of the Eighteen-Nineties*, Gray papers, National Library of Scotland, Edinburgh.

132. Lhombreaud, "Une Amitié Anglaise," p. 355.

CHAPTER 5

1. Mrs. William O'Brien [Sophie Raffalovich], "Friends for Eternity: André Raffalovich and John Gray," *The Irish Monthly* 62 (November 1934): 700-01.

2. Father Dominic Hart, "Memories of John Gray," Trudgian papers, p. 1; reprinted, in somewhat altered form, as "Some Memories of John Gray by the Reverend Dominic Hart," Brocard Sewell, ed., *The Innes Review* 2 (1975): 80-88.

3. Hart, "Memories," p. 2.

4. Ibid.

5. Gray to Raffalovich, 3 November 1898, Gray papers, National Library of Scotland, Edinburgh.

6. Frederick Baron Corvo [Frederick William Rolfe], *Hadrian the Seventh* (New York: Dover, 1969), pp. 239-43.

7. Gray to Raffalovich, 9 March 1901. "Baron Corvo was one of us. There is a district legend of him, but you must have heard all the jokes." Gray papers, National Library of Scotland, Edinburgh.

8. Christopher McElroy, Rector, Scots College, Rome, to John Flood, 9 January 2000, McCormack papers.

9. Gray to Raffalovich, 1 November 1898, Gray papers, National Library of Scotland.

10. Ibid., 8 November 1898.

11. Ibid., 27 November 1898.

12. Ibid., 5 March 1900.

13. Ibid., 10 February 1899.

14. Raffalovich to Gray, no date, Gray papers, National Library of Scotland, Edinburgh.

15. Gray to Raffalovich, 20 March 1899.

16. Ibid., 7 January 1900.

17. Rupert Hart-Davis, ed., *Letters of Oscar Wilde* (London: Rupert Hart-Davis, 1963), p. 826. Wilde describes visiting these gardens on 27 April 1900, but the site of his actual meeting with Gray is purely conjectural.

18. "Works and Days," journal of Edith Cooper and Katherine Bradley [Michael Field], 1908 [BM Add. Ms. 46798 f. 202], British Library Manuscript Collection, London.

19. John Gray, "The Lord Looks at Peter," *Blackfriars* 8 (April 1927): 238. Reprinted in Ian Fletcher, ed., *The Poems of John Gray*, The 1880–1920 British Authors Series, no. 1 (Greensboro, N.C.: ELT Press, 1988), p. 285.

20. Gray to Raffalovich, 5 March 1900, Gray papers, National Library of Scotland, Edinburgh.

21. Ibid., 10 October 1902.

22. James Langdale to Brocard Sewell, no date, Sewell papers.

23. Gray to Raffalovich, 16 December1899, Gray papers, National Library of Scotland, Edinburgh.

24. Gray to Fanny Langdale, 7 June 1902, Langdale papers.

25. Ibid., 30 September 1914.

26. Ibid., 22 May 1924.

27. Edwin Essex, O. P., "The Canon in Residence," in *Two Friends: John Gray and André Raffalovich*, ed. Brocard Sewell (Aylesford, Kent: St. Albert's Press, 1963), p. 160.

28. Mary Raphael Gray [Beatrice Hannah Gray], "A Sister's Reminiscences," in Sewell, ed., *Two Friends*, pp. 101, 104.

29. Gray to Raffalovich, 13 Oct. 1898, Gray papers, National Library of Scotland, Edinburgh.

30. Ibid., 11 October 1900.

31. Mary Raphael Gray to Helen Trudgian, 1962, Trudgian papers.

32. Gray to Raffalovich, 4 September 1902, National Library of Scotland, Edinburgh.

33. Ibid., 3 October 1902.

34. Ibid., 8 March 1903.

35. Brocard Sewell, "John Gray and André Sebastian Raffalovich: A Biographical Outline," in Sewell, ed., *Two Friends*, p. 28.

36. Gray to Fanny Langdale, 7 June 1902, Langdale papers.

37. Gray to Raffalovich, 30 November 1898, Gray papers, National Library of Scotland, Edinburgh.

38. Gray to Coralie Tinklar, his sister Sarah's new stepdaughter, 13 September 1902, John Gray Collection, John Rylands University Library of Manchester, England.

39. Gray to Raffalovich, 29 September 1902, Gray papers, National Library of Scotland, Edinburgh.

40. Ibid., 7 October 1902.

41. Ibid., 13 October 1902.

42. Ibid., 15 October 1902.

43. Ibid., 1 December 1902.

44. Ibid., 18 March 1903.

45. Ibid., 6 January 1898.

46. See Edith Cooper [Michael Field], "Works and Days," [BM Add. Ms. 46798, ff. 203-204], British Library Manuscript Collections, London. The poem was originally sent to Michael Fields on 29 December 1908; cf. Gray to Michael Field [Katherine Bradley] of that date, Henry W. and Albert A. Berg Collection, New York Public Library.

47. Found among the papers of the Michael Fields, the poem was first published by John Gawsworth in "Around My Shelves," *The Poetry Review* (January–February 1950), p. 22. Reprinted in Fletcher, ed., *Poems of John Gray*, 90.

48. Edwin Essex, "The Canon in Residence," in Sewell, ed., *Two Friends*, p. 160.

49. Ibid.

50. Ibid., pp. 160-61.

51. Mary McMenemy, a parishioner of St. Patrick's for many years, reported to McCormack by Father Anthony Ross in conversation, April 1970.

52. Brocard Sewell, *Footnote to the Nineties: A Memoir of John Gray and André Raffalovich* (London: Cecil and Amelia Woolf, 1968), p. 2 and note.

53. *Man: Journal of the Royal Anthropological Institute* 3 (1903), item number 66, pp. 117-18.

54. Gray to Raffalovich, 13 November 1902, Gray papers, National Library of Scotland, Edinburgh.

55. Ibid., 10 March 1904.

56. Moray McLaren, in an article in *The Universe* (26 May 1969), as reported in Sewell, "Gray and Raffalovich," in Sewell, ed., *Two Friends*, pp. 28-29.

57. Gray to Raffalovich, 16 November 1902, Gray papers, National Library of Scotland, Edinburgh.

58. Ibid., 4 November 1902.

59. Ibid., 11 March 1903.

60. Edwin Essex, "The Canon in Residence," in Sewell, ed., *Two Friends*, p. 162.

61. Brocard Sewell, *In the Dorian Mode: A Life of John Gray, 1866–1934* (Padstow, Cornwall: Tabb House, 1983), p. 100.

62. Published initially as *Fourteen Scenes in the Life of the Blessed Virgin Mary* (privately printed, 1903); two ensuing editions were titled *Ad Matrem* (London: Sands and Co., 1904) and (London: Catholic Truth Society, 1906). Reprinted in Fletcher, ed., *Poems of John Gray*, pp. 196-205.

    Gray produced a similar set of poems the following year, to be published as *Verses for Tableaux Vivants* (London: privately printed, 1905).

63. Gray to Raffalovich, 15 October 1902, Gray papers, National Library of Scotland, Edinburgh.

64. Gray to Raffalovich, 15 April 1903, Gray papers, National Library of Scotland, Edinburgh.

65. Gray to Margaret George, 21 September 1925, upon presenting her with a copy of *Spiritual Poems*. Collection of Margaret George, Edinburgh.

66. Gray to Raffalovich, 9 December 1903, Gray papers, National Library of Scotland, Edinburgh.

67. Ibid., 22 March 1904.

68. Gray to Longmans, 21 September 1904, National Library of Scotland, Edinburgh.

69. Raffalovich to Gray, 9 October 1904, Gray papers, National Library of Scotland, Edinburgh.

70. John Gray, ed., *Last Letters of Aubrey Beardsley* (London: Longmans, Green, 1904), pp. vii, viii.

71. Gray to Longmans, 21 September 1904, National Library of Scotland, Edinburgh.

72. Gray to Raffalovich, 6 October 1904, Gray papers, National Library of Scotland, Edinburgh.
73. Ibid., 22 October 1904.
74. Ibid., 18 December 1904.
75. Henry James to André Raffalovich, 7 November 1917, in Percy Lubbock, ed., *The Letters of Henry James,* 2 vols. (London: Macmillan, 1920) 2: 355-57.
76. 13 April 1903.
77. Gray to Sarah Tinklar, 20 July 1904, papers of Brocard Sewell.
78. Gray once confided that the plan for St. Peter's came from one he admired from the window of his sickroom in Rome; information given to McCormack by one of Gray's parishioners, Kathleen O'Riordan.
79. John Gray, *Saint Peter's, Edinburgh: A Brief Description of the Church and Its Contents* (Oxford: Basil Blackwell, 1925), p. 3.
80. Raffalovich to Gray, no date, Gray papers, National Library of Scotland, Edinburgh.
81. As is customary when joining a Third or Lay Order, Raffalovich took the new name of Brother Sebastian and Gray took that of Brother Albert. Sewell, "Gray and Raffalovich," in Sewell, ed., *Two Friends,* p. 3.
82. Mrs. William O'Brien [Sophie Raffalovich], "Friends for Eternity," p. 701.
83. Sewell, *In the Dorian Mode,* p. 113.
84. Gray to Raffalovich, 2 May 1905, Gray papers, National Library of Scotland, Edinburgh.
85. Hart, "Memories," p. 4.
86. Mrs. William O'Brien [Sophie Raffalovich], "Friends for Eternity," p. 705.
87. Walter Shewring, "Two Friends," in Sewell, ed., *Two Friends,* p. 149.
88. Peter F. Anson, "Random Reminiscences of John Gray and André Raffalovich," in Sewell, ed., *Two Friends,* p.135..
89. Ibid.
90. Gray to Raffalovich, 13 June 1905, Gray papers, National Library of Scotland, Edinburgh.

CHAPTER 6

1. Notes sent to Father Delany, O. P. by Mrs. William O'Brien [Sophie Raffalovich], Gray papers [Miscellaneous correspondence, TD 921] National Library of Scotland, Edinburgh.
2. Gray to Katherine Bradley [Michael Field], no date, quoted in Brocard Sewell, *In the Dorian Mode: A Life of John Gray, 1866–1934* (Padstow, Cornwall: Tabb House, 1983), p. 103.
3. Gray to Katherine Bradley [Michael Field], 10 June 1909, Henry W. and Albert A. Berg Collection, New York Public Library.
4. Emma Donoghue, *We Are Michael Field* (Bath, England: Absolute Press, 1988), p. 85.
5. Charles Ricketts to Gordon Bottomley, 27 July 1918, quoted in J. G. Paul Delaney, *Charles Ricketts: A Biography* (Oxford: Clarendon Press, 1990), p. 96.
6. Delaney, *Charles Ricketts,* p. 143. Following quotations from this source.
7. Joseph Darracott, *The World of Charles Ricketts* (London: Eyre Methuen, 1980), p. 45.
8. Ibid., p. 48.
9. Joseph Darracott, "Collecting," in Joseph Darracott, ed., *All for Art: The Shannon and Ricketts Collection* (Cambridge: Fitzwilliam Museum, 1979), p. 18.

10. Darrracott, *World of Charles Ricketts*, p. 112. Following quotation from this source.
11. Ibid.
12. William Rothenstein, *Men and Memories: Recollections of William Rothenstein*, 2 vols. (London: Faber and Faber, 1932) 1: 202.
13. Donoghue, *We Are Michael Field*, p. 83.
14. "Works and Days," journal of Edith Cooper and Katherine Bradley [Michael Field] [BM Add. Ms. 46782], British Library Manuscript Collections, London.
15. Donoghue, *We Are Michael Field*, p. 84.
16. Cooper and Bradley, "Works and Days," [BM Add. Ms. 46782], British Library Manuscript Collections, London.
17. Donoghue, *We Are Michael Field*, p. 103.
18. Charles Ricketts, *Michael Field*, ed. Paul Delaney (The Tragara Press: Edinburgh, 1976), p. 2.
19. Cooper and Bradley, "Works and Days," [BM Add. Ms. 46795, f. 38], British Library Manuscript Collections, London.
20. Donoghue, *We Are Michael Field*, p. 97.
21. Katherine Bradley [Michael Field], to John Gray, no date, National Library of Scotland, Edinburgh.
22. John Gray, *Spiritual Poems, Chiefly Done out of Several Languages* (London: Vale Press, 1896), p. xi, reprinted in Ian Fletcher, ed. *The Poems of John Gray*, The 1880–1920 British Authors Series, no. 1 (Greensboro, N.C.: ELT Press, 1988), p. 95.
23. Donoghue, *We Are Michael Field*, p. 122.
24. The hostess was a Mrs. McDonald. Cooper and Bradley, "Works and Days" [BM Add. Ms. 46795, f. 172], British Library Manuscript Collections, London.
25. Donoghue, *We Are Michael Field*, p. 33.
26. Ibid., p. 123, to which this account of the Fields' conversion is indebted.
27. T. and D.C. Sturge Moore, eds., *Works and Days, from the Journal of Michael Field* (London: John Murray, 1933), p. 271. The book is composed of selected entries from the journal of the "Michael Fields" and from their letters (to Gray in particular), together with a commentary by Thomas Sturge Moore, their friend and executor.
28. Donoghue, *We Are Michael Field*, p. 126. Following quotations from this source.
29. After a one-day trial on August 20, 1857, six of the poems (of which this is one) were ordered to be removed from *Les Fleurs du Mal* on grounds of obscenity; a fine of 300 (later reduced to 50) francs was imposed. The six poems were first republished in Belgium in 1866 in the collection *Les Épaves* ("*Wreakage*") but the official ban remained in France until 1949.
30. Donoghue, *We Are Michael Field*, p. 127.
31. Ibid., p. 125.
32. Ibid., p. 127.
33. Ibid. I am indebted to this source for the vivid account of the Fields's reception into the Catholic Church and the reaction from Ricketts.
34. Two poems of this title were published in the 1857 edition of *Les Fleurs du Mal*; Gray translated the one that was not banned, but it is a safe presumption he knew the second, banned, poem as well.
35. Katherine Bradley [Michael Field], to John Gray, no date, National Library of Scotland, Edinburgh. All subsequent references to the Michael Fields's correspondence, most of it undated, are to this collection.
36. Cooper and Bradley, "Works and Days" [BM Add. Ms. 46799, f. 144], British Library Manuscript Collections, London.
37. Donoghue, *We Are Michael Field*, p. 125.
38. "Modernism" entry, *New Catholic Encyclopedia*. For a more detailed discussion of Gray and Raffalovich's involvement in the Modernist crisis, see Jerusha Hull

McCormack, *John Gray: Poet, Dandy and Priest* (Hanover, N.H.: University Press of New England, 1991), pp. 197-98.

39. Bradley to Gray, 5 November 1907, National Library of Scotland, Edinburgh.
40. Donoghue, *We Are Michael Field*, p. 128.
41. Gray to Katherine Bradley [Michael Field], 17 April 1907, Berg Collection, New York Public Library. All further correspondence from Gray to the Fields is from this source.
42. Gray to Katherine Bradley [Michael Field], 17 December 1907.
43. Gray to Katherine Bradley [Michael Field], 29 December 1908.
44. Gray's letters to the Michael Fields were returned to him by their executor, Thomas Sturge Moore, after their death. It seems many of them—including this one—were destroyed. Edith Cooper refers to its contents in her journal entry reviewing 1906; "Works and Days," [BM Add. Ms. 46795], British Library Manuscript Collections, London.
45. Mary Sturgeon, *Michael Field* (London: George G. Harrap and Co., 1922), pp. 38-39.
46. Gray to Katherine Bradley [Michael Field], 23 February 1910.
47. Entry of Cooper and Bradley, 6 March 1910, "Works and Days" [BM Add. Ms. 4600, f.49], British Library Manuscript Collections, London.
48. Cooper to Gray, 11 February 1911, National Library of Scotland, Edinburgh.
49. Donoghue, *We Are Michael Field*, p. 134. This passage, including the wonderful image of the lightning rod, is indebted to this source.
50. Ibid., p. 137.
51. Ibid., p. 133.
52. Ibid.
53. Gray to Katherine Bradley [Michael Field], 13 May 1911.
54. Entry of Cooper and Bradley, 27 October 1911, "Works and Days" [BM Add. Ms. 46803, f. 150], British Library Manuscript Collections, London.
55. Edith Cooper to Gray, 12 June 1913, National Library of Scotland, Edinburgh.
56. Donoghue, *We Are Michael Field*, p. 138.
57. Ibid., p. 139.
58. Entry of Cooper and Bradley, December 1913, "Works and Days" [BM Add. Ms. 46803, f. 104], British Library Manuscript Collections, London. Gray's letters to the Michael Fields after February 1911 were not kept.
59. Donoghue, *We Are Michael Field*, p. 141, to which this paragraph is indebted.
60. Charles Ricketts to Gray, no date, Beinecke Rare Book Room and Manuscript Library, Yale University, New Haven, Conn.
61. Entry of Cooper and Bradley, 27 October 1908, "Works and Days" [BM Mss. Add. 46798, f. 182], British Library Manuscript Collections, London.
62. Gray to Katherine Bradley [Michael Field], 24 October 1908.
63. Gray to Katherine Bradley [Michael Field], 11 November 1908.
64. Gray to Katherine Bradley [Michael Field], 1 July 1908.
65. Mrs. William O'Brien [Sophie O'Brien], "Friends for Eternity," p. 703 and André Raffalovich [Alexander Michaelson], "Aubrey Beardsley's Sister," *Blackfriars* 9 (November 1928): 675.
66. R. F. Foster, *W. B. Yeats: A Life. Vol. I: The Apprentice Mage* (Oxford: Oxford University Press, 1997).
67. W. B. Yeats, "Upon a Dying Lady," *Collected Poems*, ed. Augustine Martin (London: Vintage, 1992), p. 120.
68. Information from taped conversation with Father John-Baptist Reeves, who knew both Gray and Raffalovich, McCormack papers.
69. Charles Ballantyne in conversation with McCormack, April 1970.
70. See the correspondences between Raffalovich and Francis Wright (1912–18) and Eric Gill to Raffalovich (1914–20) in the National Library of Scotland, Edinburgh. For a discussion of Raffalovich's relationship with Gill, see Fiona

MacCarthy, *Eric Gill* (London: Faber and Faber, 1989), pp. 132-34 and Robert Speaight, *The Life of Eric Gill* (London: Methuen, 1966), pp. 72-73.

71. Raffalovich to Melville Wright, 9 April 1916, National Library of Scotland, Edinburgh.

72. Raffalovich to Charles Ballantyne, 7 June 1931, National Library of Scotland, Edinburgh.

73. Firbank's biographers supplied the phrase, which mirrors Firbank's own view of Wilde. Brigid Brophy, *Prancing Novelist: A Defence of Fiction in the Form of a Critical Biography in Praise of Ronald Firbank* (London: Macmillan, 1973), pp. 274-75.

74. Father Edwin Essex, "The Canon in Residence," in *Two Friends: John Gray and André Raffalovich*, ed. Brocard Sewell (Aylesford, Kent: St. Albert's Press, 1963), pp. 153-55. It was Fr. Essex who reports Gray's attempts "to withdraw [*Silverpoints*] from circulation" by "destroying any old copies he was able to buy up."

75. Alan Neame to Brocard Sewell, 27 October 1964, Sewell papers.

76. MacCarthy, *Eric Gill*, p. 162.

77. Information from Father Anthony Ross, keeper of the Gray papers at the Dominican Chaplaincy, Edinburgh, in conversation with McCormack, April 1970.

78. Father Dominic Hart, "Memories of John Gray," Trudgian papers, p. 6. Reprinted, in a somewhat altered form, in Brocard Sewell, ed., "Some Memories of John Gray by the Reverend Dominic Hart," *The Innes Review* 2 (1975): 80-88.

79. Father Bernard Delany, "Sermon: Preached at the Mass of Requiem for Canon John Gray," in Sewell, ed., *Two Friends*, p. 175.

80. Margaret Sackville, "At Whitehouse Terrace," in Sewell, ed., *Two Friends*, p. 142.

81. Ibid., p. 144.

82. Ibid., pp. 145, 146.

83. Essex, "The Canon in Residence," in Sewell, ed., *Two Friends*, p. 165.

84. Taped conversation with Father John-Baptist Reeves, McCormack papers.

85. Sackville, "At Whitehouse Terrace," in Sewell, ed., *Two Friends*, p. 146.

86. Peter F. Anson, "Random Reminiscences of John Gray and André Raffalovich," in Sewell, ed., *Two Friends*, p. 137.

87. Leon Edel, *Henry James, The Master: 1901–1916* (Philadelphia: J.B. Lippincott, 1972), pp. 407-408.

88. Essex, "The Canon in Residence," in Sewell, ed., *Two Friends*, p. 156.

89. Anson, "Random Reminiscences," in Sewell, ed., *Two Friends*, pp. 139-40.

90. Essex, "The Canon in Residence," in Sewell, ed., *Two Friends*, pp. 155-56.

91. Anson, "Random Reminiscences," in Sewell, ed., *Two Friends*, pp. 135-36.

CHAPTER 7

1. T. S. Eliot, "Ezra Pound," in *Ezra Pound: A Collection of Critical Essays,* ed. Walter E. Sutton (Eaglewood Cliffs, N.J.: Prentice-Hall, 1963), p. 17.

2. Gray to Raffalovich, 22 March 1904, National Library of Scotland, Edinburgh.

3. T. Sturge Moore to "John Gawsworth" [Terence Ian Fytton], 21 March 1940, Reading University Library, England.

4. Fr. Bernard Delany, "A Sermon Preached at the Mass of Requiem for Canon John Gray," in *Two Friends: John Gray and André Raffalovich: Essays Biographical and Critical,* ed. Brocard Sewell (Aylesford, Kent: St. Albert's Press, 1963), p. 175.

5. A. J. A. Symons, ed., *An Anthology of Nineties Verse* (London: Elkin Mathews and Marrot, 1928), p. xx. For specific information on poems reprinted, see the bibliography of writings by John Gray at the end of this book. A typical story of

an attempt to collect Gray's nineties poetry by a young poet of the 1930s, John Gawsworth, can be found in "Two Poets 'J. G.,'" in Sewell, ed., *Two Friends*, pp. 167-72.

6. Ricketts to Gray, no date, Beinecke Rare Book and Manuscript Library, Yale University, New Haven, Conn.

7. Miscellaneous correspondence to Gray, National Library of Scotland, Edinburgh.

8. Graham Greene to McCormack, 13 October 1971.

9. Greene to his mother, 22 August 1932, quoted in Norman Sherry, *The Life of Graham Greene* vol. 1: 1904–1939 (New York: Viking, 1989), p. 426.

10. Gray to Raffalovich, 17 March 1904, Gray papers, National Library of Scotland, Edinburgh.

11. Gray's letters to Bottomley, property of Richard Lancelyn Green. Blunden to Gray, 1930–33, Special Collection, The University of Iowa, Iowa City. The libraries of Raffalovich and Gray are described in Anthony D'Offay, *Books and Autograph Letters, Mainly of the Eighteen-Nineties* I: Catalogue 1 (July 1961). Those listed here are from the inventory of McCormack from the repository in the Dominican Chaplaincy, Edinburgh.

12. For a frank account of these, see Fiona MacCarthy, *Eric Gill* (London: Faber and Faber, 1989).

13. MacCarthy, *Eric Gill*, p. 132.

14. Ibid., p. 134.

15. The above two paragraphs are indebted to MacCarthy, *Eric Gill*, pp. 141-42.

16. Ibid., p. 132.

17. Ibid., p. 129.

18. Gray to A. J. A. Symons, 6 May 1925 [Misc. GOR-GRA], Princeton University Library, Princeton, N.J.

19. *Vivis* (Ditchling, Sussex: St. Dominic's Press, 1922). Reprinted in Ian Fletcher, ed., *The Poems of John Gray*, The 1880–1920 British Author Series 1 (Greensboro, N.C.: ELT Press, 1988), p. 261.

20. Fletcher, ed., p. 262.

21. Walter Shewing, "Two Friends," in Sewell, ed., *Two Friends*, p. 150; Father Edwin Essex, "The Canon in Residence," in Sewell, ed., *Two Friends*, p. 163.

22. Peter F. Anson, "Random Reminiscences of Gray and Raffalovich," in Sewell, ed., *Two Friends*, p. 140.

23. Taped conversation with Father John Baptist-Reeves, McCormack papers.

24. Hart recounts a 200-mile trek, "Memories of John Gray," Trudgian papers, pp. 7-8. Reprinted, in an altered form, in Brocard Sewell, ed., "Some Memories of John Gray," *The Innes Review* 2 (1975): 80-88. It was by no means Gray's only walking tour of Europe.

25. Brocard Sewell, *In the Dorian Mode: A Life of John Gray, 1866–1934* (Padstow, Cornwall: Tabb House, 1983), pp. 178-88.

26. John Gray, "Winter Walking," *Blackfriars* 6 (March 1925): 148-53.

27. From the papers of Helen Trudgian.

28. John Gray, *The Long Road* (Oxford: Basil Blackwell, 1926), reprinted in Fletcher, ed., *Poems of John Gray*, p. 255.

29. Quoted in Sewell, *In the Dorian Mode*, p. 147.

30. Father Reginald Ginns to Brocard Sewell, 24 January 1968, Sewell papers.

31. Speaight, *The Life of Eric Gill* (London: Methuen, 1966), pp. 72-73, 154; and MacCarthy, *Eric Gill* (London: Faber and Faber, 1989), pp. 132-33.

32. John Gray, *Poems (1931)* (London: Sheed and Ward, 1931), reprinted in Fletcher, ed., *Poems of John Gray*, pp. 282-83.

33. "Evening," Ibid., pp. 281-82.

34. *Park: A Fantastic Story.* First published in four installments of *Blackfriars* (see bibliography), its first appearance in book form was in a limited edition of 250 copies printed by Rene Hague and Eric Gill at Pigotts, Buckinghamshire and

published in London by Sheed and Ward in April, 1932. Reprinted in Jerusha Hull McCormack, ed., *The Selected Prose of John Gray*, no. 7, The 1880–1920 British Author Series (Greensboro, N.C.: ELT Press, 1992), p. 179.

35. Ibid., p. 180.
36. Ibid., p. 291.
37. Gray to Raffalovich, 1 June 1005, Gray papers, National Library of Scotland, Edinburgh.
38. John Gray, "Winter Walking," *Blackfriars* 6 (March 1925): 151.
39. Gray, "Dods," *Blackfriars* 7 (October 1926): 640.
40. Gray, *Park*, p.217.
41. Ibid., p. 192.
42. Ibid., p. 194.
43. Ibid., p. 196.
44. Ibid., p. 197.
45. Philip Healy, "Text and Context in John Gray's *Park*: Prester John's 'Black Mischief,'" *English Language in Transition* 36, no. 4 (1993): 421. Observations on the African context of *Park* are greatly indebted to this article.
46. Gray, *Park*, p. 191.
47. Ibid., p. 192.
48. Ibid., p. 210.
49. Ibid., p. 211.
50. Ibid., p. 218.
51. Quoted in Alexandra Zaina, "The Prose Writings of John Gray," in Sewell, ed., *Two Friends*, p. 95.
52. Ibid.
53. André Raffalovich [Alexander Michaelson], "Parallels," *Blackfriars* 10 (Jan. 1929): 785.
54. McCormack, ed., *The Selected Prose of John Gray*, p. 61.
55. Healy, "Text and Context," *English Language in Transition*, 417.
56. Ibid.
57. Ibid., p. 422.
58. Gray, *Park*, p. 233.
59. Fletcher, ed., *Poems of John Gray*, p. 262.
60. Gray to Katherine Bradley [Michael Field], 7 November 1910, Henry W. and Albert A. Berg Collection, New York Public Library.
61. MacCarthy, *Eric Gill*, pp. 237-41.
62. Gray, *Park*, p. 185.
63. Ibid., p. 204.
64. Raymond Roseliep, "Some Letters of Lionel Johnson" (Ph.D. dissertation, University of Notre Dame, 1954), p. 109.
65. Gray, *Park*, p. 211.
66. Ibid., p. 223.
67. Ibid., p. 227.
68. Ibid., pp. 276-77.
69. Ibid., pp. 278-79.
70. Alan Neame to Brocard Sewell, 27 October 1964, Sewell papers.
71. Quoted in "Afterword," in Healy, ed., *Park*, p. 118.
72. Gray to Blunden, 20 February 1933, Harry Ransom Humanities Research Center, University of Texas, Austin.
73. Sewell, *In the Dorian Mode*, p. 166.
74. A suggestion articulated by Zaina, "The Prose Writings of John Gray," in Sewell, ed., *Two Friends*, p. 97.
75. "The anagram is read from the sentence Ave Maria gatia plena Dominus tecum. It is made, as you see, to tease the mind of a man like Drak." Gray to Blunden, 20 February 1933, University of Texas, Austin.

76. 24 November 1892, Peter J. Vernon, "John Gray's Letters to Pierre Louÿs," *Revue de Littérature Comparée* 53 (Janvier–Mars 1979): 96-97.
77. Ibid.
78. Anson, "Random Reminiscences of Gray and Raffalovich," in Sewell, ed., *Two Friends*, pp. 135-36. Anson slightly misquotes this famous passage from the "Conclusion" to Pater's *The Renaissance*.

EPILOGUE

1. Brocard Sewell, *In the Dorian Mode: A Life of John Gray, 1866–1934* (Padstow, Cornwall: Tabb House, 1983), pp. 136, 162.
2. Gray to Bottomley, 9 October 1929, papers of Roger Lancelyn Green.
3. Raffalovich to Norman Wright, 8 April 1930, National Library of Scotland, Edinburgh.
4. Beerbohm to Raffalovich, 17 June 1930, National Library of Scotland, Edinburgh.
5. Father Edwin Essex, "The Canon in Residence," in *Two Friends: John Gray and André Raffalovich: Essays Biographical and Critical,* ed. Brocard Sewell (Aylesford, Kent: Saint Albert's Press, 1963), p. 163.
6. Sewell, "In the Dorian Mode," p. 182.
7. Gray to Bottomley, 1 December 1933, papers of Roger Lancelyn Green.
8. Gray to Fanny Langdale, 23 December 1933, Langdale papers.
9. Brocard Sewell, "John Gray and André Raffalovich: A Biographical Outline," in Sewell, ed., *Two Friends,* pp. 45-46, to which the following passage is also indebted.
10. Reverend Dominic Hart, "Some Memories of John Gray," ed. Brocard Sewell, *The Innes Review* 2 (1975): 9.
11. John Gray, "André Raffalovich," *Blackfriars* 15 (June 1943): 406.
12. Margaret George, holograph of her memories of John Gray, National Library of Edinburgh, Scotland, and in conversation with McCormack, April 1970. Following quotation from this source.
13. Sarah Gray Tinklar to Fanny Langdale, 20 July 1934, Langdale papers. Following quotations from this source.
14. Father Bernard Delany, "Sermon: Preached at the Mass of Requiem for Canon John Gray," in Sewell, ed., *Two Friends,* pp. 175-76.
15. Essex, "The Canon in Residence," in Sewell, ed., *Two Friends,* p. 154.
16. "Works and Days," Journal of Katherine Bradley and Edith Cooper [Michael Field], 10 September 1909 [BM Add. Ms. 46799 f. 138], British Library Manuscript Collections; and Essex, "The Canon in Residence," in Sewell, ed., *Two Friends,* p. 155, to which the following quotation is indebted.
17. "Introduction," in *The Oxford Book of Modern Verse, 1892–1935,* ed. W. B. Yeats (Oxford: Oxford University Press, 1936), p. xlii.
18. Peter Anson to Norman Wright, 28 January 1935, National Library of Scotland, Edinburgh.
19. "Did we not, Darling, you and I," *Silverpoints* (London: Elkin Mathews and John Lane, 1893), p. 17, reprinted in Ian Fletcher, ed., *The Poems of John Gray,* The 1880–1920 British Author Series I (Greensboro, N.C.: ELT Press, 1988), p. 28.
20. Reported on different occasions, many years apart. To Sewell by Sister Mary Barbara, 18 March 1969; to McCormack by Father Anthony Ross, O. P., then director of the Dominican Chaplaincy, Edinburgh in April 1970. More recently by Sewell, who had it from a "hard-headed elderly friend in Edinburgh," who reported several appearances of the ghost (Sewell to McCormack, 4 November 1980).

This year, in an unsolicited email from the Rector of Scots Pontifical College in Rome, the Right Reverend Christopher McElroy, writes that a priest "tells me that John Gray is still sometimes spotted by parishioners in St. Peter's, and that he had a spooky encounter himself during a visit to the presbytery. He was standing in the bathroom when he felt as if someone was grabbing him tight from behind—but there was no one there. When he told his bishop, the late Cardinal Gray, he was told, kind of reassuringly, 'Oh yes, that would have been Canon Gray'" (4 March 2000).

BIBLIOGRAPHY

PRIMARY SOURCES

Manuscript Collections

Archives Félix Fénéon, Fonds Jean Paulhan, Institut Mémoires de L'Édition Contemporaine, Paris, France.

Archives of the Pontifical Scots College, Rome, Italy.

The British Library Manuscript Collections, London.

The Dominican Chaplaincy, George Square, Edinburgh.

Foreign Office Library (Archives), London.

General Register Office, London.

Houghton Library, Cambridge, Mass.

The John Rylands University Library of Manchester, Manchester, England.

London University Records, London.

The National Library of Scotland, Edinburgh.

New York Public Library, Henry W. and Albert A. Berg Collection, New York.

Princeton University Library, Princeton, N.J.

University of Texas, Harry Ransom Humanities Research Center, Austin, Tex.

Yale University Library, Beinecke Rare Book Room, New Haven, Conn.

Private Collections

Papers of: Jad Adams; Roger Lancelyn Green; James Langdale; Jerusha McCormack; Father Brocard Sewell; Dr Helen Trudgian.

Works by John Gray

Gray's works are arranged chronologically by year, but within the year they are listed alphabetically, as it is not always possible to establish the month in which they appeared.

1889

"Les Goncourt." *The Dial* 1 (1889): 9-13.

"The Great Worm." *The Dial* 1 (1889): 14-18.

1890

"Obituary: Dubois Pillet." *Academy* 957 (September 1890): 205.

"Sonnet: Translated from Paul Verlaine." *The Artist and Journal of Home Culture* 11 (1 August 1890): 241.

1892

de Banville, Théodore. *The Kiss*. Translated by John Gray. Performed by the Independent Theatre, 4 March 1892. Edinburgh: Tragara Press, 1983.

Bourget, Paul. *A Saint and Others: From the French of Paul Bourget*. Translated by John Gray. London: Osgood, McIlvaine & Co., 1892.

Couperus, Louis. *Ecstasy: A Study of Happiness*. Translated by A. Teixeira de Mattos and John Gray with a Translator's Note by John Gray. London: Henry & Co., 1892.

"Les Demoiselles de Sauvre." *The Dial* 2 (1892): 24.

"Dix Portraits d'Hommes par Paul Bourget." *Academy* 1061 (3 September 1892): 188.

"Heart's Demesne." *The Dial* 2 (1892): 23.

"The Modern Actor." *Albemarle* 2 (July 1892): 20-24. Reprinted as "Appendix II: The Modern Actor." In Brocard Sewell, *Footnote to the Nineties: A Memoir of John Gray and André Raffalovich*. London: Cecil and Amelia Woolf, 1968, pp. 102-107.

"Parsifal: Imitated from the French of Paul Verlaine." *The Dial* 2 (1892): 8.

"Prefatory Note." In *In the Garden of Citrons: Idyll in One Act* by J. T. Grein [Emilio Montanaro]. London: Henry & Co., 1892.

1893

"The Advantages of Civilization." *The Butterfly* 2 (November 1893): 51-56.

"Fioranzo of Maggiolo." *The Butterfly* 1 (June 1893): 69-78.

"Garth Wilkinson." *The Dial* 3 (1893): 21-24.

"A Hymn Translated from the Italian of St. Francis of Assisi." *The Dial* 3 (1893): 31-32.

"The Loves of the Age of Stone." *The Butterfly* 1 (July 1893): 142-151.

"Old Gouth." *The Butterfly* 1 (October 1893): 335-44.

"Pacidejanus Victor." *The Butterfly* 1 (September 1893): 261-75.

Silverpoints. London: Elkin Mathews & John Lane, 1893. Reprint, London: The Minerva Press, 1973.

1894

The Blackmailers. Produced at the Prince of Wales Theatre, 17 June 1894. (Never published.)

The Blue Calendar 1895. A Book of Carols. London: privately printed, 24 December 1894.

Sour Grapes. Produced at the West Theatre, Albert Hall, 17 April 1894. (Never published.)

1895

The Blue Calendar 1896. Twelve Sundry Carols. London: privately printed, 14 December 1895.

Extract from an article on Albert Chevalier. Quoted in *Albert Chevalier: A Record by Himself.* London: John Macqueen, 1895, p. 123.

Gray, John and André Raffalovich. *A Northern Aspect. The Ambush of Young Days. Two Duologues.* London: privately printed, 12 May 1895.

"A Sonnet for March." *Month* (March 1895): 428.

1896

"Battledore." *The Dial* 4 (1896): 34-36.

"The Beauties of Nature." *The Dial* 4 (1896): 15-17.

The Blue Calendar 1897. London: privately printed, 24 December 1896.

Campion, Thomas. *Fifty Songs.* Edited by John Gray. London: Hacon & Ricketts, 1896.

Drayton, Michael. *Nymphidia and The Muses Elizium.* Edited by John Gray. London: Hacon & Ricketts, 1896.

"The Flying Fish." *The Dial* 4 (1896): 1-6.Reprinted, with some changes, in *A Sailor's Garland.* Edited by John Masefield. London: Metheun, 1906.

"The Forge." *The Savoy* 2 (April 1896): 85-86.

"Niggard Truth." *Pageant* 1 (1896): 20-36.

"The Ox." *Pageant* 1 (1896): 184.

"The Redemption of Durtal." *The Dial* 4 (1896): 7-11.

Spiritual Poems: Chiefly Done out of Several Languages. London: Hacon & Ricketts, 1896.

Suckling, Sir John. *Poems and Songs.* Edited by John Gray. London: Hacon & Ricketts, 1896.

1897

Constable, Henry. *Poems and Sonnets.* Edited by John Gray. London: Hacon & Ricketts, 1897.

"Daphné." *La Revue Blanche* 12 (1897): 758-62.

"Leda." "The Swan." *The Dial* 5 (1897): 13-15.

"Light." *Pageant* 2 (1897): 113-34.

Nietzsche, Friedrich. *Collected Works.* Edited by Alexander Tille. Volume 10, *A Genealogy of Morals.* Translated by William A. Haussmann.

————. *Poems.* Translated by John Gray. New York: Macmillan Co., 1897, pp. 233-289. Reprinted: Ibid. Volume 1. London: T. Fisher Unwin, 1899.

"Nietzsche as Poet." In *Nietzsche as Critic, Philosopher, Poet and Prophet.* Edited by Thomas Common. Translated by John Gray. Part 3. "Nietzsche as Poet," London: Grant Richards, 1901, pp. 169-188.

"On the South Coast of Cornwall." *Pageant* 2 (1897): 82.

"Saint Ives, Cornwall." *The Dial* 5 (1897): 12.

1898

"Aubrey Beardsley." *La Revue Blanche* 16 (1898): 68-70.Reprint, *Aylesford Review* 8 (Autumn 1966): 95-96.

"Aubrey Beardsely: An Obituary Memoir." Edinburgh: privately printed, 1980.

"Clair de lune," *Bibelot* 5 (February 1898): 74.

The Fourth and Last Blue Almanack 1898. London, privately printed, 1898.

Goethe, J. W. von. *Satyros and Prometheus.* Translated by John Gray. Edited by Alexander Tille. Glasgow: Glasgow Goethe Society, 1898.

"Green," *Bibelot* 5 (February 1898): 78.

"A History of Universal Literature." *Month* 407 (May 1898): 512-24. (Includes two untitled translations in verse by Gray.)

"Mon Dieu m'a dit." *Bibelot* 5 (February 1898): 80-82.

"Parsifal." *Bibelot* 5 (February 1898): 80-82.

Sidney, Sir Philip. *Sonnets.* Edited by John Gray. London: Hacon & Ricketts, 1898.

1903

Fourteen Scenes in the Life of the Blessed Virgin Mary. London: privately printed, 1903. Other editions: *Ad Matrem: Poems by John Gray.* London & Edinburgh: Sands & Co., 1904; *Ad Matrem.* London: Catholic Truth Society, 1906.

"A Phial." *Venture* 1 (1903): 233-34. Reprint, *A Phial.* Edinburgh: Tragara Press, 1954.

"Some Scottish String Figures." *Man: Journal of the Royal Anthropological Institute* 3 (1903), item number 66, pp. 117-18.

1904

Beardsley, Aubrey. *Last Letters of Aubrey Beardsley.* Edited with an Introduction by the Reverend John Gray. London: Longmans, Green & Co., 1904.

"Saint Gregory the Great." *Downside Review* 23 (1904): 1.

1905

"A Pastor and Master: In Memoriam." *Month* 106 (1905): 514-16.

Verses for Tableaux Vivants. London: privately printed, 1905.

"Via Vita Veritas." *Venture* 2 (1905): 62.

1906

"The Flying Fish." Reprinted in *A Sailor's Garland*. Selected and edited by John Masefield. London: Methuen: 1906, p. 18.

"Wings in the Dark." Reprinted in *A Sailor's Garland*. Selected and edited by John Masefield. London: Methuen, 1906, p. 5.

1907

"Introduction." Catalogue of an Exhibition of Children's Toys (held at The Outlook Tower, Castlehill, Edinburgh.) Edinburgh: privately printed, 1907

1908

"The Emperor and the Bird." Published by John Gawsworth in an unsigned article, "Around My Shelves," *Poetry Review* (January–February 1950): 22. (Originally sent to the "Michael Fields" for Christmas, 1908.)

1912

"Children in they presence met." *The Westminster Hymnal*. London: Burns Oates, 1912, Hymn no. 175.

"When in the crib so weak and small." *The Westminster Hymnal*. London: Burns Oates, 1912, Hymn no. 28.

1917

"On the Holy Trinity." *The Oxford Book of English Mystical Verse*. Edited by D. H. S. Nicholson and A. H. E. Lee. Oxford: Clarendon Press, 1917, pp. 574-577. Reprinted, 1918, 1920,

"The Tree of Knowledge." *The Oxford Book of English Mystical Verse*. Edited by D. H .S. Nicholson and A. H. E. Lee. Oxford: Clarendon Press, 1917, pp. 571-74. Reprinted, 1918, 1920, 1923, 1927, 1932.

1921

"Death." *Blackfriars* 2 (May 1921): 120.

1922

Vivis. Ditchling, Sussex: St. Dominic's Press, 1922.

1924

"God-made and Machine-made." *Blackfriars* 5 (1924): 451-57.

1925

"Hymns: A Suppressed Preface." *Blackfriars* 6 (1925): 578-81.
"Man's Visible Works." *Blackfriars* 6 (1925): 450-55.
On Hymn Writing. Kensington: Cayme Press, 1925.
Saint Peter's, Edinburgh: A Brief Description of the Church and Its Contents.
    Oxford: Basil Blackwell, 1925.
Saint Peter's Hymns. Kensington: Cayme Press, 1925.
"Speciosae et Delicatae Assimilari Filiam Sion: A Poem." *Blackfriars* 6
    (January 1925): 41.
"Winter Walking." *Blackfriars* 6 (March 1925): 148-53.

1926

"Broken-borough." *Blackfriars* 7 (June 1926): 693-99.
"Charleville." *Poetry of the Nineties.* Edited by C. E. Andrews and M. O.
    Percival. New York: Harcourt, Brace and Co., 1926.
"Dods." *Blackfriars* 7 (October 1926): 637-42.
"Excursion." *Blackfriars* 7 (February 1926): 80-85.
"Hymn to the Child Jesus." *Annals of the Holy Childhood* (February 1926):
    5.
"A Hymn: Translated from the Italian of St. Francis of Assisi" ("Love Setteth
    Me A-Burning"). *Blackfriars* 7 (December 1926): 781-83.
"An Island Cloud-Factory." *Blackfriars* 7 (June 1926): 370-75.
The Long Road. Oxford: Basil Blackwell, 1926.
"The Night-Nurse Goes Her Round." *Blackfriars* 7 (March 1926):134.
Sound: A Poem. London: Curwen Press, 1926.
"Wings in the Dark." *Poetry of the Nineties.* Edited by C. E. Andrews and
    M. O. Percival. New York: Harcourt, Brace and Co., 1926.

1927

"Allanwater." *Blackfriars* 8 (May 1927): 298-303.
"Baby-Clothes." *Annals of the Holy Childhood* (November 1927): 7.
"Cyder." *Blackfriars* 8 (August 1927): 499-504.
"Helichrysum." *Blackfriars* 8 (December 1927): 725.
"The Lord Looks at Peter." *Blackfriars* 8 (April 1927): 238.
"Mane Nobiscum Domine." *Blackfriars* 8 (May 1927): 280.

"Nature-Morte." *Blackfriars* 8 (September 1927): 544.

O Beata Trinitas: The Prayers of St. Gertrude and St. Mechtilde. Translated by the Rev. John Gray. London: Sheed & Ward, 1927. Reprinted as *The True Prayers of St. Gertrude and St. Mechtilde,* 1928 and 1936.

"October." *Blackfriars* 8 (November 1927): 688-93.

"Roxburgh." *Blackfriars* 8 (1927): 104.

1928

"Charter Alley." *Blackfriars* 9 (January 1928): 30-34.

"Complaint." *Anthology of 'Nineties Verse.* Selected and edited by A .J. A. Symons. London: Elkin Mathews & Marrot, 1928, pp. 71-78.

"Crocuses in Grass." *Anthology of 'Nineties Verse.* Selected and edited by A .J. A. Symons. London: Elkin Mathews & Marrot, 1928, pp. 71-78.

Les Demoiselles de Sauve." *Anthology of 'Nineties Verse.* Selected and edited by A .J. A. Symons. London: Elkin Mathews & Marrot, 1928, pp. 71-78.

"Dialogue." *Blackfriars* 9 (May 1928): 304-308.

"Ils ont Heurté Les Portes d'Or of Henri de Régnier." *Blackfriars* 9 (September 1928): 555.

"Lean Back and Press the Pillow Deep." *Anthology of 'Nineties Verse.* Selected and edited by A .J. A. Symons. London: Elkin Mathews & Marrot, 1928, pp. 71-78.

"Mishka." *Anthology of 'Nineties Verse.* Selected and edited by A .J. A. Symons. London: Elkin Mathews & Marrot, 1928, pp. 71-78.

"On a Picture." *Anthology of 'Nineties Verse.* Selected and edited by A .J. A. Symons. London: Elkin Mathews & Marrot, 1928, pp. 71-78.

"Sound." *Anthology of 'Nineties Verse.* Selected and edited by A .J. A. Symons. London: Elkin Mathews & Marrot, 1928, pp. 71-78.

"Trespassers Will Be Prosecuted." *Blackfriars* 9 (March 1928): 164-69.

1929

"Birthday Wishes." *Blackfriars* 10 (February 1929): 847.

"Ettrickdale." *Blackfriars* 10 (April 1929): 1016.

"The Parting Guest." *Blackfriars* 10 (January 1929): 786-90. Reprinted as "Appendix II." In *In the Dorian Mode.* Edited by Sewell, pp. 222-26.

1930

"Audi Alternam Partem." *Blackfriars* 11 (May 1930): 310-11.

The Child's Daily Missal. Compiled by Dom Gaspar Lefebure, O .S. B., and Mlle Elisabeth van Elewyck. Translated by the Rev. John Gray. Lophem near Bruges, Belgium: Liturgical Apostolate, 1930.

"Evening." *Blackfriars* 11 (February 1930): 106-107.

"In North Iceland, 1914." *Blackfriars* 11 (September 1930): 558-59.
"On Aqueducts." *Blackfriars* 11 (January 1930): 22-24.

1931

"Andante." *Blackfriars* 12 (January 1931): 33-34.
"Compunction." In *An Anthology of Contemporary Catholic Poetry*. Edited by Maurice Leahy with a preface by D. B. Wyndham-Lewis. London: Cecil Palmer, 1931, pp. 61-65.
"Enough of the World is Mine." In *An Anthology of Contemporary Catholic Poetry*. Edited by Maurice Leahy with a preface by D. B. Wyndham-Lewis. London: Cecil Palmer, 1931, pp. 61-65.
"The Flying Fish (II)." In *An Anthology of Contemporary Catholic Poetry*. Edited by Maurice Leahy with a preface by D. B. Wyndham-Lewis. London: Cecil Palmer, 1931, pp. 61-65.
"Holy Communion." *Annals of the Holy Childhood* (February 1931): 1.
"The Kennet." In *An Anthology of Contemporary Catholic Poetry*. Edited by Maurice Leahy with a Preface by D. B. Wyndham-Lewis. London: Cecil Palmer, 1931, pp. 61-65.
"The Night Nurse Goes Her Round." In *An Anthology of Contemporary Catholic Poetry*. Edited by Maurice Leahy with a Preface by D. B. Wyndham-Lewis. London: Cecil Palmer, 1931, pp. 61-65.
"Ode." *Blackfriars* 12 (April 1931): 237-43.
Ode. Reprinted from *Blackfriars* 12 (April 1931): 237-43.
"Odiham." *Blackfriars* 12 (May 1931): 312-13.
Poems (1931). London: Sheed and Ward, 1931.

1932

Park: A Fantastic Story. London: Sheed & Ward, 1932. Previously published in installments in Blackfriars 12 (November1931): 682-95; 13 (January 1932): 45-51; 13 (March 1932): 158-63; 13 (April 1932): 231-42. Reprint, *Park: A Fantastic Story*. Edited with an Introduction by Bernard Bergonzi. Aylesford, Kent: St. Albert's Press, 1966.
Park: A Fantastic Story. Edited with Afterword by Philip Healy. Manchester: Carcanet Press, 1984.
"Song of the Stars." *Known Signatures*. Selected and edited by John Gawsworth. London: Rich & Cowan, 1932, pp. 54-56.
"Sound." *Known Signatures*. Selected and edited by John Gawswort. London: Rich & Cowan, 1932, pp. 54-56.

1934

"André Raffalovich." *Blackfriars* 15 (June 1934): 405-407.

SECONDARY SOURCES (SELECTED)

I. Bibliographies

Anderson, Alan. "Bibliography of John Gray." In *Two Friends: John Gray and André Raffalovich*. Edited by Father Brocard Sewell. Aylesford, Kent: St. Albert's Press, 1963, pp. 178-87.

Cevasco, G. A. "John Gray (1866–1934): A Primary Bibliography and an Annotated Bibliography of Writings about Him." *English Literature in Transition* 19 (1976): 49-63.

Fletcher, Ian. "Amendments and Additions to a Bibliography of John Gray." *English Literature in Transition* 22 (1979): 62-67.

McCormack, Jerusha Hull. "Bibliography: Works by John Gray." Ph.D. dissertation., Brandeis University, 1973, pp. 262-268.

II. Books, Parts of Books, Articles, and Studies:

Adams, Jad. *Madder Music, Stronger Wine: The Life of Ernest Dowson, Poet and Decadent*. London: I. B. Taurus, 2000.

Anson, Peter F. "Random Reminiscences of Gray and Raffalovich." In *In Two Friends: John Gray and André Raffalovich*. Edited by Father Brocard Sewell. Aylesford, Kent: St. Albert's Press, 1963, pp. 134-41.

Beardsley, Aubrey. *The Letters of Aubrey Beardsley*. Edited by Henry Maas, J. L. Duncan and W. G. Good. Rutherford, N.J.: Fairleigh Dickinson University Press, 1970.

Beckson, Karl, ed. *Aesthetes and Decadents of the 1890s: An Anthology of British Poetry and Prose*. Chicago: Academcy Chicago, 1981.

Beerbohm, Max. "Appendix A: Oscar Wilde by an American." In *Max Beerbohm's Letters to Reggie Turner*. Edited by Rupert Hart-Davis. New York: J. B. Lippincott Co.,1965.

Benkovitz, Miriam J. *Aubrey Beardsley: An Account of His Life*. London: Hamish Hamilton, 1981.

Bergonzi, Bernard. "John Gray's Park." *Aylesford Review* 7 (Winter 1965/ Spring 1966): 206-15.

———. Reprinted as "Introduction."In *Park*. Aylesford, Kent: St. Albert's Press, 1966, pp. i-xiii.

———. "John Gray." In *The Turn of the Century: Essays on Victorian and Modern English Literature*. New York: Barnes & Noble, 1973.

Bradley, Katherine and Edith Cooper [Michael Field]. *Works and Days: From the Journal of Michael Field*. Edited by T. and D. C. Sturge Moore. London: John Murray, 1933.

Cammell, Charles Richard. *Heart of Scotland*. London: Robert Hale, 1956.

Cevasco, G. A. *John Gray*. Boston: Twayne Publishers, 1982.

Croft-Cooke, Rupert. "Wilde, Gray and Raffalovich." In *Feasting with Panthers: A New Consideration of Some Late Victorian Writers*. New York: Holt, Rinehart and Winston,1967.

Darracott, Joseph, ed. *All for Art: The Ricketts and Shannon Collection*. Catalogue for an Exhibition at the Fitzwilliam Museum, Cambridge. Cambridge: Cambridge University Press, 1979.

———. *The World of Charles Ricketts*. London: Eyre Methuen, 1980.

Davray, Henry D. "Mallarmé as I Knew Him." *Horizen* 7 (May 1943): 342-353.

Delaney, J. G. Paul. *Charles Ricketts: A Biography*. Oxford: Clarendon Press, 1990.

Delany, Father Bernard. "A Sermon Preached at the Requiem of John Gray." In *Two Friends*. Edited by Sewell, pp. 173-77.

Donoghue, Emma. *We Are Michael Field*. Bath, England: Absolute Press, 1988.

Dowling, Linda. *Hellenism and Homosexuality in Victorian Oxford*. Ihtaca: Cornell University Press, 1994.

———. *Language and Decadence in the Victorian Fin de Siècle*. Princeton, N.J.: Princeton University Press, 1986.

———. "Nature and Decadence: John Gray's *Silverpoints*." *Victorian Poetry* 15, no. 2 (Summer 1977): 159-69.

Dowson, Ernest. *The Letters of Ernest Dowson*. Edited by Desmond Flower and Henry Maas. Rutherford, N.J.: Fairleigh Dickinson University Press, 1967.

Ellmann, Richard, E. D. H. Johnson, Alfred L. Bush. *Wilde and the Nineties: An Essay and an Exhibition*. Exhibition catalogue. Edited by Charles Ryskamp. Princeton, N.J.: Princeton Unversity Library, 1966.

———. *Oscar Wilde*. New York: Alfred A. Knopf, 1988.

Essex, Father Edwin. "The Canon in Residence." In *Two Friends*. Edited by Sewell, pp. 152-66.

Fletcher, Ian, ed. *The Poems of John Gray*. The 1880–1920 British Authors Series, No. 1. Greensboro, N.C.: ELT Press, 1988.

———. "The Poetry of John Gray." In *Two Friends*. Edited by Sewell, pp. 50-69.

Foldy, Michael S. *The Trials of Oscar Wilde: Deviance, Morality, and Late-Victorian Society*. New Haven: Yale University Press, 1997.

Fryer, Jonathan. *André & Oscar: Gide, Wilde and the Gay Art of Living*. London: Allison & Busby Ltd., 1999.

Gagnier, Regenia. *Idylls of the Marketplace: Oscar Wilde and the Victorian Public*. Aldershot: Scholar, 1986.

Gannon, Patricio. "John Gray: The Prince of Dreams." In *Two Friends*. Edited by Sewell, pp. 106-119.

Gawsworth, John. "Two Poets 'J. G.'" In *Two Friends*. Edited by Sewell, pp. 167-172.

Gill, Eric. *Autobiography*. London: Jonathan Cape, 1940.

"Gray, John." Foreign Office Lists: 1982–94, 1898. Privately printed, British government publication.

Gray, Mary Raphael (Beatrice). "A Sister's Reminiscences." In *Two Friends*. Edited by Sewell, pp. 100-105.

Grein, Mrs. Alice Augusta [Michael Orme]. *J. T. Grein: The Story of a Pioneer 1862–1935*. London: John Murray, 1936.

Halperin, Joan Ungersma. *Félix Fénéon: Aesthete & Anarchist in Fin-de-Siécle Paris*. New Haven, Conn.: Yale University Press, 1988.

Hanson, Ellis. *Decadence and Catholicism*. Cambridge, Mass.: Harvard University Press, 1997.

Hart, Reverend Dominic. "Some Memories of John Gray." Edited by Brocard Sewell. *The Innes Review* 2 (1975): 80-88.

Harris, Frank. *Oscar Wilde: His Life and Confessions*. New York: Garden City Publishing Co., 1930.

Healy, Philip. "Afterward." In John Gray, *Park: A Fantastic Story*. Edited by Philip Healy. Manchester: Carcanet, 1966, pp. 110-28.

————. "Text and Context in John Gray's *Park*: Prester John's 'Black Mischief.'" *English Literature in Transition* 36:4 (1993): 413-437.

Jackson, Holbrook. *The Eighteen Nineties*. London: Grant Richards, 1913.

LeGallienne, Richard. "John Gray." In *Retrospective Reviews: A Literary Log*. London: John Lane, 1896, pp. 229-32.

Lhombreaud, Roger. "Une Amitié Anglaise de Pierre Louÿs: Onze Lettres Inédites á John Gray." *Revue de Littérature Comparée* 27(Juillet–Septembre 1953): 343-57.

————. *Arthur Symons: A Critical Biography*. London: Unicorn Press, 1963.

————. "Arcades Ambo: The Poetical Friendship of John Gray and Pierre Louÿs." In *Two Friends*. Edited by Sewell, pp. 120-33. (An edited version of Lhombreaud's "Une Amitié Anglaise de Pierre Louÿs: onze Lettres Inédites á John Gray," *Revue de Littérature Comparée* 27 (Juillet-Septembre 1953): 343-357.)

McAlpine, Margaret Mary. "John Gray: A Critical and Biographical Study." Master's thesis, University of Manchester, 1967.

MacCarthy, Fiona. *Eric Gill*. London: Faber and Faber, 1989.

McCormack, Jerusha Hull. *John Gray: Poet, Dandy, and Priest*. Hanover, N.H.: University Press of New England, 1991.

————. "John Gray's Father and Father John Gray." *Durham University Journal* (December 1985): 113-20.

————. "The Disciple: John Gray/'Dorian' Gray." *Journal of the Eighteen-Nineties Society* 5 (1975–76): 13-21.

————. "Masks without Faces: The Personalities of Oscar Wilde." *English*

Literature in Transition 22 (1979): 253-69.

———. "The Person in Question: John Gray. A Critical and Biographical Study." Ph.D. dissertation, Brandeis University, 1973.

———, ed. The Selected Prose of John Gray. The 1880–1920 British Authors Series 7. Greensboro, N.C.: ELT Press, 1992.

———. "Wilde's Fiction(s)." In The Cambridge Companion to Oscar Wilde. Edited by Peter Raby. Cambridge: Cambridge University Press, 1997, pp. 96-117.

———, ed. "The Wilde Irishman: Oscar as Aesthete and Anarchist." In Wilde the Irishman. New Haven: Yale University Press, 1998, pp. 82-94.

———. ed. Wilde the Irishman. New Haven: Yale University Press, 1998.

Meadmore, William. Lucien Pissarro: Un Coeur Simple. London: Constable & Co., 1962.

Murray, Isobel. "John Gray: The Person and the Work in Question." Durham University Journal (June 1984): 261-275.

Nelson, James G. The Early Nineties: A View from the Bodley Head. Cambridge, Mass.: Harvard University Press,1971.

O'Brien, Mrs. William (Sophie Raffalovich). "Friends for Eternity." Irish Monthly 62 (November 1934): 699-706.

Raffalovich, Marc-André. [Alexander Michaelson]. "Aubrey Beardsely." Blackfriars 9 (October 1928): 609-16.

———. "Aubrey Beardsley's Sister." Blackfriars 9 (November 1928): 669-75.

———. "Edward Burne-Jones." Blackfriars 9 (March 1928): 152-59.

———. "Giles and Miles and Isabeau." Blackfriars 9 (January 1928): 18-29.

———. "Isis Unveiled." Blackfriars 9 (September 1928): 533-40.

———. "L'Affaire Oscar Wilde." Archives de L'anthropologie Criminelle de Criminologie et de Psychologie Normale et Pathologique. 10 (1895): 445-77.

———. "Letters of André Raffalovich to Edward Playfair." Antigonish Review (Winter 1971): 53-66.

———. "Oscar Wilde." Blackfriars 8 (November 1927): 694-702. Reprinted in Sewell, Footnote to theNineties, pp. 108-22.

———. "Parallels." Blackfriars 10 (January 1929): 779-85.

———. Uranisme et Unisexualité: Etude sur Différentes Manifestations de L'Instinct Sexuel. Lyons: A. Storck, 1896.

———. "Walter Pater: In Memoriam." Blackfriars 9 (March 1928): 463-71.

Reade, Brian, ed. Sexual Heretics: Male Homosexuality in English Literature from 1850–1900. New York: Coward-McCann, 1970.

Roseliep, Raymond. "Some Letters of Lionel Johnson." Ph.D. dissertation, University of Notre Dame, 1954.

Rothenstein, William. *Men and Memories: Recollections of William Rothenstein, Vol. 1: 1871–1900.* New York: Coward McCann, 1931.

Roy, G. Ross. "A Bibliography of French Symbolism in English-language Publications to 1910: Mallarmé, Rimbaud, Verlaine." *Revue de Littérature Comparée* 34 (October–December 1960): 645-59.

Sackville, Margaret. "At Whitehouse Terrace." In *Two Friends.* Edited by Sewell, pp. 142-47.

Schoonderwoerd, N. H. G. J. T. *Grein, Ambassador of the Theatre 1862–1935.* Assen: Van Gorcum & Co., 1963.

Sewell, Brocard. *Footnote to the Nineties: A Memoir of John Gray and André Raffalovich.* London: Cecil & Amelia Woolf, 1968.

———. *In the Dorian Mode: A Life of John Gray. 1866–1934.* Padstow, Cornwall: Tabb House, 1983.

———. "John Gray and André Raffalovich: A Biographical Outline." In *Two Friends.* Edited by Sewell, pp. 7-43.

———. "On Re-Reading 'Park.'" *Aylesford Review* 7 (Winter 1965/Spring 1966): 215-18.

———, ed. *Two Friends: John Gray and André Raffalovich.* Aylesford, Kent: St. Albert's Press, 1963.

Shewring, Walter. "Two Friends." *Blackfriars* 15 (September 1934). Reprinted in *Two Friends.* Edited by Sewell, pp. 148-51.

Smith, Timothy D'Arch. *Love in Earnest: Some Notes on the Lives and the Writings of the English "Uranian" Poets from 1889 to1930.* London: Routledge & Kegan Paul, 1970.

Speaight, Robert. *The Life of Eric Gill.* London: Methuen and Co., 1966.

Sturgeon, Mary. *Michael Field.* London: George G. Harrap & Co., 1922.

Sutton, Denys. "Neglected Virtuoso: Charles Ricketts and his Achievements." *Apollo* 83 (February 1966): pp. 138-47.

Symons, Arthur. "The Café Royal." In *The Café Royal and Other Essays.* Westminster: Beaumont Press, 1923.

Symons, A. J. A. "The Diner-Out." *Horizen* 4 (1941): 251-58.

Temple, Ruth Zabriskie. *The Critic's Alchemy: A Study of the Introduction of French Symbolism into England.* New Haven, Conn.: College and University Press, 1953.

———. "The Other Choice: The Worlds of John Gray, Poet and Priest." *Bulletin of Research in the Humanities* 84 (Spring 1981): 16-64.

Thornton, R. K. R. *The Decadent Dilemma.* London: Edward Arnold, 1983.

Vernon, Peter J. "The Letters of John Gray." Ph.D. dissertation, University of London, 1976.

Weintraub, Stanley. *Beardsley: A Biography.* New York: George Braziller, 1967.

W[hite], T. W. G[leeson]. "La Garde Joyeuse. 'John Gray.'" *The Artist and Journal of Home Culture* 14 (4 November 1893): 328-29.

Wilde, Oscar. *Complete Works of Oscar Wilde*. New York: HarperCollins, 1994.

———. *The Letters of Oscar Wilde*. Edited by Rupert Hart Davis. London: Rupert Hart-Davis, Ltd., 1963.

———. "The Picture of Dorian Gray." *Lippincott's Monthly Magazine,* July 1890, 3-100.

———. *The Picture of Dorian Gray*. Edited by Isobel Murray. London: Oxford University Press, 1974.

Winckler, Paul A. "John Gray and His Times." In *Two Friends*. Edited by Sewell, pp. 1-6.

Winwar, Frances. *Oscar Wilde and the Yellow Nineties*. New York: Harper, 1940.

Wyndham, Violet. "Reminiscences, by Ada Leverson: 1. The Importance of Being Oscar." In *The Sphinx and Her Circle: A Biographical Sketch of Ada Leverson, 1862–1933*. London: André Deutsche, 1963, pp. 105-23.

Zaina, Alexandra. "The Prose Works of John Gray." In *Two Friends*. Edited by Sewell, pp. 70-99.

INDEX